Desire and Discipline

Sex and Sexuality in the Premodern West

The history of sexuality is one of the newest and fastest-growing areas of scholarly and popular interest. This collection of original essays looks at sexuality in the long stretch between the twelfth and the early seventeenth centuries – a period that remains relatively unexplored, yet one that has deeply informed contemporary ideas about sex.

The volume grew out of a conference at the University of Toronto on human sexuality in the medieval and early modern world. Featuring works by world-renowned scholars, it presents a broad cross-section of current research and a diversity of theoretical, methodological, and disciplinary boundaries, including legal history, art history, textual analysis, codicological analysis, and feminist theory. Some essays focus on the universal values of the Church, and highlight the intellectual and religious homogeneity that characterized Europe for much of the period. Others are more localized and look at a specific social and historical context. As a whole the collection points to the ongoing tension between society's desire to control sexuality and people's need to express it.

Informed by contemporary trends in scholarship, including feminism, gay studies, post-colonialism, and deconstruction, these essays introduce scholars to some of the riches that are only now being unearthed in this young discipline.

JACQUELINE MURRAY is Associate Professor of History and Director, Humanities Research Group, University of Windsor.
KONRAD EISENBICHLER is Associate Professor of Renaissance Studies and Italian as well as Director, Centre for Reformation and Renaissance Studies, Victoria University at the University of Toronto.

Desire and Discipline

Sex and Sexuality in the Premodern West

Edited by
Jacqueline Murray and
Konrad Eisenbichler

UNIVERSITY OF TORONTO PRESS
Toronto Buffalo London

© University of Toronto Press Incorporated 1996
Toronto Buffalo London
Printed in Canada

ISBN 0-8020-0780-5 (cloth)
ISBN 0-8020-7144-9 (paper)

Printed on acid-free paper

Canadian Cataloguing in Publication Data

Main entry under title:

Desire and discipline: sex and sexuality in the premodern
West

Proceedings of a conference held at the University of
Toronto, Nov. 22–4, 1991.
ISBN 0-8020-0780-5 (bound). – ISBN 0-8020-7144-9 (pbk.)

1. Sex customs – Europe – History – Congresses.
I. Murray, Jacqueline, 1953–   . II. Eisenbichler, Konrad.

HQ18.E8D48 1996   306.7′094′09   C96-930483-8

University of Toronto Press acknowledges the financial assistance to its publishing
program of the Canada Council and the Ontario Arts Council.

Contents

Acknowledgments

As is the case with all projects of a collaborative nature, this collection of essays is the fruit of a long and happy process of intellectual cross-fertilization and much careful tending and nurturing. The seeds were sown in casual conversation and germinated in discussions between the two organizers/editors. Gradually the idea grew and sprouted until many flowering branches extended far afield. We hope that with the appearance of this volume the project does not come to an end but rather becomes part of a verdant field of research.

The essays here presented were originally delivered at the conference 'Sex and Sexuality in the Middle Ages and the Renaissance' (22–4 November 1991). That dynamic meeting and this volume have been made possible by the generous assistance of a number of groups and individuals. In particular, we wish to acknowledge the Social Sciences and Humanities Research Council of Canada; the Hannah Institute for the History of Medicine; the Centre for Reformation and Renaissance Studies (Victoria University, Toronto); the University of Toronto, through the Office of the President, the Office of the Vice-President and Provost, the School of Graduate Studies, the Faculty of Arts and Science, the Departments of Fine Arts and Italian Studies, the Women's Studies Programme, the Institute for the History and Philosophy of Science and Technology, and the Committee on Homophobia; Victoria University, through the Office of the President and the Office of the Principal; the University of Windsor, through the Dean of Social Science, the Department of History, and the Humanities Research Group; the Toronto Renaissance and Reformation Colloquium; and the Istituto Italiano di Cultura (Toronto). Mr

Jamie Zettle provided valuable assistance in the preparation of the typescript. We are particularly grateful to the editorial staff at the University of Toronto Press, and especially to Ms Suzanne Rancourt, whose enthusiastic and unfailing support of this project made all the difference in the world. We would also like to thank Beverley Beetham Endersby for her careful attention to detail.

Finally, we wish to thank all the scholars who have contributed their wisdom and insight to this volume and who, with grace and patience, never lost faith when events beyond our control seriously delayed the happy conclusion of this venture. To all, the editors owe an enormous debt of gratitude.

Jacqueline Murray   Konrad Eisenbichler
University of Windsor   University of Toronto

Introduction

JACQUELINE MURRAY

The study of human sexuality is one of the most rapidly expanding areas of research today. It is a field that is attracting attention from a variety of disciplines, ranging from anthropology and sociology to literary studies and history. Nor is interest limited by place or time: all cultures and historical periods are drawing scrutiny. None the less, the history of sexuality is a relatively new area of research whose inception can perhaps most conveniently be dated at the 1976 publication in French of the introductory volume of *The History of Sexuality* by Michel Foucault.[1]

In this work, Foucault presents a meandering and impressionistic reading of the history of human sexuality in the West over the course of two millennia. Concerned with issues of control and strategies of domination, he focused on how discourse both shaped sexual possibilities and limited alternatives. For him, rather than being innate, natural, and transhistorical, sexuality was the product of a time and a place – it was a specific social construction. A preoccupation with the power of words similarly influenced Foucault's understanding of Western sexuality as shaped by a culture of confession and controlled by the guilt elicited by self-examination. This examination of the self, originating in the institution of sacramental confession in the Middle Ages, was perpetuated by the secular confession of psychoanalytic self-revelation of the modern world. In his introductory volume, Foucault challenged historians to examine sexual activity in its historical context, especially those who study the period he identified as central in the development of contemporary sexual attitudes: the long centuries stretching between the decline of antiquity and the beginning of the modern world.

It is somewhat ironic, then, to note that the historical scholars who were quickest to respond to Foucault's challenge and to adopt most fully his conceptual framework were those who study the framing periods, that is, classicists and modernists. The classical and modern worlds are, indeed, useful and expedient examples for the study of how societies construct sexual possibilities. As well, they are timely, meshing nicely with the developing gay studies of the 1980s, which sought historical roots in the homosocial and homoerotic networks of Greek antiquity and the emerging gay subcultures of eighteenth- and nineteenth-century Europe.[2] Furthermore, as societies that privileged the written word and evidenced high degrees of literacy, at least among male élites, the ancient and modern worlds could be used as laboratories in which to test Foucault's theories about the role of discourse in the construction and expression of sexualities.

While Foucault's challenge to examine sexualities in their social and historical specificity remains, much of his theoretical and methodological perspective has been questioned.[3] Medievalists have criticized Foucault for his relative neglect of the long period separating antiquity and modernity, and for his cavalier and unsupported generalizations about this complex and rich society.[4] Further criticism has focused on Foucault's emphasis on the role of discourse in shaping sexuality – a perspective that virtually ignores the psychological and physical dimensions of human experience – in other words, his neglect of the role of emotion and embodiment.[5] Equally open to criticism is Foucault's masculinist perspective, his virtual exclusion of the experience of women, and his failure to recognize the profoundly different ways in which men and women experience sexuality.[6]

Another important and concomitant impetus for the study of the history of sexuality came from scholars of women's history and feminist theory. The methodological and theoretical sophistication of feminist scholarship expanded significantly during the 1980s. Issues of gender and sensitivity to women's unique experience of, and contribution to, past and present alike have now become essential components in every area of intellectual endeavour. Feminist theory, too, advances a social-constructionist position, arguing that gender differences are neither natural nor transhistorical but, rather, formed in specific historical and social contexts. By focusing on women's social rather than biological roles, feminist scholars have redressed an imbalance in traditional scholarship. However, the tendency has been to privilege the social relations of the sexes at the expense of the sexual.

Women's studies and feminist theory insert women into the equation, insisting that the implications of gender difference inform the reading of texts and the analyses of society. Similarly, gay studies and queer theory challenge heterosexist presumptions about sexual identity and question what can be considered normative in any time or place. Both these theoretical perspectives argue for broad historical inclusivity and sensitivity by scholars. Together, they have stimulated much of the current interest in the broad spectrum of human sexual behaviour in the past and present.

This is the intellectual milieu from which this collection of essays emerged. The essays developed out of a conference, 'Sex and Sexuality in the Middle Ages and the Renaissance,' organized by Konrad Eisenbichler and Jacqueline Murray, held at the University of Toronto in November 1991. Part of the rationale for the conference was to examine questions pertaining to premodern people in their biological and reproductive contexts as a complement to the wealth of studies already available on gendered social experience. This was certainly not the first time that medievalists and early-modernists had turned their attention to questions of sex and sexuality in premodern Europe. The annual Medieval Congress at Western Michigan University included the occasional session devoted to sexuality at least as early as 1982. Research in the field had also received important encouragement by the immediate success of the volume *Sexual Practices and the Medieval Church*, a collection of essays that appeared in the same year.[7] Six papers devoted to sexuality in the Renaissance were delivered to the Canadian Society of Renaissance Studies in 1987 and were published the following year.[8] Nevertheless, despite the increasing interest in this important research area, the Toronto conference was the first devoted solely and exclusively to human sexuality in the medieval and early-modern world.[9]

Despite the fact that literature on the history of sexuality has burgeoned in recent decades, the development of this field has not been without its problems. Vern Bullough's essay, which opens this volume, indicates some of the limitations of the nineteenth- and twentieth-century scholars who addressed questions of sexuality. Adhering to conventional morality, these men did not hesitate to condemn or deny historical manifestations of sexuality that did not suit their contemporary values. Furthermore, even in later decades, as Bullough's personal experience attests, the censure of colleagues could constrain research and inhibit publication. Even today, the history of sexuality remains a marginal specialization that can taint a scholar's work or inhibit his or her career.

Bullough's review of his experiences as a historian of sexuality is a cautionary tale that should remind every scholar that intellectual freedom is a tenuous privilege and remains contingent and subject to the censure and censoring of editorial boards and conference organizers. Although this situation is changing with the introduction of publication series devoted to the history of sexuality by several major academic publishers and by the founding of the *Journal of the History of Sexuality,* the current cachet of the history of sexuality nevertheless could prove fleeting unless scholars continue to assert the legitimacy of sexuality as an area of scholarly enquiry that must be free from the constraints of changing contemporary values and shifting norms. The openness of the 1990s seems far away from the repressive atmosphere of the 1950s that Bullough recalls, yet we do well to remember that, today, there are those inside and outside the academy who would restrict the research agenda or define its interpretive frame.

Bullough, one of the earliest scholars to submit premodern European sexuality to rigorous and continued scrutiny, sees a promising future for this area of research. Sexuality is so fundamental to human experience, he says, that there are myriad points of access for its study. Because sexuality is interwoven into every aspect of human life and has the potential to infiltrate and influence every aspect of society, it is a vast and complex area of research. It therefore lends itself in particular to cooperative ventures and multidisciplinary approaches, as this collection of essays attests.

The present volume is representative of a broad cross-section of research currently being pursued in that period which Foucault identified as so central to the formation of Western attitudes towards sexuality, the period stretching between the ancient and the modern world. Periodization has become something of a vexing question for scholars.[10] The subtitle of this collection has abandoned deliberately the temporal designators 'medieval' and 'Renaissance' or 'early modern' in favour of 'premodern,' a term that is gaining increasing currency as a temporal indicator. 'Premodern' stresses the social and cultural continuity of these centuries. It implies social evolution rather than abrupt changes in values and conditions. It seeks the historical inclusivity appropriate to a topic that has its roots in the movement to reclaim the margins of society and history. The distinction between 'medieval' and 'Renaissance' may arguably retain relevance for the study of intellectual and cultural movements, and even political or economic élites. However, for questions of social history, for an understanding of the great commonality of European society whose daily lives remained fundamentally unchanged until the upheavals of industrialization, distinctions such as 'medieval' and 'Renaissance' or 'early modern' seem unnecessarily and artificially delimiting.

'Premodern,' on the other hand, highlights the similarities and continuities that characterize the period stretching from Europe's recovery from the disintegration of the ancient world, a process completed by the twelfth century, to the appearance of a society that is recognizably different, sometime after the seventeenth century.[11] 'Premodern' carries with it a sense of inclusivity, and recognizes both complexity and continuity without implying social stasis. Thus, while the essays presented here cross the twelfth through early seventeenth centuries, they are rooted in a set of underlying cultural assumptions, universally embraced at the beginning of the period, and experiencing gradual modification and transformation but still visible and recognizable by its end.[12]

Geographically, this collection embraces much of premodern Europe, just up to the point at which it was starting to push beyond its ancient boundaries. Some essays focus on the universal values of the Church, defined in canon law and theology, which were disseminated across Christendom through a variety of mechanisms, including didactic strategies such as sermons or the enforcement network of ecclesiastical courts. These essays highlight the intellectual and religious homogeneity that characterized Europe for most of this period; canon law, and the values that informed it, applied equally across Christendom. Other essays are more localized and firmly rooted in a specific social and historical context, be it the refined urban atmosphere of the Italian cities or the frontier society of thirteenth-century Castile. Europe's margins are featured in essays that examine sexual attitudes and practices when, on the eve of expansion, Europeans encountered and interacted with other cultures. Finally, in their psychologized approaches to sexuality, other authors transcend notions of geographic boundaries and stress common aspects of human sexual experience.

This collection presents a diversity of theoretical, methodological, and disciplinary approaches. While most of the essays are identified with one discipline or another, ranging from legal history to art history, from textual analysis to codicological analysis, they all embrace the expansive and generous approach urged by Bullough and characteristic of interdisciplinary undertakings. This diversity accurately reflects the nature of current research on premodern sexuality. This plurality of approach is in part the happy result of relative neglect. In the wake of Foucault's original study, classicists and modernists quickly adopted his ideas and methods, and applied them to their fields of study, establishing something of a theoretical hegemony. Furthermore, adopting Foucault's unsubstantiated generalizations about the medieval and early-modern worlds, these early historians of sexuality assumed they already knew about the construction of sexuality between antiquity and the modern world. Premodernists, slower to jump on the bandwagon, have been able to avoid both theoretical conformity and interpretive excess, and have embraced a pluralistic methodology. Wary of generalizations, premodernists have avoided the pitfalls of a single, seamless interpretation, believing that the coexistence of scholarly diversity will help to reveal and explain the coexistence of historical contradiction.

The alternative to intellectual conformity is not a lack of coherence but rather a series of interwoven, complementary, and occasionally conflicting approaches, all of which contribute to a nuanced and multivalent picture of premodern sexuality. Although they have no single overarching theoretical perspective, no single interpretive framework, the essays in this volume all point to the ongoing tension between society's desire to control sex and sexuality, and people's need to express it. All the authors embrace the notion of the social construction of sexuality, although they apply it with varying degrees of flexibility. Joseph Cady challenges directly the Foucauldian denial of a homosexual identity prior to the modern period, while Robert Shephard and Guy Poirier, hesitant to posit a homosexual identity in this early period, nevertheless examine ideas and reactions surrounding premodern homosexual behaviour. Similarly, while never losing sight of the unique historical circumstances, Nancy Partner argues strongly for a psychologically informed approach to enhance our understanding of the conscious and unconscious experience of sexuality. Thus, in light of a similarity of experience, sexuality can be seen to unite human beings across time, as much as the alterity of experience stresses historical disjunction and separation.

An explicitly feminist perspective informs many of the contributions. Dyan Elliott and Ruth Karras highlight how patriarchy gendered the prevailing moral code and used it as a tool to enforce female subordination and to perpetuate the unremittingly negative evaluation of women and female sexuality embedded in so much of premodern rhetoric. On the other hand, the essays by Rona Goffen and Barrie Ruth Straus suggest how patriarchal values might have been mitigated or how women's desire might have found a voice in a period in which the modes of expression were controlled by men. Equally, questions of race and class are also addressed in some of the essays. James A. Brundage and Roberto González-Casanovas examine the legal mechanisms that could enhance social control, so that the moral code, devised by the religious élite, was imposed on diverse populations without regard for local custom and usage. The nexus of class and gender is seen in the implementation of sexual controls or in the common folk's perceptions of the sexuality of their monarchs, as examined by Carol Kazmierczak Manzione and Robert Shephard. Ivana Elbl and Guy Poirier employ race as a category of analysis in their examinations of how Europeans encountered alterity, be it the racial difference of Africans or the religious difference of Muslims.

The moral code that prescribed premodern sexual behaviour was based on a complex theology developed by the Patristic Fathers, especially Ambrose, Jerome, and Augustine. These theologians were as influenced by the ascetic philosophies of Greece and Rome as they were by the message of the gospels. Consequently, they absorbed much of the suspicion of the material world found in contemporary Stoicism, Neoplatonism, and such dualist sects as the Manicheans.[13] An unremittingly negative evaluation of the body and of human sexuality emerged from this synthesis of ancient philosophy and Christian morality. Ambrose identified sexuality with original sin, placing responsibility for the Fall onto Eve, thereby initiating the long association of women with sexual temptation and damnation. Jerome similarly connected sexual sin and original sin. He urged Christians to control their bodies, always avoiding sexual attraction and working to tame the flesh.

Augustine mitigated this harsh evaluation somewhat by recognizing sexual activity as problematic, while proposing that sexuality (the potential for sexual activity) had been a gift from God to Adam and Eve in the Garden of Eden. He argued that prelapsarian sexual expression had been controlled and subject to human reason. All of this changed, however, when sin entered the world, and Adam and Eve were expelled from Paradise. Augustine summarized the situation in *The City of God*: 'It was only after the fall, when their nature had lost its power to exact obedience from the sexual organs, that they fell and noticed the loss and, being ashamed of their lust, covered these unruly members.'[14] Thus, all of humanity was subject thereafter to their sexual desires, which were characterized as animal appetites linked to the inferior material realm. Sexual desire and temptation needed to be resisted at every turn, and each person needed to control his or her unruly members through the application of reason and the exercise of self-discipline. Sexual expression was licit only between a man and a woman, within marriage, for the purpose of procreation. The appropriate time, place, and sexual position were also prescribed. Preferable by far to this circumscribed sexual activity was the life of celibacy, in which one strove to conquer and subdue desire rather than to fulfil it.

The tension between sexual activity and a Christian mode of life was fundamental and inherent in the ideology that governed sexual activity from the fifth century onwards. From that time forward, humanity was perceived to be engaged in an enduring struggle between irrational animal appetites and the need to discipline and control those appetites through the application of reason and will power. As part of its quest for salvation, humanity struggled to free itself from sexual desire, which belonged to its lower nature. As one ascended upward, through the discipline of the flesh and the cultivation of reason and the will, sexual activity ceased, and the sexual organs were no longer unruly. Significantly, these sexual values were promoted by an élite caste of men vowed to celibacy, men who perceived themselves as at least partially successful in this struggle between desire and discipline. Not content, however, to subdue their own bodies alone, they prescribed this discipline of sexual activity across the whole of society and attempted to impose it on the sexually active laity.

In the course of the twelfth century, greater attention was devoted to understanding, refining, extending, and applying this code to every area of life, including sexual relations. Gratian's *Concordance of Disconcordant Canons* provided a legal summary of sexual relations based on earlier ecclesiastical councils, while Peter Lombard's *Book of Four Sentences* presented a theological synthesis.[15] By the middle of the thirteenth century, there was a comprehensive Christian moral code which prescribed right sexual conduct for the faithful; scrutinized deviance; and, in concert with secular officials, punished offenders.[16]

The laity, that great mass of people who married and raised children, were not easily persuaded to abandon activities that seemed so natural and fundamental to human life. The moral code, developed by those it least affected, was never really successfully imposed on the great majority of the laity. While pastoral and theological literature presented ideals of sexual behaviour, and while secular and canon law set out a means of regulating and punishing anyone who deviated from those ideals, court records show people regularly ignoring or flouting the prescriptions of Church and society alike.

The tension between prescription and behaviour is the focus of James Brundage's examination of the canon law that governed medieval sexual behaviour. Brundage shows how, as the canonists developed a moral and legal code to govern the sexual activity of the faithful, the Church also developed an efficient system of enforcement. Brundage carefully traces the implications of the modifications of the ecclesiastical courts' procedures for the enforcement of the moral code. Innovations such as the implementation of *ex officio* enquiry or the admissibility of public rumour in evidence made it easier to prosecute and convict sexual offenders. Traditional interpretations have linked these procedural innovations with the Church's attempts to address the challenges posed by heresy and usury, but Brundage argues persuasively that the goal of these procedural modifications was the prosecution of sexual offenders.

The Church's full intellectual might and judicial competence were focused on the effective imposition of its moral code on the faithful whose very behaviour would seem to indicate rebellion against these norms. This process was thoroughly embedded in the medieval understanding of the necessity to control animal appetites and subordinate the desires of the unruly flesh to the discipline of reason. It mattered little whether the discipline was internally or externally imposed, so long as individual behaviour was controlled and modified, and social order thereby preserved. Brundage's analysis of how the medieval clerical élite sought to control behaviour and impose its values across society supports Foucault's hypothesis about the ongoing repression of sexuality.

The control of sexual activity in premodern societies fell as much under secular as ecclesiastical jurisdiction. While the moral code may have developed in accordance with prevailing theological imperatives, its application and enforcement fell within the purview of secular officials as well. This intersection of secular and ecclesiastical is the focus of Roberto González-Casanovas's examination of the thirteenth-century Spanish law code, *Las siete partidas*. Despite the attempts to prescribe utopian ideals, laws are nevertheless historical documents composed in specific contexts. In *Las siete partidas* we find reflected the gendered nature of Castilian society as it assimilated the moral code of the Church and reinterpreted it to suit its specific circumstances and patriarchal agenda.

Although *Las siete partidas* is ostensibly a secular law code, ecclesiastical morality forms the underpinnings of its regulations governing sexuality. Here, once again, the tension between reason and disorder underlies the development of behavioural norms, especially those governing the relationships between men and women. González-Casanovas argues that *Las siete partidas* was an attempt by Alphonso the Wise to legitimize his rule over a diverse population and present an ideal model of human relations based on hierarchical order and reason. Sexual and gender relations reflected premodern patriarchy's assumptions about the essential nature of female subordination. Marriage was perceived as both a biological and a social institution, as a means to channel lust and perpetuate lineages. Thus, in its exposition of marriage and sexuality, *Las siete partidas* reflects the nexus of secular and ecclesiastical values, which reinforced each other in the quest for ideal behaviour governed by reason.

Human behaviour, however, is rarely ideal, and the difficulties and discrepancies that inhere in the implementation of laws are revealed in Ivana Elbl's discussion of the regulations governing the sexual behaviour of the Portuguese in West Africa in the late fifteenth and early sixteenth centuries. Both the Church and the Portuguese Crown strictly prohibited sexual relations between Portuguese traders or officials and African women. Moral strictures, however, gave way to pragmatism as Portugal faded in the distance. Various forms of informal relationships developed between Portuguese men and African women as permanent European settlements were established. Away from the social control and enforcement mechanisms of Portugal, men entered into concubinal relationships with both black and white women, and behaviour considered sexually deviant in Europe went unpunished and virtually unnoticed in the overseas colonies. Bigamy and adultery were common as men who left a legitimate wife and family in Portugal established illegitimate African families. Ultimately, even the law was modified to recognize these arrangements, and the African families gradually gained the right to inherit, in certain circumstances, the estates of their Portuguese fathers and husbands.

Elbl's examination of the Portuguese overseas provides an exciting glimpse into the 'natural' development of a sexual order in the absence of effective mechanisms to control and enforce an 'artificial' moral code. The *ad hoc* nature of the Portuguese outposts, free from social constraints and miscegenation prohibitions, shows a plurality of coexisting relations, from sexual licence and coercion to the replication of conventional relationships through stable concubinage. Distinctions based on race and class were marginal to the processes of this new sexual economy. Some individuals continued to be guided by the European morality they left behind; others greeted the absence of control as an invitation to licence. As yet this story is told only from the European male perspective; the African female version awaits recovery.

While geographic distance might have weakened society's ability to enforce conformity to the sexual norms it prescribed, there were numerous mechanisms to regulate behaviour within Europe. That is not to suggest, however, that sexual licence and the rejection of conventional sexual behaviour were unusual. Rather, the very existence of various organized enforcement systems suggests their perceived need, as Carol Kazmierczak Manzione shows in her discussion of sixteenth-century London hospitals. An examination of the minutes of the governors of two hospitals, Christ's and Bridewell, shows the effective policing of morality by secular bodies originally designed to protect society's most vulnerable and marginal members. While attempting to protect society from the chaos caused by the antisocial – vagabonds, pimps, and prostitutes – these hospitals also policed the behaviour of ordinary people accused of sexual crimes. The vulnerable and weak, such as the abandoned maid made pregnant by an abusive master, were subject to the hospital's policing of illegitimacy. But neither were more privileged members of society immune from accusations of sexual improprieties by disgruntled inferiors. The mechanisms of control, therefore, while the purview of society's élite, could occasionally be turned against those who wielded them. The governors of the hospitals were just as concerned with the maintenance of social order, free from the chaos and breakdown that accompanied undisciplined and public sexual activity, as were their predecessors in the ecclesiastical courts of earlier centuries. Here, too, public rumour continued to facilitate the prosecution of those individuals who deviated from normative behaviour.

Public rumour or gossip was a powerful social force in the premodern world, recalling Foucault's emphasis on the power of discourse. As Brundage shows, the legal recognition of public rumour as admissible, if circumstantial, evidence was entrenched by the ecclesiastical courts. Individual sexual reputation could influence social position and acceptance, and dictate whether a person was included or excluded from respectable society. Words had the potential to undermine established social structures and could lead to the dissolution of the bonds that governed a well-regulated society. Robert Shephard focuses on rumours that circulated around England about the sex lives of Elizabeth I and James I. Elizabeth set herself apart from female sexuality, adopting the persona of the Virgin Queen. While unmarried and officially chaste, Elizabeth was nevertheless the target of swirling waves of rumour about her sexual behaviour, especially during periods of political tension. Rumours also circulated about James I's homosexual proclivities, although he had in fact entered into a legitimate marriage and provided the kingdom with an heir. Shephard argues that issues of class, gender, and 'sexual orientation' account for the differing intensity of the rumours surrounding the two monarchs. He concludes that the fact that the rumours dogging Elizabeth were persistent, whereas those surrounding James were relatively rare, suggests that misogyny was a more powerful force in early-modern Europe than was homophobia.

Shephard suggests that rumours about James I's homosexual liaisons were scarce because his relationships with his favourites were not recognized as anything more than devoted friendship. This interpretation concurs with the Foucauldian assertion that homosexuality, as an identity or orientation, is a relatively recent phenomenon, emerging only in the context of the eighteenth and nineteenth centuries.[17] Certainly, in the earlier religious discourse, developed by theologians such as Thomas Aquinas, sexual acts were classified as natural or unnatural. Sodomy was only one of a number of possible sexual acts *contra naturam*, which also included masturbation, bestiality, and heterosexual intercourse beyond the legally sanctioned 'missionary' position.[18] Joseph Cady, however, argues that, if we move beyond prescriptive literature, an understanding of homosexual identity is visible long before modernists would allow. Analysing the *Mémoires-Journaux* of Pierre de l'Estoile for the years 1574–89, Cady argues that there were a variety of languages available to discuss the homosexuality found in the court of the French king Henry III, and his *mignons*. He interprets the variegated terminology used to refer to the king's homosexuality as part of an overall richness of public language in general, rather than an indication of a confusion about or absence of the notion of a homosexual identity.

Whether by sexual acts or sexual identity, those who were identified with homosexuality occupied a cultural place not dissimilar to that of heretics or others marginal to premodern Christian society.[19] Homosexuality was attributed to the Other, whether it be the religious Other of heretics or the political Other of the Templars. Guy Poirier examines the relationship between sexual deviance and alterity, in this case the Muslims of the Orient as they were portrayed in sixteenth-century French travel literature. Discussions of Muslim sexual practices, especially with regard to Christian captives, exposes not only how Europe constructed and perceived others, but also something of its own internalized cultural and sexual anxieties. Images of the castration and rape of young male captives, as part of their transformation into sexual objects for the pleasure of Muslim men, underscored European men's fear of sterility and passivity. This fear was in part linked to the evaluation of female sexuality as inferior. The possibility of feminizing men, therefore, struck at deeply rooted fears in the male psyche. Indeed, Poirier argues that the manner in which women, particularly prostitutes, were constructed as Other was not dissimilar to that of the constructed alterity of the Muslim.

The twin anxieties of sodomy and feminization underlay the fundamental understanding of what it meant to be a man in the premodern world. Masculinity and male sexuality were defined in hierarchical relation to inferior manifestations of femininity and homosexuality.[20] The moral code reflected the hierarchical evaluation of sexuality and the sexes inherent in patriarchy and was supported by contemporary Scriptural exegesis. The teachings of Paul, in particular, provided the justification for the subordination of women in general, and specifically within the marital relationship. Paul taught that a wife owed her husband complete obedience. In one area alone, that of marital intercourse, did Paul posit an equality between the spouses, who each, according to the conjugal debt, had equal claim to sexual access to the other.

Traditionally, the conjugal debt has been considered a liberating factor in the marital relationship because it accorded the wife equality with her husband. Working from an avowedly feminist perspective, Dyan Elliott offers a significantly different interpretation in her rereading of the conflicted meaning of the conjugal debt in the lives of premodern men and women. Elliott challenges both medieval and modern interpretations that the conjugal debt accorded married women a form of sexual equality in marriage. Rather, she contends that, by restricting a woman's ability to refuse her husband's sexual demands, the conjugal debt served as yet another instrument of female subordination. Elliott argues that Bernardino of Siena alone presents a significant voice of dissent in premodern discussions of female sexuality and the conjugal debt. In his sermons Bernardino explored a woman's ability to refuse her husband's sexual demands and argued that a woman should be free to tend to her own spiritual needs. His view, while an important counterbalance to the prevailing ideology of female subordination and lasciviousness, was nevertheless in the minority.

The general perception of women's lascivious nature permeated premodern society and found its expression in a variety of contexts and discourses. Nowhere was the inferior, irrational, and undisciplined nature of women more clearly exemplified than in the example of the prostitute. Ruth Karras examines the complex meanings of the medieval prostitute, from the undifferentiated lust of promiscuity to the avarice associated with sex for money. While the sins of the prostitute had various shades of meaning for medieval society, Karras finds that there was little understanding of the economic hardship that could underlie commercial sex. Women were perceived as prone to promiscuity and exemplars of the dangerous and chaotic nature of sexuality unconstrained by the moral code. Karras concludes pessimistically that the prostitute was simply at one end of a spectrum of female lasciviousness that, to some extent, incorporated all women.

Other authors are more optimistic, finding the discourse of misogyny and oppression less seamless and unremitting. Rona Goffen, for example, identifies a more sympathetic portrayal of married women in Titian's presentation of the conventional motif of the adulterous wife. The premodern evaluation of the adulterous wife was predicated on the prevailing suspicion of women's lascivious and fickle nature. Consequently, a husband was justified in suspecting his wife of adultery, presuming her guilt, and exacting punishment. Setting her analysis against the social and legal context of the sixteenth century, Goffen finds a different message underlying two of Titian's paintings that represent the theme of the adulterous wife. Through his careful structuring of *The Miracle of the Speaking Babe* and *The Jealous Husband*, Titian challenges the presumption of the wife's guilt and emphasizes the woman's vulnerability in the face of her husband's wrath. He inserts the possibility of a chaste wife wrongly accused by her unjustly suspicious husband into the charged atmosphere of premodern patriarchy and its omnipresent fear of woman's adultery. Thus, Goffen highlights the harsh rule of patriarchy that granted a husband power over his wife even unto death, yet she also reminds us that some considered that regime too harsh and sought ways to soften and mitigate it.

Marriage, not surprisingly, was the site of much of society's sexual tension. Although the only legitimate sexual relations were those between husband and wife, the double standard punished a woman's adultery while silently condoning a man's. Within marriage a woman was required to be sexually available, whatever her own physical or spiritual needs. Not surprisingly, then, Barrie Ruth Straus finds indications that some women prefered to avoid marriage altogether.

Straus examines the desires expressed by female characters in Chaucer's *Parliament of Fowls* and *Knight's Tale* to uncover a feminine response to the masculine construction of female sexual desire. She finds female characters voicing a desire to be free from marriage and its sexual requirements that complements Elliott's evaluation of the unbalanced nature of the 'sexual equality' of marriage. Elliott suggests women might want to reject sex to pursue a spiritual mode of life; Straus suggests rejection, not only of marriage, but also of its physical consequences – intercourse and childbirth. Straus hypothesizes that this female rejection is not necessarily a rejection of sexuality in favour of celibacy. Rather, she opens the possibility of the rejection of compulsory heterosexuality and the potential for female homoerotic desire. Straus suggests that, through his female characters, Chaucer may have given voice to an unarticulated female desire that is muffled in the dominant masculine discourses of the premodern world.

Chaucer wrote in the vernacular, but for most of the period the very language used to discuss sexuality and its regulation was Latin, the language of patriarchy. While mutable and flexible, Latin also carried with it certain assumptions about the need for men to exercise discipline and control over the sex/gender system. Garret Epp examines the relationship between sexual regulation and the rules of Latin grammar in Matthew of Vendôme's *Ars versificatoria*, a twelfth-century schoolroom text. Through the careful deployment of sexual language in the service of grammar and rhetoric, Matthew sought to inculcate the rules governing language and sexual conduct. Reason and discipline are dominant themes; careless literary criticism is linked with unbridled sexuality, unreasoned judgment with prostitution. Matthew perceived both rhetoric and sex as threats to the developing masculinity of his schoolboys. Both equally needed to be regulated. To inculcate his warning and instil the rules of both grammar and sexuality, Matthew deployed a startlingly explicit array of imagery, designed to warn his students about the seductive and feminizing charms of rhetoric and sodomy. Epp concludes that Matthew expected his pupils in this way 'to learn masculine control over their material, avoiding the parallel feminizations of rhetorical and moral vice.'

Language had the potential to unleash dangerous and undisciplined sexual desire. Sweet words were the tools of seduction. Nowhere was this danger more evident than in the relationship between reading and the imagination. The question of the untamed and uncontrolled imagination, which led to sexual fantasy, and ultimately to sin, was problematized as early as Jerome's confession that, in the midst of his penitential disciplines, he could not control his sexual fantasies. 'There was I, therefore, who from fear of hell had condemned myself to such a prison, with only scorpions and wild beasts as companions. Yet I was often surrounded by dancing girls. My face was pale from fasting, and my mind was hot with desire in a body cold as ice. Though my flesh, before its tenant, was already as good as dead, the fires of the passions kept boiling within me.'[21] The imagination, like language, needed to be disciplined and brought under the control of reason.

Language and texts, however, were frequently the impetus for loosening the hold of reason and could open the sexual floodgates. The experience of Abelard and Heloise or Paolo and Francesca attests to the close relationship between reading and sexual desire. Reading, then, could be transformed into a sexual act placed in the service of lust by stimulating desire and encouraging seduction or, failing that, fantasies that might culminate in masturbation. This is the question that occupies Andrew Taylor's examination of the relationship among reading, privacy, and premodern erotica. Taylor suggests that the shift from public recitation in the hall to private reading in the chamber provided individuals with the opportunity to read and reread 'the dirty bits.' Privacy and book ownership could conspire with the sweet words and feminine rhetoric, identified by Matthew of Vendôme, to evoke sexual fantasy, ultimately leading to the solitary vice.

Taylor's intriguing reflections on the complex interplay of mind, imagination, and body, and Jerome's own anguished inability to tame his mind by disciplining his flesh, converge in Nancy Partner's investigation of the erotic nature of medieval mystical experience. She urges a more interdisciplinary, theoretically sophisticated, and psychologically nuanced approach to medieval mystics, one that recognizes their individual integrity as complex human beings. Critical of modern tendencies to dehumanize mystics and to paraphrase and euphemize mystical experience, Partner contends that a recognition of the explicitly sexual nature of many mystical visions will allow for a better understanding of the impact of the imposition of the repressive moral code on the individual. The extent of the tension between the discipline of reason and the ecstasy of desire will be found in the outpouring of the unconscious, in the frankly sexualized visions of the mystics.

The essays by Bullough and Partner frame this collection of research into premodern sex and sexuality. As Bullough condemns the bowdlerism and judgmentalism that tarnished past research, so Partner pleas for more open and less euphemistic research. Together they point to a tension inherent in the study of sexuality in a period dominated by a worldview that continues to exercise remarkable influence. Despite protestations of the essentially secular nature of contemporary Western society, sexuality and spirituality, body and soul, are no more disentangled now than they were in the past. People continue to believe they have a vested interest in controlling sexuality, be it their own or that of others. The evaluation of sexualities as good or bad, moral or immoral, remains contested and matters very much to individuals and societies. These beliefs and values inform historical research and make it profoundly relevant to the present. They veil the past from the present, hiding and distorting, allowing only selective glimpses from which we moderns draw generalizations that form our own historical justification for maintaining or modifying the status quo. This is why the history of sex and sexuality is so important and yet so fraught. The challenge that faces future research into the history of human sexuality is to strike a balance between the exigencies and demands of the present and the integrity of our veiled past. This can be achieved only by continuing to embrace a plurality of theoretical and methodological perspectives and encouraging multidisciplinary research by a varied group of scholars representing a diversity of subjectivities.

NOTES

1 Michel Foucault, *Histoire de la sexualité*, vol. 1: *La Volonté de savoir* (Paris: Gallimard 1976); trans. Robert Hurley, *The History of Sexuality: An Introduction* (New York: Pantheon 1978)

2 See, for example, Jeffrey Weeks, *Sex, Politics and Society: The Regulation of Sexuality since 1800* (London: Longman 1981) and *Sexuality and Its Discontents: Meanings, Myths and Modern Sexualities* (London: Routledge 1985). For antiquity see the essay collection *Before Sexuality: The Construction of Erotic Experience in the Ancient Greek World*, eds. D.M. Halperin, J.J. Winkler, and F.I. Zeitlin (Princeton, NJ: Princeton University Press 1990). This is not to suggest that medievalists were not in the vanguard of gay studies. As early as 1980 John Boswell published his ground-breaking and controversial study of homosexuality in the Middle Ages, *Christianity, Social Tolerance, and Homosexuality: Gay People in Western Europe from the Beginning of the Christian Era to the Fourteenth Century* (Chicago: University of Chicago Press 1980).

3 A useful overview of theoretical and methodological trends in the study of the history of sexuality, with emphasis on Foucault, is presented in Gaston Desjardins, 'Histoire de la sexualité: Voir ailleurs si j'y suis. Et quelques réflexions autour de l'épistémologie foulcadienne,' *Histoire sociale/Social History* 15/49 (1992), 101–23.

4 Pierre J. Payer, 'Foucault and Penance and the Shaping of Sexuality,' *Studies in Religion/Sciences religieuses* 14 (1985), 313–20, and Elizabeth A. Clark, 'Foucault, the Fathers, and Sex,' *Journal of the American Academy of Religion* 56/4 (1986), 619–41. For example, in a recent essay collection focusing on the history of attitudes towards sexuality – *Sexual Knowledge, Sexual Science: The History of Attitudes to Sexuality*, eds. Roy Porter and Mikuláš Teich (Cambridge: Cambridge University Press 1994) – the majority of the essays (fifteen of seventeen) focus on the period after 1500. One essay surveys Greek and Roman antiquity. The

single essay ostensibly on the Middle Ages addresses questions arising from the notion of sado-masochism, its medieval origins, and modern psychological implications. It is surprising that the collection did not include examinations of medieval medical discourse or of the highly developed discourse of confession and penance that Foucault identified as so central to the development of Western sexual knowledge. In other words, the fundamental role of the Middle Ages in the development of sexual knowledge is neglected.

5 See Arthur Brittan, *Masculinity and Power* (Oxford: Basil Blackwell 1989), 48–51.

6 Victor J. Seidler, 'Reason, Desire, and Male Sexuality,' in *The Cultural Construction of Sexuality*, ed. Pat Caplan, 82–112 (New York: Tavistock 1987). See also Lois McNay, *Foucault and Feminism: Power, Gender and the Self* (Cambridge: Polity Press 1992); Lynn Hunt, 'Foucault's Subject in *The History of Sexuality*,' in *Discourses of Sexuality: From Aristotle to AIDS*, ed. Domna C. Stanton (Ann Arbor: University of Michigan Press 1992); and Catharine A. MacKinnon, 'Does Sexuality Have a History?' in ibid., 117–36.

7 *Sexual Practices and the Medieval Church*, eds. Vern L. Bullough and James A. Brundage (Buffalo: Prometheus 1982). More recently, other essay collections of particular interest have appeared, including *Sex in the Middle Ages: A Book of Essays*, ed. Joyce E. Salisbury (New York: Garland 1991), and *Handbook of Medieval Sexuality*, eds. Vern L. Bullough and James Brundage (New York: Garland 1996). The wealth of primary sources and secondary studies available on the subject of medieval sexuality in particular is presented in Joyce E. Salisbury, *Medieval Sexuality: A Research Guide* (New York: Garland 1990). In the early-modern period, there has been a tendency to link studies in sexuality more closely with gender. See, for example, *Sexuality and Gender in Early Modern Europe: Institutions, Texts, Images*, ed. James Grantham Turner (Cambridge: Cambridge University Press 1993), and *Desire in the Renaissance: Psychoanalysis and Literature*, eds. Valeria Finucci and Regina Schwartz (Princeton, NJ: Princeton University Press 1994). For a more historical rather than literary approach to early-modern sexuality, see, for example, Lyndal Roper, *Oedipus and the Devil: Witchcraft, Sexuality and Religion in Early Modern Europe* (London: Routledge 1994).

8 *Sexuality in the Renaissance/La Sexualité à la Renaissance*, ed. Jacqueline Murray, *Renaissance and Reformation/Renaissance et Réforme* 24/1 (1988).

9 A number of earlier meetings included sexuality as one aspect of themes focusing on marriage, family, and women. The Toronto conference sought to shed this context of marriage and family and move sexuality to the centre, without the interpretive implications held in contextualizing it within the fields of marriage and family or women's studies. For examples of the tendency to locate

the study of sex within the broader field of marriage and the family, see the bibliographic survey 'Recent Trends in Renaissance Studies: The Family, Sex and Marriage,' ed. Stanley Chojnacki, *Renaissance Quarterly* 40 (1987), 660–761. See also the essay collection *The Olde Daunce: Love, Friendship, Sex, and Marriage in the Medieval World*, eds. Robert R. Edwards and Stephen Spector (Binghamton: State University of New York Press 1991).

10 For example, as early as 1977 Joan Kelly highlighted the inappropriateness of the blind application of traditional periodization specifically as it applied to the experience and status of women: 'Did Women Have a Renaissance?' rept. in *Women, History and Theory: The Essays of Joan Kelly* (Chicago: University of Chicago Press 1984), 19–50. The narrow focus of 'Renaissance' on high culture and élites has been recognized in the adoption of the designation 'early modern' by social historians. This term, too, however, has the limitations of implying a sharp break with the preceding period, while being applied indiscriminately from the early sixteenth through the late eighteenth century.

11 For example, in a recent study that crosses from antiquity to the seventeenth century, John Boswell chose the title *Same-Sex Unions in Premodern Europe* (New York: Villard 1994).

12 There were many discourses which either remained unchanged from the Middle Ages or evolved slowly over the course of the sixteenth and seventeenth centuries. This is especially so for the two discourses which dominated questions of sexuality – theology and medicine – despite the Protestant and Aristotelian revolutions which might be expected to have ruptured, or at least interrupted, these discourses. For example, in a recent essay on sexual knowledge in Europe from 1500 to 1700, Patricia Crawford presents a survey of attitudes in both these discourses, yet virtually every point made by both Protestant moralists and Aristotelian-influenced medical writers can be traced to their Catholic and Galenic medieval predecessors. By considering the 'early modern' period in isolation, however, the sense of this significant continuity is lost. It is surely important to our understanding of sex and sexuality in the past that Protestant moralists provided the same sexual advice and attempted to exercise the same social control over their parishioners as had their Catholic predecessors some three hundred years earlier, or that long after Aristotelian theories of physiology and generation had prevailed in the medical schools, some doctors continued to stress the importance of female orgasm for conception. See Patricia Crawford, 'Sexual Knowledge in England, 1500–1750,' in *Sexual Knowledge, Sexual Science*, eds. Porter and Teich, 82–106.

13 Peter Brown presents a particularly insightful analysis of the early development of Christian thinking on sexuality in *The Body and Society: Men, Women, and Sexual Renunciation in Early Christianity* (New York: Columbia University

Press 1988). The teachings of Ambrose, Jerome, and Augustine on sexuality are summarized in Joyce E. Salisbury, 'The Latin Doctors of the Church on Sexuality,' *Journal of Medieval History* 12 (1986), 279–89. For the ancient context, see Aline Rousselle, *Porneia: On Desire and the Body in Antiquity*, trans. Felicia Pheasant (Oxford: Basil Blackwell 1988).

14 Augustine, *The City of God*, vols. 6–8, in *Writings of Saint Augustine*, trans. Demetrius B. Zema, Gerald G. Walsh, Grace Monahan, and Daniel J. Honan (New York: Fathers of the Church 1952), XIV.21, vol. 7: 396.

15 Gratian's *Decretum* remains available only in a nineteenth-century edition: *Corpus Iuris Canonici*, vol. 1, ed. Aemilius Friedberg, 2d ed. (Lipsiae 1879). Peter Lombard has been edited more recently: *Sententiae in IV libris distinctae*, 3d ed. (Grottaferrata: Editiones Collegii S. Bonaventurae ad Claras Aquas 1981).

16 The process by which a Christian moral code emerged has been examined comprehensively and in detail in James A. Brundage, *Law, Sex, and Christian Society in Medieval Europe* (Chicago: University of Chicago Press 1987).

17 In addition to works by Michel Foucault and Jeffrey Weeks, see also Alan Bray, *Homosexuality in Renaissance England* (London: Gay Men's Press 1982).

18 Thomas Aquinas, *Summa theologiae*, trans. Fathers of the English Dominican Province, 3 vols. (New York: Benziger Brothers 1947–8), vol. 2: 1825.

19 R.I. Moore, *The Formation of a Persecuting Society: Power and Deviance in Western Europe, 950–1250* (Oxford: Basil Blackwell 1987)

20 Thus far, there has been little research on the meaning of masculinity in the premodern world. The essay collection *Medieval Masculinities: Regarding Men in the Middle Ages*, ed. Clare A. Lees, Medieval Cultures, 7 (Minneapolis: University of Minnesota Press 1994), is an important introduction to the study of men outside their universalized and normative construction.

21 Jerome, *Ad Eustochium* (Letter 22) in *The Letters of St. Jerome*, vol. 1, trans. Charles Christopher Mierow, Ancient Christian Writers (London: Longmans, Green 1963), 140

Desire and Discipline
Sex and Sexuality in the Premodern West

Sex in History: A Redux

VERN L. BULLOUGH

Some twenty-five years ago, I gave a paper at the Society for the Scientific Study of Sex, in which I looked briefly at the state of existing historical research into human sexuality. I had intended the paper as a call to action to historians and scholars in the humanities, arguing that not only had sex in its biological sense been ignored, but also such sexually related topics as courtship, marriage, child rearing, and gender behaviour. The paper was published a year later in the *Journal of Sex Research* under a title, which in spite of its cleverness, served to emphasize my message: 'Sex in History: A Virgin Field.'[1]

In that paper, I advanced several reasons for the lack of scholarly studies, only one which I will repeat here: fear, both personal and generalized. By 'personal' fear, I meant the fear that one might be labelled as some kind of 'pervert,' a label that would make it difficult for one to get an academic position or, if one already had such a job, would lessen one's chances of getting tenure. Let me explain through personal experiences.

Personal Anxieties

Early in my career, I had been an unhappy observer of a person's being denied tenure because he was suspected by his colleagues of being homosexual. Perhaps for this reason, I followed the advice given by George Corner to William Masters when the young Masters came to him for advice about a career in sex research. Corner, a distinguished physician (and a medieval scholar as well),[2] told the would-be sex researcher to wait until he was in his late thirties, had already achieved a reputation in a 'respectable' field, had married and had a family, and then, and only then, to enter into or admit to doing sex research.[3] I did not quite follow this rule, but I kept my research into sexuality quiet, and by the time my university colleagues knew what I was doing, I was a full professor. Still, I was, if not fearful, often embarrassed by the reaction of my colleagues. For example, at a meeting of the American Historical Association in 1966 at which I gave a paper on medieval universities, I was introduced as a specialist in whores, pimps, and queers, who occasionally deigned to do real research. To protect myself against too much hostile labelling, I down-played my research into human sexuality as much as possible, and for several years I did not list most of it on my official *vita.* Undoubtedly some of my anxieties reflected my own personal insecurities. When I was invited early in 1960 to write a book on either homosexuality or prostitution, both topics I had explored, I chose to write on prostitution because I was fearful that it would be assumed by everyone that I was homosexual. Eventually, as I was better able to deal with my own insecurities, I published on the then more forbidden topics of homosexuality, lesbianism, transvestism, transsexualism, paedophilia, sado-masochism, pornography, and so on. Perhaps unconsciously I was hoping that the very variety of my sexual topics would allow me to escape any specific designation, and instead just be labelled a 'DOM,' that is, Dirty Old Man.

I never had any problems publishing the results of my research, although initially this work was not accepted by either professional medieval or general historical journals. Instead, it appeared in sociological, psychological, medical, and sexuality journals. Those historical and medieval journals to which I submitted work in the late 1950s and through the 1960s simply rejected the material as unsuitable. I do not think it ever went to referees for consideration. There was even a reluctance to have papers on sexual themes delivered at professional meetings, although times did begin to change in the late 1960s. After considerable lobbying by me, the American historian John Burnham, and others, the American Historical Association decided to devote a session at its 1970 meeting to sex in history. I was a presenter at this session which, much to my surprise, as well as that of the AHA, attracted approximately a thousand people. Encouraged by this, several medievalists, including some of the contributors to this volume, persuaded the organizers of the 1973 Kalamazoo meetings to devote a session to sexual issues in medieval studies. Since then, the field has expanded tremendously, although one of the difficulties I had in not publishing many of my early articles in professional historical or medieval journals is that they lacked the kind of peer review such journals gave them, something which I very much regretted, since my colleagues in those other fields in which I published knew human sexuality or medicine or sociology or psychology, but usually not much history. All of this background emphasizes that I do not think personal fear need be an issue in today's scholarly world.

Generalized Fear

In addition to any personal fears I might have, I noted there was also a generalized fear among scholars – namely, the fear of what we might find out about the past. This struck me one day as I was reading John Jay Chapman's essays on the Greeks, written in the 1930s. He reported that, much to his shock, the Greeks had different attitudes towards homosexuality than he did. He concluded that this was the case because the 'Attic mind was abnormal': 'But why had I not found this out before? Because the books and essays on Plato which I had been reading were either accommodated to the Greek psychology or else they were accommodated to modern Miss Nancyism — and, by the way, the two agree very sociably.'[4] In spite of Chapman's discovery (which was original only in that he wrote it up), the issue of sex in classical Greece continued to be ignored in textbooks and in scholarly research, even when I was in graduate school. As late as the 1960s, one of the best-selling books on ancient Greece, Edith Hamilton's *The Greek Way*, somehow managed to give such an idealized version of Greece that sex was not even mentioned.[5]

Unfortunately, it was not only popular idealized studies such as Hamilton's that followed the 'Miss Nancyism' denounced by Chapman, but standard reference works as well. A good example was the first edition of the *Oxford Classical Dictionary*, which in many ways was an outstanding reference work. Published in the 'enlightened' post–Second World War period, it included brief articles on women and marriage, even on adultery and sacred prostitution, but nothing on secular prostitution or on homosexuality, and the word 'sex' was banished altogether.[6]

Occasionally there was a daring popularizer who touched on the forbidden subject, but in ways which seemed to imply that, even though sex existed, it was bad. One of the best examples of this was a college-level text by Norman Cantor which appeared in 1963 and actually mentioned the word 'homosexuality,' although in 'appropriately' negative terms:

> the civilization of the Roman empire was vitiated by homosexuality from its
> earliest days. A question, uncomfortable to our contemporary lax moralists,

may be raised: Is not the common practice of homosexuality a fundamental debilitating factor in any civilization where it is extensively practiced, as it is a wasting spiritual disease in the individual. It is worth considering that another great and flourishing civilization, the medieval Arabic, where homosexuality was also widespread similarly underwent a sudden malaise and breakdown. Is there some moral psychological causation, resulting from the social effects of homosexuality that has been ignored?[7]

By making such a statement, the author emphasized that his text was more up to date than other medieval texts since it mentioned the forbidden word 'homosexual,' but at the same time he made certain that every one knew he realized just how awful such activities were. He was, of course, writing before John Boswell's or my own work on the topic appeared,[8] but, even for the time, his editorializing distorted history. The Romans never looked upon homosexuality with particular favour, and although some of the emperors certainly had homoerotic attachments, there is no evidence that Hadrian, for example, was less effective as an emperor because of his homoeroticism than those who did not share it. In fact, it was the earlier Roman emperors, when Rome was at its height, that probably had the most unorthodox sexual behaviours. Edward Gibbon, writing in an age which was somewhat more open about sex than was the United States in the first half of the twentieth century, mentioned in one of his characteristic footnotes that, of 'the first fifteen emperors Claudius was the only one whose taste in love was entirely correct.'[9] In short, it would have been much more accurate for Cantor to have said that the height of the Roman power was reached under 'sexually incorrect emperors,' and that it weakened after the more orthodox Christian emperors appeared.

Cantor, however, was simply subscribing to the simplistic view of the relation of sex to history put forth by the pioneer of modern historical writings, Leopold von Ranke. Without much documentation, von Ranke ascribed the decline of Italy at the end of the fifteenth century to pederasty and similar venial weaknesses, basically ignoring social, economic, and political realities. 'Pederasty, which extended even to the young soldiers in the army, and was regarded as venial because practiced by the Greeks and Romans, whom all delighted to imitate, sapped all vital energy. Native and classical writers ascribe the misfortune of the nation to this evil practice. A terrible rival of pederasty was syphilis which spread through all the classes like the plague ...'[10] He explained pederasts as men who curled their hair, plucked their eyebrows, and spoke to their

superiors as softly as if they were at their last breath; men who were afraid
to move their heads lest they should disarrange their hair, men who carried a looking-glass in their hat and a comb in their sleeve, or any men
who strove to sing well in ladies' society, accompanying themselves on the
viol.[11]

Perhaps von Ranke, who was of a different century than I am, ought to
be forgiven his prejudices and ignorance about sexual matters as well as
his moral outrage about unisex clothing or the behaviours now associated
with modern rock stars. Historians, however, were slow to change their
attitudes. Arnold Toynbee, as late as 1964, deplored the 'relapse into pre-
cocious sexuality' as one of the 'moral blemishes of contemporary civilization.'[12] He wanted to return to the moral standards of the nineteenth
century, when, he claimed, society had managed to postpone the age of
sexual awakening, sexual experience, and sexual infatuation far beyond
the age of puberty. 'You may tell me this was against nature: but to be
human consists precisely in transcending nature — in overcoming the
histological limitations that we have inherited from our prehuman ances-
tors ...'[13] What Toynbee did was show his historical ignorance of the reality of Victorian life, at least that outside his own privileged class. If he had
lived until today, he would use history to demonstrate that the answer to
teenage pregnancy (illegitimacy was a major Victorian problem) was just
to say no.

When I first began to read such statements, early in my career, I
ascribed them to the tendency of older historians to pontificate about the
past. Since I am now an older historian, some would even say elderly, I
worry that some in the audience may regard this paper as another elderly
professor's pontificating about the past. In part this is true, but, in my
defence, I think this is what I was asked to do, and I hope the paper is
more than that.

What I called for in my 1971 paper was a new history which went
beyond the social and intellectual history desired by James Harvey Robinson and others as they tried to expand traditional political history at the
beginning of this century.[14] My version of the new history was to include
the sexual behaviour of men and women in particular, and their biological nature in general, as well as what we now call 'gender issues.' Let me
quote myself:

... many of us dream as graduate students of finding new documents which
will radically change historical interpretations, or even change the direction
of historical studies. In my opinion the investigation of sexual behavior

offers many such opportunities to make major breakthroughs. Sex might well be a three letter word, but it exists, and has existed throughout history. For those willing to do some pioneering, the study of the history of sex offers only virgin fields.[15]

Whether my individual call had any effect is uncertain, and not particularly important; what is obvious, however, is that historians in particular, and scholars in the humanities in general, took up the investigation of sex and gender issues in the 1970s, until now there is almost a deluge of studies. Several factors, to my mind, accounted for this. One was the emergence of a strong movement for homosexual and lesbian rights which encouraged research into the past of homosexuality and lesbianism. The second wave of feminism, as it gained momentum in the 1970s, forced the broadening of the perspective of historians to questions of sex and gender. Encouraged by the new climate of opinion, graduate-school dissertation advisers who had once discouraged theses and research projects dealing with sex and gender issues (as my own had done) began to accept such topics. Professional journals of all kinds, stimulated by the growth of more specialized journals concerned with sex and gender issues, began to publish the results of the new scholarship. Publishers, seeing a market, jumped in, not only with special series but with ever more specialized journals. There is now a journal devoted specifically to the history of sexuality, the *Journal of the History of Sexuality*; many university presses are eagerly seeking manuscripts on sex and gender topics; and several presses have special series devoted to sexual topics, including the University of Chicago, Columbia University, and the Universities of California and Illinois. Almost all university presses are willing to publish manuscripts dealing with gender or sex issues. My own scholarly output in professional journals increased, in part because some of my articles which originally had been rejected out of hand by various journals as not suitable eventually came to be published, some even in the same journals that had originally rejected them. Medieval studies in general has seen, if not an explosion, at least increasing interest in the topic. Joyce E. Salisbury's bibliography of studies in medieval sexuality, published in 1990, listed some 815 items, of which 288 are articles and 237 are books, most published within the past twenty years. The rest of her listings fall under the category of primary sources: history, law, literature, religion, and science.[16]

Naturally, I was pleased to see that Jim Brundage and I led the list of modern authors, but to emphasize that the materials for sex and gender studies have been around for a long time, the most significant author/ editor was J.P. Migne. In fact, so great is the interest that Brundage and I have recently published *A Handbook of Medieval Sexuality*, which attempts to serve as a more detailed guide to sex and gender studies in the Middle Ages.[17]

Definitions, Interpretations, and Sources

Even though more of us are studying sexual and gender issues in the medieval period, problems remain. One is quite simply what constitutes a sexual topic. Salisbury, for example, indicates that she has restricted her sources to what she calls 'love consummated,' and therefore has left out courtly love and religious love. Instead, she attempted to include works discussing or describing sexual contact or attitudes towards sexual contact, and thus listed works dealing with intercourse, fornication, adultery, homosexuality, prostitution, and bestiality. She also included many works on medieval gynaecology, not because we consider such a subject sexual but because medieval people did. On the other hand, she listed works on transvestism and cross-dressing, although it was not considered to have anything to do with sex in the Middle Ages, unlike the case in the twentieth century. Compilers of bibliographies have to make choices, and Salisbury made intelligent ones.

Obviously those mentioned in Salisbury's bibliography are looking for different things in medieval records than were past researchers. Historians have always recognized that each generation writes its own history; usually we believe this is so because each generation looks at history from a different perspective and is seeking different kinds of answers. In recent years it is the feminists and gays who have been seeking new kinds of answers.

Some, recognizing that most of the source material was written by men who had certain assumptions about sex, have come to believe that it is impossible to get an accurate picture of sexuality in the past. Some of these have turned to deconstructionism and the philosopher Michel Foucault as a guide. Foucault, who had planned a six-volume study of sexuality in civilization, had only published three volumes before he died in 1984. Two of these volumes dealt with Graeco-Roman civilization and were based heavily on primary-source material. The first volume, which was more general, presented little research about sexuality and no conclusive evidence, but set sexuality in the midst of nowhere and made conclusions about it which were not necessarily historically accurate. Foucault, however, was not interested in history or in explaining how assumptions developed or the reasons for them, but, rather, was engaged in the construction of his own myths of the past, which might or might not be true. He held that, since past history had been written almost entirely by males who bought into the assumptions of a heterosexual normality, the view of history could have little validity to the homosexual or feminist, and so all of history had to be reinterpreted.[18]

Foucault had both good and bad effects on the study of sexual and gender issues in history. He emphasized to the historically oriented researchers that their research was really a centre-piece to the understanding of the place of sex in the contemporary world, and this realization came as more and more was being published about sex in history. History could become the cutting edge for the reassessment of the past that the more militant gays and feminists wanted. There was also a more negative consequence – namely, the attempt to create new mythologies by those more radically discontented with the status quo.

Some of this was tied into the question of nature versus nurture. One of the issues in the scholarship of the 1980s, for example, was just how much homosexuality and lesbianism were social constructs. Some went so far as to claim that the origin of modern homosexuality came as late as the eighteenth century; others chose to place it later, in the nineteenth century; still others tried to place it earlier.[19] It is almost essential for a researcher to have some understanding of the conflict in order to arrive at where she or he stands, since the stance might well influence the conclusions. I would hold that, while there are strong biological factors at work in human sexuality, there is also a complex of psychological, sociological, and cultural factors involved. There are probably also critical periods during which sociopsychological factors have greater influence than the others, but it is not yet clear what agents are at work. To me, this implies that same-sex relationships always existed; in fact, I would hold that, potentially, we are all bisexual, but that the meanings of such relationships are culturally and socially influenced.

This issue emphasizes one of the potential dangers in the study of medieval sexuality and gender issues, that is, separating it from other aspects of medieval life or failing to put it in the context of the time. This area is where the medievalist plays such an important role, and the sexologist has to take a back seat. Some forms of medieval literature seem to approach the subject of sexuality directly, as James Brundage and John T. Noonan have demonstrated through their study of canon law, or Danielle

Jacquart and Claude Thomasset through their study of medieval medi-cine.[20] For the most part, however, information about sex and gender issues appear serendipitously, and the importance of potential references have to be recognized by the researcher. This is simply because, even with all the new bibliographical tools, it is difficult to find materials that were not previously indexed. Moreover, since most indices never listed such topics as homosexuality or lesbianism, or even used the term 'sexual intercourse,' finding such material is not easy. For this reason, it is impor-tant that medievalists as a group acquire some expertise in sexual matters. Most of us carry on research in our own specialized area, but, since sexual and gender issues are so much a part of being human, most medievalists will occasionally run across something directly pertaining to sexuality which has not yet been widely recognized by others. My message to those who do read something or hear something is to make note of it and either investigate it further or pass the information along to a colleague who might want to do so. The sources for medieval history are so vast that it is only by the work of the specialists in various areas of medieval studies contributing their occasional findings that a more comprehensive under-standing of medieval sexuality will come about. This makes it important to communicate our findings to others, either through writing them up or telling others about them.

We also need to keep in mind that sex and gender issues are very broadly defined. Much of the current research has concentrated either on homosexuality or prostitution in the medieval period or on more gen-eral gender issues. I will pass over these, and look at how serendipity has influenced some of my own research and why scholars such as myself owe so much to others.

Serendipitous Findings

One of the issues that nineteenth- and early twentieth-century scholars of the marriage and the family devoted a lot of ink to was the so-called *Jus Primus Noctis*, or 'Right of the First Night,' which might, in feminist terms, be called an attempt to cloak rape with some elements of respectability.[21] In spite of the vast literature on the topic, there is no mention of it in Sal-isbury's bibliography. Where can we find information about the existence of such a custom when it was not written in any tribal, Roman, canon, or civil laws?[22] All kinds of medieval sources might give some information, but who can read them all. Happily, I found an important reference by lis-tening to a paper on Count Gerald of Aurillac presented by M.F. Skinner at the 1990 Fordham University medieval conference.[23] The story of the count's life originally had been written by Abbot Odo (879–942), the founder of the Cluniac movement, as an effort to encourage the noble laity of the time to emulate the life of Gerald, who had been one of them. In the story, Odo recounts how Gerald became sexually attracted to one of his serfs:

> He was tortured, therefore, allured, and consumed by blind fire. Overcome at length he sent word to the mother of the girl that he would come by night. [Although he still prayed to be delivered from temptation] ... Gerald came to the agreed place, and the girl entered the room; because he was cold he stood at the hearth facing her; divine grace looked on him and this same girl appeared to him so deformed that he could not believe it was she whom he saw, until her father asserted it was so.[24]

We are told that Gerald backed away from his assignation and rode off in relief, musing at the divine miracle of her transformation which allowed him to stay celibate. To me, and to those in attendance, it seemed obvious that her family had made great efforts to make her look unattractive in the hope of saving her from rape by the master, since they were otherwise unable to defy the wishes of the lord. In effect what the story serves to emphasize is that a powerful noble could more or less violate with impunity women under his control. It was an accepted fact of life. I suspect I always knew, or at least suspected, that this was the case, but this instance provides additional insight. This is only one case, and many more are needed before we can arrive at some basic conclusions, but I think it is significant in indicating the very real basis for the so-called right of the first night – namely, power and authority to take whom the lord wished.[25]

All kinds of things appear in medieval source material which bear on modern sexual problems. For example, Robert of Brunne (or Robert Mannying), in his poem 'Handling Synne,' based on William of Wadington's *Manual des pechiez*, reports that a man and wife who sought refuge from their enemies in a monastery engaged in sexual intercourse with such abandon that they aroused the ire of God, and the result was what is sometimes called 'Penis captivus,' in which the couple could be separated only by praying to God. A similar incident is recorded in the life of Saint Guignerus.[26] Both of these references come from published works which I happened to run across, but many more exist in manuscript. Guy de Beaujouan, for example, found a medieval medical manuscript dealing in some detail with the various positions for sexual intercourse, while searching through a manuscript collection in Spain.[27] Keep alert for serendipitous discoveries.

Sex and Gender Issues

One area of medieval studies with which I have long been concerned is the presence of strong gender bias and the limitations put on the female.[28] From medieval source materials, it seems quite clear that women were praised for trying to become more manly, while men were denounced if they showed feminine weakness. One of the interesting illustrations of these ideas appears in attitudes towards cross-dressing.[29] My findings that many women saints successfully impersonated males, only to have their true sex uncovered at their death, illustrate how women could achieve higher status by denying their sex. Perhaps because I was looking for examples, the more I examined the medieval sources, the more cross-dressing women I found. Again, friends and colleagues in the medieval field sent me examples. One came to my attention from a note by a fellow medievalist. This was *Le Roman de silence*, which, though written in the thirteenth century by Heldris de Cournuälle, was not discovered until the 1960s and published in full in 1972.[30] It recounts the story of a girl raised as a boy, her adventures, and her ultimate return to the feminine role. It also tells about the struggle she underwent between her true nature, as a female, and her nurture (as a male), and how it was resolved. Again, without colleagues to feed me this kind of information, my studies would have been severely weakened.[31]

It was not only cross-dressing which emphasized the higher status of the male, but also sex changes. Jane Schulenberg, another medievalist, sent me several references to medieval sex changes. Again, one of them comes from saints' lives, this time, the life of Abban. Let me quote:

> Now the king was old at this time, and he had no heir except a daughter whom his wife bore that very night. And he requested Abban to baptize her. And he perceived the sadness of the king at having no heir. 'If God pleases,' said Aban, 'thou shalt have an heir.' 'Nay,' said the king, 'that is impossible for me owing to my age.' Abban took the infant in his hands, and prayed earnestly to God that the king might have an heir; and the girl that he immersed in the font he took out as a boy, and laid it on the king's bosom. 'Here is thy son,' said he. And the king was exceedingly glad, and so were the people of the country, at these miracles.[32]

A similar miraculous change of sex was attributed to the intervention of Saint Gerald, Abbot of Lismore, who was being held a prisoner by a pagan king. In this case, the king's only child, a daughter whom the king had tried to pass off as a son, had died. The king promised Saint Gerald an abbey rich in lands and goods if they could raise up his 'son' from the dead. Saint Gerald prayed for such a miracle:

> O Eternal God, Who art the protector of all that trust in Thee, Who takest away the anguish of Thy faithful peoples, Who didst dry up the Red Sea for the captive Israelites and miraculously loosed Peter from his bonds, have mercy and loose us also, who are prisoners of these barbarians, from this perilous pass into which we are come by the death of the King's daughters, insomuch as Thou mayest make of this dead maiden, by Thy marvelous power a living youth, granting to him quick motion and sense through our minister ... Be it son or daughter, may God Who giveth life to all, and to Whom all things are possible, vouchsafe to raise thee up a male child.

Inevitably, to the amazement of all, a royal youth rose from the bier.[33] Still another such miracle appears in the collection of Theodore of Appoldia.[34] I have found no similar change into females, and this seems to emphasize the importance and status and role of males vis-à-vis females.

This does not mean that males were not able to impersonate women, but they did so as part of what might be called 'fun and games.' This is most evident in the case of Ulrich von Lichtenstein, a thirteenth-century knight from Styria, whose case I found more or less accidentally. Ulrich is best remembered for his narrative poem, *Frauendienst*, or *Autobiography in Service of Ladies*.[35] This German predecessor of Cervantes's *Don Quixote* includes an episode in which Ulrich, in order to honour his lady and all women, disguises himself as the goddess Venus and travels from Venice, through northern Italy, to Styria, Austria, fighting jousts all the way. Apparently, on first impression, some thought he was a woman and, before one joust, a countess attempted to kiss him. When he moved his veil aside for her to do so, she laughed and said.

> Why you're a man!
> I caught a glimpse of you just now.
> What then? I'll kiss you anyhow.
> From all good women everywhere
> I'll give you a kiss. Because you

wear a women's dress and honor thus
us all, I'll kiss for all of us.[36]

Possible Sado-Masochism and Other Medieval Sex Practices

Medieval views of cross-dressing are easy to demonstrate, and they had much in common with the views held of women's role and place in our own society until fairly recently. But how much can we apply current sexual terminology to the medieval period? This is a difficulty I faced when studying sado-masochism. Although the terms were coined in the nineteenth century,[37] I would hold that the concept is deeply embedded in Western culture, and it is this historical tradition which helps explain the phenomenon today. But did medieval sado-masochism have the same sexual overtones as modern analysts put upon current practices? I would hold, in fact, that it did to some extent, and if we accept that sexuality is culturally and historically influenced, then such a recognition is logical.[38] I recognize the dangers of trying to read the medieval mind, but even though we might interpret things in a different way than they did, the influence of the cultural setting remains important.

Let me amplify. Quite obviously there are many elements in medieval society which emphasize both the importance of suffering and the need to give punishment. Among the early ascetics in the Egyptian desert, for example, there was a widespread belief that those who had not suffered in this world were condemned to suffer in the next, and by implication any suffering endured on this earth would result in a corresponding purification of one's soul in the next.[39] Although asceticism is not, in and of itself, necessarily masochistic, there is a line between the physical and mental training necessary to achieve greater self-control and sado-masochistic pleasure, between self-denial and self-punishment, but it is not always clear what that line is. Some of the early Christian ascetics seem to have crossed that line and, if one is to believe the descriptions of Palladius, that line was crossed often.

For example, Palladius reported that Macarius the Younger (394 C.E.) left his regular cell every year during the forty days of Lent, practising self-mortification in dark underground holes. The opening for these cells was only large enough to wiggle inside, and, once there, it was possible to sit up but impossible to straighten out the legs. Even this suffering was not enough for Macarius, and one day when he was

sitting in the cell, a gnat stung him on the foot. Feeling the pain, he killed it

·with his hands, and it was gorged with his blood. He accused himself of act-
ing out of revenge and condemned himself to sit naked in the marsh of
Skete out in the great desert for six months. Here the mosquitoes lacerate
even the hides of wild swine just as wasps do. Soon he was bitten all over his
body, and he became so swollen that some thought he had elephantiasis.
When he returned to his cell after six months, he was recognized as Macarius only by his voice.[40]

One of the modern classics of sado-masochism is a novel, *Miss High
Heels*, in which the main character achieves ecstasy through having his
hands and feet locked into boxes filled with fleas that bit him while he
was cross-dressed. 'I was in seventh heaven: pain and pleasure were inex-
tricably mixed.'[41] For the sado-masochist these extreme practices create a
state of ecstasy. The individuals involved rid themselves of their old-style
body, slowly transforming the flesh through fasting and maceration until
they arrive at a new psychological insight in which it is believed the dei-
fied body is capable of overcoming the problems of space, of treating suffering with contempt, of passing through the centuries of time, and
ultimately of acquiring the substance and power of the angels. One of the
better descriptions of this process was recorded by Saint Jerome:

> There I sat, solitary, full of bitterness; my disfigured limbs shuddered away
> from the sackcloth, my dirty skin was taking on the hue of the Ethiopian's
> flesh; every day tears, every day sighing; and if in spite of my struggles sleep
> would tower over and sink upon me, my battered body ached on the naked
> earth ... Yet that same I, who for fear of hell condemned myself to such a
> prison, I, the comrade of scorpions and wild beasts, sat there, watching the
> maidens in their dances; my face haggard with fasting, my mind burnt with
> desire in my frigid body, and the fires of lust alone leaped before a man pre-
> maturely dead. So destitute of all aid, I used to lie at the feet of Christ, water-
> ing them with my tears, wiping them with my hair, struggling to subdue my
> rebellious flesh with seven days' fasting ... and the Lord Himself is witness,
> after many tears, and eyes that clung to heaven, I would sometimes seem to
> myself to be one with the angelic hosts.[42]

I would hold that suffering and punishment have been so much a part of
the Western Christian tradition that it is understandable why we have
what is called the 'sado-masochistic personality' in our own society. Saints'
lives are full of similar incidences, although none of these is listed in Salisbury, probably because she did not make the same leap between the cul-

tural connections of medieval and contemporary sado-masochism that I did.

It might well be that, because of my studies of sex, I have become like the proverbial person who saw sex in everything. Perhaps I do, but I hope I do not stretch my sources or read too much into them. Still, those interested in sexuality do see things differently. For example, Rupert of Etux (d. 1129) reported a dream in which he worshipped the crucifix and in which Jesus seemed to return his gaze and accept his salutation. Rushing to the altar, Rupert embraced and kissed the image. 'I held him. I embraced him. I kissed him for a long time. I sensed how seriously he accepted this gesture of love, when, while kissing, he himself opened his mouth that I might kiss more deeply.'[43] Frances Wack called this an example of unabashed eroticism. I would agree, but what it indicates to me, aside from its homosexual implications, is that deep kissing, or what is popularly called 'French kissing,' is no new development. It, like so many other things, has medieval antecedents.

Certainly, medieval people thought that sex was a normal part of life, even though they might not have subsumed under the category of sexual behaviour everything that we now do. Sexual dysfunction was held to have important consequences. Canonists, however, distinguished between permanent impotence, which was assumed to be natural, and temporary or relative impotence, attributable to sorcery or witchcraft, and in fact the fear of temporary impotence might well have been one of the major reasons for the growing hostility to witchcraft. Even this belief was not hard and fast, and the physician increasingly in the later medieval period was called upon to deal with impotence. By the end of the medieval period, physicians had been able to recognize, classify, explain, and treat sexual dysfunction, in the process removing much of it from the field of witchcraft. In short, the medieval period also saw the beginning of the medicalization of sexual behaviour which reached its height in the nineteenth and twentieth centuries.[44]

Some Tentative Conclusions

Although both medicine and law were examining sexual behaviour in a much more effective way than it had ever been examined before, and theologians continued to write about what was natural and what was unnatural, the medieval period was far from the age of specialists. This means there is a vast unexplored literature out there, from art to music, from folklore to literature, from science to theology, which can throw new light on sexuality in the Middle Ages. As I have tried to emphasize, the study of sexuality in history is much too broad a subject for any one of us to know it all. It is only through interaction with one another at conferences, through collections of papers, and through serendipity that we can further expand our knowledge. Medievalists, I believe, have a tremendous amount to contribute to this branch of knowledge, and we can all do so from our own particular area of expertise. There are certainly pitfalls, and I have mentioned some of them, and there is a minimal knowledge base about sex, which is important, but this is not difficult to achieve, and having done so we can contribute from our own particular areas of expertise. All of us, in short, should recognize that sex is an integral part of what it is to be human, that it has tremendous influence on our own self-perceptions, and we should look for it in our research. If you do not know what to do with your data, or need help in interpreting, I am certainly available, but so are many of the others who contributed to this book.

NOTES

1 Vern L. Bullough, 'Sex in History: A Virgin Field,' *Journal of Sex Research* 8/2 (1972), 101–16

2 See, for example, George Corner, *Anatomical Texts of the Early Middle Ages: A Study in the Transmission of Culture* (Washington, DC: Carnegie Institution of Washington 1927).

3 Masters has often summarized the advice in his talks, but for Corner's own recollection see George W. Corner, *Seven Ages of a Medical Scientist: An Autobiography* (Philadelphia: University of Pennsylvania Press 1981), 213.

4 John Jay Chapman, *Lucian, Plato, and Greek Morals* (Boston: Houghton Mifflin 1931)

5 Edith Hamilton, *The Greek Way* (New York: Norton, many printings)

6 *The Oxford Classical Dictionary*, eds. by M. Cary, J.D. Denniston, J. Wright Duff, A.D. Nock, W.D. Ross, and W.H. Scullard (Oxford: Clarendon Press 1949)

7 Norman Cantor, *Medieval History: The Life and Death of a Civilization* (New York: Macmillan 1963)

8 John Boswell, *Christianity, Social Tolerance, and Homosexuality* (Chicago: University of Chicago Press 1980). Earlier I had written on the topic in a somewhat different vein: Vern L. Bullough, *Sexual Variance in Society and History* (New York: Wiley 1976; Chicago: University of Chicago Press, 1980). I did not, and still do not, agree with Boswell's thesis that the early-medieval Church was tol-

erant of homosexuality. It was not, but it was not until after the Gregorian reforms that the papal hierarchy was able effectively to move against those who strayed from the Church doctrine. For details, see ibid., 175–204, 317–413.

9 Edward Gibbon, *The Decline and Fall of the Roman Empire*, ed. James Bury (repr. New York: Heritage Press 1944), 59 n. 26, and 1475.

10 Leopold von Ranke, *History of the Latin and Teutonic Nations, 1494–1514*, rev. trans. by G.R. Dennis (repr. London: George Bell 1909).

11 Ibid.

12 Arnold J. Toynbee, 'Why I Dislike Western Civilization,' *New York Times Magazine*, 18 May 1964.

13 Ibid.

14 James Harvey Robinson, *The New History* (New York: Macmillan 1912)

15 Bullough, 'Sex in History,' 114–15

16 Joyce E. Salisbury, *Medieval Sexuality: A Research Guide* (New York: Garland 1990)

17 Vern L. Bullough and James Brundage, *A Handbook of Medieval Sexuality* (New York: Garland 1996)

18 See Michel Foucault, *History of Sexuality: An Introduction* (New York: Pantheon 1978). The English translation left out the French subtitle, best translated as 'the will to power,' which is a better key to the theme of the book. For discussion see James Miller, *The Passion of Michel Foucault* (New York: Simon and Schuster 1993); D. Megil, 'Foucault, Structuralism and the Ends of History,' *Journal of Modern History* 51 (1979), 453–503. There is a vast literature on the topic.

19 There is a vast literature on this. See Bullough, *Science in the Bedroom: A History of Sex Research* (New York: Basic Books 1994), 225–40. For the depth of the discussion see four issues of the *Journal of Homosexuality* 28 (1995) devoted to 'The Biology of Sexual Preference.'

20 James Brundage, *Law, Sex and Christian Society in Medieval Europe* (Chicago: University of Chicago Press 1987); John T. Noonan, *Contraception: A History of the Treatment by Catholic Theologians* (Cambridge, MA: Harvard University Press 1965); Danielle Jacquart and Claude Thomasset, *Sexuality and Medicine in the Middle Ages*, trans. Matthew Adamson (Princeton, NJ: Princeton University Press 1988). There are many more. See Bullough and Brundage, *Handbook*.

21 See E. Westermarck, *The History of Human Marriage*, 3 vols., 5th ed. (New York: Allerton 1922), vol. 1: 166–206, for a general discussion. Paolo Mantegazza, who, after being unable to find any written law describing such a right, simply concluded that it was a custom more binding than a law (*Gli amori degli uomini*, 1885, translated into English as *The Sexual Relations of Mankind* by Samuel Put-

nam [New York: Eugenics 1935], par 2, ch. xi, 208). The most exhaustive study was by K.J. Schmidt, *Jus Primae Noctis: Eine Geschlictliche Untersuchung* (Freiburg: Harden 1881), who held that the whole idea was only a learned superstition deriving from the practice of *culagium*, a requirement that a serf get permission to marry, and sometimes pay a fee.

22 The only possible legal reference was among the Scots where the *Chronicle* of Boece reports that King Ewen II (about A.D. 875) established the rights of the first night. Boece, however, wrote at the beginning of the sixteenth century, and his history included many fabulous narratives, of which this was one. See H. Boece, *The Chronicles of Scotland*, trans. Walter Seton, R.W. Chambers, and E.C. Batho (Edinburgh: Blackwood 1938), Book III, ch. vi. Still, a Scottish lawyer as late as 1930 would argue that such rights existed: H. M'Kechnie, 'Jus Primae Noctis,' *Judicial Review* 42 (1930), 435–8.

23 M.F. Skinner, 'Speaking Out: Men, Women, and Spiritual Authority: 750–1150,' paper delivered at Fordham University, 1990.

24 John of Salerno, *The Life of St. Odo of Cluny*, ed. Gerald Sitwell (including *Odo's Life of St. Gerald*) (London 1858), 109

25 Naturally I proceeded to write up the finding. See Vern L. Bullough, 'Jus Primus Noctae,' *Journal of Sex Research* 28 (February 1991), 163–6.

26 The Mannyng text was edited by F.J. Furnival. I did not find this reference myself, but it was published by J.D. Rolleston in '*Penis captivus*: A Historical Note,' *Janus* 39 (1936), 196–201. Medieval descriptions are probably inaccurate, and this might well be a legendary tale, although in an uncircumcised man it is possible for the foreskin to become entangled in such a way as to act as a tourniquet, engorging the penis, and making it extremely painful to withdraw or move. The second incident is in *Acta Sanctorum* (Antwerp: Bolandist Society 1643), March, vol. 3: 459. This too was reported by others, including C. Grant Loomis, *Bulletin of the History of Medicine* 7 (1939), 93–7. Both were recently reprinted in *Sex in the Middle Ages: A Book of Essays*, ed. Joyce Salisbury (New York: Garland 1991), 232–8.

27 Guy Beaujouan, 'Manuscrits médicaux du Moyen Âge consérves en Espagne,' *Mélanges de la Casas de Velazquez* 9 (1972), 173

28 Vern L. Bullough, 'Medieval Medical and Scientific Attitudes Toward Women,' *Viator* 4 (1972), 485–501. For a more comprehensive overview, see Vern L. Bullough and Bonnie Bullough, *The Subordinate Sex* (Urbana: University of Illinois Press 1973), and Vern L. Bullough, Brenda Shelton, and Sarah Slavin, *The Subordinated Sex*, rev. ed. (Athens: University of Georgia Press 1988).

29 Vern L. Bullough, 'Transvestism in the Middle Ages: A Sociological Analysis,' *American Journal of Sociology* 79 (1974), 1381–94. For a different view which appeared about the same time, see John Anson, 'The Female Transvestite in

Early Monasticism: The Origin and Development of a Motif,' *Viator* 5 (1974), 1–32. My view is both more political and more sexological than Anson's.

30 The romance exists in only one manuscript, Mi.Lm.6, which is deposited on loan in the Muniments Room of the University of Nottingham. Its contents were first published in a series of articles by Lewis Thorpe, its discoverer, in *Nottingham Medieval Studies*, beginning in 1962, and the articles were brought together in book form and amplified in Lewis Thorpe, *Le Roman de silence* (Cambridge: W. Haffer 1972). It has since been translated into modern English: See Heldris de Cournuälle, *Le Roman de silence*, trans. Regina Paski, vol. 63 in the Garland Library of Medieval Literature (New York: Garland 1991).

31 I used the account in Vern L. Bullough and Bonnie Bullough, *Cross dressing, Sex, and Gender* (Philadelphia: University of Pennsylvania Press 1993).

32 *Bethada Náem nérenn: Lives of Irish Saints*, ed., trans.,and annotated by Charles Plummer (Oxford: Clarendon Press 1922), vol. 2: 8, xiii, 28

33 Interestingly this text had been translated by G.G. Coulton and appeared in his *Life in the Middle Ages* (Cambridge: Cambridge University Press 1967), vol. 1: 8–9, but I had either missed it or forgotten it until it was again brought to my attention.

34 *Acta Sanctorum*, August vol. 1: 652

35 Ulrich von Lichtenstein, *Frauendienst, oder: Geschichte und Liebe des Ritters und Sängers*, trans. Ludwig Tieck (Stuttgart 1812). It was translated into English verse by J.W. Thomas: *Ulrich von Lichtenstein's Service of Ladies* no. 63 of the University of North Carolina Studies in Germanic Languages and Literature (Chapel Hill: University of North Carolina Press 1969).

36 Ibid., Quatrain 538, p. 110

37 See Richard von Krafft-Ebing, *Psychopathia Sexualis*, translation of the seventh German edition by Charles Gilbert Chaddock (Philadelphia: F.A. Davis 1894).

38 See Vern L. Bullough, Dwight Dixon, and Joan Dixon, 'Sadism, Masochism, and History,' in *Sexual Knowledge, Sexual Science: The History of Attitudes to Sexuality*, eds. Roy Porter and Mikuláš Teich, 47–62 (Cambridge: Cambridge University Press 1994).

39 Jacques LeCarrier, *The God Possessed*, trans. Roy Monkcom (London: George Allen and Unwin 1963), 173–4

40 Palladius, *The Lausiac History*, trans. and annotated by Robert T. Meyer (Westminster, MD: Newman Press 1965), 18:4, p. 59

41 *Miss High Heels* (n.p., 1931; repr. New York: Grove Press 1969), 138

42 Saint Jerome, *Ad Eustachium, Epis*, xxii, in Migne, *PL*, xxii. This particular translation relies heavily upon that of Helen Waddell in *The Desert Fathers* (repr. Ann Arbor: University of Michigan Press 1957), 27.

43 *PL*, 168: 1601. See also Peter Dinzelbacher, 'Über die Entdeckung der Liebe in Hochmittelalter,' *Saeculum* 32 (1981), 285–308, and especially Mary Frances Wack, *Lovesickness in the Middle Ages: The Viaticum and Its Commentaries* (Philadelphia: University of Pennsylvania Press 1990), 24.
44 See Michael McVaugh, 'Medicalization of Sexual Behavior in the Middle Ages,' an unpublished paper given at the American Association for the History of Medicine, Cleveland, Ohio, May 1991.

Playing by the Rules:
Sexual Behaviour and Legal Norms
in Medieval Europe

JAMES A. BRUNDAGE

This paper examines the medieval European experience with a perennial problem – namely, the relationship between the behavioural expectations enunciated by the norms that society imposed to govern human activities and the recalcitrant realities of human conduct.

I will not greatly surprise you, I am sure, if I disclose that serious disparities between the two were common, and that the gap between the prescribed ideal and actual experience was often very wide indeed. The medieval Church, for example, banned premarital intercourse, and society scorned the woman (but usually not the man) who yielded her virtue before the importunities of her betrothed and the urgent promptings of her own flesh. Yet many couples went to their weddings accompanied by their children, and pregnant brides, so far as we can tell, were no rarity in medieval villages.[1] Indeed, since the marriage rules of the Church itself, in their classic form, rested the validity of marriage solely upon the consent of the couple, this often enough had the effect of legitimizing unpremeditated exchanges of marital intent uttered amid the heat and passion of adolescent sexual gropings. When the circumstantial details of individual marriages emerge from the dry and dusty records of the ecclesiastical courts, they uncover couples who claim that they exchanged marital consent in a bedroom, sometimes while actually in bed with each other, or in a kitchen, a storeroom, a shed, a garden, near a hedge, in a field, or under a tree – in short, under circumstances that were, to say the least, informal, and suggest that marital consent may well have been incidental to premarital sexual intimacy. In some regions, at least, local custom appears to have sanctioned trial marriages in which couples lived together for a period prior to formal exchanges of marital consent.[2] The venerable norms that banned premarital intercourse, in short, diverged significantly from what real people did in real time.

Similarly the rules that prohibited fornication between unmarried partners and adultery between married persons and third parties were so widely disregarded that ordinary people could, and frequently did, treat these high-flown theories of the clerks as having scant relationship to daily life. People generally found it hard to believe that such everyday and natural behaviour could be sinful at all, much less mortally so, and the opinion that fornication was no sin appears among the heretical propositions condemned at Paris in 1277.[3] Even devout and learned writers refer (seemingly with sighs of resignation) to 'average incontinence' as a benchmark against which the seriousness of other deviations from the norms of sexual behaviour must be measured and conceded that it was scarcely possible to find an adult who had not broken the rules against fornication.[4]

The clergy, as well as the laity, commonly fell short, often far short, of observing the rules binding them, rules that theoretically obliged everyone in major orders to renounce marriage, which was the sole approved setting for legitimate sex, and in addition to abstain from any and every sort of overt genital sexual activity, marital or non-marital, homosexual or heterosexual, mercenary or gratuitous, long-term or short-term, solitary or social.[5] These rules not merely held up the austere values of a self-selected ascetic élite for emulation by the vastly more numerous and heterogeneous ranks of the clergy at large, but sought to make their observance mandatory.

Canon law in its classical period prescribed a battery of harsh penalties for infractions of these rules, penalties so disproportionate to the offences, indeed, that by an all-too-familiar paradox they seem foreordained to be applied erratically in practice. While direct overt resistance to the new rules about clerical celibacy concocted late in the eleventh and early twelfth centuries was relatively short-lived, passive resistance persisted throughout the high Middle Ages. Although clerics in major orders ceased to marry, many of them substituted concubines for wives and continued to produce families, albeit illegitimate ones, much as before.[6] Arguably the real losers in the process were the women and children.[7]

Obviously the norms of sexual conduct prescribed by councils, popes, and synods presented serious problems, since the public at large, including many of the clergy, as well as the laity, conspicuously failed to observe their terms. What I want to explore here are the ways in which the medieval Church sought to bridge the gap between precept and practice, or, in other words, the means it devised to enforce its rules on sexual behaviour.

If they were to be effective in modifying behaviour, the sexual rules of the medieval Church required some workable enforcement system. We may begin our analysis by dividing the enforcement strategies available to the medieval Church into two broad categories, formal and informal. Informal enforcement mechanisms included persuasion through sermons, admonitions, and teaching; personal pressures generated by family, social superiors, employers, peers, and associates; and the internal checks on conduct that sprang from conscience, shame, and fear. Formal enforcement mechanisms, on the other hand, comprised actions brought in the courts to penalize offenders, as well as the instructions that confessors gave and the sanctions that they might impose upon those who sought absolution for their sexual transgressions.

During the second half of the twelfth century, Pope Alexander III (1159–81) embraced an analysis, based apparently on the intentionist ethics of Pierre Abelard, that distinguished between two subcategories of formal enforcement mechanisms: those applied in the external forum (sometimes called the 'public forum'), in other words, in Church courts, and those applied in the internal forum, that is, the private judgments rendered in confession and the sacrament of penance.[8] During the early Middle Ages, the Church had relied more heavily on informal enforcement mechanisms than on formal ones to implement its notions of appropriate sexual conduct; by the close of the thirteenth century, however, juristic processes and public sanctions in the external forum had come to play a more prominent role than they previously had done in the enforcement of the Church's sexual norms. In this paper I propose to examine some of these formal enforcement mechanisms that medieval ecclesiastical courts employed to implement the Church's sexual norms.

Increasing reliance on formal and public sanctions to compel sexual offenders to atone for their faults and mend their ways required development of a more elaborate court system than the early medieval Church had possessed. It further required Church authorities to develop mechanisms of coercion to compel compliance with court decisions and judgments. Elaboration, growth, and maturation of concern with enforcing the sexual norms, in other words, went hand in hand with development, growth, and maturation of the ecclesiastical courts during the twelfth and thirteenth centuries. This was, I think, no coincidence; rather, increasing anxiety to enforce the norms of sexual conduct constituted one crucial factor that helped drive the Church's leadership during this period both to create procedures specifically designed to deal with the special problems that deviant sexual conduct presented and to revamp the courts themselves so as to make them more professional and more competent than they previously had been.

The procedural changes involved in dealing with sex offences largely concerned the law of evidence. Not all deviations from the Church's norms for sexual behaviour constituted crimes justiciable before the courts. While all sex offences were sins, a great number of them – such as entertaining lascivious fantasies, masturbation, wet dreams, and the like – were solely matters of conscience, for which the 'internal forum' of the confessional was the appropriate venue for private adjudication by the confessor, who was empowered to impose punishment in the form of an appropriate penance and impart sacramental absolution of guilt.[9]

Twelfth-century jurists only gradually drew a distinction between sexual crimes in the rigorous sense of the term and other types of sexual sins and offences.[10] When they did so, they relied, as canonists and theologians so often did, on the ideas of Saint Augustine. Gratian's definition of 'crime' in his *Decretum* (completed *ca* 1140), for example, is entirely Augustinian: 'A crime, however, is a serious sin, eminently deserving of accusation and condemnation.'[11] The anonymous author of the *Summa Coloniensis* (written *ca* 1169) similarly distinguished 'crimes' from other sins by their consequences. A 'crime' consisted of an action that gave rise to a formal complaint (*accusatio*), which, if proved, entailed a public penalty (*dampnatio*) that might result in exclusion from the ranks of the clergy.[12] Johannes Teutonicus (d. 1245), in his *Glossa ordinaria* (completed in 1216) to the *Decretum*, drew the observations of his predecessors into a systematic taxonomy of offences. Johannes distinguished four different meanings of 'crime,' although he also noted that some writers favoured a fivefold distinction.[13] As Johannes saw these matters, 'crime' in its broadest sense included all sins, mortal and venial. A more restrictive definition would limit the term to those sins that produced *infamia*. A person tainted with *infamia* was disreputable and was in consequence barred from holding certain highly esteemed public offices or dignities, ecclesiastical or civil, and forbidden to exercise important functions, such as bringing accusations in court, making a valid will, or serving as a witness.[14] A third approach discriminated between offences on the basis of intention; in this sense, 'crime' meant only those sins committed deliberately. Finally, in a specifically ecclesiastical sense, 'crime' meant sins so serious that they warranted exclusion from the clerical estate.[15]

Within the universe of crimes, sexual crimes presented particularly difficult juristic problems. Since sex offences characteristically occurred in
private, so that the only witnesses were usually the parties themselves,
these crimes were exceptionally difficult to prove unless the participants
confessed to them. If a confession was not forthcoming, the reigning
canonical procedural law at the end of the twelfth century, the so-called
accusatory procedure, required that a competent person must lay a complaint before the court and support that complaint by *plena probatio*.[16]
This procedure *per accusationem* raised two formidable difficulties. First, a
complainant had to be forthcoming; yet, serious legal disincentives discouraged many potential accusers from taking the grave risks that bringing an accusation about sexual misconduct involved. Among other
things, the complainant became liable for the costs of the case, which
was bound to be a discouraging prospect for all but the very wealthy. Furthermore, should the accuser be unable to furnish adequate proof of the
accusation, he or she could be penalized under the *lex talionis* for bringing a false accusation.[17] Moreover, the standard of proof demanded in
criminal proceedings was extraordinarily high: *Plena probatio* in criminal
matters, according to the standard authorities, must consist of evidence
'clearer than the light of day.'[18] In criminal matters that meant sworn tes-
timony from two qualified and credible eyewitnesses.[19] In practice it was
often impossible to meet this standard in cases against alleged sex
offenders.

Church authorities clearly found this situation frustrating. It meant
that, although, as Pope Innocent III (1198–1216) once put it, 'it is in the
public interest that crimes not remain unpunished,' nevertheless sexual
crimes often did remain unpunished, both because few accusers were
willing to brave the hazards of preferring charges and because competent
witnesses were seldom available. This contradiction between the public
policy (to punish sex crimes) and the prevailing rules of procedure
(which hindered implementation of that policy) seemed to require some
resolution. The result was a series of significant modifications of the rules
of criminal procedure during the thirteenth century. One set of changes
sought to overcome the initial handicap that required an accuser to take
up the burden of pressing the case, while another set of changes lowered
the standard of proof required for conviction.

The first set of changes, inaugurated by Innocent III and adopted by
the Fourth Lateran Council in 1215, involved the elaboration of a new
process for initiating criminal actions, the procedure *per denunciationem*,
in which no public accuser was required. Instead, action against a suspect

might be initiated through a *denunciatio,* in which the complainant remained anonymous and thus secured immunity from the liabilities that accompanied formal accusation. Alternatively, in an even more radical break with past practice, an ecclesiastical judge might proceed *per inquisitionem* to initiate an *ex officio* inquiry on his own authority when common belief or report (*fama*) suggested to him that someone somewhere was having fun – and breaking the law.[21]

Desirable, or even necessary, as these mechanisms no doubt seemed from the point of view of law enforcement, we may consider their implications for personal liberty ominous. But these procedural novelties (however we choose to regard them) unquestionably made it far easier to take action against those suspected of infringing the sexual regulations of the medieval Church and placed formidable weapons in the hands of ecclesiastical authorities who wished to prosecute irregular sexual behaviour.

It seems clear, as Richard Fraher has argued, that these innovations were adopted largely in reaction to the frustration that authorities so often experienced when they attempted to enforce their repeated prohibitions against clerical concubinage.[22] The new procedural modes not only enabled bishops and their officials-principal to take action against priests who were living in sin without waiting for an accuser to take the initiative, but also allowed them to prefer charges against laypersons who violated the rules against fornication, seduction, extramarital cohabitation, bigamy, irregular marriages, incest, frequenting prostitutes, and all the other varieties of sexual turpitude that depraved ingenuity or diabolical inspiration might suggest for finding sexual pleasure outside of the chaste and fleeting embraces permitted in the marriage bed. Historians have usually linked the introduction of criminal procedure *per denunciationem* and *per inquisitionem* to thirteenth-century campaigns against heresy and usury. Although these procedural innovations clearly did facilitate the repression of unorthodox theological opinions and may well have made it easier to proceed against money-lenders, it is almost certainly true that their actual impact on thirteenth- and fourteenth-century society was in fact far greater in the field of sexual behaviour than it was anywhere else.

The new procedural forms made it much easier to hale offenders against prevailing standards of sexual behaviour into court. Coupled with these procedural changes was a new doctrine of proof that made it easier to convict defendants once they got there. Here, too, widespread public knowledge or belief again played a key role. As early as the 1180s, Pope Lucius III (1181–5) had approved, and indeed praised, the imposition of extrajudicial sanctions, in the form of a boycott of services, against priests who were generally known to live with concubines.[23] Teachers of canon law, however, were leery of this decretal – 'extremely difficult and dangerous,' one commentator called it, for he feared that it tended to undermine regular legal process by encouraging irregular penalties imposed outside of, or even in defiance of, prevailing juridical norms.[24]

Nevertheless, Pope Innocent III used his predecessor's decision as the foundation for major modifications in the law of evidence. If a priest openly flaunted his relationship with a concubine and made no attempt to conceal it, Innocent ruled in an 1199 decision, then neither complaint nor further evidence was required to convict such a notorious offender. A judge could simply summon him to court, charge him with the crime of concubinage, and forthwith pronounce sentence for the crime without calling a single witness.[25] The notoriety of the offence was all the evidence required. The Pope hastened to add, however, that imposition of sanctions was the business of the ecclesiastical courts, not the community at large. Pope Innocent sought, in addition, to restrict the fallout from this judicial bombshell by adding important qualifications. Judges, he admonished, must distinguish carefully between notorious behaviour of this sort and mere rumours, widespread suspicion, or common belief that a priest had engaged in irregular conduct with a female companion. Where common fame (*fama*), rather than open and flagrant misbehaviour (*notorium*), was at issue, a judge should require the suspect to clear himself of suspicion by swearing a purgative oath in which he solemnly denied that his conduct was improper and thereby put his soul's salvation in peril if he lied.

Teachers of canon law in the universities quickly seized upon these landmark decisions and built upon them an elaborate jurisprudence of evidence.[26] They distinguished delicately, painstakingly, between concepts such as *notorium* and *fama, manifestum,* and *evidentia.*[27] These careful distinctions were not just schoolroom exercises to sharpen the wits of fledgling lawyers; they also had the power to change the lives and fortunes of men and women. Conduct that a judge deemed flagrant (*notorium*) furnished evidence sufficient, not only to initiate judicial proceedings, but also to convict a defendant of the crimes with which he was charged and subject him to the penalties prescribed by law – a judge might strip him of clerical rank and position, for example, and, with it, of benefice and income as well; part him from his companion at bed and board; take away his children; break up his home; in short, destroy both his honour and his fortune, without a single witness being heard.

Conduct that a judge deemed less than flagrant, that he considered merely the subject of common gossip, general belief, and widespread acceptance (*fama*), on the other hand, might be sufficient to warrant prosecution, with all the agony and hardship that entails, but conviction required more than this. Nevertheless, the standard of proof required for conviction was also lowered when common fame asserted guilt. Whereas earlier criminal procedure required the evidence of two witnesses to prove an accusation, the new criminal procedure of the early thirteenth century considered that *fama* itself constituted circumstantial evidence that probable cause for action existed.[28] Thus, under the new rules, widespread suspicion created a presumption that simply required corroboration, rather than the full-fledged proof by two witnesses that the accusatory procedure demanded. This difference in consequences is not trivial, but determining whether reports of conduct amounted to *notorium*, or simply constituted *fama*, was a matter of judicial discretion. Prospective judges learned in the law schools the guidelines for drawing these vital distinctions, and the fine doctrinal hairlines that their teachers spun in lecture and in disputation found frequent application in the chambers of consistory courts from Aberdeen to Antioch, Cracow to Coimbra.[29]

The new law of evidence in the thirteenth century, like the new procedures for prosecuting crimes, seems designed in large part to cope with difficulties that arose from sexual misconduct, among both the clergy and the laity. These innovations, however, were far from cost-free, for they substantially reduced the procedural protections that canon law had long afforded to accused persons in order to make it easier to prosecute and convict offenders against sexual morality. This shift suggests that popes and councils at the beginning of the thirteenth century as a matter of deliberate policy assigned higher priority to restraining offenders against the Church's norms of sexual behaviour than to protecting individuals against wrongful prosecution and conviction.[30]

These procedural changes, as I remarked earlier, have often been linked to the Church's preoccupation in the early thirteenth century with other issues, notably heresy and usury.[31] While the new procedures were used against heretics and usurers, of course, two kinds of circumstantial evidence (ironically enough) seem to indicate that sex offenders were the primary targets of these radical changes in established criminal procedure. First and foremost, the decretals that enunciated the new and less exacting standards of proof were often written to resolve cases that involved sex offenders. This would seem to indicate *prima facie* that the standards themselves were initially devised in order to combat lust, rather than greed or doctrinal deviance.[32] And second, where substantial bodies of evidence survive to tell us what the courts were actually doing with the new procedures, it is abundantly clear that prosecutions for adultery, fornication, and other sexual offences were far more numerous than prosecutions for heresy or usury.[33] It might be objected here that this simply means that fornication and adultery were common, while heresy and usury were not – the means, the opportunity, and the urge to engage in copulation are, after all, everywhere available; require no special learning or equipment; and do not ordinarily demand access to surplus capital. It seems to me, however, that this objection cuts both ways. While I would certainly agree that a burning desire to engage in unorthodox theological speculation, or to make money without doing hard physical labour in return for it, no doubt afflicts fewer people than do the lures and urges of the flesh, none the less it seems likely that, for precisely that reason, ecclesiastical authorities deemed measures that would discourage sexual misbehaviour a particularly urgent priority on the moral and legal agenda of a Christian society.

Coupled with the new criminal procedures that made prosecution of sexual offences considerably easier and more likely to succeed, we also find substantial innovation during the thirteenth century in the structure and administration of the ecclesiastical courts themselves. Those changes, and most particularly the ones at the lower levels of the organization, also had the effect of making it easier than it previously had been for Church authorities to detect, prosecute, and punish sexual offenders.

Much of what I shall say here about the Church courts will draw upon the experience of the Church in England, and that for two reasons. First, records of medieval ecclesiastical courts survive more plentifully in England than elsewhere in Western Christendom.[34] And second, records of the English Courts Christian have been studied and their contents analysed in greater detail than those from other regions; hence, the record material there is not only richer but also more accessible than it is elsewhere.

It would be rash to assume that the practices of the English courts were representative of what happened in other regions; indeed, as Robert Brentano has shown, ecclesiastical administration in Italy differed markedly from that in England, while Charles Donahue, Jr, has detailed significant differences between the ways that ecclesiastical courts in France handled marriage cases and those practised in their English counterparts.[35] None the less, the English evidence at least supplies detailed evidence about patterns of operation there and suggests that similar patterns may have prevailed on the Continent as well.

The local courts of archdeacons and bishops are particularly important in this context, for those were the tribunals that heard the vast majority of cases involving sex offences. Prior to the twelfth century, bishops normally exercised their judicial powers, and especially their criminal jurisdiction, in diocesan synods.[36] Bishops were expected to meet with the clergy of their dioceses in synod at reasonably regular intervals, and it was a usual part of the business in these assemblies to deal with offences against ecclesiastical discipline, as well as with other pastoral concerns.[37] Towards the end of the twelfth century, many bishops seem to have felt overburdened with routine judicial business, which consumed an inordinate amount of their time and pre-empted other pastoral concerns. In consequence they commenced to delegate much, and ultimately almost all, of their judicial business to one member of their households who soon came to be known nearly everywhere simply as 'the official,' or sometimes 'the official-principal' to distinguish him from other officials in the bishop's entourage.[38] The bishop's official-principal typically had substantial formal training in canon law and, by the mid-thirteenth century, had in many, perhaps most, dioceses become a full-time judge who occupied a prominent place in diocesan administration. The court over which the official-principal presided was styled the bishop's consistory.[39]

Within the diocese, at a lower level than the bishop, one or more archdeacons kept their eyes on the habits and morals of the faithful, both clerical and lay, and, when so minded, could hale offenders against sexual morality into their own courts for punishment.[40] By the early thirteenth century – say, 1210 or thereabouts in England – archdeacons, like bishops, commonly had their own 'officials' to whom they delegated the bulk of the judicial business that came before them.[41] By the late thirteenth century, the courts of archdeacons and their officials had secured a major role in the enforcement of the laws governing sexual morality and handled substantial numbers of routine prosecutions for fornication, adultery, and other common sex offences.[42] In the court of the official of the archdeacon of Sudbury, in the late thirteenth century, for example, sex and marriage cases comprised nearly two-thirds of the recorded actions, while they accounted for almost 90 per cent of the cases in a rural dean's court in the diocese of Worcester in 1300. Likewise, across the Channel, in Normandy, irregular sexual behaviour furnished the ecclesiastical court of Cerisy with the overwhelming majority of its business during the decade between 1314 and 1323.[43]

When defendants in such cases were found guilty – and almost all those charged were convicted – judges generally required them to pay fines and court costs. In addition, offenders were often subjected to some type of ritual humiliation, such as parading round the parish church bare-chested and bearing a lighted candle before Sunday Mass, for example, in order to expose them to the scorn and derision of their neighbours and kin. This common coupling of shame with financial penalties was plainly designed to deter others from committing carnal offences.[44] Whether it actually achieved that goal may be doubted, but there is little question that expensive and degrading punishments for behaviour that many ordinary people (and a few theologians) regarded as natural and blameless stirred up resentment against those who imposed these sentences.[45]

> The archdeacon [declared one twelfth-century poet]
>> Is a feather-clad eagle,
>> Given to rapine.
> From far off he spots his prey,
>> Circles round it,
>> Swoops, and feasts off plunder.[46]

Two hundred years later, Chaucer pungently described another such, you may recall, in the *Friar's Tale*:

> Whilom ther was dwellynge in my contree
> An erchedekan, a man of heigh degree,
> That boldely dide execucion
> In punysshynge of fornicacioun.
> ...
> But certes, lecchours did he grettest wo;
> They sholde syngen if that they were hent,
> ...
> For er the bishhop caughte hem with his hook,
> They weren in the erchedeknes book ...[47]

It was no wonder that archdeacons were so bitterly disliked and that the question 'Can an archdeacon be saved?' supplied theological faculties in the universities with ripe material for ribald, and probably entertaining, disputations.[48]

An essential element in this proliferation of ecclesiastical courts was the appearance from the late twelfth century onwards of a corps of professional jurists to staff these tribunals. Both bishops' and archdeacons' courts, as we have seen, commonly employed judges with formal training in the law. In addition, the courts furnished employment for numerous other legally trained personnel, including advocates, proctors, and notaries, in addition to scribes, clerks, apparitors, and other subordinate functionaries who did not require specifically legal training. Some of the men who filled subordinate roles (especially in courts that sat in university towns, but probably elsewhere as well) were apt to be law students serving something like an apprenticeship in the courts.[49]

Ecclesiastical law was, in modern economic terms, a growth industry from the second half of the twelfth century onwards. Not only did it supply numerous opportunities for employment, and often lucrative employment at that, but also the market for law-related jobs seems to have expanded sharply and steadily for nearly two hundred years, from the time of Gratian at least up to the Black Death. In addition to enticing economic opportunities, careers in ecclesiastical law offered other inducements to hungry and ambitious young men. Canon law smoothed access to power and influence: many canon lawyers became bishops or archbishops, some became cardinals, a few became popes. At lower levels in the ecclesiastical structure, levels at which ordinary mortals could realistically aim, legally trained men secured canonries, prebends, and benefices of every kind out of all proportion to their numbers among the ranks of the clergy. And, in the more formally legal sphere of activity, judgeships in growing numbers offered a winning combination of prestige, power, security, and steady income. Private practice as an advocate brought many a man ample fortune and, for some, even furnished entrée into the ranks of the nobility. Proctors and notaries, while not usually as well rewarded or as highly regarded as advocates, none the less often appear comfortably well off. Qualifications in canon law opened many doors, and its practitioners were key figures in the reshaping of Christian society during the high Middle Ages.

All of these developments – the proliferation of courts; the legal profession's growth in numbers, prosperity, and influence; the enhanced role of law in the late medieval Church and society; as well as the development of inquisitorial procedure and the diminution of procedural safeguards for defendants that accompanied it – rested in considerable part upon the need to implement the medieval Church's laws concerning sexual conduct. Those sexual regulations were, in sum, a critical factor in shaping both the institutional and the psychological structures of the world of the high Middle Ages.

NOTES

1 Barbara Hanawalt, *The Ties That Bound: Peasant Families in Medieval England* (New York: Oxford University Press 1986), 194–7

2 Jean-Luc Dufresne, 'Les Comportements amoureux d'après le registre de l'officialité de Cerisy,' *Bulletin philologique et historique (jusqu'à 1610) du Comité des travaux historiques et scientifiques* (1973), 134–5; Richard H. Helmholz, *Marriage Litigation in Medieval England* (Cambridge: Cambridge University Press 1974), 29, 92; *Select Cases from the Ecclesiastical Courts of the Province of Canterbury, c. 1200–1301*, ed. Norma Adams and Charles Donahue, Jr, Selden Society Publications, vol. 95 (London: Selden Society 1981), 104, 122, 129

3 Bartholomew of Exeter, *Penitentiale* 69, ed. Adrian Morey, in *Bartholomew of Exeter, Bishop and Canonist: A Study in the Twelfth Century* (Cambridge: Cambridge University Press 1937), 236–7; Thomas of Chobham, *Summa Confessorum* 7.2.5.2–3, ed. F. Broomfield, Analecta medievalia Namuricensis, vol. 25 (Louvain: Éditions Nauwelaerts 1968), 341–4; *Chartularium universitatis Parisiensis*, eds. Heinrich Denifle and Emile Chatelain, 4 vols. (Paris: Delain Frères 1889–97), vol. 1: 553, no. 183; Robert E. Lerner, *The Heresy of the Free Spirit in the Later Middle Ages* (Berkeley and Los Angeles: University of California Press 1972), 17–18

4 Thus, Gratian, *Decretum* C. 15 q. 8 c. 1, and Johannes Teutonicus, *Glossa ordinaria* ad v. *caetera* and to D. 2 de pen. c. 5 v. *ex qua minus*; likewise, Huguccio, *Summa* to D. 25 d.p.c. 3 v. *sit sine peccato*, in B.N. lat. 3891, fol. 29va, and Vat. lat. 2280, fol. 26ra: 'Immo pauci adulti inueniuntur sine carnali delicto, scilicet fornicationis, ut di. l. quia sanctitas (D. 50 c. 16) et ita nullus potest eligi sine peccato, unde patet quod non sic accipitur ibi in epistula pauli nomen criminis, sed sensus est ibi'; cf. Stephen of Tournai, *Summa* to D. 89 d.p.c. 5 v. *propinquis*, ed. Johann Friedrich von Schulte (Giessen: Emil Roth 1891; repr. Aalen: Scientia 1965), 110–11. Note also the plaintive reflections of Guibert of Nogent in *Self and Society in Medieval France: The Memoirs of Abbot Guibert of Nogent (1064?–ca. 1125)*, ed. and trans. John F. Benton (New York: Harper Torchbooks 1970), 65–6. Gratian's *Decretum* and the rest of the *Corpus iuris canonici* are cited from the standard edition by Emil Friedberg, 2 vols. (Leipzig: Tauchnitz 1879; repr. Graz: Akademische Druck-u. Verlagsanstalt 1959). Citations to the *Glossa ordinaria* on the *Decretum* and other canonistic texts refer to the vulgate version printed in the *Corpus iuris canonici*, 4 vols. (Venice: Apud Iuntas 1605).

5 Gabriel Le Bras, *Institutions ecclésiastiques de la chrétienté médiévale*, Histoire de l'église depuis les origines jusqu'à nos jours, vol. 12 (Paris: Bloud et Gay 1959), 168; Christopher N.L. Brooke, 'The Gregorian Reform in Action: Clerical Marriage in England, 1050–1200,' *Cambridge Historical Journal* 12 (1956), 1–20

6 Berhnard Schimmelpfennig, 'Ex fornicatione nati: Studies in the Position of Priests' Sons from the Twelfth to the Fourteenth Century,' *Studies in Medieval and Renaissance History* 2 (1980), 3–50

7 James A. Brundage, *Law, Sex, and Christian Society in Medieval Europe* (Chicago: University of Chicago Press 1987), 214–23, 314–19, 401–5, 474–7, 567–9

8 See Stephan Kuttner, 'Ecclesia de occultis non iudicat: Problemata ex doctrina poenali decretistarum et decretalistarum a Gratiano usque ad Gregorium PP. IX,' in *Acta Congressus iuridici internationalis VII seculo a decretalibus Gregorii IX et XIV a Codice Iustiniano promulgatis,* 5 vols. (Rome: Pontificium Institutum Utriusque Iuris 1935–7), vol. 3: 244, and *Kanonistische Schuldlehre von Gratian bis auf die Dekretalen Gregors IX.,* Studi e testi, vol. 64 (Vatican City: Biblioteca Apostolica Vaticana 1935), 4–6, 19–22.

9 Hostiensis, *Summa aurea una cum summariis et adnotationibus Nicolai Superantii* 5.54 De penitentia et remissione § 11 (Lyons: Joannes de Lambray 1537; repr. Aalen: Scientia 1962), fol. 271ra–rb

10 Richard M. Fraher, 'Preventing Crime in the High Middle Ages: The Medieval Lawyers' Search for Deterrence,' in *Popes, Teachers, and Canon Law in the Middle Ages,* eds. James Ross Sweeney and Stanley Chodorow (Ithaca, NY: Cornell University Press 1989), 214 and n. 8

11 D. 81 c. 1 § 1: 'Crimen autem est graue peccatum, accusatione et dampnatione dignissimum'

12 *Summa 'Elegantius in iure diuino' seu Coloniensis* 2.6, eds. Gérard Fransen and Stephan Kuttner, Monumenta iuris canonici, Corpus glossatorum, vol. 1 (Vatican City: Biblioteca Apostolica Vaticana, 1969–90), 42–3: 'Quid sit crimen? Crimen est quod accusatione uel dampnatione dignum est. Accusationem autem si comitetur probatio, depositio sequatur.' Rufinus's definition in his *Summa* to D. 25 d.p.c. 3 v. *vel crim. inf.,* ed. Heinrich Singer (Paderborn: F. Schöningh 1902; repr. Aalen: Scientia 1963), 60, is very similar, although a few lines farther on, commenting on the term *criminale,* he simply equated crime with mortal sin.

13 Here Johannes no doubt had in mind Gratian's fivefold definition in D. 25 d.p.c. 3 §§ 4–6 of the *Decretum.*

14 On *infamia* and its consequences, see esp. Peter Landau, *Die Entstehung des kanonischen Infamiebegriffs von Gratian bis zur Glossa ordinaria,* Forschungen zur kirchlichen Rechtsgeschichte und zum Kirchenrecht, vol. 5 (Cologne and Graz: Böohlau 1966), and F. Migliorino, *Fama e infamia: Problemi della società medievale nel pensiero giuridico nei secoli XII e XIII* (Catania: Giannotta 1985).

15 Johannes Teutonicus, *Glossa ordinaria* to D. 25 d.p.c. 3 v. *nomine autem:* 'Gratianus uolens exponere auctoritatem Apostolis "Oportet episcopum esse sine crimine" [Tit. 1:7], assignat hic plures significationes huius nominis, "crimen";

licet his quidam quinque significationes assignent, ego non assigno nisi quatuor. Dicitur enim quando crimen omne delictum siue mortale siue ueniale, siue ex deliberatione procedat, siue ex ignorantia, secundum quod dicitur "Nemo sine crimine uiuit" et hanc significationem innuit ibi, nomine autem criminis. Quandoque dicitur crimen infamia procedens ex crimine, prout ibi sumitur in epistola ad Titum. Quandoque dicitur crimen solum id quod ex deliberatione procedit, siue illud sit mortale, siue ueniale, prout ibi sumitur "criminis appellatio," etc. [D. 25 d.p.c. 3 §4]. Quarto modo dicitur crimen solum id quod est dignum depositione, prout ibi sumitur, "alias, ea demum." Ioan<nes Teutonicus>.'

16 The following discussion of criminal procedure draws heavily upon studies by Richard M. Fraher, formerly my pupil, now (at least in these matters) my guide. See, in addition to 'Preventing Crime in the High Middle Ages' (*supra* note 10), '"Ut nullus describatur reus prius quam convincatur": Presumption of Innocence in Medieval Canon Law,' in *Proceedings of the Sixth International Congress of Medieval Canon Law*, eds. Stephan Kuttner and Kenneth Pennington, Monumenta iuris canonici, Subsidia, vol. 7: 493–506 (Vatican City: Biblioteca Apostolica Vaticana 1985); 'The Theoretical Justification for the New Criminal Law of the High Middle Ages: "Rei publicae interest, ne crimina remaneant impunita,"' *University of Illinois Law Review*, 1984, 577–95; and 'Conviction According to Conscience: The Medieval Jurists' Debate Concerning Judicial Discretion and the Law of Proof,' *Law and History Review* 7 (1989), 23–88.

17 Tancredus, *Ordo iudiciarius* 2.7.5 and 2.8, in *Pillius, Tancredus, Gratia libri de iudiciorum ordine*, ed. Friedrich Christian Bergmann (Göttingen: Vandenhoeck & Ruprecht 1842; repr. Aalen: Scientia 1965), 157–8, 162–4

18 Gratian C. 2 q. 8 c. 2, citing Cod. 4.19.25. Citations from Justinian's *Code* and the other texts of the *Corpus iuris civilis* refer to the critical edition by Paul Krueger, Theodor Mommsen, Rudolf Schoell, and Wilhelm Kroll, 3 vols. (Berlin: Weidmann 1872–95). For a further details see Wieslaw Litewski, 'Les Textes procédureaux du droit de Justinien dans le Décret de Gratien,' *Studia Gratiana* 9 (1966), esp. 78–84. Medieval lawyers were extremely reluctant to venture general definitions of 'proof' and 'evidence'; see Jiří Kejř, 'Pojem soudního důkazu ve středověkých právních naukách,' *Stát a právo* 13 (1967), 187 (English summary).

19 Gratian, C. 2 q. 1 c. 2; Tancredus, *Ordo iudiciarius* 3.7, ed. Bergmann, 228–9; Fraher, 'Preventing Crime in the High Middle Ages,' 216

20 X 5.39.35 med.: 'et publicae utilitatis intersit, ne crimina remaneant impunita ...'

21 X 5.1.17 (1206) and 5.1.24 = 4 Lateran (1215) c. 8. See further Winfried Trusen, 'Der Inquisitionsprozeß: Seine historischen Grundlagen und frühen

Formen,' *Zeitschrift der Savigny-Stiftung für Rechtsgeschichte,* kanonistische Abteilung 74 (1988), 168–230.

22 Fraher, 'Preventing Crime in the High Middle Ages,' 222–4

23 X 3.2.7

24 Nicholas de Tudeschis (also known as Panormitanus or Abbas Siculus), addition to *Glos. ord.* to X 3.2.7 v. *Vestra*: 'Famosum est tum propter materiam intrinsecam ipsius, tum propter materiam extrinsecam, scilicet notorii, et utraque est multum difficilis et periculosa.'

25 X 3.2.8: 'Nos igitur consultationi tuae taliter respondemus, quod, si crimen eorum ita publicum est, ut merito debeat appellari notorium, in eo casu nec testis nec accusator est necessarius, quum huiusmodi crimen nulla possit tergiversatione celari.'

26 Thus, e.g., Tancredus, *Ordo iudiciarius* 2.7.1–5, ed. Bergmann, 150–8; Geoffrey of Trani, *Summa perutilis et valde necesarii ... super titulis decretalium* to X 2.19 § 7 (Lyons: Joannes Moylin, alias de Cambray, 1519; repr. Aalen: Scientia 1968), 207–8.

27 Bernard of Pavia, *Summa decretalium* 2.12.4, ed. E.A.T. Laspeyres (Regensburg: Josef Manz, 1860; repr. Graz: Akademische Druck-u. Verlagsanstalt 1956), 44; Johannes Andreae, *In quinque decretalium libros novella commentaria* to X 3.2.7 (Venice: Apud Franciscum Franciscium 1581; repr. Torino: Bottega d'Erasmo 1963), fol. 9ra–rb; Filippo Liotta, *La continenza dei chierici nel pensiero canonistico classico da Graziano a Gregorio IX,* Quaderni di 'Studi Senesi,' vol. 24 (Milan: Giuffrè 1971), 357–9.

28 Tancredus, *Summula de criminibus,* ed. Richard M. Fraher, in *Bulletin of Medieval Canon Law* 9 (1979), 29–31, and *Ordo iudiciarius* 2.7.1, ed. Bergmann, 151–2; Hostiensis, *Summa aurea,* lib. 2, tit. De probationibus § 6 (fol. 97va) and tit. De testibus § 7 (fol. 100va–vb); William Durandus, *Speculum iudiciale,* Lib. 3, Partic. 1 tit. De notoriis criminibus § 3.3–4 (Basel: Apud Ambrosium et Aurelium Froebenios Fratres 1574; repr. Aalen: Scientia 1975), vol. 2: 46

29 How closely the actions of courts and judges corresponded to the doctrines of the academic jurists is a matter of considerable interest, but it is also a matter on which speculation remains difficult, even hazardous. More studies of ecclesiastical court records will be needed before it is possible to pronounce with great confidence on this issue, but studies to date generally seem to indicate that judges were indeed conscious of the rules spelled out by the academic authorities and for the most part apparently respected them: Richard H. Helmholz, *Marriage Litigation in Medieval England,* Cambridge Studies in English Legal History (Cambridge: Cambridge University Press 1974), 187–9; Charles Donahue, Jr, *Why the History of Canon Law Is Not Written* (London: Selden Society 1986), 21–2

30 John Langbein has noted disquieting parallels between these medieval developments and certain twentieth-century innovations in American criminal procedure: 'The Constitutio criminalis carolina in Comparative Perspective: An Anglo-American View,' in *Strafrecht, Strafprozeß und Rezeption: Grundlagen, Entwicklung und Wirkung der Constitutio criminalis carolina*, eds. Peter Landau and Friedrich-Christian Schroeder (Frankfurt am Main: Vittorio Klostermann 1984), 215–25.

31 See the discussion in Fraher, 'Preventing Crime,' 226–8.

32 E.g., X 3.2.7–8

33 Michael M. Sheehan, 'The Formation and Stability of Marriage in Fourteenth-Century England,' *Mediaeval Studies* 33 (1971), 234; Charles Donahue, Jr, 'Roman Canon Law in the Medieval English Church: Stubbs vs. Maitland Reexamined after 75 Years in the Light of Some Records from the Church Courts,' *Michigan Law Review* 72 (1974), 656–60.

34 Charles Donahue, Jr, *Records of the Medieval Ecclesiastical Courts: Reports of the Working Group on Church Court Records, Pt. 1: The Continent*, Comparative Studies in Continental and Anglo-American Legal History, vol. 6 (Berlin: Duncker & Humblot 1989), 23–5.

35 Robert Brentano, *Two Churches: England and Italy in the Thirteenth Century* (Berkeley: University of California Press 1968; repr. 1988), 62–173; Charles Donahue, Jr, 'What Causes Fundamental Legal Ideas? Marital Property in England and France in the Thirteenth Century,' *Michigan Law Review* 78 (1980), 59–88, and 'Institutional History from Archival History: The Court of Canterbury Rolls,' in *The Weightier Matters of the Law: Essays on Law and Religion – A Tribute to Harold J. Berman*, eds. John Witte, Jr, and Frank S. Alexander, American Academy of Religion, Studies in Religion, No. 51 (Atlanta: Scholars Press 1988), 33–55.

36 Paul Hinschius, *Das Kirchenrecht der Katholiken und Protestanten in Deutschland*, 6 vols. (Berlin: J. Guttentag 1869–97) 3: 582–603; Christoper R. Cheney, *English Synodalia of the Thirteenth Century* (London: Oxford University Press 1968), 1–33; Colin Morris, 'From Synod to Consistory,' *Journal of Ecclesiastical History* 22 (1971), 115–23

37 The Fourth Lateran Council (1215) c. 6 reiterated earlier enactments that required bishops to hold diocesan synods at least once a year, and this provision was incorporated in the *Liber Extra* at 5.1.25; for the conciliar text see *Constitutiones Concilii quarti Lateranensis una com commentariis glossatorum*, ed. António García y García, Monumenta iuris canonici, Corpus glossatorum, vol. 2 (Vatican City: Biblioteca Apostolica Vaticana 1981), 53.

38 Paul Fournier, *Les Officialités au Moyen Âge: Étude sur l'organisation, la compétence et la procédure des tribunaux ecclésiastiques en France de 1180 à 1328* (Paris: E. Plon

1880; repr. Aalen: Scientia 1984); Anne Lefebvre-Teillard, *Les Officialités à la veille du Concile de Trente*, Bibliothèque d'histoire du droit et droit romain, vol. 19 (Paris: R. Pichon et R. Durand-Auzias 1973); Winfried Trusen, 'Die Gelehrte Gerichtsbarkeit der Kirche,' in *Handbuch der Quellen und Literatur der neueren europäischen Privatrechtsgeschichte*, vol. 1: *Mittelalter (1100–1500): Die Gelehrten Rechte und die Gesetzgebung*, ed. Helmut Coing, 467–75 (Munich: C.H.Beck 1973); Christopher R. Cheney, *From Becket to Langton: English Church Government, 1170–1213* (Manchester: Manchester University Press 1956; repr. 1965), 147–8, and *English Bishops' Chanceries, 1100–1250* (Manchester: Manchester University Press 1950), 20–1; Dorothy M. Owen, 'The Records of the Bishop's Official at Ely: Specialization in the English Episcopal Chancery of the Later Middle Ages,' in *The Study of Medieval Records: Essays in Honour of Kathleen Major* (Oxford: Clarendon Press 1971), 189–205. This at least was true for most of Europe north of the Alps. In Italy titles such as 'vicar' or 'diocesan vicar' often designated a functionary who performed many of the same duties as an official-principal: Brentano, *Two Churches*, 76–8.

39   Bishops usually reserved a few particularly sensitive matters for their own personal judgment in what came to be known as the Court of Audience. Even when a bishop sat personally as a judge, however, he often relied upon his official-principal for advice about legal technicalities.

40   On archdeacons and their courts see generally Hinschius, *Kirchenrecht*, vol. 2: 183–205, as well as Alexander Hamilton Thompson, 'Diocesan Organization in the Middle Ages: Archdeacons and Rural Deans,' *Proceedings of the British Academy* 29 (1943), 153–94; and Cheney, *From Becket to Langton*, 145–6. Archdeacons in Italian dioceses (which typically were far smaller than those elsewhere), however, rarely exercised an independent jurisdiction of their own: Brentano, *Two Churches*, 66–8.

41   Cheney, *From Becket to Langton* 147, and *English Bishops' Chanceries*, 145–6; Trusen, 'Gelehrte Gerichtsbarkeit,' 471–2, 482–3.

42   Thus, e.g., the Synod of Salisbury (1238–1244) c. 53, and 2 Winchester (1247?) c. 53, in *Councils and Synods with Other Documents Relating to the English Church, II: A.D. 1205–1313*, 2 vols., eds. Sir F.M.Powicke and C.R. Cheney, (Oxford: Clarendon Press 1964) vol. 1: 285–6, 411; Michael M. Sheehan, 'Marriage and Family in English Conciliar and Synodal Legislation,' in *Essays in Honour of Anton Charles Pegis*, ed. J. Reginald O'Donnell (Toronto: Pontifical Institute of Mediaeval Studies 1974), 210.

43   Antonia Grandsden, 'Some Late Thirteenth-Century Records of an Ecclesiastical Court in the Archdeaconry of Sudbury,' *Bulletin of the Institute of Historical Research* 32 (1959), 62–9; Frank S. Pearson, 'Records of a Ruridecanal Court of 1300,' in *Collectanea*, ed. Sidney G. Hamilton, Worcester Historical Society Pub-

lications 31 (1912), 69–80; Jean-Luc Dufresne, 'Les Comportements amoureux d'après le registre de l'officialité de Cerisy,' *Bulletin philologique et historique (jusqu'à 1610) du Comité des travaux historiques et scientifique* (1973), 131–56.

44 On deterrence as a conscious goal of medieval legal process see Fraher, 'Preventing Crime,' *supra*, note 7.

45 On the belief that fornication between unmarried persons is no sin see, e.g., Thomas of Chobham, *Summa* 7.2.5.2–3, ed. Broomfield, 341–4, and Raymond of Penyafort, *Summa de penitentia* 3.34.22, ed. Xavier Ochoa and Aloisio Diez, Universa biblioteca iuris, vol. 1, Tomus B (Rome: Commentarium pro religiosis 1976), col. 817. This teaching was among those condemned at Paris in 1277: *Chartularium universitatis Parisiensis*, 1: 553 (No. 473).

46 My translation of 'Apocalypsis Goliae episcopi,' lines 109–12, in *The Latin Poems Commonly Attributed to Walter Mapes*, ed. Thomas Wright, Camden Society First ser., vol. 16 (London: Camden Society, 1841; repr. New York: Johnson Reprints 1968), 7: 'Est aquila, quae sic alis innititur, / archidiaconus, qui praedo dicitur; / qui videt a longe praedam quam sequitur, / et cum circumvolat ex rapto vivitur.'

47 Geoffrey Chaucer, *Friar's Tale*, lines 1301–18.

48 Charles Homer Haskins, *The Renaissance of the Twelfth Century* (Cambridge, MA: Harvard University Press 1927; repr. New York: Meridian Books 1958), 51. On the excesses of archdeacons see, e.g., Cheney, *From Becket to Langton*, 152–3.

49 See my study 'The Bar of the Ely Consistory Court in the Fourteenth Century: Advocates, Proctors, and Others,' *Journal of Ecclesiastical History* 43 (1992), 541–60.

Gender Models in Alfonso X's *Siete partidas*: The Sexual Politics of 'Nature' and 'Society'

ROBERTO J. GONZÁLEZ-CASANOVAS

Introduction: The Political Rhetoric of the *Partidas*

This paper examines the function of sexual roles as social and political models, as well as didactic and propagandistic texts, in part IV of Alfonso X of Castile's legal code, the *Siete partidas* (1256–63). Such a study takes as its critical points of departure the reinterpretation of Alfonso's juridical works as literature of exemplarity, as undertaken by Seniff, López Estrada, and Stone. In addition, the present study is influenced by a broad spectrum of historicist theories that embrace cultural politics (Montrose), the social anthropology of gender (Jehlen), feminist critique (Fisher and Halley), sociolinguistic criticism (Fowler), ethical narratology (White), secular mythography (Frye), didactic rhetoric (Hampton), and communal reception (Jauss). The methodology developed by cultural historicists can help us read Alfonso's legal utopia as a series of rhetorical, political, and poetic operations that deal with the king's authority in the text as judge and the court's (and people's) reception of the text as a privileged model of reading and enacting justice in society. By combining these two critical approaches – the literary textuality of the laws as a utopia and the historical contextuality of their interpretations by Alfonso's contemporaries – it is possible to appreciate the original rhetorical impact that the *Siete partidas* were meant to have in court and nation as a vernacular encyclopedia of law and custom, mirror of society, and model of what medieval scholastics and Renaissance humanists would term the Christian Republic or Commonwealth.

Alfonso X's *Siete partidas* reworks and reinterprets various late-medieval humanistic concepts of nature and society. The Wise King's vernacular legal code, which was never enforced during his lifetime, in effect functions as a utopian mirror for society; in it, all the various estates and conditions of human life are discussed and related to a patriarchal scheme of order, hierarchy, and harmony that is equally based on Graeco-Roman and Judaeo-Christian codes of justice. It is important to note the secular context of authority within which this utopia would unfold. Hence, the physical, social, political, and ethical models for sexual roles in the *Siete partidas* are not predicated only on penitential traditions of canon law as formulated by Church institutions (as in Raymond of Peñafort's *Summa de casibus poenitentiae*), but also on the natural science and moral philosophy of pagan antiquity as developed at Italian legal and medical schools (Bologna and Naples) and among Arabic and Latin scholar-translators at royal courts and *scriptoria*, such as those of Frederick II of Sicily and Alfonso X of Castile himself (for parallels between the latter, see the studies by Montes and R.S. López).

Natural Law and Social Utopia in the *Partidas*

The interpretation of the *Siete partidas* as a cultural and literary text, one that offers its readers both models of didactic literature and myths of human perfection, owes much to the critical work of Dennis Seniff, Francisco López Estrada, and Marilyn Stone. Seniff emphasized the need to employ interdisciplinary approaches to Alfonso X's non-fictional texts as literary creations that embody, interpret, and exemplify both learned and popular traditions of wisdom. To such an extent had Alfonso's court internalized biblical, scholastic, and Islamic notions of the rational order of creation that new vernacular law books of Castile came to represent a secular and popular synthesis of natural law that preceded that of Thomas Aquinas. As Seniff observes, 'Even a cursory examination of the legal corpus of Alfonso X of Castile ..., reveals that currents of natural law, far from appearing exclusively in the *Summa theologica*, had already become part of Iberian thought by 1262, ... some five years before the [*Summa theologica*] was begun' (p. 162). To this concept of a didactic *summa* in the vernacular for popular diffusion, as advocated by Seniff, one must now add the complementary interpretation of the *Siete partidas* as a prehumanist utopia that has been developed by López Estrada. What Alfonso's utopia represents is not only a social model but also a political text that provides its own internalized gloss of the legal categories as problems in human relations (López Estrada, 208). What is most valuable in López Estrada's analysis is his recognition of a utopian rhetoric of instruction and formation that can truly be termed humanistic:

> The legislators of the *Partidas* composed the work by employing a theory of law involved with political science; and this is propitious for approaching a utopia. They are jurists as fond of humanistic considerations as of the merely legal preventive formula; that is, they pay more attention to the humanistic spirit of the whole than to the letter of the particular case ... That is the 'creative' sense of the *Partidas*: that the letter endow the understanding with the greatest clarity, and this is a linguistic merit that acquires the status of literature, due to its place at the origins of [Spanish] literature, as it applies to a legislative content that seeks in the *letter* the firmness of its communication, that the law acquire the highest literary status so that in this also it may be exemplary and normative. (pp. 212–13; my translation)

At the same time that López Estrada was formulating this utopian reading of the *Partidas*, Stone was noting the didactic rhetoric of Part 4 of the *Partidas*. Her observations stress the practical unity of semantic and ethical considerations in Alfonso's elaboration of his legal text; beyond this common rhetorical objective, Stone also often finds a common literary subjectivity that combines social and cultural contexts of virtue and vice into traditional forms of counsel and example. For Stone, the uniqueness of the *Partidas* 'lies in the many explanations included after the laws themselves to clarify the meaning of the rules. In that sense, the *Siete partidas* may be seen as an ethical guide intended to foster certain moral attitudes' (p. 147). This point is also made by López Estrada, who underscores the similarity of many sections of the *Partidas* to medieval didactic subgenres, such as the *castigos* and *espejos*, or books of counsels and mirrors for princes (p. 208).

Gender Models: Religious Tradition, Political Authority, and Social Order

Any study of the Fourth Partida, which treats domestic relations, should begin with the symbolic place it occupies in Alfonso X's book of laws. The order of the seven Partidas reflects the logical and axiological progression from the theological and moral priority of canon law in human affairs (First Partida), to the philosophy of political order to be reflected by the ruling classes (Second Partida), to the norms of justice to be exemplified by the administrators of legislation (Third Partida), to the social basis of natural law found in the family (Fourth Partida), to the civic obligations to be exercised in the settlement of disputes (Fifth Partida), to the economic virtues to be practised in questions of inheritance (Sixth Partida), and finally to the ethical problems posed by those offences against the social order that merit official condemnation and punishment (Seventh Partida). If Alfonso's law code represents a utopia, then the Fourth Partida on matrimony and social relations constitutes the most important part of the Wise King's program for communal order and harmony. As the Alfonsine jurists themselves note: 'we have placed it in the middle of the Seven Partidas of this book, just as the heart is placed in the middle of the body ...' (SP P. 4, prol.; Scott, 877).[1] The Fourth Partida consists of a combination of idealistic and pragmatic considerations that makes for a balance between the legal extremes to be found in the First and Seventh Partidas: the First ratifies the spiritual and ecclesial foundations of canon law so as to project a social hierarchy based on the supremacy of a clerical patriarchy of celibate men, whereas the Seventh catalogues the social transgressions, vices, and crimes to be controlled by legal prohibitions and punishments against men and women; the First establishes the harmony that prevails within a Christian Republic of priests and monks, whose chastity leads to a human order that mirrors the divine, while the Seventh comes to identify sexual sins with natural appetites and social vices that threaten disorder for the community as well as destruction for the individual.

Within this highly structured presentation of the various types of legislation and their proper contexts, one finds an important subtext on social equilibrium. This message combines the binary opposition of order and disorder with the triangular dialectic of nature, society, and politics. For the modern reader of this medieval utopia, two dynamic forces emerge at opposite poles that define human relationships through the attractions and repulsions which they effect: on the one hand, the Alfonsine jurists constantly focus on the sexual sphere that not only includes the biological drive in man and woman to join and reproduce, and thereby maintain both the species and society, but also involves the cultural definition of traditional roles and relations of dominance according to gender; on the other hand, the Alfonsine sages continuously refer to the moral sphere that not only reflects the theological and philosophical search for a universal meaning on which to base all levels of human authority, but also responds to the need to establish political institutions to regulate social and economic transactions according to a code of legitimate power, which is exercised for reasonable ends and in the service of the common good. What is striking in this rhetorical apparatus of the legal order is the degree to which the Alfonsine jurists exercise polysemous and ambiguous interpretations of nature, society, and politics. In effect, they often confuse issues of sexuality and morality, gender and community, culture and reason.

In the selected passages from the Fourth Partida, which deal with matrimony, royal marriage, natural (and social) obligations, friendship and community, and the definitions of woman and family (see the corresponding five sections of the appendix to this paper), one can recognize that the attempts made by the Alfonsine jurists to define utopia at the same time serve to ratify the status quo. The issue of order or disorder dominates the texts on the proper relationships between men and women in the various contexts of creatures and Christians, citizens and subjects. It is important to apply historicist criteria to these juridical norms in three ways: as didactic texts on the interpretation of authority, as mediating discourses on the exercise of power, and as performative communications on the reception of exemplarity. The passages from the *Siete partidas* offer various models of sexuality and morality for a contemporary readership of literate and semiliterate members of the court society, royal bureaucracy, and clerical intelligentsia. These models correspond to relations of family and community as the basic categories of human institutions. The problems that arise in their interpretation depend on the relative balance between the universal application of a common morality and the particular circumstances of a culture-defined gender. As Jehlen notes: 'Culture, society, history define gender, not nature ... The introduction of gender into the critical discussion multiplies its concerns and categories ... to produce a newly encompassing account of cultural consciousness that is also newly self-conscious' (pp. 263n, 272). For these reasons, it is necessary to note the functions of the ideological code, sociological model, and ethical rhetoric in the Alfonsine laws.

The passages on matrimony (see section 1 of the appendix) combine rhetorical strategies that correspond to the clerical traditions of biblical mythopoesis, scholastic symbol, providential history, and etymological parable. First, matrimony is said to be a divine institution established in Paradise in terms that constitute a paraphrase of the book of Genesis: woman here serves as man's companion and mate; her function and very reason for existing is male-defined, for it is decreed by God the Father, designed to please men, and destined to maintain the species. Second, matrimony is affirmed to be the highest sacrament of the Church as a result of its historical precedence over the other sacraments and its social importance as a biological mechanism for human survival that maintains the divine order of creation and as a morally sanctioned channel for male lust that avoids the worldly disorder of unbalanced animal appetites; these criteria, which depend upon clerical traditions of biblical exegesis and penitential theology, reduce women to a gender role based on positive and negative notions of sexuality that correspond to views of creation before and after the Fall. Third, matrimony is shown to have developed as a providential device in history to restore balance in the cosmos (replacing fallen angels), in humanity (supplanting lust), in society (nurturing children), and in morality (sanctioning natural bonds between couples). From the sanctity of a sacrament, the jurists thus descend to the expediency of a social prophylactic: for marriage was established 'to avoid quarrels, homicides, insolence, violence, and many other very wrongful acts which would take place on account of women if marriage did not exist' (SP P. 4, T. 12, prol.; Scott, 886).[2] Such a further clerical apology for official male–female relations serves to promote a mechanical gender role for women as some sort of divinely appointed regulator of male drives; this view depends on a scholastic interpretation based on moral legalism which contrasts with the more dynamic gender role of woman as mediatrix found in this period in Marian devotion, female hagiography, and affective modes of spirituality (the last, studied by Bynum). Fourth, the very name of matrimony is reduced to a negative reflection upon the burdensome role played by woman in the sexual process of reproduction and familial office of child rearing. Matrimony as an official institution of Church and State, according to both canon and civil law, is thus transformed by the logocentric imagination of a patriarchal ideology into an implicit parable on the subjection of woman, with her physical and social limitations, to man, who once married can enjoy the pleasures of animal lusts without the risk of falling into sin and exercise political power over his household without responsibility for menial tasks. What such appeals to the authority of the Bible (creation), the Church (sacrament), the Church Fathers (moral reason), and human society (natural reason) show is not only the eclectic culture of the Alfonsine jurists, but also the hybrid ideology of the Wise King, whose claim to power must be justified before the cultural pluralism of a diverse national population and diverse royal court. Alfonso's audience, and his group of collaborators, embrace Christians, Muslims, and Jews, as well as clerical and lay scholars from Western and Oriental traditions of learning.

In contrast to the passages on matrimony from the Fourth Partida, the references to royal matrimony found in the Second Partida (see section 2 of the appendix) show another aspect of social utopia that is aristocratic rather than clerical, contemporary rather than historical, and practical rather than symbolic. These images of royal order depend equally upon courtly convention and moral philosophy drawn from the wisdom tradition of classical antiquity and the Bible. The authorities cited, Cato and Solomon, underscore the common humanist and biblical tradition shared by learned Christians, Muslims, and Jews at Alfonso's intellectual and administrative court. Although matrimony itself is understood in the Fourth Partida in light of the patriarchal order of creation and society as established by clerical tradition, royal matrimony is interpreted in the Second Partida according to a mixed patriarchal and communal model that is based both on sapiential tradition and on practical experience: 'a king who thus honors, loves, and watches over his wife, will be loved, honored, and cared for by her, and, for that reason, will offer a good example to all in his country. But ... he must place her in company of such men and women as love and fear God, and know how to preserve his honor and hers' (SP P. 2, T. 6, L. 1; Scott, 299).[3] In these apparently more universal categories of human culture, men and women are accorded equal importance in the exemplarity of their relations and in the mutual benefits of their good actions.

It is significant that, leaving aside various corollaries to matrimony and sections on children, the central passages on family consist of two glosses: one, in the Fourth Partida itself, on the etymology of matrimony (vs. patrimony), has already been cited (see section 1 of the appendix); the other, on the concepts of *paterfamilias* and *materfamilias*, occurs in a sort of miscellaneous appendix to the law code towards the end of the Seventh Partida (see section 5 of the appendix). The first passage affirms the biological basis for familial and social bonds in the physical labour of the woman in conceiving, bearing, and rearing children; this constitutes a type of scholastic commentary on creation and procreation that relates the notions of suffering and toil to the condition of fallen humanity in society and to the responsibility of woman for man's fall in Paradise. The second passage acknowledges the social reality of male and female heads of household, which corresponds both to the pragmatic traditions of Roman legislation (revived in the Middle Ages by Bolognese jurists) and to the historical circumstances of some women in Reconquest Castile (studied by Dillard):

By the word 'family' is understood the master, his wife, and all those who live under him, and over whom he has control; as, for instance, his children, servants, and other descendants: for that is a family where more than two men live under the orders of the master ... The person who is the master of the house is called *paterfamilias*, although he may have no children, and a woman who lives honorably in her own house and is of good habits, is called *materfamilias*. (SP P. 7, T. 33, L. 6; Scott, 1473)[4]

Here one should first of all note the privileged status of the Roman model of the extended family or household, rather than the matrimonial one (based on sexuality and theology), as the basic sociopolitical unit of the state. One should further note, however, the gendered contexts of this passage, which defines *paterfamilias* in socio-economic terms of the master of a household (whether or not he is married or has children), but restricts *materfamilias* to the moral definition of an independent woman who lives virtuously alone. Is this the case of a double standard on the part of jurists who may be male clerics or on the part of a king who subscribes to a chivalric patriarchy? While these may be plausible explanations, it is worth recalling that Alfonso's self-consciously enlightened and pragmatic approach to legislation throughout the *Siete partidas*, with its appeals to Roman reason and Oriental wisdom, may here serve to acknowledge by implication another type of female head of household. This type of woman is recognized by the law code, but she does not merit the title of *materfamilias*: for she is the legally sanctioned concubine or *barragana* of medieval Castile (SP P. 4, T. 14, L. 1–3), who would be regarded as a semi-independent woman with legal power over her children (known as 'natural' but not 'bastards').

The passages on friendship (see section 4 of the appendix) represent the ideological and ethical centre of the Alfonsine utopia as the best model of social harmony, one that transcends the self-interest of nature and politics. At the same time, these passages constitute historical and cultural texts on the Alfonsine model of secular enlightenment, which is based on the wisdom of the world as epitomized by Aristotle. It is Aristotle (as interpreted by Averroes) who in medieval Iberia represents the point of contact between Christian and Islamic forms of scholasticism based on Graeco-Roman natural and moral philosophy. What is significant is that the Alfonsine interpretation of this Aristotelian ideal of friendship is conspicuously patriarchal and hierarchical, since it goes beyond matrimonial and familial relations, and distinguishes between degrees of partial and complete bonds of affection and esteem:

Natural friendship is that a father and a mother feel towards their children and a husband has for his wife. Not only human beings who are endowed with reason have this, but also all other animals who possess the faculty of procreation, ... and persons who are natives of one country have also a natural friendship for one another ... The second kind of friendship is more noble than the first, because it can exist among all men who are kindly disposed; and it is superior to the former, for it arises solely from beneficence, while the other originates in a debt of nature ... (SP P. 4, T. 27, L. 4; Scott, 1004–5)[5]

Women here appear in the conventional gender roles of wives and mothers, whose relations with men operate on a common level of animal or creaturely affection. The classical notion of the friend as companion of the heart and mind is then combined by the Alfonsine jurist with the chivalric notion of the companion in the exercise of arms and virtues; this occurs in a reference to a Spanish feudal custom of always respecting the friendship of a fellow noble unless formally challenged by him (ibid.). This combination of moral philosophy and chivalric honour translates into asexual and supranatural categories of human exemplarity that transcend biological appetites and social contracts so as to privilege courtly codes and political interests.

The passages on community (see section 4 of the appendix) also depend upon Aristotelian distinctions between the properly natural and social dimensions of human relationships. This notion of community is the logical and ideological extension of the ideal of friendship. Where there is true friendship, beyond marriage and family, one finds a community that approximates a utopia: 'Aristotle stated that if true friendship existed among men, they would have no need of courts or magistrates to judge them, because friendship would cause them to do and observe what justice orders and directs' (SP P. 4, T. 27, L. 1; Scott, 1003).[6] Here is a curious instance of a law code pointing beyond itself to the vision of a society made up of friends who need no laws. The utopian model of this text thereby implies a dystopian interpretation of its context in contemporary society, in which such a great reform of legislation as the *Siete partidas* is required. For it seems that the people are so far from realizing the Aristotelian ideal of community that their every action, relation, and intention must be regulated by Church and Court. The Alfonsine utopia thus emerges as a nostalgic representation of a classical golden age of moral philosophers, as well as a conservative projection of an aristocratic élite whose formation in true chivalry and courtesy enables them to transcend the negative prohibitions of laws so as to enact the positive counsels of their code.

What is significant in this regard is the lack of reference in Alfonso's humanist and aristocratic subtext to any of the contemporary models of evangelical perfection and apostolic community which constitute the socially revolutionary paradigms of the properly late-medieval utopias (noted by Ozment, 208). These models were being advocated by Franciscan and Dominican preachers, as well as by marginal (and at times heretical) groups of pious laymen and -women such as the Albigensians and the beghards and beguines, in various attempts to renew the Church or Christian Republic as the manifestation in the world of the utopian City of God and mystical Kingdom of Christ. Hence, the choice of utopias in the thirteenth century reflects both ideological and cultural positions of power. These involve hierarchical or communal authority, aristocratic or egalitarian relationships, and patriarchal or heterosocial bonds of loyalty. It is interesting to note that Alfonso's appeal to what he perceives as the more universal grounds of society in philosophy and chivalry, precisely what should unite his diverse Christian and Muslim subjects, proves to be the more conservative and gendered utopia, as it refers to classical and Oriental paradigms of wisdom and virtue interpreted by male sages and heroes. It is the contemporary movement of Church reform, not Alfonso's efforts at enlightenment, that is responsible for some measure of revolution in the cultural definition of gender roles, as more ordinary men and women take an active part in creating communities that would transcend the limitations of sexual, social, and political bodies. Alfonso's utopia is circumscribed by the textual boundaries of legal traditions, the contextual frontiers of Reconquest Iberia, and the metatextual barriers of a patriarchal aristocracy ruled by philosopher kings. In contrast, the utopia of the apostolic movement of his time seeks to transcend the historical, social, and political parameters of Christendom. In order to achieve transcendence, this utopia requires the imitation and re-enactment of the charismatic examples of Christianity offered by the Apostles and the Virgin Mary in Scripture and Church tradition, by male and female saints in history and legend, and by religious and lay communities of pious men and women in various contemporary societies.

Conclusion: Patriarchal Order and the Discourse of Power

In the Fourth Partida, the Alfonsine jurists consider matrimony, family, friendship, and community according to mixed criteria: they combine the utopian morality of the Christian Republic with the gendered culture of the clergy and court. Such a conflict of interpretative interests leads the modern critic to go beyond the legal text, political contexts, cultural intertexts, and ethical subtext in order to address metatextual questions of authority, mediation, and reception posed by the Partidas. On the one hand, one recognizes the hermeneutic problem of defining the 'natural order': Is it to be found exemplified in creation or revelation? Is its true scope cosmic and universal or human and anthropological? Is its justification spiritual and theocentric or religious and anthropocentric? Is it manifested primarily in physical existence or social lifestyles? Is its underlying power a biological drive or a political self-interest? Is its defining concept an idealistic vision of self-transcendence by members of the Christian Commonwealth or a utilitarian strategy for survival in the contemporary world dominated by aristocratic men? On the other hand, one encounters the rhetorical problem of applying the social and political exemplarity: To what extent is courtly tradition or popular experience at the heart of the social norms represented? Who is to be responsible – the clerical experts, a philosopher king, the nobles at court, or the patriarchs of the community – for interpreting the paradigms of social and sexual morality? From where in the prevailing ideological code – Christian theology, some 'natural reason,' ecclesiastic or aristocratic tradition, the political status quo, or social utility – is the criterion for right action to be drawn and developed? Such metacritical questions imply that the dialectic of nature, society, and politics addresses an ideal reader who would represent the culturally heterogeneous, physically heterosexual, intellectually orthodox, and politically pragmatic subject of Alfonso's legislation and utopia. But is this ideal reader the same as the contemporary one envisaged by the Wise King? In other words, is such complexity a modern form of scholastic dialectic predicated upon the critical awareness of ideologically and culturally defined issues of sexuality, gender, and dominance? What is certain is that in one important respect it is valid to apply concepts of cultural historicity and political textuality to the *Siete partidas*, for in reinterpreting traditional legislation in terms of social utopia Alfonso X and his jurists in effect privilege the interpretative and normative functions of human law. For modern historicist critics this represents a fascinating attempt by a medieval patriarchal ruling order self-consciously to read and rewrite itself. Alfonso X's model of royal propaganda would transpose human nature into humanist enlightenment, transform contemporary society into an exemplary community, and translate worldly politics into a Christian utopia.

The Alfonsine concept of human nature as a biological equilibrium and of society as a political balance influences the legal treatment of sexuality. The terms in which the entire law code defines the phenomenon of sexuality include: biblical views of the Fall, penitential theology, religious vows, carnal appetites, gender roles, matrimonial contracts, family structure, social relations, courtly obligations, and issues of legitimate inheritance. With respect to the Wise King's approaches, as a worldly, enlightened monarch, to sexual relations in contemporary society, it is still necessary to confront the text of the *Siete partidas*, not only with the metacritical issues of interpretation noted above, but also with a series of provocative yet unresolved questions of cultural history that merit further study: (1) To what extent does this juridical 'realism' reflect the ethos of courtly love or the pragmatism of Graeco-Roman (and Graeco-Arabic) legislation? (2) Is this type of tolerant attitude meant to extend beyond aristocratic circles to the populace as a whole? (3) What effect should these laws have on the policies of socioreligious relations and on issues of repopulation in the extensive frontier areas just reconquered from the Moors? (4) How can traditional views on the natural (physical) appetites of sexuality and the equally natural (social) operations of human culture be reconciled to the contemporary circumstances of a pluricultural and multilevel frontier society? (5) How is it possible, according to clerical, classical, and Oriental ethics, to integrate fallen creatures and physical disorder into the utopian society being designed by natural reason and royal fiat? Such questions point to the historical challenges, doctrinal complexity, and political dilemmas that serve as background to Alfonso X's *Siete partidas*. In this ambitious work the Wise King attempts to elaborate, not just a legal code that would embrace all categories and situations of society, but also a political utopia that would project onto the heterogeneous peoples of the Reconquest a common image of human wisdom and royal enlightenment. As a legal text on justice, the *Partidas* raises the problem of how to embrace all forms of life, as they in fact exist in contemporary society, and subject them to a hierarchical order interpreted by a Christian philosopher king. As a utopian text on exemplarity, the *Siete partidas* elaborates an ideal model of human relations and responsibilities on earth that claims to be based on a spiritual or sapiential order. In the process of reconstructing the myth of the universal rule of reason, the Wise King attempts to legitimize his own secular power and consolidate his authority over all the men and women among his diverse peoples.

APPENDIX

Selected passages from the *Siete partidas* – original text, with translations

Note: Quotations are taken from Alfonso X el Sabio, *Las siete partidas*, ed. Gregorio López [with Latin glosses of 1555 ed.], 4 vols. (Madrid: Benito Cano 1789); translations are from the S.P. Scott edition, 3 vols. (Chicago: American Bar Association 1931).

1. On matrimony

Nuestro Señor Dios ... fizo muger, que le diesse [al ome] por compañera, en que fiziesse linaje; e establesció el casamiento de ellos ambos en el Parayso; e puso ley ordenadamente entre ellos, que assí como eran de cuerpos departidos según natura, que fvessen uno quanto en amor, de manera que non se pudiessen departir, guardando lealtad uno a otro; e otrosí, que de aquella amistad saliesse linaje, de que el mundo fuesse poblado, e él [Dios] loado, e servido. (SP P. 4, prol.; GL II, 453)

Our Lord ... [created] woman and gave her as a companion by whom [man] might have descendants; and He established them both in Paradise in marriage and promulgated it as a law between them that while their bodies were different by nature, they should be one by love, so that they could not be divided, preserving faithfulness to one another; also that from this affection offspring be born by which the world might be peopled and He Himself praised and served. (SP P. 4, prol.; Scott, 877)

[E]sta orden del Matrimonio ... es uno de los más nobles e más honrados de los siete Sacramentos de la Sancta Eglesia. E porende deue ser honrrado e guardado como aquel que es el primero ... E otrosí como aquel que es mantenimiento del mundo, e que faze a los omes beuir vida ordenada naturalmente, e sin pecado, e sin el qual los otros seys Sacramentos non podrían ser mantenidos, nin guardados. E por esso lo pusimos en medio de las siete partidas deste libro; assí como el coraçón es puesto en medio del cuerpo ... (SP P. 4, prol.; GL II, 453)

[T]his regulation of matrimony ... is one of the noblest and most honorable of the seven Sacraments of the holy Church, and for this reason it should be honored and observed, as being the first ... [A]lso, as it is the support of the world, and causes men naturally to live a regular life and one free from sin, and without which the other six sacraments can neither be maintained nor observed. For this reason we have placed it in the middle of the Seven Partidas of this book, just as the heart is placed in the middle of the body ... (SP P. 4, prol.; Scott, 877)

[L]os Santos Padres muestran otras razones [por establecer Dios el casamiento] ... La primera fue para cumplir la dezena orden de los Angeles ... La segunda por desuiar pecado de lujuria. La tercera es por auer mayor amor a sus fijos, seyendo ciertos de ellos que son suyos. La quarta por desuiar contiendas, e homezillos, e soberuias, e fuerças, e otras cosas muy tortizeras, que nascerían por razón de las mugeres, si casamiento non fuesse. (SP P. 4, T. 12, prol.; GL II, 465)

[T]he holy fathers ... assigned other, spiritual reasons for [God establishing matrimony] ... The first was to supply the tenth order of angels ... The second, to avoid the sin of lust ... The third, so that a man may have greater love for his children, he being certain that they belong to him. The fourth, to avoid quarrels, homicides, insolence, violence, and many other very wrongful acts which would take place on account of women if marriage did not exist. (SP P. 4, T. 12, prol.; Scott, 886)

[L]a razón por que llaman Matrimonio al casamiento, e non Patrimonio, es ésta. Porque la madre sufre mayores trabajos con los fijos ... E demás desto, porque los fijos, mientra son pequeños, mayor menester han de la ayuda de la madre, que del padre. (SP P. 4, T. 2, L. 2; GL II, 466)

[T]he reason why marriage is called matrimony, not patrimony, is because the mother endures greater hardships with children than the father ... [I]n addition to this, because children, while they are small, have greater need of the assistance of the mother than of the father. (SP P. 4, T. 2, L. 2; Scott, 886)

2. On royal matrimony

[D]eue el Rey catar que aquella con quien casasse aya en sí quatro cosas. La primera, que venga de buen linaje. La segunda, que sea fermosa. La tercera, que sea bien acostumbrada. La quarta, que sea rica ... E si tal non la pudiere fallar, cate que sea de buen linaje, e de buenas costumbres: ca los bienes que se siguen destos dos, fincan siempre en el linaje, que della desciende; mas la fermosura e la riqueza pasan más de ligero. (SP P. 2, T. 6, L. 1; GL I, 393–4)

[The] king should consider that she whom he marries be endowed with four qualities. First, she should come of good family; second, she should be handsome; third, she should have good habits; fourth, she should be wealthy ... [I]f he cannot find one like this, he should see that his wife is of good family and good habits, for the benefits from these two qualities will all abide in the line descended from her, but beauty and riches pass away more easily. (SP P. 2, T. 6, L. 1; Scott, 298)

[E]l Rey que desta guisa honrrare, amare e guardare a su muger será él amado e honrrado e guardado della, e dará ende buen exemplo a todos los de su tierra. Mas para fazer estas cosas bien e cumplidamente, ha menester que le dé tal compañía de omes e de mugeres que amen e teman a Dios, e sepan guardar la honrra dél e della. Ca naturalmente non puede ser que non aprenda ome mucho de aquellos con quien biue cotidianamente. E por esto dixo Catón el sabio en castigando su fijo: Si quisieres aprender bien, aue vida con los buenos. E esso mismo dixo el Rey Salomón, en manera de castigo: Que el que oviesse sabor de fazer bien, que se acompañasse con los buenos, e se arredrasse de los malos. (SP P. 2, T. 6, L. 1; GL I, 394–5)

[A] king who thus honors, loves, and watches over his wife, will be loved, honored, and cared for by her, and, for that reason, will offer a good example to all in his country. But, so that these things may be well and thoroughly accomplished, he must place her in company of such men and women as love and fear God, and know how to preserve his honor and hers. For, naturally, it cannot be but that a man learns much from those with whom he daily lives. For this reason Cato the Wise advised his son: 'If you desire to acquire information properly, associate with the good.' King Solomon said the same thing, by way of advice: 'He who wishes to do good, should associate with good men, and avoid those that are wicked.' (SP P. 2, T. 6, L. 1; Scott, 299)

3. On natural relationships or obligations

Naturaleza tanto quiere dezir como debdo que han los omes vnos con otros, por alguna derecha razón en se amar, e en se querer bien. (SP P. 4, T. 24, L. 1; GL II, 599)

Natural relationship means an obligation which men are under to others to love and cherish them for some just reason. (SP P. 4, T. 24, L. 2; Scott, 990)

Diez maneras pusieron los Sabios antiguos de naturaleza. La primera e la mejor es la que han los omes a su señor natural ... La segunda es la que auiene por vasallaje. La tercera por criança. La quarta por caballería. La quinta por casamiento. La sexta por heredamiento. La setena por sacarlo de captiuo, o por librarlo de muerte o deshonrra. La octaua por aforramiento, de que non rescibe precio el que la aforra. La nouena, por tornarlo Christiano. La dezena por morança de diez años, que faga en la tierra, maguer sea natural de otra. (SP P. 4, T. 24, L. 2; GL II, 600)

The ancient wise men established ten kinds of natural obligation. The first and best is the relation men sustain towards their natural lord ...; the second is derived from vassalage; the third arises through nurture; the fourth springs from knighthood; the fifth, from marriage; the sixth, from inheritance; the seventh, from rescue from captivity, liberation from death or dishonor; the eighth, from emancipation, for which the party granting it received no reward; the ninth, by becoming a Christian; the tenth, by ten years' residence in a country, although the party may be a native of another. (SP P. 4, T. 24, L. 2; Scott, 991)

4. On friendship

Amistad es cosa que ayunta mucho la voluntad de los omes, para amarse mucho.

Ca segund dixeron los Sabios antiguos, el verdadero amor passa todos los debdos. (SP P. 4, T. 27, prol.; GL II, 629)

Friendship is something which induces persons to love one another greatly, for, as the wise men of the ancients declared, true love is the most important of all obligations. (SP P. 4, T. 27, prol.; Scott, 1003)

[A]mistad, segund dize Aristóteles, es vna virtud que es buena en sí, e prouechosa a la vida de los omes ... E concordia es vna virtud que es semejante a la amistad. E desta se trabajaron los Sabios, e los grandes Señores, que fizieron los libros de las leyes, porque los omes biuiessen acordadamente ... [D]ixo Aristóteles que si los omes ouiessen entre sí verdadera amistad, non aurían menester Justicia nin Alcaldes que los judgassen: porque aquella amistad les faríe complir, e guardar aquello mismo, que quiere e manda la Justicia. (SP P. 4, T. 27, L. 1; GL II, 629–30)

[F]riendship, according to Aristotle, is a virtue which is intrinsically good in itself and profitable to human life ... Concord is a virtue similar to friendship, which sages and the great lords who made the books of the law favored bringing about so that men might live together in unity ... Aristotle stated that if true friendship existed among men, they would have no need of courts or magistrates to judge them, because friendship would cause them to do and observe what justice orders and directs. (SP P. 4, T. 27, L. 1; Scott, 1003)

Aristóteles, que fizo departimiento naturalmente en todas las cosas deste mundo, dixo que eran tres maneras de amistad. La primera es de natura. La segunda es la que ome ha a su amigo, por uso de luengo tiempo, por bondad que aya en él. La tercera es la que ome ha con otro, por algund pro o por algund plazer que ha dél, o espera auer. E amistad de natura es la que ha el padre o la madre con sus fijos, e el marido a su muger: e esta non tan solamente la han los omes, ... mas avn todas las otras animalias, que han poder de engendrar ...: e amistad han otrossí segund natura, los que son naturales de una tierra ... La segunda manera de amistad es más noble que la primera, porque puede ser entre todos los omes, que ayan bondad en sí: e porende es mejor que la otra, porque ésta nasce de bondad tan solamente, e la otra de debdo de natura ... La tercera manera de amistad ... non es verdadera amistad ... E avn y ha otra manera de amistad, segund la costumbre de España, que pusieron antiguamente los Fijos dalgo entre sí, que non se deuen deshonrrar nin fazer mal vnos a otros, a menos de tornarse la amistad, e se desafiar primeramente. (SP P. 4, T. 27, L. 4; GL II, 631)

Aristotle, who established natural distinctions between all things in this world, said there are three kinds of friendship: first, that of nature; second, that a man has for his friend, from intercourse of long duration by the affection which he has for him; third, that a man has for another for some advantage or pleasure which he obtains or expects to obtain from him. Natural friendship is that a father and a mother feel towards their children and a husband has for his wife. Not only human beings who are endowed with reason have this, but also all other animals who possess the faculty of procreation, ... and persons who are natives of one country have also a natural friendship for one another ... The second kind of friendship is more noble than the first, because it can exist among all men who are kindly disposed; and it is superior to the former, for it arises solely from beneficence, while the other originates in a debt of nature ... The third kind ... is not true friendship ... There is another kind of friendship which exists by the custom of Spain, which, in former times, nobles established with themselves when they agreed not to dishonor or injure each other, without first renouncing their friendship and issuing a challenge ... (SP P. 4, T. 27, L. 4; Scott, 1004–5)

5. Definitions of woman and family

Vsamos a poner en las leyes deste nuestro libro, diziendo: Tal ome, que tal cosa fiziere, aya tal pena. Entendemos por aquella palabra que el defendimiento pertenesce también a la muger como al varón, maguer que non fagamos y emiente della ... [P]or esta palabra que es dicha Muger ... se entiende también la virgen que ha de doze años arriba, como todas las otras. (SP P. 7, T. 33, L. 6; GL III, 521)

We are accustomed to insert in the laws of this our book words like the following: 'Such-and-Such a man who commits such-and-such an act, shall suffer such-and-such a penalty'; and we mean by this that the punishment shall apply to a woman as well as to a man, although no mention of her is made ... By the word 'woman' is understood a virgin more than twelve years of age, and all others. (SP P. 7, T. 33, L. 6; Scott, 1473)

[P]or esta palabra Familia se entiende el señor della, e su muger, e todos los que biuen so él, sobre quien ha mandamiento, assí como los fijos e los siruientes, e los otros criados. Ca Familia es dicha aquella en que biuen más de dos omes al mandamiento del señor, e dende adelante ... E aquél es dicho Paterfamilias que es señor de la casa, maguer que non aya fijos. E Materfamilias es dicha la muger, que biue honestamente en su casa, o es de buenas maneras. (SP P. 7, T. 33, L. 6; GL III, 521–2)

By the word 'family' is understood the master, his wife, and all those who live under him, and over whom he has control; as, for instance, his children, servants, and other descendants: for that is a family where more than two men live under the orders of the master ... The person who is the master of the house is called paterfamilias, *although he may have no children, and a woman who lives honorably in her own house and is of good habits, is called* materfamilias. *(SP P. 7, T. 33, L. 6; Scott, 1473)*

NOTES

1 'Lo pusimos en medio de las siete partidas deste libro; assí como el coraçón es puesto en medio del cuerpo ...' (SP P. 4, prol.; GL II, 453)

2 'Por desuiar contiendas, e homezillos, e soberuias, e fuerças, e otras cosas muy tortizeras, que nascerían por razón de las mugeres, si casamiento non fuesse' (SP P. 4, T. 12, prol.; GL II, 465)

3 '[E]l Rey que desta guisa honrrare, amare e guardare a su muger será él amado e honrrado e guardado della, e dará ende buen exemplo a todos los de su tierra. Mas ... ha menester que le dé tal compañía de omes e de mugeres que amen e teman a Dios, e sepan guardar la honrra dél e della' (SP P. 2, T. 6, L. 1; GL I, 394)

4 'Por esta palabra Familia se entiende el señor della, e su muger, e todos los que biuen so él, sobre quien ha mandamiento, assí como los fijos e los siruientes, e los otros criados. Ca Familia es dicha aquella en que biuen más de dos omes al mandamiento del señor, e dende adelante ... E aquél es dicho Paterfamilias que es señor de la casa, maguer que non aya fijos. E Materfamilias es dicha la muger, que biue honestamente en su casa, o es de buenas maneras' (SP P. 7, T. 33, L. 6; GL III, 521–2)

5 '[A]mistad de natura es la que ha el padre o la madre con sus fijos, e el marido a su muger: e esta non tan solamente la han los omes, ... mas avn todas las otras animalias, que han poder de engendrar ...: e amistad han otrossí segund natura, los que son naturales de una tierra ... La segunda manera de amistad es más noble que la primera, porque puede ser entre todos los omes, que ayan bondad en sí: e porende es mejor que la otra, porque ésta nasce de bondad tan solamente, e la otra de debdo de natura ...' (SP P. 4, T. 27, L. 4; GL II, 631)

6 '[D]ixo Aristóteles que si los omes ouiessen entre sí verdadera amistad, non aurían menester Justicia nin Alcaldes que los judgassen: porque aquella amistad les faríe complir, e guardar aquello mismo, que quiere e manda la Justicia' (SP P. 4, T. 27, L. 1; GL II, 629–30)

WORKS CITED

Primary Texts

SP   = Alfonso X, *Las siete partidas* [1256–63]
GL   = *Las siete partidas*, 4 vols. Ed. Gregorio López [Latin glosses of 1555 ed.]. Madrid: Benito Cano 1789
Scott = English tr. of *Las siete partidas*, 3 vols. Trans. S.P. Scott. Chicago: American Bar Association 1931

Studies:

Bynum, Caroline Walker. *Jesus as Mother: Studies in the Spirituality of the High Middle Ages*. Berkeley: University of California Press 1982

Dillard, Heath. *Daughters of the Reconquest: Women in Castilian Town Society, 1100–1300*. Cambridge: Cambridge University Press 1984

Fisher, Sheila, and J.E. Halley, eds. *Seeking the Woman in Late Medieval and Renaissance Writings*. Knoxville: University of Tennessee Press 1989

Fowler, Roger. *Literature as Social Discourse: The Practice of Linguistic Criticism*. Bloomington: Indiana University Press 1981

Frye, Northrop. *The Great Code: The Bible and Literature*. New York: Harcourt Brace Jovanovich 1982

Hampton, Timothy. *Writing from History: Rhetoric of Exemplarity in Renaissance Literature*. Ithaca, NY: Cornell University Press 1990

Jauss, Hans Robert. *Toward an Aesthetic of Reception*. Trans. T. Bahti. Minneapolis: University of Minnesota Press 1982

Jehlen, Myra. 'Gender.' In *Critical Terms for Literary Study*, eds. F. Lentricchia and T. McLaughlin, 263–73. Chicago: University of Chicago Press 1990

López Estrada, Francisco. 'El sentido utópico de las *Partidas*.' In *Las utopías*, 205–14. Madrid: Casa Velázquez, Universidad Complutense, 1990

López, Roberto Sabatino. 'Entre el Medioevo y el Renacimiento: Alfonso X y Federico II.' *Revista de Occidente* 43 [extraordinario 11] (December 1984), 7–14

Montes, Eugenio. 'Federico II de Sicilia y Alfonso X de Castilla.' *Anejo de Revista de Estudios Políticos* 10 (July/August 1943), 1–31

Montrose, Louis. 'Professing the Renaissance: Poetics and Politics of Culture.' In *The New Historicism*, ed. H.A. Veeser, 15–36. New York: Routledge 1989

Ozment, Steven E. *The Age of Reform (1250–1550): An Intellectual and Religious History of Late Medieval and Reformation Europe*. New Haven: Yale University Press 1980

Seniff, Dennis P. 'Introduction to Natural Law in Didactic, Scientific, and Legal Treatises in Iberia.' In *The Medieval Tradition of Natural Law*, ed. H.J. Johnson, 161–78. Kalamazoo: Western Michigan University, Medieval Institute, 1987

Stone, Marilyn. *Marriage and Friendship in Medieval Spain: Social Relations According to the Fourth Partida of Alfonso X*. New York: Lang 1990

White, Hayden. *The Content of the Form: Narrative Discourse and Historical Representation*. Baltimore: Johns Hopkins University Press 1987

'Men without Wives': Sexual Arrangements in the Early Portuguese Expansion in West Africa

IVANA ELBL

The early overseas expansion took Portuguese men away from home for weeks, months, and, in the case of long-term or permanent postings overseas, even years. These prolonged absences necessarily resulted in sexual deprivation. During the time at sea, which accounted for the better part of any ship-borne expedition, the men were simply sundered from all female company. During their stay in Africa or off the coast of Africa, extramarital sex with African women, slave or free, constituted in most cases the only opportunity for sexual gratification. While many Portuguese and other European men may have found this alternative acceptable, pleasant, or even preferable to the sex life available to them at home, both ecclesiastical and secular law saw any sexual arrangements other than marriage as illicit and condemnable. The canon law considered almost all extramarital sex as fornication[1] and viewed occupations requiring long absences from the marriage bed with great suspicion.[2] It looked with particular disfavour at extramarital sex with non-Christians, and prescribed Draconian penalties for offenders caught in the act.[3] Moreover, in Portugal, as in many other parts of Europe, and especially southern Europe, extramarital sex with non-Christians was deemed illegal, by not only the religious but also the secular law, and was sometimes punishable by death.[4]

The sexual arrangements of the participants in the early Portuguese expansion in West Africa were thus overshadowed by an irreconcilable tension between biology and law. The long absence from home did nothing to curb sexual needs, and in practice both the religious and the secular proscriptions were mostly disregarded. The individual participants as well as those whom they served, especially the Portuguese Crown and the Church, were deeply troubled by the contradictory demands presented, on the one hand, by the obvious need for sexual fulfilment and the need to populate the overseas holdings, and, on the other hand, by the ideal of chastity and continence.

To rely on self-disciplined adherence to the ideal was very unrealistic. Abundant evidence shows that the sexual drive of the men and women of medieval Portugal far exceeded the limits set by the Church. Of the five major political crises which shook Portugal in the fourteenth and fifteenth centuries, four were in some way connected with the sexual misbehaviour of the royal persons.[5] Extramarital relations were extremely common, as reflected by the seemingly endless streams of petitions to legitimize children born out of wedlock to both lay and ecclesiastical parents.[6] In 1466, the members of a Bohemian embassy commented in wonderment on the fact that many members of the Portuguese clergy seemed to be lawfully married, that is, lived openly with their common-law wives.[7] On a darker note, the royal chanceries reveal that many criminal and civil cases in which royal intervention was sought had a sexual context, whether it was seduction, adultery, or various types of sexual assault.[8] Concubinage and prostitution were regarded with great complacency both by the authorities and by the public.[9] As a matter of fact, long-standing concubinage was hardly distinguishable from common-law marriage (casamento da pública fama) and a simple exchange of vows was an accepted form of marriage ceremony, although in the fifteenth century it became increasingly common to seek nuptial blessing (casamento de benção), as pressure to have marriages solemnized by the Church increased.[10] Both the popular and the Court culture were preoccupied with the pleasures of love and sex.[11] Queen Phillipa, the pious wife of D. João I of Avis, was reportedly so concerned about the sexual looseness of the Portuguese Court that, in order to prevent further immorality in her household, she counselled the king to marry off a number of her maids-in-waiting to eligible courtiers. The king paired the young people at random and had them wed in a mass ceremony held in the queen's chambers.[12]

Queen Phillipa's solution might have been an ideal way out of the problem. If married men accompanied by their wives could have been sent overseas, there might have been less cause for concern about extraordinary and mass lapses in officially defined sexual morality. However, as was often the case in frontier situations, very few Portuguese women ventured overseas in the early period. At first, most of the enterprises took the form of ship-borne expeditions. Eventually, as island set-tlements and permanent Crown outposts came into existence, conditions were created which allowed women to join their men. However, few did or were allowed to by either the Crown or their husbands, who hoped to return to Portugal in a not-so-distant future. This expectation was not unrealistic. The Crown employed sailors and other ship's personnel on a single-voyage basis[13] and rotated its overseas staff every three or four years.[14] The separation was obviously not seen by the Crown as sufficiently long to warrant the company of family members.[15] Wives were implicitly excluded from mainland outposts such as the Arguim factory or São Jorge da Mina because the instructions governing these outposts make no reference to either transport or suitable accommodation for wives, although they do describe in minute detail all arrangements for the men, down to the number of shirts they were allowed to take with them to Africa.[16]

Only royal officials dispatched to govern the settlements in the Cape Verde Islands and the Gulf of Guinea, such as hereditary captains or governors, would sometimes bring their wives and children with them, mostly because they were expected to remain at their post for the rest of their lives, and their heirs might inherit the office. In the early 1500s, the Crown began appointing married men to the *capitanías* or ordering bachelor captains to marry, often under pressure from the inhabitants of the settlements, who obviously believed that married men would act more responsibly and have a higher stake in the defence and orderly running of their post.[17] In 1500, Fernão de Mello, the newly appointed captain of São Tomé, impressed his contemporaries by bringing his wife and children to the island and housing them in a strong, stone tower,[18] a residence designed to serve as protection from both foreign attackers and unruly colonists, many of whom were *degredados*, men and women exiled to the island for crimes which would otherwise have merited a death penalty. Mello's predecessor, the previously widowed Alvaro de Caminha, spent his years on the island with a much-loved concubine, Ursula, and a female slave, Isabel.[19]

In the main settlements of the Cape Verde Islands, it was quite common for both the principal residents and ordinary inhabitants to be married.[20] Often the wives were not only deeply involved in the business affairs of their husbands but also seem to have invested in slave trading on their own.[21] However, it is impossible to say whether they had been brought from Portugal or married their husbands while already in Africa. Because African slaves took Christian names after baptism, and sometimes adopted their masters' surnames as well,[22] the records do not even allow us to distinguish which of the wives may have been native Portuguese and which *creolas* (white Portuguese born in Africa); *pardas* (daughters from marriages between Portuguese fathers and African mothers); or black women, either free or slave. Some of the *degredados* sent to São Tomé in the first wave of settlement in 1493 were accompanied voluntarily by their wives.[23]

The Portuguese authorities made repeated efforts to stimulate white marriages or marriages between Christian partners in the Portuguese settlements. Respectable women without dowry were sometimes sent to the islands to find husbands, but unless a marriage was already arranged, they could find themselves reduced to concubinage.[24] More frequently, unattached Portuguese females who found themselves in the tropics were *degredadas*, women convicted of a crime and exiled from Portugal. The Crown's hope was that they would marry fellow *degredados* or other Portuguese settlers and remain in Africa to populate Portuguese island settlements.[25] However, the *degredados* of both sexes were often so anxious to go back to Portugal after they had served their sentence that those who had married sought explicit reassurance from the authorities that the marriage would not stand in the way of their return.[26] To assure a permanent white settlement on São Tomé, the Crown attempted to use teenagers pulled from the ranks of the Castilian Jews who sought refuge in Portugal after their expulsion from Spain. In 1492, 2,000 newly baptized Jewish adolescents of both sexes were dispatched to the island under the supervision of Alvaro de Caminha,[27] in the hope that they would intermarry with the *degredados* and create a balanced population base.[28] The plan, however, did not work very well: many died, and the surviving Portuguese and young New Christians found each other unattractive as marriage prospects, partly because of firmly engrained prejudices,[29] and partly because both seemed to prefer African consorts.[30]

The attraction that the Europeans felt for African women may explain the predominance of interracial marriage in the early expansion, at least as much as the scarcity of white women does. The fact that many Portuguese preferred African partners to the available European ones is quite interesting, because it has often been assumed that black Africans were aesthetically unattractive to Europeans. The early experience in West Africa suggests the very opposite: while swarthy skin in a white person may have been considered a detriment to physical beauty, black African women were often described by contemporary Europeans as attractive, sensuous, and very intelligent.[31]

However, interracial marriages between free and consenting partners were rare and often not recognized by the Portuguese authorities, because they involved non-Christian African women and Portuguese men who illegally settled on the mainland among the Africans and became integrated into their social and political frameworks in the same fashion as other long-distance traders. Marriage was one of the accepted ways through which strangers could be integrated into African societies. The Portuguese who chose this route, and who became known as *lançados*, continued to take pride in their Portuguese and Christian heritage and lifestyle, but they soon came to imitate the family forms of their African neighbours, including polygamy. Some of the *lançados* eventually rejected even the last trappings of their European origins, including Christianity and European dress, and became known as *tangosmaos* (a derogatory term meaning approximately 'worshippers of fetishes').

The Portuguese Crown repeatedly forbade Portuguese subjects to settle on the mainland, ostensibly to protect them from putting their immortal souls in danger by being corrupted by un-Christian ways.[32] The Crown would periodically order all *lançados* to leave the mainland and return to Portugal or to a Portuguese-held territory.[33] To obey such an order could mean leaving an African family behind. First of all, the African wife might be unwilling to leave her kin and people. Second, her kinsfolk might be reluctant to let her go and could prevent her from leaving because, in many African societies, the kin retained rights to the woman unless the marriage agreement stated otherwise.[34] The *lançado* traders had to buy the permission of the male kin of their wives or concubines even if they wanted the spouses to accompany them on their business journeys in the neighbouring regions.[35] Third, for a number of reasons the marriage might not be recognized by the Portuguese Church and secular authorities.

The Church frowned upon marriages between Christians and non-Christians because, technically, holy matrimony could not exist between them: marriage was, above all, a spiritual union and only secondarily a physical one.[36] In practice, however, most canonists grudgingly agreed that such unions were *de facto* marriages, and therefore not invalid.[37] However, the important element was the notion of marriage in the non-Christian partner's society.[38] As divorce was relatively easy to arrange in many African societies, and as many African societies were, at least in principle, polygamous, it was assumed that such marriages were not necessarily permanent, and that they were closer to concubinage than to marriage.[39] The Portuguese secular authorities would be, above all, concerned with the fact that the *lançados* 'bought' their wives by paying bridewealth to their kin. The wives could thus be perceived more as slaves than as wives. Given the fact that *lançados* returning to a Portuguese-controlled territory usually had to pay a hefty fine for breaking the law against settling on the mainland and for avoiding taxes, a fine that usually amounted to one-half of the declared property, chances were good that, if labelled a slave, the wife could be confiscated by the Crown authorities as part of the fine. Moreover, should the Church not recognize the marriage as valid, the *lançado* would be exposed to charges of multiple fornication with an unbeliever, a sin which called for severe punishment from both secular and Church authorities. However, if the wife had converted to her husband's religion, the union would be legal, provided her conversion to Christianity was deemed satisfactory. All in all, it was safer for the *lançados* not to flaunt their African families in so unfriendly a territory. Later in the sixteenth century, however, *lançados* visiting the Cape Verde Islands would routinely bring their African wives or concubines with them.[40] Outside the Upper Guinea mainland, most acknowledged interracial unions developed out of a lasting slave–master relationship or concubinage.

Marriage was not, however, the main objective of most Portuguese men visiting or stationed in Africa. Most of them intended to return to Portugal to rejoin their families or to start a new one there. While in Africa, they sought temporary solace, not a lifelong commitment. They obtained gratification either by making an arrangement with their African hosts or by resorting to sex with their female slaves. The African hosts were rather understanding about the whites' needs. The white men without wives appeared to lack 'a proper relationship to the forces of creation'[41] and their hosts often tried to solve the visitors' problem by offering either a permanent solution in the form of brides or a temporary one by arranging casual sex.[42] When Cadamosto, a young Venetian trader, decided to sell his merchandise to the *damel* of Kayor in Senegal and agreed to wait a while for the *damel* to assemble the payment, the latter felt obliged to give Cadamosto '... una garzona de annj 12/ in 13/ negra e molto bella' (a twelve- to thirteen-year-old girl, black and very beautiful) for the service of his 'camara' (bedchamber). Cadamosto accepted and sent the girl to his ship.[43] Overall, he found Wolof and Manding women and girls very attractive and very sensuous.[44]

Cadamosto's frank digressions about his sexual feelings are unique in the sources and have probably to do with the fact that he visited Africa as a very young man and that he completed the draft of his narrative only a few years later. The only other such intimate firsthand evidence comes from another young foreign merchant, Eustache de la Fosse, who travelled to the Gold Coast in 1479. He is the only source explicitly referring to sexual activities. He included the word for 'le jeu d'amour' (love play), *choque, choque*, among the fourteen or so words comprising in the minidictionary of essential terms that we find in his report.[45] The circumstances of his learning the term were doubly unlucky, one could say. While selling his merchandise, he was invited into a hut full of women, whose haggling apparently stupefied him so much that he walked out, leaving his merchandise behind. When he returned, the women and the merchandise were gone. In their place he found an attractive young girl, who inquired whether he was interested in *choque, choque* and then proceeded to disrobe, 'pensant que je voulais faire l'amour avec elle, ce dont je n'avais nullement l'intention, tellement j'etais ennuyé de la perte de mes deux basins, qui restèrent perdus' (... thinking that I wanted to make love to her, which I did not intend in the slightest, so much was I annoyed at the loss of my two basins, which remained lost).[46] Obviously, de la Fosse did not refrain from sex out of chastity or concern about continence: at first annoyed by the loss of merchandise, he seems to have later regretted just as much missing his opportunity to engage in a 'jeu d'amour.'

The need for sexual gratification of the Portuguese men travelling to or stationed in Africa could not be denied, and even the Crown felt compelled to address it, albeit reluctantly. One such attempt may have consisted in the hiring of a few 'castle women' (*mulheres do castelo*) for its main overseas outposts, Arguim and São Jorge da Mina. Ostensibly, their job was to provide mundane services, such as washing and cooking,[47] but the fact that they were unattached, in some cases of slave status,[48] and that they drew relatively high salaries,[49] suggests that they may have been expected to look after other physical needs of the male members of the garrison as well. By paying potential part-time prostitutes merely for being available, the Crown technically would not be committing or contributing to a sin. According to medieval canonists and theologians, prostitution was a form of work, even if condemnable. As long as the prostitute did not derive pleasure from it, she was entitled to making a living from her activity.[50] The customer was, of course, guilty of the sin of fornication. A member of the garrison who would decide to call on a 'public woman' would thus be making a personal moral decision, and the Crown would be blameless. The castle women were few, however, one for about ten men,[51] and there is no direct evidence that they were even moderately attractive or that they indeed did provide sexual services.

The second solution was more typical of the overall pattern. From the 1490s, at the very least, the Crown began assigning slaves to its employees or to those dispatched to Africa by its order, for example, the *degredados*. These slaves, called *escravos/escravas da ordenança* or *do ordenado*, were supposed to provide personal services. In addition, the Crown acknowledged the right of its employees to purchase slaves *para o seu mantimento* (for their upkeep) or would pay salaries in slaves instead of cash. While these slaves might be of either sex, most Portuguese were issued or allowed to buy at least one female slave. While the records of the royal factories stress that such slaves were supposed to carry out work similar to that of the castle women,[52] the sources describing the situation in São Tomé are much more blunt: the female slaves were given to both the voluntary and the involuntary settlers to increase the population of the island.[53]

This official stamp of approval for concubinage and casual sex represents a major departure from both the teachings of the common law and the proscriptions of the Portuguese secular law. The general Church proscription of extramarital sex could not be debated away. However, many governments and Church authorities in fifteenth-century Europe acknowledged that, if men could not bring themselves to continence and were not in a position to act out their passions in the marriage bed, it was better if they committed fornication with prostitutes and other 'public women,' rather than compounding their sin by corrupting 'honest women.'[54]

The problem was that female slaves could not be automatically considered 'public women,' women who could be expected to provide sex outside of marriage on request or on a transaction basis. According to the Portuguese law, a master could be charged with rape if he forced his female slave into a sexual act without her consent. If he was convicted, the consequences could be severe: the penalty for rape was death and confiscation of property.[55] However, as slaves normally could not testify against free persons, and especially their masters, except when called upon to do so before the Inquisition,[56] legal protection for the victim was rather theoretical.

Moreover, in many societies, not excepting medieval Portugal, forcible sex with socially inferior females drew substantially lighter penalties or was seen as an unavoidable, or even acceptable, vice.[57] The niceties of courtly love led some late-medieval 'love experts' to suggest that socially low-ranking women were incapable of love, and therefore unworthy of courting. Because amorous persuasion would be wasted on them, their social betters should, if unable to control their passion, simply proceed to having sex with them without any prior obfuscations.[58] The Portuguese *cortes* frequently demanded that the king deal with the sexual violence and unbridled passions that members of the nobility tended to display when lodging with townspeople and peasants and, despite the threats of excommunication, even when staying in convents.[59] Given the vulnerability of low-born women, and even nuns, it is not clear why slave women should have been the object of any greater consideration.

An odd twist of cross-cultural interaction made black slave women, however, even more open to sexual abuse. In slave-owning African societies the master usually had an unquestioned right of sexual access to his female slaves.[60] Many African slave women thus may have expected sexual services to be required of them. The Portuguese would interpret such acceptance of fate as moral looseness or excessive sexual appetite, and rapidly come to place black slave women at the same level as prostitutes.[61] The law corpus of D. Manuel reflected this view by creating a provision that the mandatory death sentence for rape had to be confirmed by the Crown in the case of black slaves and prostitutes.[62]

The laws against sex with non-Christians could in theory have offered some protection, but, as Saunders has pointed out, the appropriate charges were seldom laid when a free Christian Portuguese male was involved with a black, non-Christian woman.[63] Moreover, the Crown repeatedly ordered all its slave-owning subjects to have their slaves baptised within a set period of time after purchase.[64] For children, this period was one month; for adults and adolescents over ten years of age, six months. Adult slaves who did not wish to be baptised had to be informed of their right to refuse. However, their refusal to convert and the reasons for it had to be registered with the appropriate bishopric for the masters to be exempted from obeying the royal order.[65] As a result, many slave women would be baptised shortly after arrival at their final destination, and those who consorted with these nominal Christians were not exposing themselves to any special legal sanctions. Only *lançados* and *tangosmaos* associating with non-Christian African women would be open to official censure.

The legal position of slave women who had sex with their masters or other free men, as well as that of free concubines, was extremely precarious.[66] Theoretically, their behaviour constituted a violation of both secular and ecclesiastical law. They were kept at their sex partner's sufferance and could be dismissed at any time. The law would always take the side of the legitimate wife or heirs. Should the master be married, his wife could launch an adultery complaint, with unpleasant consequences for the female slave, whether the latter was a willing or an unwilling party in the situation. Female slaves who voluntarily had sex with married men who were not their masters might suffer severe physical punishment. Wives whose husbands had liaisons with their female slaves could easily force them to sell the slave or obtain a court injunction ordering them to do so.[67] Because of the legal entanglements in Portugal as well as in the Crown outposts on the African mainland, the masters were thus seldom willing to acknowledge paternity of children born of casual sex with slaves or admit any obligation to their slave sex partners.[68] The position of a slave concubine was thus extremely vulnerable both legally and socially.

Concubinage took different forms in different settings. In the context of royal factories, relationships with slave women were clearly expected to be temporary and casual. Such women fell into the category of the necessities of life, together with clothing, housing, and communal ovens.[69] The sexual irregularity was never explicitly acknowledged by the representatives of the Crown, who merely allowed the staff and residents to purchase or be assigned the authorized number of slaves of both sexes.[70] As a result, no bond was expected to develop between the men and their female slaves. Many Crown employees resident in São Jorge da Mina treated their female slaves with almost callous indifference. Apparently, once they tired of one slave, they would sell her to another member of the garrison or to the visiting African merchants, and would purchase a replacement, either locally or from São Tomé.[71] Selling the escravas or escravos da ordenança to the African merchants near the end of one's spell of duty seems to have been a common practice among the São Jorge residents, aimed at increasing the profits from their stay in Africa. Out of thirty-four ranking members of the São Jorge da Mina outpost, fifteen sold their female slaves during their term in office, and twelve sold male slaves that had been assigned to them.[72] The Crown made no attempt to regulate the frequency of such transactions as long as the staff members declared all of them.[73] This does not mean, however, that no members of the garrison developed emotional attachments to their female 'allocations.' Some indeed paid considerable amounts to have them shipped to Portugal before the end of their spell of duty in Africa,[74] and others apparently accorded their female slaves the status of common-law wives.[75] Overall, however, the royal factories, in particular São Jorge da Mina, had a rather dismal reputation when it came to the commitment to slave women and sex partners drawn from among the surrounding African population.[76] The reason was, at least in part, that the Crown was almost obsessively concerned with the smuggling of gold out of Mina[77] and was therefore not interested in sponsoring the growth of a Portuguese or half-Portuguese population near the outpost.[78] Therefore, unlike in the case of the island settlements, it did not encourage *de facto* marriages or permanent concubinage. On the contrary, it tried to ensure that the resident Portuguese developed as few personal ties to Africa as possible.

In the island settlements, especially those in the Gulf of Guinea, the function of the slave women assigned to the would-be settlers was quite different: they were supposed to serve as surrogate wives and to produce as many children as possible.[79] However, in order to prevent promiscuity or polygamy, the settlers were not supposed to hold more than one nubile female slave, a policy which was frequently disregarded.[80] Many of the relationships between masters and their *escravas de ordenança* none the less acquired the character of permanent rather than casual concubinage, and thus almost the status of common-law marriage. In some cases, formal marriage took place.[81] Race was not a factor in whether the relationship would be casual or long-term. White women (whether they were in Africa voluntarily or as *degredadas*) as well as captive ex-Jewish girls were involved in casual or lasting sexual relationships about as often as were their enslaved African counterparts.[82]

The emotional ties between masters and concubines could become quite strong, even where more than one concubine was involved. The will of the ageing captain of São Tomé, Alvaro de Caminha, reveals his deep attachment to and affection for Ursula, the mistress of his household, who, however, does not seem to have been his wife: he never refers to her in the document as 'minha mulher' (my wife) or 'minha viúva' (my widow), and carefully avoids specifying the nature of their relationship. Yet, for all practical purposes, the dispositions of the will treat her as his wife: she was to inherit all the furnishings of his São Tomé house and she was left a significant amount of money to serve as her dowry should she decide to remarry or to enter a convent in Portugal. Caminha also suggested a suitable marriage partner, and provided her with an introduction and an emotional personal plea for admission to a specific convent, should she choose to become a nun. She was also invited to select from among Caminha's female slaves one to take to Portugal with her as her personal servant. In addition, he gave her two hand-picked male slaves and confirmed her ownership of two slave children, whom he had given to her previously as a gift.[83] Caminha also manumitted one of his female slaves named Isabel, in recognition of her 'serviços' to him. He provided her with money, formally bequested a slave child from the Benin to her, and made arrangements for her future.

Isabel was almost certainly a baptised African, because she is referred to only by her first name and is labelled *escrava* (slave). Ursula appears to have been a former Jew, because her cousin, Marinheira, is identified in the will as one of the *moças*,[84] the term in its local context usually designating the young ex-Jewish women sent to São Tomé. Ursula might have been previously emotionally involved with one of the executors of Caminha's will and a trusted servant of his, because Caminha designated him as the candidate for Ursula's hand, left him money, and begged his forgiveness for unspecified wrongs.[85] Ursula, Isabel, and their slave entourage were expected to leave São Tomé together after his death, on the first available ship, and give each other friendly support when in Portugal.[86]

Unlike in Portugal, where owners seldom acknowledged their children from liaisons with slave women, in the island settlements both recognition of the offspring and acknowledgment of responsibility for their upbringing were readily forthcoming. Alvaro de Caminha, for example, made generous provisions for a yet-unborn child which he thought he might have fathered out of wedlock with a Portuguese woman named Ines Fernandes. The ageing Caminha was none too sure of the woman's claim but, as he obviously had had sex with her, he decided to give her the benefit of the doubt. He instructed his principal heir and co-executor of his will, Pedro Alvares de Caminha, to make sure that Ines indeed gave birth and that the child survived. The child was to be sent to Portugal, entrusted to a good widow, and raised to enter a religious order. Should the child die while still in São Tomé, the mother was to be given nothing more than one *escrava da ordenança* and one of Caminha's own female slaves, valued at 4,000 *réis*.[87] Caminha's doubts about the child's parentage are clearly reflected in this arrangement.

Both the sons and daughters the settlers had from their *escravas da ordenança* were usually raised in their fathers' households, and boys were often sent to schools in Portugal.[88] Children of both sexes could inherit their fathers' property, or at least the part of it located in Africa.[89] However, unless their mothers' slave status had been revoked[90] and a *bona fide* marriage had taken place, the progeny was still considered illegitimate and could hold on to property only if there were no challengers. Given the fact that many of the settlers and *degredados* left a family in Portugal and then raised another in the island, there was much room for inheritance quarrels from the very beginnings of the settlement.[91] In the first decades, the usual solution was to give the legitimate children their father's property in Portugal and most of his liquidity, whereas the illegitimate offspring would inherit land and other property in the tropics that could not be easily sold for cash.[92] As in Portugal, however, the rights of the legitimate heirs usually prevailed, because the Portuguese inheritance law, the Crown statutes, and the general sentiment demanded so. The Portuguese civil laws were ill equipped to handle claims arising from such situations (most of which were condemned by the Church law) and would oscillate wildly between a stark denial, at least in theory, of the rights of the female partners in such illicit unions and of their offspring,[93] and *ad hoc* common-sense solutions in practice.

The matter was complicated by the fact that those Portuguese men who chose to remain in Africa permanently or for long periods of time seldom remained contented with only one concubine. Once their households were established, both the *lançados* and the island settlers started to gravitate towards a polygamous pattern, keeping a principal wife or a principal concubine, and a number of female slaves as servants and casual sex partners. Some of the arrangements had a distinctly African cultural imprint, consistent with either a matrilineal or matrilocal family pattern. The *lançado* sexual arrangements serve as an example of the former: extramarital sex did not draw heavy sanctions in many African societies,[94] especially matrilineal ones, because inheritance rules favoured the children of one's sister rather than direct offspring,[95] and the Portuguese thus felt that their amorous liaisons did not violate local customs very much, even though they were aware that the competing African men did not view the matter with much sympathy.[96] Yet open clashes and challenges seem to have been few as long as the favours were properly negotiated with the appropriate relatives.[97]

In São Tomé, sexual arrangements, if left to themselves, drifted towards the matrilocal pattern. In an attempt to explain why he did nothing to eradicate concubinage during his term of office, Alvaro de Caminha explains in his will that, when he arrived in São Tomé in 1493, he found many free black women *amancebadas* (living in concubinage or whoredom) with both white and black men. As supplies were running drastically short, and these women, who had land under cultivation, had more food at their disposal than anybody else, Caminha billeted a number of his men with them, and further assigned slaves of both sexes to serve the men and expand the scale of agricultural activities. As a result of these living arrangements, many of the free and slave women became or remained *mancebas* of both the Portuguese and the black slaves.[98] This is quite consistent with the matrilocal pattern where the women are the owners and cultivators of the land and the men essentially outside members of the society. However, the matter weighed heavily on Caminha's conscience, and he instructed his appointed successor, Pedro Alvares de Caminha, to apply all the statutes of the law regarding concubinage and make the settlers surrender all superfluous sex partners.[99] Pedro Alvares was hardly in a position to comply, however, because he was not confirmed in office by the king. Under the captaincy of Fernão de Mello, the informal sexual arrangements continued unchallenged and, by the middle of the sixteenth century, there were '... mais has amãcebadas que as casadas' (more 'loose' than married women).[100]

Partly because there was no other alternative, both secular and ecclesiastical authorities were forced to tolerate a much higher degree of sexual permissiveness than they normally would, even in such a relatively sexually 'unrestrained' country as Portugal. In Portugal, rape was punishable by death and confiscation of all property, public concubinage by confiscation of a small portion of property, and, for repeated offenders, by whipping and incarceration. Fornication with a married woman drew the penalty of perpetual exile and confiscation of property in the case of a noble offender, and death in the case of a commoner. Fornication with a virgin or a widow automatically called for marriage.[101] The latter rule, however, was perverted in the islands into a licence to rape the prospective bride. The authorities were very lax in dealing with rapes and abductions whose purpose was a forced marriage or concubinage, and civil and Church courts kept passing such cases back and forth between each other like the proverbial hot potato.[102]

Similarly, promiscuity and public sexual display were seldom punished, to the dismay of Church representatives fresh off the boat from Europe. Promiscuity and casual concubinage outside the master–slave relationship were very common, especially in the island settlements in the Gulf of Guinea.[103] The authorities blamed the mixing of races, and even the demeanour and dress of women. The confessors were instructed to promote the values of chastity and modesty in young women from mixed relationships,[104] and the Crown authorities tried to ban what they considered provocative outfits, such as African wrap-skirts which tied in the front and thus constituted a great temptation for the men to untie them. European-style skirts, much less suitable for the tropical climate but also considered somewhat more difficult to remove, were to be worn by all women, slave or free, under the threat of substantial punishment.[105]

Given the degree of sexual permissiveness and opportunity for sex, it might seem quite remarkable that there still remained room for flourishing prostitution and other forms of sex for pay. In the island settlements, prostitution was distinguished from concubinage mostly because it did not involve a master–slave relationship, and therefore required payment. In the opening decades, the slave–master relationship was not seen as *mancebía* (living in whoredom) as long as it did not involve an excessive number of female slaves. Only free women living with men in a non-binding relationship and accepting favours from them, or women requiring pay or upkeep for their services, were seen as *mancebas* (whores). However, by the mid-sixteenth century, there were '... muitas mulheres que publicamente se daõ por dinheiro ...' (many women giving themselves openly for money).[106] The Crown tried to deal with them by separating them from the 'honest' population and by exiling them back to Portugal (irony of ironies),[107] but without much success.

The Church kept denouncing all Christians living in relationships other than proper or common-law marriage as *amancebados* (living in whoredom), and demanded that they regularize the relationships and dismiss superfluous or illicit sex partners.[108] While some of the bishops boasted of their achievements in reforming the morality of the island population, any success was invariably short-lived.[109] This is not surprising, given the fact that the local representatives of both Church and Crown often took vigorous advantage of the loose sexual arrangements. The potential extent of sexual misbehaviour of the persons in authority is rather graphically documented in the mud-slinging matches which often accompanied power struggles between Crown and Church representatives or internal infighting within the two groups. Thus, in 1551, the vicar-general of the Cape Verde Islands was accused of keeping two whores, both white. One of them was a young widow originally committed to the care of João Correa, captain of the island; the other a nun sent to Santiago by the queen to be cured of leprosy.[110] The accusations which nearly cost D. Gaspar Cão his bishopric were even more colourful: D. Gaspar apparently condoned both lay and clerical concubinage, and himself displayed great incontinence. He allegedly kept many *mancebas*, married, single, and widowed, and 'for the love of these whores,' like a man ruled by women, showered favours on some of the settlers and injustice on others.[111] The bishop defended himself, claiming that he had always stringently admonished all those guilty of the sin of concubinage and that he himself led a pristinely chaste life. It was his accusers who, according to him, were guilty of sexual sins and of violence and immorality.[112] Many such accusations were doubtlessly exaggerated, or even fabricated, but it does not detract from the fact that sexual arrangements in the island settlements remained very flexible. In the later centuries, most European visitors would comment in surprise on the looseness of sexual morals in the Portuguese African settlements.[113]

Biology thus clearly won its battle with law. Pragmatism, rather than abstract ideals, came to determine the sexual arrangements in the early expansion. The 'men without wives' hardly suffered any sexual deprivation while in Africa; rather, the contrary. The problem was with their partners, many of whom were slaves and whose consent was not required. While sexual access was accepted as one of the claims that a master could have on his female slave in Africa, and while it can be argued that the female slaves may have expected such demands to be made of them, this phenomenon came to be reflected in Portuguese law, through a mechanism akin to cultural relativism, as something specifically pertaining to black slave women. A foundation was thus laid for racially differentiated legal treatment. However, despite the fact that sexual mistreatment and forced sex (or what we today see as such) certainly did occur on a regular basis, many of the concubinages led to *de facto* marriages in which the position of the women was quite strong, and mutual affection ran deep. Such relationships were seldom monogamous, however, and family formation was heavily influenced by African patterns. The sexual arrangements of the early overseas expansion thus constitute, among other things, a fascinating instance of cross-cultural blending.

NOTES

1 For the evolving position of the Roman Catholic Church on extramarital sex see James A. Brundage, *Law, Sex, and Christian Society in Medieval Europe* (Chicago and London: University of Chicago Press 1987), sections on non-marital sex, sexual offences, and sex and the clergy.

2 Ibid., 506–7. Long-distance merchants who were away from home for more than a year at a time were particularly suspect.

3 Among the suggested penalties were castration and death: ibid., 207 and 461. Whether such penalties were actually routinely applied is a different matter. As a rule, while the punishments prescribed by the canonists for sexual offences were harsh, the actual treatment of penitents was very lenient.

4 In Modena, for example, the punishment for intercourse with Saracens was death and confiscation of all property, unless the Christian offender was a prostitute, in which case the death penalty was commuted to life imprisonment: ibid., 518. A similar regulation was embodied in the fifteenth-century corpus of Portuguese law *Ordenaçoens do Senhor Rey D. Affonso V* (Coimbra: Real

Imprensa da Universidade 1792), liv. 5, tit. 25, and repeated in the early six-teenth-century compilation, *Ordenaçoens do Senhor Rey D. Manuel* (Coimbra: Real Imprensa da Universidade 1797), liv. 5. tit. 21.

5 The end of the reign of D. Affonso IV and the reign his son, D. Pedro, were overshadowed by the adulterous and tumultuous relationship between D. Pedro and Inês de Castro, his wife's lady-in-waiting. To end the scandalous relationship, D. Affonso IV murdered Inês, who by that time had two sons by D. Pedro. After he had become king, D. Pedro had his lover's body exhumed, married her corpse, and forced the entire court to pay homage to it. His son, D. Fernando, angered both the King of Castile and the King of Aragon when he successively broke off the engagements to their daughters to marry Leonor Teles, an already married noblewoman. This bigamous rela-tionship led to several wars with Castile, and to the civil war which brought the dynasty of Avis to the Portuguese throne. The only child of the marriage between D. Fernando and Leonor Teles was deemed illegitimate because the union was bigamous. The pretext for the Portuguese–Castilian war over Castilian succession in 1474–8 was the supposed illegitimacy of the heiress, D. Juana, whose was allegedly a product of an adulterous relationship between the queen, a sister of D. Affonso V of Portugal, and her lover. Finally, both the tragic struggle between the young D. Affonso V and his uncle D. Pedro, regent during Affonso V's minority, and the great conspir-acy of the nobles of the realm against D. João II, can be seen as conse-quences of an illegitimate relationship between D. João I and his base-born concubine, from which sprung the House of Bragança, whose members were key actors in both conflicts.

6 D. João II (1385–1433) issued more than 2,000 letters legitimizing children born out of wedlock; D. Duarte (1433–8), his successor, more than 300: A.H. de Oliveira Marques, *A sociedade medieval portuguesa*, 2d ed. (Lisbon: Livrária Sá Da Costa 1971), 124. From 1398 to 1438, two archbishops, five bishops, thir-teen masters and priors of the three military orders, and large numbers of ordinary clergy and both male and female members of religious orders had their illegitimate progeny legitimized. Many of the applicants petitioned repeatedly, often for children born of different mothers with whom the father lived simultaneously: ibid., 125. Oliveira Marques's source was an unpublished dissertation of H.C. Baquero Morenas, 'Subsídios para o estudo da sociedade medieval portuguesa (moralidade e costumes),' Faculdade de Letras de Lis-boa, 1961, in particular 207–10 and 145–61.

7 *The Travels of Leo of Rozmital through Germany, Flanders, England, France, Spain, Portugal and Italy, 1465–1467,* ed. and trans. by M. Letts (Cambridge: Cam-bridge University Press 1957), 113. They also noted that priests who were to say

the mass for the first time were accompanied by women and girls who were their '*special friends*' (ibid.: emphasis added).

8 Arquivo Nacional da Torre do Tombo, Lisbon (hereinafter cited as ANTT), Chancelaria de D. João I; Chancelaria de D. Duarte; Chancelaria de D. Affonso V; Chancelaria de D. João II; and Chancelaria de D. Manual. Summaries of documents or a complete subject guide to these collections is not available, but partial coverage is provided by such works as A. Braacamp Freire, 'A Chancelaria de D. Affonso V,' *Archivo Historico Portuguez* 2 (1904), 479–87, and 3 (1905), 62–74, 130–54, 212–36, 401–40.

9 Oliveira Marques, *A sociedade*, 126

10 Ibid., 115–17

11 Ibid., 108–13; A.H. Oliveira Marques, *Portugal na crise dos séculos XIV e XV* (Lisbon: Presença 1986), 485–6

12 Fernão Lopes, *Chronica de El-Rei D. João I*, vol. 6 (Lisbon: Escriptorio 1898), ch. cxxxix, 55–6. On the queen's personal qualities see ibid., vol. 5 (Lisbon: Escriptorio 1897), ch. xcviii, 128–9.

13 *Regimento das Cazas das Indias e Mina*, ed. Damião Peres (Coimbra: Faculdade de Letras, Universidade de Coimbra 1947), 71–4

14 The length of service in Africa was not set by a clearly defined policy, but the records of discharge (*cartas de quitação*) show that the captains or factors of the Arguim and Mina outposts served for approximately three or four years before they were replaced. For Arguim, for example, see A. Braacamp Freire, 'Cartas de quitação del-Rei D. Manuel,' *Archivo Historico Portuguez* 1 (1903), 203, doc. 203 (Affonso da Moura, 1492–95); 2 (1904), 353–4, doc. 235 (Fernão Soares, 1499–1501); 8 (1910), 400–1, doc. 642 (Gonçalo de Fomsequa, 1505–8); 2 (1904), 354, doc. 237 (Francisco de Almada, 1508–11). In each case, the length of service was counted in years, months, and days. No two of the periods are exactly identical.

15 The Church was of a different opinion. See Brundage, *Law, Sex, and Christian Society*, 506–7.

16 *Regimento*, 19–20

17 In 1512, the principal residents of Santiago, the main island of the Cape Verde archipelago, successfully petitioned the Crown to appoint only married men as captains, or, should that be impossible, to grant the post to candidates able to make a sufficiently large safety deposit, which was to be forfeit should they neglect their duties: A. Brásio, ed., *Monumenta Missionaria Africana: Africa Occidental*, 2a sér, vol. 2 (Lisbon: Agência Geral do Ultramar 1963), doc. 16, 47–8.

18 Valentim Fernandes, *O Manuscrito 'Valentim Fernandes,'* ed. A. Baião (Lisbon: Academia Portuguesa da História 1940), 122 and 126

19 On Caminha's relationship with Ursula see his will: J.M. de Silva Marques, *Descobrimentos Portugueses: documentos para a sua história*, vol. 3 (Lisbon: Instituto de Alta Cultura 1971), doc. 331, 501, 506, and 514. On his family status and relative age see ibid., doc. 339, 546–7.

20 The 1513–15 customs registers mention a number of wives, ranging from spouses of prominent officials and residents to those of artisans and sailors: ANTT, Núcleo Antigo, no. 757, fo. 44v, 70v, 83v, 84v, 87v, 118v. These references are only to those instances where the register explicitly identifies a female customs-payer as somebody's wife. The status or attachment of the other women mentioned in the register cannot be established, because in this period Portuguese women retained their maiden patronym, rather than taking their husband's name.

21 See *supra* note[20]. The most prominent female slave traders, however, appear to have been unattached, either widowed or single. The maverick among these was Dona Brisyda, a woman who, in partnership with her neighbour Joham Vidão, equipped in 1513 and 1514 two ships to trade for slaves in Guinea: ibid., fo. 22 and 40.

22 A.C. de C.M. Saunders, *A Social History of Black Slaves and Freedmen in Portugal, 1444–1555* (Cambridge: Cambridge University Press 1982), 90

23 Silva Marques, *Descobrimentos*, vol. 3, doc. 331, 513. In his will, Alvaro de Caminha, the first captain of São Tomé, pleaded that arrangements be made to repatriate these women should they so desire: ibid.

24 A considerable amount of data on these matters can be derived from official denunciations and reports of royal or ecclesiastical inspectors, because such information was considered particularly damaging for the accused. Thus, Fr. João Monserate, chaplain of D. João III, severely criticized in his 1551 report to the king the vicar-general of the Cape Verde Islands for his public sexual incontinence and corruption of respectable women. The vicar-general's principal concubine was a widowed white woman sent from Portugal to the care of João Correa, captain of the island, so that she might eventually be married. The vicar-general took her to his house and persuaded her to become his concubine (*manceba*) by dressing her in silk and surrounding her with servants. Fr. João had as much contempt for her apparently willing part in the matter as he had for the vicar-general's behaviour: Brásio, *Monumenta*, 2a sér., vol. 2, doc. 127, 417.

25 For references to this policy see the will of Alvaro de Caminha: Silva Marques, *Descobrimentos*, vol. 3, doc. 500–15.

26 Caminha implored the Crown not to renege on his promise that they would be allowed to return to Portugal, given to the *degredados* at the time of their marriage: Silva Marques, *Descobrimentos*, vol. 3, p. 513, doc. 331. His cousin, Pedro Alvares de Caminha, made a similar plea after Alvaro's death, claiming

that many of the men were reformed characters and deserved to return: ibid., doc. 339, 547. The Crown was obviously reluctant to comply, partly because of the cost of repatriation and partly because allowing married couples to return would have defeated the main objective — populating the island.

27 Fernandes, *O Manuscrito*, 122. The mortality among these young people was appalling. By the beginning of the sixteenth century two-thirds of them had died: ibid.

28 Silva Marques, *Documentos*, vol. 3, doc. 331, 512 and 513. See also J.M. Azevedo e Silva, 'A mulher no povoamento e colonização de São Tomé (séculos XV–XVII),' *A mulher na sociedade portuguesa. Visão histórica e perspectivas actuais.* Actas do Colóquio, Coimbra, 20–22 março (Coimbra: Faculdade de Letras da Universidade de Coimbra 1986), vol. 2: 231.

29 Azevedo e Silva, 'A Mulher,' 231. In his will, Caminha commented that many of the 'moças' (ex-Jewish girls) and their male counterparts remained single: Silva Marques, *Descobrimentos*, vol. 3, doc. 331, 513.

30 Fernandes, *O Manuscrito*, 122. His informant, a sailor who visited the island 'many times' before December 1506, noted that white women tended to mate with black men, and white men with black women.

31 See, for example, Luís de Cadamosto, *Viagens de Luís de Cadamosto e de Pedro de Sintra* (Lisbon: Academia Portuguesa da História 1947), 35, 47–8.

32 Brásio, *Monumenta*, 2a sér, vol. 2, doc. 47, 149. Several decades later, Almada commented on the sorry spiritual state of his fellow Portuguese who became *lançados* in areas which were not regularly visited by the Santiago clergy: '... estão muitos de nossos, lançados, vivendo em pecado mortal, sem se apartarem dele, morrendo nele por falta de médicos da alma [... there are many of ours, *lançados*, who live in mortal sin from which they do no extricate themselves and die in it for the lack of physicians of the soul]': A. Alvares d'Almada, 'Tratado breve dos rios de Guiné do Cabo Verde,' in Brásio, *Monumenta*, 2a sér., vol. 3: 329.

33 Ibid., 2a sér, vol. 2, docs. 28, 44 (p. 143), 47, 52 (p. 163), 100, and 105.

34 João Ferreira, a *lançado* originally from Crato in Portugal and an expert interpreter, married a daughter of the 'Gran-Fula,' the ruler of a Fula state on the middle Senegal River, but needed a special permission from his father-in-law for her to accompany him on his travels: Almada, 'Tratado,' 253.

35 Ibid., 326

36 Gratian, for example, summarily declared that marriage could not exist between a Christian and an infidel: Brundage, *Law, Sex and Christian Society*, 238. Other canonists, however, reluctantly acknowledged such unions provided they were deemed lawful in form: ibid., 265–6.

37 Ibid., 195, 340, and 380

38 The canonists varied on this point. Some considered only the Christian matrimony indissoluble, whereas other marriages could be dissolved because they were neither *ratum* nor *perfectum* outside the context of Christianity: ibid., 267. Pope Celestine III declared that a Christian convert could put a non-Christian wife aside and marry a Christian one: ibid., 340. Innocent III, however, sharply reversed this ruling and declared all marriages indissoluble. In case of polygamous relationships, Innocent III demanded that only the first wife be kept and the others dismissed: ibid., 340 and 380.

39 Almada commented with dismay that 'when they want divorce, the father returns the gift which they had given him, and the daughter is free to do as she wants. The blacks do not have limits on how many wives they have; it depends on their possibility and on how much bridewealth can they afford to give the parents': Almada, 'Tratado,' 263.

40 Ibid., 326

41 P.D. Curtin, *Economic Change in Precolonial Africa. Senegambia in the Era of the Slave Trade* (Madison: University of Wisconsin Press 1975), 5

42 This attitude could sometimes result in embarrassing situations. For example, one black ruler was so impressed by a mass and sermon delivered at his court on Christmas Day by a proselytizing priest that he made him an offering of 'hũa escrava mossa muito boa e fermoza' (a very good and beautiful slave girl). The missionary effort had obviously not been very successful: Almada, 'Tratado,' 310.

43 Cadamosto, *Viagens*, 35

44 Cadamosto, *Viagens*, 47–8

45 Eustache de la Fosse, 'Viagem de Eustache de la Fosse à Costa Ocidental de Africa,' in Brásio, *Monumenta*, 2a sér, vol. 1, doc. 73, 470–1

46 Ibid., 472

47 J.L. Vogt, *Portuguese Rule on the Gold Coast, 1469–1682* (Athens: University of Georgia Press 1972), 46–7

48 In 1508, one out of three castle women serving in Arguim was a slave: ANTT, Núcleo Antigo, no. 888, fos. 132–4.

49 In Arguim, the castle women earned 5,000 *réis* per year in 1508: ANTT, Núcleo Antigo, no. 888. fos. 132, 133, 134. In São Jorge da Mina they earned as much as 12,500 *réis* in 1529: Vogt, *Portuguese Rule*, 46. The level of these salaries does not compare all that unfavourably with those of even high-ranking *Casa da Guiné* officials stationed in Portugal in the late 1480s – the *almoxarife do almazém* earned only 10,000 *réis*: Silva Marques, *Descobrimentos*, vol. 3, doc. 232, 349; the scribe of the treasury and factory 20,000 *réis*: ibid., doc. 231, 343; and the head of the entire *Casa da Guiné*, its treasurer and factor, 40,000 *réis*: ibid., doc. 217, 333.

50 V. Bollough and B. Bollough, *Women and Prostitution: A Social History* (Buffalo: Prometheus Books 1987), 120; J. LeGoff, *Time, Work and Culture in the Middle Ages* (Chicago: University of Chicago Press 1980), 66–7 (quoting Thomas of Chobham); Brundage, *Law, Sex, and Christian Society*, 393 and 523.

51 In Arguim there were in 1508 three castle women and at least thirty male members of the garrison: ANTT, Núcleo Antigo, no. 888, fos. 101–38 (some fos. are missing); in 1529 there were four castle women in São Jorge da Mina and fifty-one male members of the garrison: Vogt, *Portuguese Rule*, 46.

52 Vogt, *Portuguese Rule*, 46–7

53 Azevedo e Silva, 'Mulher,' 230–1, quoting C. Espírito Santo, *Contribução para a história de São Tomé e Príncipe* (Lisbon: Grafitécnica 1979), 20. In 1506, Fenandes's informer related that the king had ordered that each *degredado* was to be given a black male or female slave to be of such help and service as the *degredado* might want: Fernandes, *O Manuscrito*, 122. The orders were to assign each specified settler 'uma escrava boa' (a good slave woman) or 'uma escrava moça boa' (a good slave girl): Silva Marques, *Descobrimentos*, vol. 3, doc. 331, 507, 512, 513.

54 Brundage, *Law, Sex, and Christian Society*, 522; Oliveira Marques, *A sociedade*, 127–8.

55 Saunders, *A Social History*, 102

56 Ibid., 116

57 For example, in the medieval Chinese moral code, sex crimes against servant women were worth, on average, 100 or 150 per cent fewer demerits than sex crimes against their social betters. Sex offences against prostitutes were ten times less serious than those against married women from a good family: R. Tannahill, *Sex in History* (New York: Stein and Day 1980), 196–7.

58 Bullough and Boullough, *Women and Prostitution*, 136

59 Oliveira Marques, *A sociedade*, 124

60 P.E. Lovejoy, *Transformations in Slavery: A History of Slavery in Africa* (Cambridge: Cambridge University Press 1983), 5–6, 8; I. Kopytoff and S. Miers, 'African "Slavery" as an Institution of Marginality,' in *Slavery in Africa. Historical and Anthropological Perspectives*, eds. S. Miers and I. Kopytoff (Madison: University of Wisconsin Press 1977), 31–2

61 Such opinion was consistent with the tendency of some canonists and lay moralists to regard all women frequently engaging in extramarital sex as 'whores,' a label which Gratian, for example, considered synonymous with 'prostitutes.' Gratian adopted Saint Augustine's view that frequent extramarital sex, not acceptance of payments for sexual favours, was what defined a prostitute: Brundage, *Law, Sex, and Christian Society*, 248.

62 Saunders, *A Social History*, 102

63 Ibid.

64 Ibid., 90

65 Brásio, *Monumenta*, 2a sér., vol. 2, doc. 25, 69

66 Often the only indicator of whether a concubine was a slave or a personally free servant would be the name; at baptism, slaves were given Christian first names but not surnames: Saunders, *A Social History*, 90.

67 Ibid., 103.

68 Ibid., 90–2

69 Vogt, *Portuguese Rule*, 47

70 Ideally, the Crown expected three residents to share one female slave: ibid. In reality, however, most of the higher-ranking members of the garrison had one or several female slaves at their disposal. Gonçalo Roiz de Sequeira, *alcaide* of São Jorge da Mina went through seven female slaves between 1495 and 1499: Silva Marques, *Descobrimentos*, vol. 3, 525, and Lopo Soares, the outgoing captain, kept three female slaves, one white and two black, during his stay: ibid., 521 and 537.

71 For the pattern of purchases and resales see Silva Marques, *Descobrimentos*, vol. 3, doc. 336, 520–40.

72 Ibid., 520–41

73 The rich data on slave ownership among the members of the São Jorge da Mina garrison in 1495–9 has been preserved because, at the end of Lopo Soares's turn as captain of the outpost, the ranking residents were required to make a sworn declaration, stating all the purchases, sales, and other transactions involving payments in gold: ANTT, Núcleo Antigo, no. 867; published as doc. 336 in Silva Marques, *Descobrimentos*, vol. 3: 520–41.

74 The prices of slaves sent to Portugal were often 30–40 per cent higher than those sold internally in São Jorge da Mina or to the visiting African merchants. Compare tables 40–4 in I. Elbl, 'The Portuguese Trade in West Africa, 1440–1521,' PhD thesis, University of Toronto, 1986, 632–6.

75 The outpost's factor, Gil Matoso, lived with an 'escrava branca' (white slave woman), Isabel Matosa, who not only carried his name and required substantial upkeep but also was entitled to sell slaves in her own name: Silva Marques, *Descobrimentos*, 3, doc. 336, 537.

76 African women who found themselves pregnant by white men often resorted to abortion or infanticide. As a result, the growth of racially mixed population in the neighbourhood of São Jorge da Mina was kept in check, despite the fact that concubinage between the Portuguese men and African women was widespread: Brásio, *Monumenta*, 1a sér., vol. 3 (Lisbon: Agência Geral do Ultramar 1953), 90; C.R. Boxer, *Race Relations in the Portuguese Colonial Empire, 1415–1825* (Oxford: Clarendon Press 1963 repr. Westport 1985), 11.

77 Intensive searches of all traffic to or from Mina were mandatory: (*Regimento*, 15, 23–4). Draconian penalties were prescribed as punishment for the smuggling of gold. See for example ANTT, Corpo Cronológico, parte II, maço 39, doc. 155, and Brásio, *Monumenta*, 2a sér., vol. 2, doc. 28, 79–92.

78 In 1502, the Mina officials boasted that the African village attached to the fortress was growing daily as 'more and more [people] came to serve the Portuguese king': ANTT, Corpo Cronológico, parte I, maço 3, doc. 119. The Crown, remaining concerned about the damage to its gold trade caused by illicit exchanges between ships' crews, the fortress garrison, and the black population (ANTT, Corpo Cronológico, parte I, maço 8, doc. 72), did not try to dismantle the village, only to prevent miscegenation (Boxer, *Race Relations*, 11).

79 Azevedo e Silva, 'A Mulher,' 230–1; Fernandes, *O Manuscrito*, 122

80 Sometimes, the official reason was a loss of the previous allocation as a result of death, debilitating sickness or escape (Silva Marques, *Descobrimentos*, vol. 3, doc. 336, 504) but often no reason was required. In 1499, for example, Alvaro de Caminha confirmed Afonso Lopes, a free black, in the possession of the female slave he had previously married and of one additional one, both of whom were to accompany him to Portugal. Similarly, he gave Pero de Manícomguo one female slave and an entitlement to another; Pero was to choose one as his wife and remain in São Tomé. The gift was explicitly designed to curb any temptation Pero might have to return to his native Kongo (ibid., 507–8).

81 Silva Marques, *Descobrimentos*, 507 and 508

82 Alvaro da Caminha, for example, had as his principal concubine an ex-Jewish woman, but he also kept a black concubine and several female slaves. In addition, he had an illicit sexual relationship with a white Portuguese woman, Ines Fernandes, who became pregnant by him: Silva Marques, *Descobrimentos*, vol. 3, doc. 331, 504 and 512. Similarly, Lopo Soares, the captain of São Jorge da Mina in 1495–9, kept an expensive white slave imported from Portugal and two black slave women: ibid., doc. 336, 521 and 537. Portuguese women who had joined their husbands in exile often came, after the death of their spouses, to live in concubinage with other Portuguese men: ibid., doc. 331, 507.

83 Ibid., 501.

84 Ibid., 505. Marinheira was also left money in Caminha's will, but he was not as fond of her as of Ursula or Isabel. Whereas the other two women were recommended to the care of his sisters in Faro, Marinheira was either to join Ursula or go wherever she willed: ibid., 501 and 505. Caminha obviously felt that Marinheira was troublesome, or simply had too much will of her own.

85 Ibid., 501

86 Ibid., 501 and 514

87 Ibid., 512

88 Azevedo e Silva, 'A mulher,' 238

89 As a result of liberal inheritance practices, in the first half of the sixteenth-century the children from mixed relationships came to control much of the land in São Tomé and to constitute a mulatto aristocracy: Fernandes, *O Manuscrito*, 123; Azevedo e Silva, 'A mulher,' 231.

90 In 1515, D. Manuel manumitted all female slaves who had been given to settlers by the order of D. João II during the first attempt to populate São Tomé. The manumission extended to their offspring: Brásio, *Monumenta*, 1a sér., vol. 1, doc. 87, 331–2. In 1517, the manumission was also extended to the male slaves and their progeny: ibid., doc. 107, 376.

91 For various examples see Silva Marques, *Descobrimentos*, vol. 3, doc. 331, 507 and 511.

92 Such a solution was employed for example in the case of an illegitimate mulatto daughter of Joâne Meemdez. Her father died without a chance to revise the will he had made in Portugal, and thus effectively disinherited his daughter. Alvaro de Caminha, as captain of São Tomé, none the less ordered that the girl be given the slaves owed to her father by way of salary. The rest of his property was to be accounted for and kept until it could be made clear whether his Portuguese wife or other legitimate heirs were still alive: Silva Marques, *Descobrimentos*, vol. 3, doc. 331, 507.

93 The Crown went to great lengths to assure orderly processing of estates of the deceased and of determining and locating legitimate heirs: *Regimento*, 72 and 131; 'Regimento do Thesoureiro-Geral dos Defuntos de Guiné e das Ilhas de Cabo Verde,' doc. 32 in Brásio, *Monumenta*, 2a sér., vol. 2: 103–13.

94 Almada, 'Tratado,' 324, 333

95 Ibid., 238, 248–9

96 Boxer, *Race Relations*, 10

97 Almada, 'Tratado,' 326

98 Silva Marques, *Descobrimentos*, vol. 3, doc. 331, 513

99 Ibid., 514

100 Brásio, *Monumenta*, 2a sér., vol. 2, doc. 160, 462

101 Oliveira Marques, *A sociedade*, 126

102 Azevedo e Silva, 'A mulher,' 233

103 Brásio, *Monumenta*, 2a sér., vol. 2, doc. 155, 443–5; doc. 160, 462–3

104 Azevedo e Silva, 'A mulher,' 238–9

105 Ibid., 233

106 Brásio, *Monumenta*, 2a sér., vol. 2, doc. 155, 443

107 Ibid., 443–4

108 Bishop D. Gaspar Cão describes some of these 'solutions,' which invariably

penalized the woman: thus, Manuel Fernandes, a merchant who kept a Moorish female slave, was pressured into selling her and removing her from his house. Henrique Fernandes, who had an illicit relationship with a mulatto woman, was presented with the choice of either marrying her or letting her go, and he chose to go into hiding until she died in childbirth. In another such case, the man simply packed and returned to Portugal. In only one of the cases mentioned by D. Gaspar did the ecclesiastical sanction result in marriage: Azevedo e Silva, 'A Mulher,' 236.

109 Ibid., 233
110 Brásio, *Monumenta*, 2a sér., doc. 127, 417
111 Ibid., 1a sér., vol. 3: 7–13; quoted in Azevedo e Silva, 'A Mulher,' 235
112 Azevedo e Silva, 'A Mulher,' 233 and 235–6
113 T, Bentley Duncan, *Atlantic Islands. Madeira, the Azores and the Cape Verdes in Seventeenth-Century Commerce and Navigation* (Chicago: University of Chicago Press 1972), 234

Sex in Tudor London: Abusing Their Bodies with Each Other

CAROL KAZMIERCZAK MANZIONE

This day Mary Lee sent into this house by warrant from Master Justice Collins being examined & confessed that she was delivered of a child begotten in whoredom by one Anthony Shippe dwelling in Holborne within the great gate and saith he hath ... diverse and sundry times the use and carnal knowledge of her body in his own house at which times usually he would send his wife to Market and she further saith that the child which she was so delivered is now dead. Ordered that she shall be punished which was done accordingly.'[1]

Mary Lee's offence was twofold: she had sex many times with a married man, and even worse, she had an illegitimate child. By judgment of the governors of Bridewell, her activities warranted punishment, which was most likely whipping, the standard punishment for people found guilty of sexual indiscretions. What makes this and hundreds of similar cases of particular interest is not the offence nor the punishment, but the responsible agency, Bridewell, one of the three royal hospitals founded in 1552. Since medieval times, and well past the sixteenth century, various church courts had jurisdiction over marriage, sexuality, and family life in general. Why were Bridewell and Christ's Hospital, newly created secular institutions, authorized and charged to investigate and punish sexual offenders?

Before examining the operations of the royal hospitals, there are two essential perspectives that first require discussion: London's population increase and the changing attitudes towards the poor. London was experiencing a remarkable growth in population by the mid-sixteenth century, owing largely to the influx of a significant number of poor people. This urban expansion was not always welcomed and at times actively discouraged as London's new inhabitants not only were poor but were the vagrant poor, mostly jobless and desperate, engaging in begging and other crimes to support themselves. In 1552, the Common Council concluded that the situation was serious and dangerous, stating that the 'great number of beggars, vagabonds, idle and suspect person [had] increased within this city and the commonwealth thereby much impaired, and evil rule much enhanced and grown, and the ability and surety of the said city much decreased and diminished.'[2] In concert with the Crown, alarmed officials, feeling overwhelmed by the poor and needy, responded by founding the three royal hospitals. Although these hospitals, Bridewell, Christ's and St Thomas, were founded together to address the issue of poverty, each was created to handle a different clientele. Bridewell was founded '... to be a workhouse for the poor and idle person be now set a work and relieved at the charges of the citizens.'[3] Christ's Hospital was founded as an orphanage and school for '... the fatherless children & other poor men's children that were not able to keep them ...'[4] St Thomas the Apostle Hospital was founded as a place to tend to the needy and sick of London, in other words to act as a hospital in the modern sense of the word. A few years later, another medical establishment, St Bartholomew's Hospital, neighbouring Christ's, was added to the other three.[5] However, only two of these establishments, Bridewell and Christ's, found themselves in the business of attempting to regulate sexuality in London: the minutes of their courts of governors serve as the primary source for this essay.

By 1552, poverty was no longer considered a pitiable and benign predicament but had become a condition that posed a danger to society. The poor were basically divided into two categories: the needy poor and the undeserving poor. The needy poor were the traditional objects of charity – orphans, foundlings, widows, the elderly, and the infirm – the groups taken care of by Christ's and St Thomas hospitals. The undeserving poor were the able-bodied beggars, rogues, prostitutes, and bawds who were held to be responsible for their condition, which was believed to be the result of laziness, immorality, or a general sinful nature; they were the residents of Bridewell. Bridewell and Christ's hospitals represent the dual nature of attitudes towards the poor. The deserving poor were to be assisted compassionately, and the undeserving poor were to be punished, shown the error of their ways, and assisted only if repentant. This system necessitated the creation of a mechanism for determining the proper subjects of charity, and that constituted the bulk of the business of the royal hospitals. The governors had no doubts that they could effectively and wisely make such judgments as they were the same wealthy, élite men who ran the City as aldermen, masters of the twelve great guilds, and church wardens. As such, few would question their expertise, experience, or motives, and few would find fault with whatever activities they deemed necessary to exercise their mandate, thereby preventing the calamitous breakdown of good order that was so feared.[6]

In essence, therefore, London's response to its perceived crisis of over-crowding and poverty was to institutionalize the problem by having the responsibility turned over to the hospitals However, they went further than just making the problem less visible; the governors believed that they could reform their charges by teaching and preparing the children of Christ's for apprenticeships in honest professions and giving training to the undeserving poor in order that they might acquire job skills and an opportunity to redress their moral deficiency. Bridewell punished those they believed to be whores, but it went even further; it also attempted to reform these women by forcing them to reside with the hospital, learn honest ways, and, it was hoped, became respectable wives and mothers. 'Their punishment would consist of being put in the pillory or stocks, whipping at the cart's tail or whatever; it was only after their punishment that their reformatory detention at Bridewell was to begin.'[7] In other words, poverty should be a temporary situation rectified by education, hard work, and job training administered by enlightened, dedicated, caring officials.

Given the daunting responsibility outlined above, how in fact did Bridewell and Christ's operationalize their missions? Bridewell had a more difficult charge as it attempted to regulate the more unsavoury aspects of sexuality in the City, most prominently, prostitution. For example, on 24 January 1562, Agnes Weye and Margery Upton were brought into Bridewell by the bailiffs of Westminster upon the order of Secretary Cecil because they were 'common strumpets and whores' and were whipped.[8] Rose Talwothe was transferred to Bridewell by the governors of St Bartholomew's Hospital because she was discovered to be 'a common harlot & night walker.'[9] The primarily concern was with preventing the escalation of prostitution and its associated evils of beggary, bastards, and bawds, which were feared because they carried the potential for the break-down of good order and were symbolic and symptomatic of London's uneasy transition from a medieval city to a world commercial centre. The correlation was clear: prostitution equals crime, especially beggary and thievery. On 26 February 1575, Jane Robinson was delivered to Bridewell for correction, not only for being 'a common harlot,' but also for 'having ribald songs and filthy talk'[10] which annoyed neighbours, and therefore disturbed the peace.

Bridewell's reach went beyond the prostitutes or their customers; bawds and those who passively or actively aided illicit sexual activity were also disciplined at Bridewell, as was the case with Margaret Rodes, a widow living in Smithfield. She confessed that she went out for a drink while a boarder, Blanche Rogers, and an unidentified man 'abused their bodies together.' Margaret also confessed 'that she hath offended and lived lewdly as a bawd and is very sorry and will put the wench out of the house.'[11]

But it wasn't just the beggars, prostitutes, and bawds that were disciplined; quite proper and respectable Londoners could also find themselves ordered to appear before the governors to answer charges. Londoners who engaged in sex outside of marriage were perceived to pose a substantial threat to the peace, social harmony, and good order of the City. As explained in the wardmote inquest of Farringdon Without, adulterers and fornicators caused 'the high displeasure of Almighty God, the great offence of the neighbors, the evil example of all other malefactors in the like case offending, and against the peace of our said sovereign Lady, the Queen.'[12]

Given these assumptions, any creative domestic arrangements that did not fit society's concept of marriage ran the risk of discovery. This was situation with Jasper Palmer, a goldsmith found himself pleading for mercy in January 1560 for the 'abusing of Joan Mills who being a maiden he hath defiled and of long kept and maintained'[13] The fact that Palmer was a goldsmith, and a member of one of the most powerful and wealthiest guilds, did not prevent his exposure and punishment.

Who made the complaints is as interesting and informative as the offenders. There were a variety of motives for informing on employers, spouses, and business associates. London still was small enough for people to know each other and have interpersonal conflicts, and having an opponent embarrassed by a public accusation of sexual indiscretion may have been hard to resist. On the 30 March 1562, Richard Rayes and Mary Paternoster claimed that 'their mistress and one Allen were naughty together, their said master being out of the town.'[14] This accusation backfired upon the denouncers; they were the ones punished, specifically for slander, by Bridewell's governors. This episode is also revealing in that servants, for whatever motive, could bring forth an allegation against their masters and mistresses and that officials would seriously investigate the charges. One's social position in the community didn't make one immune from public disclosure of fornication or adultery. It seems that anyone could bring a real or imagined accusation of sexual impropriety against anyone else. The same was probably as true for Tudor London as L.R. Poos noted for medieval England: 'Behind the formal means of regulating sexuality in later-medieval England there thus must have lain multiple networks of informing, gossip, rumor, talebearing and, on occasion, lies about neighbors' sex lives among community inhabitants.'[15]

Spouses could also inform on each other. On 12 August 1560, John Martin, a brewer, asked the governors to examine his wife, Joan, 'for that she is suspected to use the company of others beside her husband, namely Jackson.'[16] Martin's motive seems to have been a desperate attempt to maintain his family and force his wife to behave. Ellen Kitchen confessed to 'committing whoredom' with William Wycliff, goldsmith, and because she was 'very penitent & sorry was remitted punishment & delivered to her husband.'[17] It is of further interest that Mistress Kitchen was brought into Bridewell by Sir Martin Bowes, goldsmith and governor, whose action may have been prompted less by a desire to punish adulterous wives than by the urge to settle a personal or business dispute with a rival.

Robert Mownte found himself answering charges at Bridewell on 27 October. Mownte, a seventy-two-year-old haberdasher, was accused by his servant, Agnes Stone, 'that he attempted to abuse her and hath kissed her,' to which he admitted to kissing her twice. He posted sureties for his appearance at the next court. On 5 November, he was to be punished: 'should have been whipped but for his age and other causes is now spared.'[18] There are a number of interesting aspects to this case besides the leniency shown because of the advanced age of Master Mownte. First, it is notable that this offence was committed upon that very day that Mownte made his first court appearance, so that prompt and immediate disputation was possible, and probably not unusual. Second, his servant knew where to go to make effective complaint; she first brought her problem to Mr Bragge, who was a governor of Bridewell in this year, something she must have already known. Third, the fact that it had not advanced beyond the stage of kissing and attempted abuse wouldn't have exempted Mownte from a whipping.

Tudor London was densely populated, and finding privacy to 'abuse your body' with anyone else must have presented quite a challenge. It seems that people didn't necessarily hesitate to seize the moment when the opportunity presented itself. People lacking access to a bed resorted to public places such as alleys, ditches, and even walls, that sound neither romantic nor comfortable. Of course, public fornication couldn't be tolerated, as was the situation of John Standyle, tailor, and Anne Foster, alias Russell, who found themselves taken to Bridewell on 8 October 1578 because they were 'taken in Bores Head alley in Fleet Street committing whoredom.'[19] This was probably not a case of a client and prostitute having to make do, as Anne Foster was not identified in the records as a whore, which she surely would have been if she were so suspected.

A more interesting situation was when Master Smith, tailor, was out of the house, and his servants made the most of his bed. John Goodyson and Thomas Sawoode shared the favours of Joanne Cox and Joanne Yonge in combinations that are unclear as the records overuse pronouns, leaving the reader in confusion as to who was doing what to whom and to what portion thereof. It is small wonder that the clerk was confused: 'he confessed that he hath offended with his master's two maids and also that his fellow Thomas Sawoode likewise was in bed with him and then at the same time and that then they had carnal copulation together.' In addition, John confessed he went to try out Anne Flude's bed, and she also confessed 'that John Goodyson had the use of her body in her bed twice & never more.' Anne also volunteered that John 'had the use of Joanne Coxe half a dozen times.' Joanne Yonge confessed 'that John and Thomas lay with her & Joanne Coxe together all in one bed & she saith that the same Thomas had the use of her body twice or thrice once in her master's bed & in other places of the house.' Joanne Cage had a lengthier tale to tell. She confessed

> that the said John had the use of her body never but twice but she saith that he hath oftentimes requested to abuse her body but she said she would never grant him. She saith he had the use of her first about a twelve month past. She saith that all her fellows knew that he lay with her thus, and he lay with her first in her master's bed. She saith John Hawle, Henry Lambe, Christopher Thorneton & Thomas Wheate knew that she had lain with the said John.[20]

This matter concludes with an order for correction for the entire group.

Similar to the practice in regular law courts, a person had to shown to be guilty; accusation did not always equal guilt. Elizabeth Wheatley was brought before the governors on 12 January 1562 because she was suspected of aiding her daughter in prostituting themselves. She was released because 'no matter could be proved against her.'[21]

As shown above, sexual licentiousness and the prostitution, crime, and general disruption of community peace that seemed to result from unrestricted sexuality caused great concern, as they served to weaken the family, the core of the state. It is almost goes without saying but none the less bears repeating that the family was seen as an embodiment and metaphor for the state: 'The family was not only the fundamental economic unit of society; it also provided the basis for political and social order. It is well-known that in this period the family served as a metaphor for the state; in conventional political thought the king was a father to his people, the father king in his household.'[22]

However, the most serious consequence of sexuality outside of marriage, and that having the most disruptive effect, was illegitimate children. These children were, by definition, outside of a family, and therefore had no real place in society. In addition to protecting the sanctity of the family, there was a very practical and financial interest in policing illegitimacy; public charity was expensive. 'Improper sexual relationships were, in the eyes of ecclesiastical law, crimes to be formally punished. They brought with them tensions, quarrels, and disrepute, but for those involved and their neighbors and kindred unwanted children were potentially their most serious consequence.'[23] Christ's found itself involved in policing sexuality because of the cost of raising and tending to the needs of orphans, some of whom were abandoned and illegitimate children. As previously stated, Christ's Hospital was designed to be an orphanage and school for poor children, orphans, foundlings, and illegitimate children. The governors of Christ's got involved in the lives of pregnant and new mothers because the hospital was obligated to support the illegitimate children of single mothers. If the fathers could be identified, then the City would be relieved of the cost of supporting those children. The governors spent a lot of time and energy and were relentless in locating and forcing fathers to pay for their illegitimate children. In order to qualify for assistance, unmarried mothers needed to go before the governors and name the father and recount the circumstances of their impregnation. More often than not, the women's stories were believed, and the men had to prove their innocence; the women didn't necessarily have to prove the men guilty. It may have also been the situation that the governors gave women the benefit of the doubt because they were uncertain whether the confessions detailed circumstances that were ordinary seduction or rape, and proving rape was even more difficult in the sixteenth century than it is today. Madelyn Soper, who was a servant, gives the following account of what appears to be rape: 'that Robert Odam the bell ringer of the Royal Exchange the week after low Sunday last did aline her up into the turret there and shut the door and there bound her hands with a great rope and bused her body against her will and she saith also that being so high she could not be hear although as she saith she tried very loudly.'[24] Odam admitted to having 'abused her body but it was with her will.'[25] No further entry is made, and the matter was dropped without further action and without concluding who told the truth.

Giving women the benefit of the doubt in a sexual dispute was, to a certain degree, self-serving because, if a man was determined by the governors to be the father of a bastard and forced to pay 'child support' or marry the mother, then the citizens of London were spared the cost of maintaining that child. This was an important consideration, given the often desperate fiscal straits of Christ's Hospital, and every pence and shilling made a difference to the survival of the orphanage. It may have been a bit naïve that most of the women's stories were believed, but it may also have been that they had simply told the truth.

The information provided by the women testifying before Christ's governors was quite remarkable in the details surrounding the circumstances of their children's conception, especially in regards to particular times and places. For example, at the 14 October meeting of the Court of Governors in 1570, Margaret Cale claimed that Henry Carie 'hath gotten her with child the first time that he abused her was ... about iii weeks before Easter last ... and again abused her xiii days after Easter ...'[26] These records are in marked contrast to what Martin Ingram notes for Church courts: 'the examination of offenders in court were often very briefly recorded, amounting to little more than a bare statement of denial or confession.'[27]

Christ's had a set procedure for examining the mothers of illegitimate children that resembles that of other legal structures.

And that two governors or more, whereof the treasurer to be one ... shall also at any time examine all single women or others being brought into this house with child; and cause the parties whom they accuse to be sent for before them; and upon his or their confession, to cause him or them to enter into bands with sureties to the mayor and commonalty, to see the same child kept from the charge of this city and hospitals; and to see the woman provided for, from that time until she be delivered and churched; with such other covenants as the case shall require. And if the said parties do not confess the fact, and the same by all resumptions likely to be true, they shall be committed toward, there to remain until further trial may be had thereof; or else put in surety to answer this court from time to time, until the truth may be known.[28]

The surety that fathers were required to post could be quite hefty. Hugh Robertson was required to post a bond of ten pounds on 12 August 1570, more than many people paid for yearly rent.[29] If a man refused to post a surety, he could be incarcerated in either Bridewell's or Christ's stockhouse until he did, or confessed to his action.

An interesting point in the procedure outlined above was the expectation that a father not only support the child after birth but also support his pregnant partner until the child was born. This expectation seems to have been a standard arrangement, as Houlbroke notes that, in the Norwich Church courts, 'the judge could order him to meet the expenses of confinement and purification, to support the child, and to provide the woman with a dowry.'[30] For example, Thomas Newman, brewer, on behalf of James Aborrow, his apprentice, agreed to provide Katherine Ouerton 'vi pence weekly until she be brought abed and then during he laying on child-bed to allow her xx shillings.'[31]

Masters were financially liable for the cost of their servants' illegitimate children, for they were responsible for their proper conduct; the master is assumed to be at fault as well because he is answerable for the breakdown of discipline in his own house. Richard Eckells, on behalf of his servant, Humphrey Lowthe, 'promised to bring into this house monthly for one whole year from midsummer next coming the sum of iis. viiid.'[32]

Servants and apprentices make frequent appearances in these records, as one would expect, because most households had them, and they were young and unmarried, and had opportunities to engage in sexual liaisons that were not available to their rural counterparts. It may not have been uncommon for servants to engage in sexual relationships with each other, and the practice might reflect a change of urban courtship patterns in this group, its intention being to lead eventually to marriage. Given the current level of interest in the sexual abuse and exploitation of dependents and subordinates by men in authority, one would have expected to find more evidence of fornication between servants and masters. There are such cases in the minutes, but it is not as prevalent as one would imagine. One could argue such cases would not be reported, and that the establishment would work to protect men, especially respectable men, from public exposure. However, these liaisons had the most potential for being the most disruptive, because marriage wouldn't be possible to legitimize offspring and the moral climate in Tudor London would not have permitted the governors to wink and look the other way. It has already been noted how difficult it was to keep an affair secret, and there were always neighbours, family, and business associates who might be willing to use this information to their advantage and make an accusation to the authorities. Still, some masters did have affairs with servants, fathering children. 'Alice Bruster, servant with William Saywell ... declared that her said master got her with child and she said that he promised her marriage and abused her half a dozen times in the shop & other places.'[33] That same day, Saywell was called before the court, where he denied the charge of fathering Alice's child and making a proposal of marriage. At the next regular court day, 26 November 1569, the accused still declared his innocence and that he 'never had to do with Alice Bruster.'[34] At the same court, Alice maintained that three witnesses, Mistress Benlew, Goodwife Robinson, and Mistress Claiden, heard William Saywell say to them that, if Alice 'would have kept the matter secret that he would have allowed to her two shillings or forty pence a week.' The two principals and the three witnesses were ordered to appear at the next court, where, on 10 December, Saywell finally admitted the fact and promised 'to keep her the time she lay in child bed and further to giver her £20 ... or else marry her.'[35] Alice seems to have seduced by the anticipation of marriage and a better life, a prospect that was irresistible to a servant, even if Master Saywell was insincere and desperate to hide his guilt.

Masters were not let off easily. Jeram Lambert, butcher, agreed to provide a dowry of forty pounds to his servant, Margaret Janys, whom he impregnated, 'but also in presence of this said court upon his knees asked God's mercy.'[36]

Although it didn't seem necessary, or even vital, to showing veracity, having a witness greatly added to the credibility of a particular case and accents the difficulty of conducting an illicit affair in private, away from curious eyes. Cicely Somerset's witness reported that she observed Richard Rily, a gardener, 'in the night time came to the windmill in St Georges Field with a great dog lead in his hand and fetched out one Cicely ... after whom she looked out and saw the same Riley abuse her body in a pit.'[37] Witness could not only collaborate for the accusers, but suspected fathers could also present witnesses to clear themselves, as was the circumstance of Hugh Robertson. The same Hugh Robertson who was required to post a surety of ten pounds was found to be innocent of getting Alice Harcot with child 'upon Bartholomew Day in the forenoon' when neighbours testified that he was with them on the day and time in question.[38]

Some days, the governors had to be creative and Solomon-like in their solutions to paternity questions. Rachel Griffin came to court in January or early February 1572 claiming that Henry Norrison got her with child, having abused 'her on midsummer evening [24 June] in the kitchen and divers times before that and that he promised her marriage.'[39] The record of this matter is a bit garbled, but it appears that Robert Wheatly also had sexual relations with Rachel. With paternity uncertain, the court ordered both Wheatley and Norrison to pay her an allowance during her pregnancy, and child support, thereby holding both equally responsible. Neither man could evade his responsibility by claiming that, since the other could be the father, neither one could be held liable.

What the minutes of the courts of governors of both Bridewell and Christ's hospitals illustrate beyond the regulatory attempts to control poverty and sexuality was the creation of an alternative justice system which provided a speedy, flexible, and timely response to issues brought before them. In essence, the governors oversaw a legal system that had the power to order accused persons to appear, demanded sureties, decided guilt or innocence, and levied punishment in the form of fines and corporeal punishments. Although the governors instituted set procedures to handle cases, in what appeared to be in a relatively impartial manner, they avoided being trapped into being rigid and overly procedure-bound. Christ's and Bridewell came to be arenas in which ordinary citizens could use the system to settle personal disputes quickly and without cost.

The governors were allowed very wide latitude to do whatever they felt necessary to solve the problem of poverty, even if it began to trample a bit on individual rights of people who were not poor. In order to address a troubling social problem, the leadership of the government of the City of London embarked on a rather remarkable and admirable program of social welfare. They believed they were striking at the heart of the problem by attempting to regulate and control poverty with the end goal of eradicating it altogether. However, before they could realize that goal, they recognized they also had to manage the conditions that were associated with poverty – beggary, prostitution, and illegitimate children. This, in turn, necessitated controlling irregular sexuality, not only of the poor and needy, but of all London citizens, regardless of socio-economic status. In other words, a chain of administration resulted from a basic assumption, and from there the governors assumed myriad responsibilities whenever they felt the need. They decided civil and criminal cases by creating an alternative justice system to serve these needs. They gave themselves the authority to do whatever they deemed necessary to eliminate poverty from London, a scourge they felt was jeopardizing their peace and security. No one would object to their assuming a broad range of powers; after all, they were the same men who were in control of the economic, political, and religious environment of the City. This system began with the best of intentions but, over time, the potential for abuse increased: 'the governors of Bridewell were given wide powers – which, in the late seventeenth century were to be challenged as violating the basic legal rights of the individual.'[40]

The records of Bridewell and Christ's hospitals demonstrate that there was in place in the sixteenth century a concerted effort at moral policing, which is traditionally associated with the Puritan Commonwealth of the seventeenth century. Although there are obviously a lot more cases contained within the minutes of both institutions that couldn't be covered in this essay, there is strong evidence that both men and women were held accountable for their actions. People who were discovered 'having the use of each other's bodies,' or 'abusing' their body with someone else, were punished, regardless of gender, or social or economic status. Poor women were not left to face the public shame and consequences of fornication, adultery, or unintended pregnancies alone; assistance was available, and dedicated to preventing them from descending into beggary or prostitution. Of course, the governors did not succeed in ending poverty and the social problems associated with it. None the less, they were remarkable for having conceptualized the complex and interrelated problems of poverty and endeavouring to create a systematic, complex, and sympathetic response to a social problem. The governors advanced beyond merely providing money in an impulse of Christian charity to the poor; they began a rational social-welfare system.

NOTES

1 Guildhall Library [GL], MF512/IV, 20 September 1598. The records of Bridewell Hospital are on microfilm, and the folio numbers are sometimes missing or unreadable; reference, therefore, is made by dates. The new year starts on 1 January. I have modernized spelling and punctuation, with the exception of last names.
2 Quoted from Charles Pendrill, *Old Parish Life in London* (London: Oxford University Press 1937), 215
3 John Stow, *A Survey of London*, ed. Charles Lethbridge Kingsford from the 1603 edition (1908, repr.: Oxford: Oxford University Press 1971), vol. 2, 143.

4 John Howes, *Contemporaneous Account, in Dialogue-Form of the Foundation and Early History of Christ's Hospital and of Bridewell and St Thomas' Hospitals* (printed from the original manuscript of 1582 & 1587: London: January 1889), 24. I had the opportunity to compare this printed book with the original manuscript, and it is a faithful transliteration.

5 Carol Kazmierczak Manzione, *Christ's Hospital of London, 1552–1598: A Passing Deed of Pity* (Selingsgrove: Susquehanna University Press 1995), 25–38

6 Ibid., 121–37

7 J.A. Sharpe, *Crime in Early Modern England, 1550–1750* (London and New York: Longman 1984), 186

8 GL, MF511/I, 24 January 1562

9 GL, MF511/II, 9 February 1575

10 Ibid., 26 February 1575

11 GL, MF511/III, 24 January 1578

12 GL, MS 3018/I, folio: 66, 24 October 1599

13 GL, MF510, 23 January 1560

14 GL, MF511/I, 30 March 1562

15 L.R. Poos, 'Sex, Lies, and the Church Courts of Pre-Reformation England,' *Journal of Interdisciplinary History* 35/4 (Spring 1995), 585

16 GL, MF510, 12 August 1560

17 GL, MF511/I, 4 December 1561

18 GL, MF512/III, 27 October and 5 November 1578

19 GL, MF511/III, 3 October 1578

20 GL, MF511/II, 6 November 1574

21 GL, MF511/I, 12 January 1562

22 Susan Dwyer Amussen, *An Ordered Society: Gender and Class in Early Modern England* (Oxford and New York: Basil Blackwell 1988), 1

23 Ralph Houlbrooke, *Church Courts and the People during the English Reformation, 1520–1570* (New York: Oxford University Press 1979), 76

24 GL, MS 12806/II, 2 September 1571

25 Ibid.

26 Ibid., 14 October 1570

27 Martin Ingram, *Church Courts, Sex and Marriage in England, 1570–1640* (New York: Cambridge University Press 1987), 263

28 'The Order of the hospitalls of K. Henry the viiijth and K. Edward the vith, viz. St Bartholomew's, Christ's, Bridewell, St Thomas's by the Maior, Cominaltie, and Citizens of London, Governours of the Possessions, Revenues, and Goods of the sayd hospitalls,' in *Memoranda, References, and Documents Relating to the Royal Hospitals of the City of London*, ed. J.F. Firth (London: reprinted by Benjamin Pardon, 1803), 84

29 GL, MS 12806/II, 12 August 1570
30 Houlbrooke, *Church Courts,* 77
31 GL, MS 12806/II, 17 February 1571
32 Ibid., 22 June 1566
33 Ibid., 19 November 1569
34 Ibid., 26 November 1569
35 Ibid., 10 December 1569
36 Ibid., 28 February 1568
37 Ibid., 9 December 1571
38 Ibid., 9 September 1570
39 Ibid., undated Court Meeting sometime between 29 December 1571 and 9 February 1572
40 Sharpe, *Crime in Early Modern England,* 186

Sexual Rumours in English Politics: The Cases of Elizabeth I and James I

ROBERT SHEPHARD

The sex lives of political leaders have attracted public interest ever since Old Testament times. In different ages, however, people have construed the significance of illicit sexual activities by those leaders in different ways. Numerous politicians in twentieth-century Western democracies have found their ambitions damaged or destroyed once allegations of sexual improprieties became public knowledge. For a king in early-modern Europe, however, having mistresses was almost a royal prerogative. The fact that a king intended to become *pater patriae* in the most literal sense was normally taken to be a reassuring sign of his active, virile, masculine character. Among male subjects, it could even produce a kind of psychological identification with their king. After Samuel Pepys had a dream in which he held Charles II's mistress Lady Castlemaine in his arms and 'was permitted to use all the dalliance I desired with her,' he wrote in his diary that it was 'the best that ever was dreamed.'[1] Female subjects may have had fantasies of their own. Only when a royal mistress was perceived to be an agent of another country or of a subversive movement – as with Charles II's French mistresses, or with Anne Boleyn – did criticism become widespread.

But what about the political effects of sexual transgressions on the part of monarchs who did *not* fit their age's gender norms for rulers? In this study, I will examine the gossip and rumours that spread about the sexual lives of two such rulers of England. Elizabeth I was an unmarried woman. According to present-day conceptions, James I was homosexual. In both their cases, rumours circulated concerning their real or imagined sexual activities outside the bounds of marriage. And in both cases, the effect of these rumours was to diminish their political standing, even to undermine the legitimacy of their rule. Yet there were also important differences between the salacious stories that spread about these two monarchs. The frequency and intensity of the rumours about Elizabeth were much greater than those about James.[2]

Engaging in scandalous gossip about the powerful may well be a universal pastime. But rumours and gossip frequently reflect people's underlying anxieties and most deeply held assumptions, as shaped by their particular historical circumstances. In addition, unless the form that the scandal takes is somehow felt to be appropriate to its target, it will lack sufficient plausibility and spice to be passed on.[3] Analysing these rumours can therefore help lead us to a deeper understanding of attitudes about sex and gender in this era, as well as providing insights into the interpenetrations contemporaries perceived between sexuality and power, and between private morality and public reputation.

I

When Elizabeth Tudor came to the English throne in 1558, she found herself confronting a difficult situation. As the female ruler of a patriarchal society, she embodied what Louis Montrose has termed 'a contradiction at the very center of the Elizabethan sex/gender system.'[4] Moreover, she succeeded her sister Mary, whose reign many had come to see as a failure. Elizabeth thus had to overcome not only ideological prejudices against women rulers, but also empirical evidence that seemed to confirm the common wisdom. As a consequence, she faced immediate pressures to marry.[5]

Elizabeth's decision about marriage would have consequences that were personal as well as political. Women were expected to get married in early-modern England, and one of the monarch's most important duties was to produce offspring – preferably male offspring – who would ensure a clear succession to the throne. On the other side of the balance sheet, however, a wife was expected to 'obey' and 'serve' her husband, as the marriage ceremony in the Anglican Prayer Book put it.[6] The acquisition of a king consort would thus have been bound to diminish Elizabeth's own independence and authority. Finally, Christian morality tolerated sex only between married partners, and the double standard dictated that an aristocratic woman who engaged in sex outside of marriage gravely impaired her honour. If she was a queen regnant, she lost her nation's honour as well, and thereby called her own right to rule into question, as

Mary Queen of Scots would discover a decade later, after her escapades with Bothwell.

As is well known, Elizabeth chose to solve the marriage problem by *not* marrying. Instead, she consciously developed the persona of 'the Virgin Queen,' which became progressively more elaborate as her reign continued.[7] This persona formed part of a more complex image which legitimated Elizabeth's rule by portraying her as different from and superior to ordinary women.[8] In sexual terms, the price Elizabeth paid for transcending the standard gender role for women was abstinence. Breaking her implicit vow of celibacy would jeopardize the more than feminine (but, at most, only partially masculine) image that she had cultivated. By the same token, accusations that Elizabeth was engaging in illicit sex involved a questioning of – if not a direct attack upon – her image, and indeed the legitimacy of her whole regime.

Rumours and gossip about alleged sexual misbehaviour on the part of Queen Elizabeth began soon after she came to the throne. As Christopher Haigh has pointed out, their frequency tended to peak at moments of national crisis: in particular, during the uncertain years soon after her accession, when her romance with Robert Dudley (later raised to the peerage as the Earl of Leicester) was at its most intense, and in the years following the Northern Rising of 1569.[9] But such stories appeared throughout her reign. In 1585, a German visitor to the English Court, Lupold von Wedel, matter-of-factly noted that 'they say the Queen for a long time has had illicit intercourse' with Leicester, followed by affairs with Sir Christopher Hatton and Sir Walter Ralegh.[10] As late as 1601, a maid to an English captain's family in the Dutch cautionary town of Flushing was asserting that Elizabeth had had a child by the second Earl of Essex.[11] (Elizabeth was sixty-eight years old at the time.) When one analyses the contents of these stories, three major themes emerge, separately or in combination. The sexual activity is usually alleged to affect the distribution of political power within the realm; the succession to the throne; or the queen's personal fitness to rule.

Sex was directly linked with politics in assertions that Elizabeth made decisions about political rewards based on sexual attraction. The most explicit and detailed exposition of such claims came in some statements supposedly made in 1587 by one John Pole, an imprisoned counterfeiter and probable acquaintance of Christopher Marlowe. According to an informant's account, Pole stated that

... the quene allwaies from time to time hath most liberally geven to such

manner of persons as coulde doe beste & have been best weaponed, chiefly
the Earle of Leicester who was the common bull of the Courte, he may
spend 50,000 pounds a yeare; as much my Lord Chauncellor [Hatton]; some
8 or 10,000 a yeare Sir Walter Raliegh; the kinges yerely revenue he said did
not amount to somuche [*sic*] as one of those two carped [i.e., carpet]
knightes may spende ...

   Allso others the quene preferred, as Sir W. Pickeringe, Sir Thomas Hen-
neage & Mr. Paggington [i.e., Packington] & others whose names I forgete &
gave them greate giftes, which had the use of her at their pleasure, but she
gave not so large unto them for that they proved not so well in discharginge
their busines as the other three before mencioned.[12]

In Pole's marvellously reductive formulation, there was a direct, propor-
tional relationship between the gifts and preferments courtiers received
and their success at satisfying the queen sexually.

   Other scandalmongers suggested that the queen was being dominated
by her alleged lovers. In 1562, one Edmond Baxter reportedly asserted
that 'my lord Robert [Dudley] dede kepe the quenes grace.'[13] Ten years
later, a London butcher was telling people that 'the Erle of Leic[ester]
kepeth Her Majesty.'[14] By casting Elizabeth as a mistress who was being
'kept' by Dudley, they implied that he and not she was really in charge of
the relationship and, of course, the country as well. The alleged lover,
who was supposedly leaping into the non-existent husband's side of the
bed, was in effect usurping the political role of king consort as well.

   Implicit in such criticism was the view that sexual favouritism violated
the accepted standards for political advancement. Similar views exist at
the present day, of course; sleeping one's way to the top is not right. But
the standards that such behaviour violates today are not the same as they
were then. In our bureaucratic age of civil-service regulations, personnel
departments, and search committees, credentials and experience are supposed to be the basis for hiring and promotion. In early-modern
England, the criteria were different. From the standpoint of the old aristocracy, one's family lineage should be the paramount standard. Under
Elizabeth, however, the wrong people were getting ahead for the wrong
reasons. These were the assumptions underlying the comments attributed by a witness to Edmond Mather, who was accused in 1571 of plotting
to kill the queen and free Thomas Howard, the fourth Duke of Norfolk,
who was then in the Tower of London awaiting execution: 'What pyttye
weare yt, sayd he, that so noble a man as he [i.e., Norfolk] should dye
now in so vyle a woman her dayes, that desyrethe nothinge but to fede

her owne lewd fantasye, and to cutt off such of her noblylite as weare not perfumed, and courtelyeke to please her delycate eye, and place such as were for her tourne, meaneing daunsers, and meaning you, my Lord of Lecester, and one Mr Hatten, whom he sayd had more recourse unto her Majestie in her pryvye chamber, than reason would suffre, yf she weare so vertuouse and well inclined, as some naysythe [i.e., noiseth] her ...'[15] In the case of this partisan of the blue-blooded Howard family, it is hard to tell what bothered him more: his belief that the queen was 'feeding her lewd fantasy,' or the family backgrounds of her alleged paramours. Leicester and Hatton, the two major favourites of the first half of Elizabeth's reign, also figured in some comments reported to Lord Burghley the following year by Matthew Parker, Archbishop of Canterbury. In a letter whose tone quivers with indignation, Parker wrote that an unidentified man had made various offensive statements about Elizabeth to two officials, who 'hathe it in wryting, that this villain should utter most shamefull wordes agaynst her, viz., that th'Erle of Leicester and Mr Hatton should be suche toward her, as the matter is so horrible, that they wold not wryte down the wordes, but wold have uttered them in speeche to your Lordship if ye wold have been at leisure.'[16]

A second theme in the sexual rumours about Queen Elizabeth centres less on the alleged sexual misbehaviour itself than on the consequences of the alleged sex – namely, alleged children. As early as 1560, Anne Dowe, a wandering handywoman, was telling people in Essex that 'Dudley and the quene hadd played by legerdemayne together,' and that she had a child by him. When one of the individuals with whom she was talking objected that the queen had no child yet, Dowe reportedly replied, 'If she have nott, he hath putt one to makyng ...'[17] Similar stories about Elizabeth's supposed illegitimate children continued to circulate right down to the end of her life, as we have already seen. Soon after the Northern Rising, one Marshame was condemned to lose both of his ears or pay a hundred-pound fine for saying that 'my Lord of Leicester had two childerne by the Quene.'[18] In 1580, a labourer from Maldon named Thomas Playfere was reported for saying that the queen had two children by the Earl of Leicester.[19] The following year, a servant to a Catholic gentleman in Norfolk credited Elizabeth and Leicester with no fewer than five children.[20] In 1585, an immigrant Huguenot leatherdresser from Picardy found himself in trouble for insisting to the patrons of a Southwark alehouse that 'wee say in our countrey that the Quene of England is a whore & hath had two children.'[21] A Dorset man by the name of Edward Fraunces made perhaps the most inventive use of such tales in 1598. He tried to seduce Elizabeth Baylie with the following come-hither line: '... The beste in England [i.e., the queen] had muche desyred the plesure of the fleshe, and had allso three bastardes by nobell men of the Courte. And theirfore he needed not to be ashamed to aske her such a question, nor she to denye him in that respecte ...'[22] She turned him in to the authorities instead.

This concern about illegitimate children is understandable when one remembers how unsettled the succession to the Crown was during Elizabeth's reign. Her decision not to marry preserved her own independence, but it also guaranteed the end of the direct Tudor line. As a consequence, Elizabeth faced pressures throughout her reign to change her mind about marriage, or at least to name a successor, both of which she steadfastly refused to do.[23] Yet the cloudy succession question would have become even murkier if Elizabeth had indeed had an illegitimate child or children.

The position of a reigning queen differed in this respect from that of a king. Because paternity could never be proved for certain, the claims of a king's illegitimate offspring by one of his mistresses could always be rejected if this was desired. A queen consort, of course, was supposed to maintain absolutely unblemished chastity, because a child of hers by another father would have no royal blood, while the same uncertainty about paternity would make it difficult to displace the child from the line of succession. Anne Boleyn and Catherine Howard had both learned that suspicions of adultery could be fatal to a queen consort. For a queen regnant, however, the problem was different. A child's *maternity* was capable of empirical verification, by witnesses at the birth. The illegitimate child of a reigning queen would definitely contain the royal blood, and thus would have a strong claim to the throne if no legitimate heir of her body existed. In northern Europe, however, the succession of illegitimate offspring had never become accepted to anywhere near the extent that it had in Renaissance Italy, so such a child in England would have created a royal mess politically.[24] Given a system in which legitimate blood relationship played a major role in the inheritance of estates and kingdoms, the double standard made a certain kind of sense.

Elizabeth, as an unmarried woman exercising power in her own name, was already operating outside of her age's normal gender and political roles. Her refusal to marry or to name a successor created political anxiety about the future. The possibility that an illegitimate claimant might appear exacerbated that anxiety still further. Given these circumstances, it is not surprising that rumours about the queen's supposed children surfaced repeatedly as the years passed and Elizabeth still remained unmarried. Some of these stories directly addressed the latent concerns about the succession. For example, in 1574, Antonio de Guaras, the Spanish diplomatic agent in England, reported rumours of an intrigue to secure the succession for 'the son of the Earl of Hertford [heir to the Grey claim to the throne] whom they would marry to a daughter of Leicester and the queen of England, who, it is said, is kept hidden, although there are bishops to witness that she is legitimate.'[25] Hinted at here was the possibility of a secret or counterfeit marriage between Elizabeth and Leicester. The anonymous authors of *Leicester's Commonwealth* put a slightly different twist on this story a decade later, asserting that Leicester was scheming to put forward one of his own 'brood' of bastards, '(whereof he hath store in many places, as is known) to the lawful succession of the crown under color of that privy and secret marriage, pretending the same to be by her Majesty, wherein he will want [i.e., lack] no witness to depose what he will.'[26]

In the later years of Elizabeth's reign, as Carole Levin has pointed out, stories began to spread that the queen had had one or more illegitimate children, only to order them killed.[27] In these rumours, the earlier fears that Elizabeth may have had offspring conjoined with frustration and anger that the queen, now past child-bearing age, had left the succession question as unsettled as she had found it. A bastard might have been better than nothing. These tales reflect a heightened animus against Elizabeth. In them, she stands accused of a double sin: first, having illegitimate children and, then, committing infanticide. These stories suggest that she had been both sinful in the past and deficient in providing for her nation's future.

Finally, the rumours about Elizabeth's alleged sexual affairs had the effect of implying that she was not fit to rule in the present. Some of the talebearers expressed this judgment explicitly. In 1562, Edmond Baxter ran together sexual, social, and political criticism when he averred that 'the queen was a naughtie woman and cold not rule hir realme nor justice was nott ministered, and that my Lord Keper [Sir Nicholas Bacon] was a naughtie man & a wreche, and yet for all that he was fayne to knele on his knees and call hym good honerable lord.'[28] In Baxter's view, the whole government of England had become infected by the queen's misbehaviour. It was a hypocritical sham, a world turned upside down in which legitimate authority had vanished. Vice could not be named directly, and even insisted on being acclaimed as virtue.

To take another case, in 1601 a man named William Knyght wrote a letter detailing 'monsterus and unnaturall speches of her Majesty' allegedly uttered in Germany by the Puritan scholar Hugh Broughton. This letter included one of the more lurid versions of the tale of murdered illegitimate children, in which the newborn infants had supposedly been cast immediately into a roaring fire and incinerated. But it also accused Broughton of saying that 'he coulde nott fynde in his hartt to praye for her Majesty, sayinge she was a athyiste and a maynttener of athysme, and therffor mentt nott to comm into the realme untyll her Majestys deathe.'[29] Here the queen's alleged 'naughtiness' had expanded into a total negation of God, in reaction to which the only righteous response was to flee the kingdom.

A similar view came from the opposite end of the religious spectrum in Cardinal William Allen's *Admonition to the Nobility and People of England and Ireland*, published in 1588. In Allen's catalogue of Elizabeth's failings, he devoted a section to her 'unspeakable and incredible variety of luste,' with Leicester 'and divers others.' Despite Elizabeth's claim that she would die a maiden queen, said Allen, she 'forced the verie parliament it self to give consent and to provide by a pretended lawe ... that none should so muche as be named for her successor duringe her life, savinge the naturall, that ys to saie bastard borne childe of her owne bodie.' According to Allen, these sexual violations showed 'how shamefully she hath defiled and infamed her person and cuntry,' through 'her shamefull incontinency & pernitious obstinacy against the honor and good of the whole realme.'[30] These reasons contributed to Allen's conclusion that Elizabeth must be deposed. From perspectives such as Allen's or Broughton's, the queen's sexual misdeeds were part of an all-embracing pattern of transgression, and it is difficult to tell whether issues of gender, politics, or religion were the deepest determinant.

II

Between them, Mary and Elizabeth ruled England for fifty years. By the end of Elizabeth's reign, dissatisfaction with so prolonged a period of rule by women was becoming evident. In 1597, the French ambassador recorded his impression that Elizabeth's rule was 'little pleasing to the great men and the nobles, and if by chance she should die it is certain that the English would never again submit to the rule of women.'[31] In 1603, they were relieved of their burden. Elizabeth died, and despite the long-standing anxieties about the succession, the Crown passed smoothly to James VI of Scotland. The English received James rapturously. He was an experienced, adult, male ruler. He had already provided for the succession by siring three children. Yet, in James's case too, there would be a discrepancy between the gender role expected of a king and the real man sitting on the throne. Although James had done his heterosexual royal duty by marrying and having children, his erotic inclinations plainly lay in the direction of pretty young men. A series of handsome and never terribly bright Adonises rose to prominence at James's Court. And in James's case as well, rumours and gossip linked his sexual proclivities to perceived political failings.

For one thing, James did not possess the warrior virtues that remained an important component of the masculine gender role for aristocrats and royalty, as defined by the code of honour. By the early 1600s, the mounted knight had become a figure of chivalric romance, but professional armies had not yet come into existence. Most military officers still came from noble or gentle backgrounds, and it was not long since kings had routinely led their nation's armies in the field. Yet James dashed the hopes of those who wanted their new king to be a great warrior. His tendency to faint when swords or knives were unsheathed in his presence was notorious. After becoming king of England, James quickly moved to sign a peace treaty with Spain, ending almost two decades of conflict. He took as his motto *Beati pacifici* – 'Blessed are the peacemakers' – and gloried in being called the *rex pacificus*. Late in his reign, James's reluctance to defend his son-in-law the Elector Palatine against German Catholics, which would have embroiled England in the Thirty Years War on the Protestant side, caused terrible frustrations among militant Protestants.

To some, James's sexual inclinations seemed connected to these other masculine shortcomings. Sir Anthony Weldon asserted in the course of his caustic character sketch of the king that James 'naturally ... hated women.'[32] Sir John Oglander noted in his commonplace book that James 'loved young men, his favourites, better than women, loving them beyond the love of men to women. I never yet saw any fond husband make so much or so great dalliance over his beautiful spouse as I have seen King James over his favourites, especially the Duke of Buckingham.'[33] He added that, during James's first visit to the Isle of Wight, in the course of which the king attended a drill by the soldiers stationed there, he noticed that James 'was much taken with seeing the little boys skirmish, whom he loved to see better and more willingly than men.'[34] The hint of pederasty in this comment contrasts with the behaviour that would have been appropriate for a real man and a real king. James should presumably have identified more with the men than with the boys – although in a wholly non-sexual way, of course, responding to the guns for their literal rather than their symbolic significance.

James lavished an astonishing array of grants and honours upon his major favourites: in particular, upon Robert Carr, later Earl of Somerset, in the early 1610s, and George Villiers, later Duke of Buckingham, after 1615.[35] This led some to speculate that the monarch's gifts had been granted only in return for sexual favours. Soon after Carr appeared on the scene, Lord Thomas Howard described the behaviour of James towards the new favourite as follows: 'The Prince [i.e., James] leaneth on his arm, pinches his cheek, smoothes his ruffled garment and, when he looketh at Carr, directeth discourse to divers others.'[36] Francis Osborne went further, to the very verge of explicitness: 'The love the K. shewed [his favourites] was as amorously conveyed as if he had mistaken their sex, and thought them Ladies ... Nor was his love, or what else posterity will please to call it, (who must be Judges of all that History shall inform) carried on with a discretion sufficient to cover a less scandalous behaviour; for the King's kissing them after so lascivious a mode in publick, and upon the theater as it were of the World, prompted many to imagine some things done in the Tyring-house that exceed my expressions no less than they do my experience: and therefore left floting upon the Waves of Conjecture, which hath in my hearing tossed them from one side to the other.'[37]

In the anonymous pamphlet 'Tom Tell-Troath,' which appeared in 1622, the author portrayed a hypothetical 'notoriously wicked ... absolute and dissolute' prince, whom some may have felt resembled their own monarch uncomfortably closely. In his bedchamber, the libeller wrote, this evil prince could 'kisse his Minions without Shame, and make his Grooms his Companions without Danger: Who, because they are acquainted with his secret Sins, assume to themselves as much Power and Respect as Catholick Princes use to give their Confessors. A Pack of ravenous Currs, that know no Difference between the Commonwealth, and one of their Masters Forrests, but think all other Subjects Beasts, and only made for them to prey upon, that lick theire Masters Soares not whole, but smooth, and bark at every Man that dares be found circled with these sweete Beagles.'[38] As had been the case with Elizabeth, the presumption was that the king was not distributing honours and office to the deserving – by whatever standard – but rather was misusing his royal authority to reward those who would gratify his sinful sexual urges.

The sinful aspect appeared most prominent to the young Puritan Simonds D'Ewes, who in 1622 described in his diary a conversation he had

had with a former college friend who was visiting him in London, where he was attending the Inns of Court. 'Of things I discoursed with him that weere secrett as of the sinne of sodomye, how frequente it was in this wicked cittye, and if God did not provide some wonderfull blessing against it, wee could not but expect some horrible punishment for it; especially it being as wee had probable cause to feare, a sinne in the prince as well as the people, which God is for the most part the chastiser of himselfe, because noe man else indeed dare reprove or tell them of ther faults.'[39] D'Ewes went on to claim that the king had prevented the punishment of a Frenchman guilty of buggering a knight's son, and that James's dislike of Sir Edward Coke stemmed from Coke's knowledge of the king's sexual misdeeds.

However, while stories and gossip about James's homosexual proclivities did occasionally appear, they are far less numerous than the tales alleging sexual transgressions on Elizabeth's part. In fact, contemporary allegations about James's homosexuality are surprisingly hard to come across. After the examples cited above, the well goes dry very quickly, and some of the examples we just considered are not even truly contemporary. Weldon, Osborne, and Oglander were all writing well after James's reign was over. Perhaps they were simply recalling matters that had been subjects of common conversation in the Court or the countryside. But, on the other hand, Weldon and Osborne – frustrated courtiers who became bitter enemies of the Stuarts, and who published most of their works under the Commonwealth – may have been embroidering their recollections for propaganda purposes. Nor were most of the contemporary commentators dispassionate observers. The Howards resented having to work through Carr and Villiers to obtain rewards and offices to which they felt their aristocratic lineage entitled them. As for 'Tom Tell-Troath,' its author was a virulently anti-Catholic critic of James's foreign policy of the early 1620s. Some scholars have attributed the work to Thomas Scott, a one-time chaplain to James who finally left the country because of his outspoken opposition to the Spanish Match. If Scott was indeed the author of 'Tom Tell-Troath,' then he wrote that work only after having become seriously estranged from James over religio-political issues.

Most interesting of all, while the State Papers, Domestic, preserve dozens of reports to the Privy Council and other officials concerning hostile comments and libels regarding James I, sexual allegations appear in none of them. Typically, the slanderous comments about James involved criticism of his perceived attitudes about religion: generally that he was too sympathetic to Catholics, or at least was an insufficiently militant Protestant. Other slanders included a variety of complaints, such as that 'his Ma^{ty} had no such minde of the Church as hee had of sweareing & hunting,' as one Thomas Ashton was charged with saying in 1619.[40] A vicar in Yorkshire was accused of stating that 'the king is a foole, and good for nothing but to catch dottarells, and further sayed he could make as good a king of cloutes ...'[41] Late in James's reign, a prisoner in the Marshalsea found himself in trouble for telling a fellow inmate 'that he would kicke him about the yard the next daye, ... and him that woare the Crowne of England if he talk so to him.'[42] But allegations about James engaging in homosexual activity cannot be found among them.

To take another example of abusive comments regarding James, in 1608 the government suppressed a play by John Marston known as *The Silver Mines*, now lost. According to the French ambassador, the play 'slandered their King, his mine in Scotland, and all his favourites in a most pointed fashion; for having made him rail against heaven over the flight of a bird and have a gentleman beaten for calling off his dogs, they portrayed him as drunk at least once a day.'[43] While it would certainly be interesting to know exactly how the favourites were slandered, the general thrust of the satire appears to have been characteristic anti-James fare, with the criticism focusing on monopolies, in this case the one for silver mines in Scotland; on his inordinate love of hunting; and on his drinking habits. After the Thirty Years War began, public criticism centred on the Spanish Match and on the danger into which James's lack of militancy was supposedly placing international Protestantism.

How can we account for the relative paucity of rumours and gossip about James's homosexuality? One possibility is that government officials systematically purged such reports from the records, precisely because they were so dangerous politically. This hypothesis cannot be dismissed out of hand. The political machinations behind the fall of Anne Boleyn are still being debated today, owing to the thoroughness with which the conspirators covered their tracks.[44] But, on the whole, this explanation seems unlikely. The amateurish, unbureaucratic nature of government in this period would have made such an Orwellian cleansing of the records difficult. The contrasts with the Boleyn case are noteworthy too. Whatever they were, the schemes that resulted in her disgrace and execution were the work of a very small group, who enforced a strict silence upon themselves. Rumours about James's homosexuality would presumably have arisen from a number of sources both within and outside the Court, and therefore would likely have been recorded in a wide range of private letters and papers as well as in official reports, none of which appears to be the case.[45]

Another possibility is, of course, that people were afraid they would be severely punished if they spoke or wrote about James's homosexuality and therefore kept quiet, in effect censoring themselves. In one possible instance, when Robert Carr, Earl of Somerset and previously one of James's major favourites, was ordered to stand trial for the poisoning of Sir Thomas Overbury, he hinted that he would make some revelations that the king would regret. James reportedly reacted to this threat with considerable agitation. But in the end, Carr held his tongue about whatever he had been referring to, and he received relatively light treatment and an eventual pardon.[46] Fear might also account for the fact that of the small collection of comments about James's homosexuality by contemporaries that we do find, so many were not written down until well after his reign was over. In the final analysis, however, this explanation seems implausible as well. The men and women of Tudor and Stuart England were notoriously outspoken. The record is full of individuals who – out of principle or anger or drunkenness – made all sorts of derogatory statements about public figures, including monarchs. And human nature would appear to be against this hypothesis too, for the more scandalous a story, the more likely it is to be repeated as soon and as often as possible, especially when it fits the observed facts reasonably well.

The remaining possibility – and on balance, by far the most likely one – is that most of James's contemporaries did not see his behaviour towards his favourites as signifying a sexual relationship between them. At first sight this seems incredible, for, from a twentieth-century perspective, the homoerotic nature of these relationships appears blatantly obvious. But we possess models of sexuality, deriving ultimately from Freud, that emphasize the pervasiveness of sexuality in the human psyche. According to these conceptions, there is a smooth continuum between liking and loving, and all human interaction partakes of some element of libido or Eros. But the models of same-sex friendship and sexuality available to the early seventeenth century were quite different. The reasons for most contemporaries' peculiar blindness about James will become clearer as we consider those models.

For one thing, as Alan Bray has shown, sodomy was regarded in Renaissance England with a supernatural horror that linked sodomites with sorcerers, heretics, Papists, and traitors.[47] Bray further argues, however, that the very fearsomeness and loathsomeness associated with homosexuality made people very slow to recognize the mundane same-sex relationships in their midst. Evidence for this can be found in the minuscule number of prosecutions for sodomy despite the extreme revulsion the act inspired, and in the lack of spontaneous harassment of individuals whom we would likely categorize as homosexual.[48] If this was true regarding people of ordinary status, then it must have been all the more true of the king, for how could the very embodiment of order and authority be engaging in acts that repudiated nature and God's own Creation? James's reign was not glorious, but neither was it disastrous on a scale that only divine wrath could explain; and while James gave his subjects much to complain about, he was a complacent pedant and no monster of iniquity. James did not relish Puritans, but he was a strong defender of staunchly Protestant theology in the Church of England. In short, he showed none of the 'signs' that were supposed to mark a sodomite; therefore, he must not be one.

Second, most people in early Stuart England had no concept of homosexuality as a distinct sexual orientation; that is, as a fundamental, permanent, and indeed defining part of one's overall personality. Such an understanding of sexuality and personality emerged on a widespread basis only in the late nineteenth century, following the advent of modern psychology. In other words, in the dominant discourse of the time, individuals sometimes committed homosexual acts, and some individuals were perhaps more susceptible to this temptation than others; but this was a sin of which all persons were theoretically capable, and there were no 'homosexuals' as such. One consequence of this view was that sodomites could be identified only by being caught in the act. The fact that in this period people commonly slept in the same bed with others of the same sex made this a difficult proposition. To most people, there was no sense that other kinds of behaviour – such as the supposed effeminacy or affectations that characterize the modern stereotype of gay males – were giveaways that revealed a person's sexual orientation. James's pattings of cheeks and smoothings of garments, and even his kisses, thus would not necessarily have been perceived in the ways they likely would be today.

Finally, the Renaissance had revived from classical antiquity the convention of passionate but Platonic friendship between males. Such relationships could be emotionally intense, but the attraction was understood to be spiritual rather than carnal. As a result, when contemporaries interpreted close personal relationships between males, they had available a ready-made category that left sexuality out of the picture entirely.

James's sexual life thus appears to have been a much bigger issue for later historians – with their very different conceptions of sexuality and homosexuality – than it was for most of his contemporaries. As we have seen, some of them were already 'modern-minded' enough to extrapolate from his public behaviour towards his favourites to presumed sexual acts in private. Some made this a feature of retrospective condemnations of his reign, after the Civil War broke out. Looking at the available evidence in the broadest context, it seems likely that we must recognize the existence in the early seventeenth century of more than one conceptual model for understanding the nature of homosexuality. Some scholars have attempted to show that at least some individuals in this period recognized or self-identified with a permanent homosexual orientation, and the examples presented above tend to support this.[49] The quotations from Simonds D'Ewes and the Puritan author of 'Tom Tell-Troath' raise the intriguing possibility that Calvinist concepts of predestination and reprobate souls may have provided the basis for a rudimentary concept of a permanent sexual orientation. But those who were operating within the age's dominant discourse about sexuality appear not to have recognized what we would term James's homosexuality. While many contemporaries condemned the corruption and immorality of James's Court, the idea that these qualities somehow had their roots in James's sexual nature was predominantly a later invention, based on a new understanding of sexuality.[50]

III

When one compares the sexual rumours that circulated about Elizabeth with those about James, and the relationship of these rumours to politics, two major similarities appear. First, the underlying concern in most cases was that political rewards and public offices were being granted according to inappropriate, sexual criteria. Not only were the unworthy being advanced, but the worthy were being held back. For example, Osborne cited Sir Henry Rich as one individual who 'refused [James's] favour upon those conditions [his favourites] subscribed to, ... Rich losing that opportunity his curious Face and Complection afforded him, by turning aside and spitting after the King had slabbered his mouth ...'[51] It was widely accepted at the time that the favour of the prince was an unpredictable but essential element in monarchical government. However, the almost universal view was that the monarch's favour ought to be granted on the basis of qualities other than sexual ones. Not unnaturally, the individuals who felt this most intensely were disgruntled courtiers – such as Weldon, Osborne, and the Catholic authors of *Leicester's Commonwealth* –

who were able to rationalize away their failures by asserting that the game was being played by rigged, sexual rules. In such a context, political failure could even be transformed into a badge of virtue.

Second, in the cases of both Elizabeth and James, the fact that their alleged lovers were male gave the rumours of sexual liaisons an added political significance. The mistresses of a king were of course in a position to influence or manipulate him. But custom barred women from public office in early-modern England (with the sole exception of the monarchship itself, when no male successors were available), and it was rare for a woman to be granted a title of honour in her own right. A royal mistress was therefore always in a dependent position. A male lover, on the other hand, could be named to high office, receive titles of honour, build an independent power base, and eventually become a potent political player in his own right, as Leicester, Hatton, Essex, Carr, and Buckingham demonstrated. Male lovers of the monarch were thus potentially of greater political significance than royal mistresses were, and accordingly they attracted greater attention and were more likely to be the subjects of rumours and gossip.

But the contrasts between the sexual rumours about Elizabeth and those about James are also striking. This is particularly noticeable when one considers the frequency of the rumours about Elizabeth, and the lurid details they often contained, compared with the relatively sparse, bland, and indirect comments about James. It is also significant that the sources of the rumours in James's case were almost universally individuals who had political or religious grievances against the king, as well as the opportunity to observe him at close range. By contrast, numerous ordinary people who had no discernible personal or religious motivation nevertheless invented or repeated stories about Elizabeth's supposed sexual transgressions. This suggests that Elizabeth, as an autonomous, unmarried woman wielding royal power, was perceived as more of an anomaly than was James, a homosexual male in the same position. As such, she tended to be scrutinized more critically and denigrated more easily; her sexual life was more subject to derogatory and demeaning fantasy. As a consequence, Elizabeth had to present herself as someone extraordinary: as the Virgin Queen who was the secular successor to the Virgin Mary; as the mother and wife to her entire country. The image was dazzling, but the strain sometimes showed, particularly towards the end of her reign. No doubt, too, the persona was so superhuman that the temptation to deflate it must have been great. By claiming perpetual chastity, Elizabeth appeared to be putting herself above normal human nature, thereby

almost inviting speculation that the reality was different. Not unexpectedly, such claims attracted a flood of stories and gossip about rampant
sexual activity on her part, just as had occurred with nuns and monks in
the Middle Ages. On the other hand, for a male ruler such as James to
legitimize himself, all he had to do was to present himself as being ordinary, which is a much easier role to carry off.

Elizabeth's own deliberate use of eroticism as a technique of ruling also
helped make her vulnerable to accusations of illicit sexual activity. Her
decision to use sex appeal for political purposes is understandable. Given
the age's assumptions about the natural submissiveness of females, keeping control over her male ministers and courtiers was a difficult task. The
conventions of courtly love, with their emphasis on male service to a
dominant mistress, were thus a useful tool in her armoury, as was her customary flirtatiousness with the men surrounding her. But presenting herself in such a way brought along with it all the negative baggage
associated in the Judaeo-Christian tradition with women's sexuality. While
this behaviour was politically helpful, it therefore had its drawbacks too,
which emerged in one form in sexual rumours and innuendoes. And this
was not a minor political liability, for the double standard proclaimed
that a woman who was merely reputed to engage in sex with a man other
than her husband suffered severe damage to her honour.

Finally, if it was a greater transgression in this period for a monarch to
be an independent woman than a homosexual man, then it follows that,
in social practice, misogyny was more potent than homophobia. This may
seem odd, given the vehemently hostile comments about sodomy that
one finds practically every time the subject is mentioned. But if ordinary
homosexual activity was largely invisible to contemporaries, then this paradox makes more sense. And many indications point in that direction:
the tiny number of prosecutions for sodomy; the general absence of the
endemic gaybashing and derogatory jokes about gays and lesbians that
we see today; the highly conventional nature of most of the hostile references to homosexuality; as well as the unexpectedly small number of
rumours and reports about James I's homosexuality, as discussed in this
study. Indeed, in James's case, xenophobia about his Scottish origins produced far more material for scandalmongers and satirists than his sexual
orientation did. A woman's femaleness, on the other hand, was always evident, and carried with it all the problematic and threatening features
attributed to powerful women by a patriarchal culture. When it came to
persecution and scapegoating in the early modern period, witches – who
were predominantly female – were far more frequent targets than sod-

omites were. And with regard to the sexual behaviour of rulers, Elizabeth's alleged transgressions were the subject of rumours and gossip much more often than were James's.

NOTES

1 *The Diary of Samuel Pepys*, 11 vols., eds. Robert Latham and William Matthews (Berkeley: University of California Press 1970–83), vol. 6: 191 (15 August 1665)
2 Because concealing seditious or treasonable words was a serious crime, local officials frequently sought to protect themselves by reporting any suspect speeches or writings that came to their attention to the Privy Council or other officials of the central government. One aspect of my search for sexual rumours and gossip about these two sovereigns therefore centred on examining the *Acts of the Privy Council* as well as the original documentation for all of the scores of 'libels' and 'slanders' about Elizabeth and James noted in the volumes of the *Calendars of State Papers, Domestic* for their reigns. These sources also provided a rough cross-section of the whole country. In addition, I cast my net widely in the published and unpublished documentary sources from the period.
3 For overviews of psychological and sociological research on gossip and rumour, see Gordon W. Allport and Leo Postman, *The Psychology of Rumor* (New York: Henry Holt 1947); Tamotsu Shibutani, *Improvised News: A Sociological Study of Rumor* (Indianapolis: Bobbs-Merrill 1966); and Ralph L. Rosnow and Gary A. Fine, *Rumor and Gossip: The Social Psychology of Hearsay* (New York: Elsevier 1976). A survey of recent research which has challenged and refined Allport and Postman's conclusions can be found in Ralph L. Rosnow, 'Inside Rumor: A Personal Journey,' *American Psychologist* 46 (1991), 484–96. Max Gluckman emphasized the role that scandalous gossip can play in enforcing traditional values and conduct in 'Gossip and Scandal,' *Current Anthropology* 4 (1963), 307–16.
4 Louis Adrian Montrose, '"Shaping Fantasies": Figurations of Gender and Power in Elizabethan Culture,' *Representations* no. 2 (Spring 1983), 77
5 The most thorough gender-based analysis of Elizabeth and her strategies of political self-presentation is Carole Levin, *The Heart and Stomach of a King: Elizabeth I and the Politics of Sex and Power* (Philadelphia: University of Pennsylvania Press 1994). For discussions of the 'marriage question' that focus on its gender implications, see pp. 39–65 in the above work; Allison Heisch, 'Queen Elizabeth I and the Persistence of Patriarchy,' *Feminist Review* no. 4 (1980), 47–53; and Christopher Haigh, *Elizabeth I* (London: Longman 1988), 10–16.

6 *The First and Second Prayer Books of King Edward VI*, Everyman's Library (London: J.M. Dent 1910), 411

7 On the 'Virgin Queen' aspect of the cult of Elizabeth, see Heisch, 'Queen Elizabeth,' 49–50; Haigh, *Elizabeth I*, 19–20; and Carole Levin, 'Power, Politics, and Sexuality: Images of Elizabeth I,' in *The Politics of Gender in Early Modern Europe*, eds. Jean R. Brink, Allison P. Coudert, and Maryanne C. Horowitz, Sixteenth Century Essays and Studies, vol. 12 (Kirksville, MO: Sixteenth Century Journal Publishers 1989), 97–100. Helen Hackett, *Virgin Mother, Maiden Queen: Elizabeth I and the Cult of the Virgin Mary* (New York: St Martin's Press 1995), is a book-length study of the subject whose publication came too late for me to be able to consult it for this essay.

8 Heisch, 'Queen Elizabeth,' 49–54; Haigh, *Elizabeth I*, 20–4

9 Haigh, *Elizabeth I*, 155–6

10 'Journey through England and Scotland Made by Lupold von Wedel in the Years 1584 and 1585,' trans. Gottfried von Bülow, *Transactions of the Royal Historical Society*, n.s. 9 (1895), 263, 265

11 Sir William Browne to Sir Robert Sidney, 7 November 1601, in Great Britain, Historical Manuscripts Commission, *De L'Isle and Dudley MSS.*, 5 vols. (London: HMSO 1925–66), vol. 2: 540. Browne ordered the maid to be whipped, but in private, to prevent the story from spreading further.

12 Statement by John Gunstone of assertions made by John Pole, 1590?, SP 12/273/103, Public Record Office, London. This is probably the 'writing' referred to in the *Acts of the Privy Council of England*, n.s., 32 vols. (London: HMSO 1890–1907), vol. 20: 28–9. In my transcriptions of manuscripts, I have silently modernized the usages of i/j and u/v and the conventions of capitalization, punctuation, and numeration.

13 Examination of Robert Garrerd, 19 January 1563, SP 15/11/86

14 Sir Rowland Hayward and William Fleetwood to Lord Burghley, 26 July 1571, SP 12/80/9

15 William Murdin, *A Collection of State Papers relating to Affairs in the Reign of Queen Elizabeth from the Year 1571 to 1596* (London: William Bowyer 1759), 203–4

16 Thomas Wright, ed., *Queen Elizabeth and Her Times*, 2 vols. (London: Henry Colburn 1838), vol. 1: 440

17 Lord Robert Rich and Thomas Mildmay to Sir William Cecil, 13 August 1560, SP 12/13/21. See also F.R. Emmison, *Elizabethan Life: Disorder* (Chelmsford: Essex County Council 1970), 41.

18 Wright, *Queen Elizabeth*, vol. 1: 374

19 Emmison, *Elizabethan Life*, 41–2. As the other examples that I have presented show, however, Emmison is incorrect in asserting that such rumours came only from Essex.

20 Rev Thomas Scot to the Earl of Leicester, March 1581, SP 12/198/34

21 Examination of Richard Dennall, 28 June 1586, SP 12/190/56

22 Confession of Basyll Baylie and Elizabeth Baylie, 28 December 1598, SP 12/269/22

23 On the implications for the succession of Elizabeth's decision not to marry, see Heisch, 'Queen Elizabeth,' 47–53; Haigh, *Elizabeth I*, 10–19; and Levin, 'Power, Politics, and Sexuality,' 103–5.

24 In what was probably a fortunate development for England, the death in 1536 of the seventeen-year-old Henry Fitzroy, Duke of Richmond and Henry VIII's illegitimate son by Elizabeth Blount, prevented England from having to find out how strong the claim of such a contender to the throne would have been.

25 *Calendar of State Papers, Spanish, 1568–1579* (London: Public Record Office 1894), 491

26 *Leicester's Commonwealth: The Copy of a Letter Written by a Master of Art of Cambridge (1584) and Related Documents*, ed. D.C. Peck (Athens: Ohio University Press 1985), 130

27 Levin, 'Power, Politics, and Sexuality,' 103–5. See also Emmison, *Elizabethan Life*, 42.

28 Examination of Robert Garrerd, 19 January 1563, SP 15/11/86

29 William Knyght to [?], 2 April 1601, SP 12/279/48

30 Cardinal William Allen, *An Admonition to the Nobility and People of England and Ireland concerninge the Present Warres, Made for the Execution of his Holines Sentence, by the highe and mightie Kinge Catholike of Spaine* ([Antwerp: A. Conincx?] 1588), 19, 20

31 [Andre Huralt, Sieur] de Maisse, *A Journal of All That Was Accomplished by Monsieur De Maisse, Ambassador in England from Henri IV to Queen Elizabeth, Anno Domini 1597*, eds. G.B. Harrison and R.A. Jones (Bloomsbury: Nonesuch Press 1931), 11–12

32 Sir Anthony Weldon, *The Court and Character of King James* (London: J. Collins 1651), 125

33 Sir John Oglander, *A Royalist's Notebook: The Commonplace Book of Sir John Oglander*, ed. Francis Bamford (London: Constable 1936), 196

34 Ibid., 198

35 Regarding the rise of Robert Carr, see P.R. Seddon, 'Robert Carr, Earl of Somerset,' *Renaissance and Modern Studies* 14 (1970), 49–59; and D. Harris Willson, *King James VI and I* (New York: Henry Holt 1956), 336–44. On the magnitude of James's grants to Carr, see Lawrence Stone, *The Crisis of the Aristocracy, 1558–1641* (Oxford: Clarendon Press 1965), 444, 475. Regarding the grants and income enjoyed by George Villiers, see Roger Lockyer, *Buckingham: The Life and Political Career of George Villiers, First Duke of Buckingham, 1592–1628* (Lon-

don: Longman 1981), 20, 25–7, 61–3, 119–21, 412–14, 460; and Stone, *Crisis,*
475.

36 Sir John Harington, *Nugae Antiquae,* 2 vols., ed. Thomas Park (London: Vernor
and Hood 1804), vol. 1: 392

37 Francis Osborne, 'Traditionall Memoyres on the Raigne of King James I,' in
Works (London: Allen Bancks 1673), 534–5

38 'Tom Tell-Troath,' in *Harleian Miscellany,* 8 vols. (London: T. Osborne 1744–6),
vol. 2: 415

39 *The Diary of Sir Simonds D'Ewes,* ed. Elisabeth Bourcier (Paris: Didier 1974),
92–3 (29 August 1622)

40 Information of Thomas Swanne, 18 January 1619, SP 14/105/51. For criticisms
of James's passion for hunting, see G.P.V. Akrigg, *Jacobean Pageant; or the Court
of King James I* (Cambridge, MA: Harvard University Press 1962), 159–61.

41 Examination of Thomas Wetherall, 28 October 1620, SP 14/117/41

42 Statement by Robert Mortlocke regarding speeches by John Bailye, 1625, SP
14/189/58

43 Quoted in George Chapman, *The Conspiracy and Tragedy of Byron,* ed. John
Margeson, The Revels Plays (Manchester: Manchester University Press 1988),
276

44 See, for instance, the sharply contrasting interpretations of Anne's fall in E.W.
Ives, *Anne Boleyn* (Oxford: Basil Blackwell 1986), 335–418, and in Retha War-
nicke, *The Rise and Fall of Anne Boleyn* (Cambridge: Cambridge University Press
1989), 191–233.

45 In a few instances (e.g., SP 14/122/111, 14/123/64, and 14/127/59), the supporting examinations detailing the exact nature of the slanderous comments
about James have disappeared. But it is not uncommon for such enclosures to
have gone missing, so this is a weak foundation upon which to build a massive
conspiracy theory.

46 Beatrice White takes at face value James's expressed fear that Carr might try to
implicate him somehow in Overbury's murder: *Cast of Ravens: The Strange Murder of Sir Thomas Overbury* (London: John Murray 1965), 150–3, 168–74, 182–4.
Yet such a charge would appear to have been easy for the king to deny. As
Akrigg has pointed out, however, James's real concern may have been about
other damaging disclosures Carr might make: *Jacobean Pageant,* 200. The possibility of Carr charging him with homosexual importunities or acts might have
been among them.

47 Alan Bray, *Homosexuality in Renaissance England,* 2d ed. (London: GMP Publishers 1988), 19–30. See also Caroline Bingham, 'Seventeenth-Century Attitudes
toward Deviant Sex,' *Journal of Interdisciplinary History* 1 (1971), 447–68.

48 Bray, *Homosexuality,* 68–9, 76–8. Bray further shows that the rare prosecutions

for sodomy can be linked to very specific circumstances, such as the disturbance of public order, a period of crisis calling for a scapegoat, or parents outraged by a sexual approach to a son (pp. 71–5). B. Burg has used the infrequency of sodomy prosecutions to argue that 'in early Stuart England people were relatively tolerant of homosexuality,' unless other, more serious political or moral offences were also involved: 'Ho Hum, Another Work of the Devil: Buggery and Sodomy in Early Stuart England,' in *Historical Perspectives on Homosexuality*, eds. Salvatore J. Licata and Robert P. Petersen, Research on Homosexuality, vol. 2 (New York: Haworth Press, Stein and Day 1981), 69. But evidence that contemporaries showed positive tolerance for acts they recognized as homosexual is thus far lacking. Given the highly charged negative ideas associated with sodomy in this era, it therefore seems more plausible that contemporaries failed to see or interpret such acts than that they saw them and gave a wink and a nod.

49 See, for example, Joseph Cady, '"Masculine Love," Renaissance Writing, and the "New Invention" of Homosexuality,' in *Homosexuality in Renaissance and Enlightenment England: Literary Representations in Historical Context*, ed. Claude Summers, 9–40 (New York: Haworth Press 1992; simultaneously issued as *Journal of Homosexuality* 23, nos. 1/2 [1992]); and Giovanni Dall'Orto, '"Socratic Love" as a Disguise for Same-Sex Love in the Italian Renaissance,' in *The Pursuit of Sodomy: Male Homosexuality in Renaissance and Enlightenment Europe*, eds. Kent Gerard and Gert Hekma, 34–65 (New York: Haworth Press 1989; simultaneously issued as *Journal of Homosexuality* 16, nos. 1/2 [1988]). These essays present suggestive although ultimately inconclusive evidence and interpretations.

50 Maurice Lee, Jr, traces the negative judgments of James I that were typical among historians until recently in part to anachronistic revulsion towards James's homosexuality, and in part to susceptibility to Weldon's scurrilous but entertaining gossip: *Great Britain's Solomon: James VI and I in his Three Kingdoms* (Urbana, IL: University of Illinois Press 1990), xi–xiv, 233–5, 255–7.

51 Osborne, 'Traditionall Memoyres,' 535. Since Rich in fact was raised to the peerage as the Earl of Holland in 1623, two years before the end of James's reign, one has to be sceptical about the accuracy of Osborne's anecdote. But what is important here is the perception of politics the anecdote embodies, rather than its literal truthfulness; and of course the same applies to all the gossip and rumours we have been considering.

The 'Masculine Love' of the 'Princes of Sodom' 'Practising the Art of Ganymede' at Henri III's Court: The Homosexuality of Henri III and His *Mignons* in Pierre de L'Estoile's *Mémoires-Journaux*

JOSEPH CADY

The materials about Henri III and his male favourites, or *mignons*, in the *Mémoires-Journaux* of the French Court official Pierre de L'Estoile (1546–1611) are of major significance in the history of sexuality, though they have never been studied in detail before.[1] As far as we know now, they are the frankest and most extensive Renaissance depictions of homosexuality and are also the earliest sustained sample we have of personal and popular writing about the subject in the post-classical West. Otherwise, the kinds of accounts of homosexuality we find in L'Estoile's work do not start to appear in any numbers until the long eighteenth century – for example, in the letters and memoirs of figures like 'Madame' (Duchess of Orléans and sister-in-law of Louis XIV) and the Duc de Saint-Simon in France and Mrs Thrale (Hester Lynch Thrale, later Mrs Piozzi) in England, and in anonymous satires like the British *The Town Display'd, in a Letter to Amintor in the Country* (1701) and *The Women-Hater's Lamentation* (1707).

Furthermore, these texts suggest authors and audiences who were quite aware of the existence of what we would now call a 'homosexual orientation' – that is, of the fact that some people are predominantly or exclusively attracted to their own sex and are identifiable by that desire – and as such they pose a major challenge to the dominant argument about sexual orientation in the current historical study of sexuality, which holds that homosexuality is a relatively new historical 'invention.' Popularized first by the work of Jeffrey Weeks, Michel Foucault, and Alan Bray, this vaguely conceived view seems at a minimum to say that earlier periods such as the Renaissance had no significant conception of, or language for, homosexuality as a distinct, categorical, sexual orientation – especially one directed towards adult age-peers – and ultimately to hold that a *de facto* homosexual orientation did not even exist in the age. If homosexuality 'existed' at all in the Renaissance, this argument implies, it was only as a transient and unremarkable 'act' of an 'undivided,' implicitly bisexual, sexuality, an item of 'behaviour' that anyone could perform, unconnected to any inner inclination or directionality and typically age-asymmetrical, occurring only between markedly older and younger partners. Elsewhere I have labelled this position 'new-inventionism' and criticized it through studies of the earlier term 'masculine love,' which I have argued was a prominent Renaissance language for a male homosexual orientation, and of the Renaissance's practice of using the noun 'love' as a term of desire in a male–female context only, making it the age's *de facto* language for a heterosexual orientation.[2] I want to continue that critique here by illustrating the persistent and various ways L'Estoile's *Mémoires-Journaux* materials about Henri III reveal the age's definite awareness of a distinct homosexual orientation. Since the chief figures in these texts are men, most of the *Mémoires-Journaux*'s references are to male homosexuality. But a few mentions of lesbianism also occur, indicating that the age recognized the existence of a general 'homosexuality' as well.

L'Estoile's *Mémoires-Journaux* has long been regarded as an invaluable source for the study of French social history of the high Renaissance – for example, historians have found an almost perfect correspondence between the observations in those texts and independent data, like the Registers of Paris for the same years.[3] Eleven volumes long in the complete, authoritative edition, which was not published until the end of the nineteenth century, the *Mémoires-Journaux* extends from 1574 to 1611 and covers the entire reigns of Henri III (1551–89, r. 1574–89) and Henri IV (1553–1610, r. 1589–1610). Called in manuscript 'Registre-Journal d'un Curieux' (The Account Book and Journal of a Curious Man) – the text was given its present title by the nineteenth-century editors[4] – the *Mémoires-Journaux* combines two kinds of documents kept by L'Estoile, a descendant of prominent lawyers and officers of the Crown, who served for much of his life as clerk-in-chief of the Paris Parlement.

The first, and larger, component of the work is a diary in which L'Estoile chronicles the tumultuous political events of the period and records myriad other aspects of contemporary French life: from Court and city gossip to fashions in food, clothing, and amusements; to prices, crops, and the weather; to disease and the state of medicine. The second component, usually affixed to his diary entries at the appropriate dates, is

L'Estoile's extensive scrapbook collection of writings about noteworthy contemporary events and controversies that, in this era before systematic journalism, were circulated hand to hand or through public posting or in pamphlet form. Almost all these scrapbook materials are anonymous, and most are broadsides and satires. Some are in Latin, suggesting that they were written most immediately for the Court or other educated circles such as the Parlement or the Church. The large majority, however, are in French and are clearly directed at a broader popular audience. In any case, there is no difference in attitude between the Latin and French texts, and L'Estoile himself makes no significant distinction between them. He includes both, where available, in the same scrapbook section, and he typically describes these materials as 'distributed and made public everywhere in Paris' at the time.[5]

The civil wars, or Wars of Religion, that gripped France from the 1560s to the 1590s are, of course, the dominant political context for the *Mémoires-Journaux* sections dealing with Henri III, which take up the first three volumes and part of the fourth. Most of L'Estoile's scrapbook materials reflect the outlook of the opposition Holy League, the ultra-Catholic force founded by Henry of Guise in 1576 (when the Crown first granted Protestants religious freedom), ostensibly to defend Catholicism against the Huguenots, but largely a device by which the House of Lorraine-Guise hoped to take over the throne. The League's conflict with the Crown spanned more than twenty years and culminated in the armed rebellion of the Paris League against the monarchy, lasting from 1588 (a year before the assassination of Henri III) until 1594 (when it was finally defeated by Henri IV). Throughout this struggle L'Estoile shared the position known as *politique*, which, while Catholic in faith and critical of Henri III's policies, supported the monarchy against the League for reasons of national stability and tradition. This stance is inevitably reflected in the *Mémoires-Journaux*, but, rather than overriding its materials, seems largely responsible for the remarkable relative balance scholars have seen in the work. For example, while L'Estoile's diary is usually more circumspect or restrained about the king than are the more blatant and strident scrapbook materials – whose anonymous authors he sometimes calls 'foolish and wicked' and which he frequently introduces with terms like 'filthy' and 'obscene'[6] – L'Estoile still provides many sympathetic examples of popular grievances against the Crown.

At least forty-five different *Mémoires-Journaux* items between 1576 and 1589 concern the sexuality of Henri III and his *mignons*. Given the absolute stigma attached to manifest homosexuality at the time, almost all these materials condemn the subject, with a few exceptions, such as the Amadis Jamin poems I discuss below. My discussion here will cover the most representative or revealing texts. In terms that would be easily recognizable to a modern reader, the most literal and frank statement of an awareness of a homosexual orientation in the *Mémoires-Journaux* appears in one of the twenty-six satiric verses L'Estoile appends to his diary entry about a 7 April 1583 procession of the king and his Congregation of Penitents of the Annunciation of Our Lady. The king had established this confraternity of penitents from among his followers in the previous month (the members were chiefly the *mignons*, together with several respected nobles and public officials), and the group provoked much public outcry for its perceived hypocrisy; L'Estoile had described its founding in a detailed March diary entry. The quatrain focuses on the problem of the king's childlessness, which especially alarmed the Catholic faction because the Huguenot Henri of Navarre was close in the line of succession (and Navarre did become heir apparent in the following year, after the death of the king's brother, the Duke of Alençon). 'The King has become a penitent,' the poem states, 'because he doesn't have children' (that is, to beg God to send him offspring). 'But the actual reason he doesn't have any,' it continues, 'is that he really doesn't tend that way.'[7] The poem fairly bluntly indicates an awareness, not just of homosexuality, but of a heterosexuality/homosexuality distinction. Using what new-inventionism mistakenly maintains is only a modern sexual vocabulary, it recognizes a male-to-female sexual 'tendency' (that is, orientation) that can result in children, and a male-to-male one that cannot.

The same clear distinction is made, if more figuratively, in two other *Mémoires-Journaux* pieces. Another of the April 1583 attacks on the penitents, alluding to the confraternity's official title, says of the king: 'He has chosen our Good Lady / As his religious patron. / But, on my soul, he likes / A blond young man better.'[8] Symbolically evoking the king's 'liking' for men, the poem also seems clearly to recognize a heterosexuality/ homosexuality distinction in the contrast it poses between the choices of a 'Lady' or a 'young man.' (New-inventionism typically takes 'young man' references like this literally. But, as John Boswell has pointed out in discussing other earlier writing about male homosexuality, these usually did not designate actual age-asymmetrical situations but were meant, rather, to symbolize male beauty in general, as 'girl' in heterosexual literature has often been a metonym for 'female.'[9] For example, in the particular situation discussed here, the parties were almost age-peers – the *mignons* were in their twenties, and Henri III was thirty-two.)

The same awareness of orientation is registered in the governing metaphor of a long anonymous poem that circulated at Court in December 1581 and that L'Estoile calls 'A Courtier's Libel,' a generic title he gives to several similar scrapbook satires of Court mores. Cast as an exposé report by a Court attendant to a curious out-of-town friend, the poem uses the imagery of marriage to describe a ubiquitous and exclusive homosexuality at Court, providing as well one of the few depictions of lesbianism in the *Mémoires-Journaux*. Reflecting what we would now call the 'compulsory heterosexuality' of the age, the king and the *mignons* had to marry, and the poem assumes knowledge of the king's practice of orchestrating the marriages of his chief favourites to keep them near him, sometimes promising or giving them titles at the same time. The two *mignons* mentioned here are Saint-Luc – whose marriage to a Mademoiselle de Brissac had been arranged, L'Estoile notes in his diary for February 1578, 'by the will and express command of the King'[10] – and La Valette, the king's final favourite, whom he had betrothed to the queen's sister in October 1581 and, then, in the next month, made the Duke d'Epernon. This 'Courtier's Libel' that followed in December implicitly portrays these marriages and betrothals as fronts for an actual pervasive homosexuality. The speaker has been preoccupied, he begins, by 'these fine marriages ... at this Court.' But these marriages, he notes, are not the familiar kind. With his special private access, he has learned that the real nuptials at court are not between men and women but strictly between members of the same sex. 'By my faith,' he tells his friend, 'these nuptials are superb! / ... But what marriages these are, / You've never seen the like. / One man marries another, / And women mate similarly. / ... The King has repudiated / Saint-Luc, his first bridegroom, / And, seeking a new adventure, / Has married La Valette.'[11] The success of the poem's satire rests in part on the fact (and on the audience's knowledge) that, in this public culture, marriage pertains only to male–female sexuality, and thus this dimension of the poem both registers an awareness of a distinct 'heterosexuality' and establishes it as this culture's official sexuality. At the same time, the use of marriage as a metaphor to describe the Court's actual pervasive same-sex coupling – with all its connotations of an established, and presumably enduring, institution – implicitly defines same-sex attraction as the kind of substantial and lasting desire we would now call an orientation. This point is then only reinforced by the fact that the king is presented as 'marrying' and 'remarrying' only other men.

To modern readers, the other frankest indications in the *Mémoires-Journaux* of awareness of a homosexual orientation might be their many explicit, bawdy references to male homosexual sex. In several broadsides the king and the *mignons* are bluntly described as 'fucking' each other (through verbs like 'enfiler,' to pierce or run through, and 'estoquer,' to thrust). For instance, another April 1583 attack on the confraternity of penitents declares, 'Two by two they go coupled, / Devoutly enough. / But I call them foul / When they fuck each other.'[12] Similarly, the 1581 'Courtier's Libel' declares that 'The King fucks his *mignons*, / Makes them his bedmates.'[13] Sometimes the focus is on the *mignons*' sex with each other. One 1578 sonnet portrays them as 'Comrades / In perverted spirit, fucking each other.'[14] Occasionally, the blunter 'foutre' and 'fesse' are used, as in another April 1583 quatrain against the penitents that satirizes their ritual self-flagellation: 'If these fuckers, fucked in the ass, / Want to stop being fucked / And crave a good whipping and beating instead, / Doesn't that show some style?'[15]

Not surprisingly, jibes about 'ass' ('cul') are popular in this strand of the *Mémoires-Journaux*. For example, in an anonymous broadside poem called 'The Mignons in 1577,' Quélus, one of the king's first favourites, is described as 'advancing [at the Court] totally through his ass.'[16] After Quélus died of injuries suffered in a fight with followers of the Duke of Guise in April 1578, Saint-Luc (mentioned in the 1581 'Courtier's Libel' above) replaced him in the king's affections, and a 1578 sonnet in part attacks him in the same terms. The title adds a parenthetical anagram of Saint-Luc's name, so that its last word is 'cul': the complete title reads, 'A Sainct-Luc (Cats in Cul)' (1:340). Additionally, another long 'Courtier's Libel' for September 1579 calls the king 'a dealer in ass.'[17] Furthermore, another April 1583 satire on the penitents' self-flagellation proclaims, '*Mignons*, ... / Don't just thrash your backs. / It's your ass that's offended.'[18] With its play on 'behind' and 'rear,' 'derrière' sometimes replaces 'cul' in these texts. For example, the same September 1579 'Courtier's Libel' reports that 'the derrière / ... is the way / Of our court.'[19] In addition, a satiric April 1578 poem mentions another *mignon*, Maugiron, who was killed in the same brawl as Quélus, declaring that 'Samson's strength was his hair, / And Maugiron's was his rear.'[20] Relatedly, in a February 1578 quatrain about an earlier fight between Quélus and Bussy d'Amboise (the favourite of the Duke of Alençon), Quélus is described as 'not knowing how / To take men from the front; / If he'd taken Bussy from behind, / He'd really have stuffed it to him.'[21] Another poem, in Latin, from August 1580, makes fun of the casualties suffered by the *mignons* in their siege of the city of La Fère that summer: 'If they couldn't protect their behinds, / They can scarcely protect their fronts.'[22]

These bawdy materials cover possibilities besides anal intercourse as well. For instance, though the 'A Sainct-Luc (Cats in Cul)' sonnet mentioned above spotlights 'ass' in its title, the poem itself dramatizes mutual masturbation, with the *mignon* coming in the hand of the king. The poem is a comment on Saint-Luc's recent marriage to Mademoiselle de Brissac. As mentioned above, in my discussion of the December 1581 'Courtier's Libel,' the king arranged the marriages of his *mignons* to keep them near him, often offering them titles at the same time, and knowing observers recognized these matches as fronts for an ongoing homosexuality (as L'Estoile further hints in his 1578 diary entry about Saint-Luc's marriage, when he particularly adds that 'the bride was ugly and ... deformed').[23] These points also dominate the sonnet against Saint-Luc, which, like the April 1583 quatrain about the king discussed earlier, uses childlessness as sign of homosexuality. The angry speaker declares, 'Saint Luc, ... you can't / Get any offspring with de Brissac; / Your semen is lost in the chubby hand / Of the Great Man who promises to make you a duke.'[24]

Though these bawdy *Mémoires-Journaux* materials highlight sexual acts, they should not be mistaken for a view of homosexuality as only a kind of transient 'behaviour,' as new-inventionism argues. The quantity of these gibes alone suggests that a homosexual 'tendency' was perceived in Henri and his favourites (to use the language of the April 1583 quatrain against the king), a likelihood further supported by the *Mémoires-Journaux* relative lack of bawdy heterosexual materials concerning them. More subtly, the degree of alarm in these texts also implies a recognition of homosexual orientation. In the sexual world envisioned by new-inventionism, there really would be no need to be vexed by homosexuality, because there would never be homosexuality for very long – homosexual 'act' and heterosexual 'act' would follow each other in a constant cycle, and during the heterosexual phase traditional culture's imperative of biological procreation could be met. The consternation about homosexuality in these bawdy texts thus *ipso facto* indicates awareness of a homosexual orientation, that is, of the fact that some people have persistent homosexual feelings and do not 'convert' automatically to heterosexuality. Even without these other implications, it would be tautological to reason from these particular texts that their culture therefore saw homosexuality as only a form of 'behaviour' – their subject, explicit sex, requires that they focus on sexual 'acts' in the first place.

A smaller number of *Mémoires-Journaux* items are at almost the opposite pole from these bawdy materials and work entirely by suggestion instead, and a homosexual orientation can be detected in these texts as well. Here no explicit sexuality is depicted or mentioned, but deep-set desire and attachment are clearly implied, either through language too heightened for any other kind of situation or through the more obvious kind of innuendo in which the author drops hints or allusions he assumes the audience will easily catch. Vivid examples of the first approach appear in a set of twenty-four memorial sonnets about the *mignons* that a poet named Amadis Jamin presented to the king on 10 August 1578 and that L'Estoile inserts at the end of his scrapbook for that year. These concern the several *mignons* killed in the April 1578 brawl between the *mignons* and followers of the Duke of Guise in which, as mentioned earlier, Quélus, the king's first favourite, and another named Maugiron, were mortally wounded. This is one of the most noticed incidents in the *Mémoires-Journaux*; besides including the Jamin sonnets, L'Estoile devotes a lengthy diary entry to the event and then appends to it seventeen of the 'great number of epitaphs, commemorations, ballads, and Latin and French poems [that] were made public and distributed in Paris and at the Court' about the episode.[25]

The last five of the Jamin sonnets are cast in the voice of the king. These contain a number of striking, extravagant declarations that transcend even the occasional hyperbole of the conventional friendship-elegy and that cannot be explained as the customary rhetoric of Court flattery either, since they are spoken by a king about his subjects. Furthermore, if we imagine these exclamations to be spoken by a man about a woman instead (that is, if we put them to 'the heterosexuality test'), they would unhesitatingly be read as romantic. In one sonnet, for instance, the king calls the *mignons* a 'perfect creation destroyed / By death' whose 'sepulcher is my heart.'[26] In another he addresses them 'in heaven' as 'your Henri, / Sad, pensive, musing, alone, and grieving, / Who vents his life and soul in tears.'[27] In another he wishes 'to cast off my body ... / And fly to them / ... in heaven, / Revelling in their presence, their faces always in sight!'[28] And in the last he declares, 'I think and think of you at every hour / And see and gaze on you every night in my dreams ... / I cannot and will not live without you ... / My soul does not stir without thinking of you ... / My ear hears nothing but your names.'[29] There were special circumstances to the composition and disposition of these sonnets as well, and these, too, clearly imply that they express a profound (and recognizably forbidden) 'tendency' in the king. In introducing the sonnets L'Estoile notes that 'they say [the king] himself commissioned' them, and a final note appended to them, apparently written by Jamin himself, mentions presenting the poems to the king and adds that he 'regarded them favourably and locked them in his cabinet himself.'[30] The sonnets' sympathetic portrait of the king and the *mignons*, one of the rare ones in the *Mémoires-Journaux*, is no doubt explained by the royal commission, and the fact that the king then appears to have concealed the poems seems a final confirmation of fact that they express a taboo homosexual longing. L'Estoile does not explain how he came to have a copy of the hidden manuscript.

As with many of his diary entries, L'Estoile's own account of the brawl and the *mignons'* deaths is more restrained than the scrapbook documents. None the less, the heightened diction and telling specifics of his description of the king's behaviour at the loss of Quélus and Maugiron – Quélus lingered for thirty-three days before dying – imply the same kind of romantic passion evoked more blatantly in the Jamin sonnets:

> The King went to see [Quélus] every day, never budging from his bedside, and promised a hundred thousand francs to his surgeons if he should recover ... None the less, he passed from this world to the next, with the words 'Oh! my king, my king!' always on his lips, ... while speaking nothing of God or of His mother. In truth, the King showed an amazing friendship for Maugiron and him: he covered their dead bodies with kisses, clipped their blond locks and had them taken away for safekeeping, and removed Quélus's earrings, which he himself had given him, putting them on with his own hand. .
>
> These and similar kinds of behaviour (unworthy in truth of a lofty king) gradually caused contempt for this prince and provoked malice against his *mignons*, who possessed him.[31]

The king's constant attendance on Quélus, Quélus's deathbed impiety in reserving his last words for the king, the king's ardour over Quélus's and Maugiron's bodies, his putting the gift of the earrings on Quélus himself – all clearly exceed the 'friendship' context in which L'Estoile tries to place them, as his adjective 'amazing' seems pointedly to suggest; and, again, if we put this passage to 'the heterosexuality test,' it would without hesitation be read as a love scene. L'Estoile's conclusion then comes close to admitting this situation openly, especially his choice of verb to describe the *mignons'* influence over the king. In its strict dictionary sense, 'posséder' might be translated as 'dominate,' but L'Estoile seems to want the word's suggestion of romantic 'possession' as well, a 'possession' usually characteristic only of what we would now call an orientation.

Some of the broadsides L'Estoile appends to his diary entry work by a similar kind of suggestiveness. One Latin epitaph for Quélus notes that he had 'the love of the King, / the great love of the King.'[32] Another, in French, addressed to the king, declares that 'Quélus was uniquely beloved by you.'[33] Yet another, closer to bluntness, holds that Quélus was 'loved too much by his King.'[34] Additionally, a few *Mémoires-Journaux* materials of this kind work by literary or symbolic allusion; these come closest to traditional innuendo, in assuming a bond of private knowledge between speaker and audience that will easily penetrate the speaker's code. For example, another bawdy April 1583 document about the confraternity of penitents uses an allusion to the *Aeneid* to deride yet again the anal intercourse between the king and the *mignons*. The king sometimes called the *mignons* 'his children,'[35] and this quatrain declares, 'The great King of the Gauls / Adopted his *mignons* as his sons. / He had a good reason. They have carried this father, / As Aeneas did his, on their backs and shoulders.'[36] A related, though more transparent, kind of document is an anonymous May 1585 sonnet issued by the League called 'On the Duke d'Epernon's Cancer.'[37] As mentioned in my discussion of the December 1581 'Courtier's Libel,' in November of that year the king made his final favourite, the *mignon* La Valette, the Duke d'Epernon, after having betrothed him to the queen's sister in the preceding month. In a May 1585 diary entry, L'Estoile reports that the Duke d'Epernon was suffering from a 'dangerous throat tumour' and, echoing his 1578 description of the king's behaviour at Quélus's deathbed, mentions that 'the King went immediately to see him, to look after him and dress his wounds himself.'[38] He then inserts the League sonnet, which compares the king to a sun that abandons all the other signs of the zodiac for Cancer: 'The Lion, the Ram, the Virgin, the Fish, / The Goat, the Bull, the Archer, even the Twins, / No longer feel his dear presence: / He loves, he treasures Cancer alone.'[39]

The *Mémoires-Journaux*'s frequent mentions of the king's and the *mignons*' 'effeminacy' might also be read as references to a homosexual orientation, given the term's exclusive association with male homosexuals now. For example, a long anonymous 1576 broadside poem ironically entitled 'The Virtue and Purity of the Mignons' castigates the *mignons* as 'these effeminates, ... these vile effeminates,' and an angry anonymous 1577 sonnet baldly calls them 'effeminate men.'[40] However, in the Renaissance the word 'effeminate,' when applied to a man, did not automatically connote homosexuality, but instead had a diversity of meaning it lacks today. For instance, the term sometimes designated a kind of hyper or helpless male heterosexuality, a usage that, of course, no longer exists.

Donne's remark that he is called 'effeminat' because he 'love[s] womens joyes,' in his epigram 'The Jughler' (1587?–1596?), belongs to this Renaissance tradition.[41] Furthermore, these particular accusations of 'effeminacy' were surely spurred in part by the occasional transvestite behaviour or 'other-sex appearance' of the king and the *mignons*, and transvestitism is not the same as homosexuality. The king sometimes appears in female dress in the *Mémoires-Journaux*. For instance, in a February 1577 diary entry, L'Estoile reports that 'at his jousts, tournaments, ballets, and grand masquerades, the King was usually dressed as a woman, opening his doublet to expose his throat, around which he wore a necklace of pearls and three silk collars ... like the ladies of his Court.'[42] Relatedly, the *mignons* are frequently compared to women in their finery. For example, in a July 1576 diary entry, L'Estoile remarks that 'the people detested' the *mignons* in part 'for their effeminate, lewd make-up and dress': 'These fine *mignons* wear their hair long, curled and recurled artificially, with little velvet bonnets on top of it, like the whores of the brothels.'[43]

But several factors suggest that in the *Mémoires-Journaux* 'effeminate' did signify only 'homosexual,' in the association the term came exclusively to have in later periods. First of all, the larger context of the entire work implies the point, since 'effeminate' is applied there only to men who have been clearly depicted as attracted to other men throughout it. More specifically, some *Mémoires-Journaux* texts compare the king and the *mignons* to women, not just cosmetically, but sexually (as in the allusion to 'whores' above), as if to say that their sexual desires are more properly those of heterosexual women. For example, another angry anonymous 1577 sonnet against the *mignons* uses the language of 'femaleness' to characterize them in what is clearly a homosexual situation. In this poem, another of the *Mémoires-Journaux*'s frankly bawdy pieces, the alarmed speaker writes to a friend about the *mignons*, who are sexually menacing him. He baldly and repeatedly calls them 'cunts': 'I'm as horrified of these hated cunts / As I am of fucking a common whore. / I don't dare attack these well-armed cunts. / ... The thought of being a bugger disgusts me. / ... I'm afraid of being swallowed up by these ravenous cunts. / ... I'd rather give myself to some rich widow.'[44]

Until recently, 'sodomy' in earlier discourse was usually automatically assumed to mean 'homosexuality' and also was thought to have been the most common premodern way of referring to the subject. 'Sodomy' has also figured prominently in new-inventionism, where, conversely, the term has played a major role in its denial that an earlier homosexual orientation 'existed.' New-inventionism's views that 'there was no' discrete homosexuality in the past and that sexuality was understood then only as 'acts' or 'behaviour' have been based chiefly on the facts that, in earlier laws (the situation still largely applies in present law), 'sodomy' technically referred to any biologically non-procreative sexuality (for example, heterosexual oral or anal intercourse as well as homosexuality) and that those laws use only the language of 'act' or 'behaviour' – and not, for example, of 'inclination' or 'tendency' – to refer to sexuality. (Here new-inventionism overlooks the fact that this technical 'sodomy' still includes all homosexuality but only some heterosexuality, so effectively still differentiates a separate 'homosexuality'; it also misses the circular reasoning underlying its second point – since in the Western tradition laws are directed only against acts and not against feelings, laws by definition speak about sexuality only as 'act' or 'behaviour' and not as feeling or orientation.) If we limit ourselves for the moment only to literal mentions of 'sodomy,' those in the *Mémoires-Journaux* depart in different ways from both the older and the new-inventionist views of the term. Exact 'sodomy' references appear only rarely; and, when they do, they show no influence of the legal model but instead refer only to same-sex eroticism.

The clearest example of this usage in the *Mémoires-Journaux* occurs in L'Estoile's scrapbook for 1581, in another of the work's few mentions of lesbianism. In his manuscript, shortly after the long December 1581 'Courtier's Libel' I discussed above, L'Estoile inserted a copy of an anonymous verse dialogue between two women, entitled 'La Frigarelle' after a female character in that 'Libel.' The editors do not reprint the poem, pleading its length (eighty-two verses), but they do include L'Estoile's introductory remarks as well as a biblical passage he appended to it. L'Estoile notes that this poem 'portrays the love between a great lady and a young woman' and was 'well-known at Court.' He then groups it with the preceding 'Courtier's Libel' as 'libels describing a Court of Sodom and our courtiers' and ladies' vile affections, against nature, such as we read about in the first chapter of Saint Paul's Epistle to the Romans.'[45] Then, following the poem in the manuscript, L'Estoile wrote out a French translation of verses 26 and 27 of the first chapter of Romans, the section that reads (in the 1611 King James version), 'Even their women did change the natural use into that which is against nature: and likewise also the men, leaving the natural use of the woman, burned in their lust one toward another; men with men working that which is unseemly.'[46] These materials overflow with indications that, for L'Estoile and his assumed audience, 'sodomy' signified only same-sex sexuality: his use of its language to describe the clearly homosexual content of 'La Frigarelle';

his subsequent phrase 'against nature,' an epithet traditionally reserved for homosexuality; and, of course, his final reference to Saint Paul and the care he then takes to write out the biblical verses, which refer, of course, only to same-sex eroticism and, with their terminology of 'leaving' and 'burning,' suggest a determined and passionate orientation rather than an occasional pleasurable 'act.'

The other notable mention of 'sodomy' in the *Mémoires-Journaux* does not similarly carry its own explanation within it, but its homosexual meaning is implied by its contexts as well as suggested ambiguously by its source. Another of the most noticed events in the *Mémoires-Journaux* was the king's inauguration, on 1 January 1579, of an Order of the Knights of the Holy Spirit from among his *mignons* and other followers. As I shall discuss in detail below, L'Estoile devotes a lengthy diary entry to the event and appends several scrapbook materials about it. Among these is an anonymous poem with the fully capitalized title 'GOD SPEAKS' that, according to L'Estoile, was affixed to the door of the Church of the Augustinians as the king and his knights were assembled inside for the ceremony solemnizing the Order. The poem is an adaptation of chapter 1, verses 10 to 17, of the Book of Isaiah, in which Isaiah calls the Israelites 'rulers of Sodom' and 'people of Gomorrah' before transmitting God's words of wrath to them. The opening line of 'GOD SPEAKS,' directed at the king and his favourites, declares, 'You, princes of Sodom, listen to the Lord,' mimicking in condensed form Isaiah's call to Israel.[47] The rest of the poem is devoted to God's lament about the general corruption of the Court and follows the Old Testament original fairly closely.

Since there is nothing manifestly homosexual, or even sexual, about the evils God decries in the body of the poem – when specified at all, they are religious, political, or humanitarian – this particular 'sodomy' reference might at first seem to uphold new-inventionism's view that, to earlier periods such as the Renaissance, 'sodomy' signified 'a general unlawfulness' rather than a specific 'homosexuality.'[48] On the other hand, to evoke the general kind of corruption described in the body of the poem, the poet presumably could have drawn on a number of other biblical precedents or relied on another kind of source entirely (for example, Latin satire). It may therefore have been Isaiah's 'sodomy' reference that determined the poet's use of it as his model here, a reference that to him and his milieu carried a homosexual meaning which he knew he could exploit to stoke his audience's anger at the king. This possibility seems also to be supported by the poet's significant condensation of Isaiah's opening announcement – note that he omits any reference to a 'Gomorrhan people' to focus entirely instead on the king and his favourites as 'princes of Sodom.' Even if this particular possibility must remain ambiguous, the poem's larger and immediate contexts strongly suggest that 'princes of Sodom' here can be read as roughly equivalent to our 'male homosexuals' now. The *Mémoires-Journaux* as a whole certainly supports that interpretation, with its host of other homosexual depictions of the king and his favourites. And, as I shall discuss shortly, L'Estoile inserts 'GOD SPEAKS' right after two texts in which male homosexuality is a frank and central issue. Of additional interest is the suggestion in both these 'sodomy' references that the Bible, and not the law codes stressed by new-inventionists, was the strongest influence on people's understanding and use of 'sodomy' language in the age.

If we go beyond literal 'sodomy' references here to include language that was customarily associated with it, then the *Mémoires-Journaux* does support the older view that such terminology was one of the most popular earlier ways of denoting same-sex sexuality. 'Buggery' was often used interchangeably with 'sodomy' in premodern sexual commentary – for example, in his *The Third Part of the Institutes of the Laws of England* (1628), Sir Edward Coke entitles the chapter proscribing same-sex sexuality 'Of Buggery, or Sodomy'[49] – and 'bugger' references abound in the *Mémoires-Journaux*. Occasionally the term seems simply to indicate 'a man who gets fucked,' with no necessary suggestion of sexual orientation – for example, that seems to be the meaning of the sexually menaced speaker of the 1577 sonnet I discussed earlier in which the *mignons* are repeatedly called 'cunts' when he cries, 'The thought of being a bugger disgusts me.'[50] However, most often 'bugger' in the *Mémoires-Journaux* has no association with a specific sexual role, but is rather used generically to mean something like our 'gay male' now (or, more accurately, something like the modern derogatory term 'faggot'). For example, the anonymous sonnet 'The Mignons in 1577' (the one that described Quélus as advancing at Court 'totally through his ass') labels another, Sagonne, as 'a real bugger.'[51] The same phrase is used for La Valette/d'Epernon in another long Court exposé that L'Estoile inserts right after the December 1581 'Courtier's Libel' and simply calls its 'Sequel': 'La Valette ... / ... the most beloved ... / ... is a real bugger.'[52] The king is freely called a 'bugger' in this material as well. For example, in his diary entry for 26 January 1589, when hostility to the king was at a peak after the assassinations of the Duke and Cardinal of Guise in the preceding month, L'Estoile states, 'Even all the sons of good mothers in Paris spew insults and taunts at the King, calling him "Henry of Valois, bugger, son of a whore, tyrant."'[53]

Similarly, the term adds even more spice to the bawdy 1578 'A Sainct-Luc (Cats in Cul)' sonnet I discussed earlier. In the opening line Saint-Luc is called a 'little bugger' and, after having been described as coming in the king's hand, in the last line is dubbed the 'beloved' of 'a bigger, master, bugger.'[54]

A revealing addition here is the term 'bougeron,' which sometimes appears rather than, or in tandem with, 'bougre' in the *Mémoires-Journaux*. The word no longer exists in modern French, but, since the suffix 'on' often functions in French as an intensifier of a root noun, in Renaissance French 'bougeron' seems to have meant something like what in modern terms we might call a 'superbugger.' The word seems to have functioned as a way for commentators either to make a real distinction (say, between a 'average' or 'run-of-the-mill' 'bugger' and a hyper or obsessed one) or simply to underscore their disgust through exaggeration.[55] For example, later in the December 1581 'Sequel,' La Valette/d'Epernon is called 'a superbugger' and not just 'a real bugger,' and the speaker declares 'Do you want ... / ... to last as a favourite? / First of all, you've got to be ... / ... an expert superbugger.'[56] Similarly, in an anonymous 'Ballad on the Mignons' Battle of 27 April 1578,' the battle in which Quélus and Maugiron lost their lives, one of the prototypical Parisians whom the narrator describes as speeding to view the corpses is called 'Mister Superbugger, / Great friend of the King.'[57] Additionally, another of the April 1583 quatrains attacking the king's confraternity of penitents uses both 'bougre' and 'bougeron.' Referring to the hoods that were part of the penitents's habit, it declares: 'It's a good thing / They cover their faces; / Otherwise you could spot / The buggers and superbuggers among the good men.'[58] In the same vein, the December 1581 'Sequel' describes the Court as 'Home / To buggers, whores, and superbuggers,' and the speaker of the 1578 'A Sainct-Luc (Cats in Cul)' sonnet is so angry that he calls Saint-Luc a 'superbugger' and 'little bugger' all in one breath – the poem's complete, overloaded, opening accusation reads, 'Saint-Luc, you superbugger, little bugger, you can't / Get any offspring with de Brissac.'[59]

The *Mémoires-Journaux* also contains designations of homosexuality that have left our vocabulary entirely, but that were major ways of denoting the subject in the period. One of these is the phrase 'masculine love,' which, as mentioned, I have found to have been widespread in the Renaissance as a categorical term for a male homosexual orientation. 'Masculine love' appears in another of L'Estoile's scrapbook documents about the inauguration of the Order of the Knights of the Holy Spirit. In the substantial diary entry he devotes to this event, L'Estoile reports different factions' views of the king's reasons for founding the Order. He notes that, to the general populace, the Order was an attempt by the king to strengthen his defences against the League, while to the Huguenots, in the wake of the St Bartholomew's Day Massacre, the Order was yet another royal strategy to entrap them. The League, in contrast, saw the Order as nothing more than what we might now call a covert homosexual clique and spread a public rumour to that effect. 'The others,' L'Estoile says, 'more malicious, slandering these actions of their prince, attributed them to sex and said that the entire ceremony was nothing but a cover for the love affairs of the King and his *mignons.* This was the language of the heads of the League, who intentionally spread this rumour among the people.'[60]

Immediately after these remarks, L'Estoile inserts a Latin verse dialogue by an unidentified League sympathizer, in which a prototypically named 'Stranger' to Paris queries an 'Inhabitant' as they watch the new Order parade through the streets after the investiture ceremony (it is right after these two texts that L'Estoile puts the aforementioned 'GOD SPEAKS'). A capitalized 'Masculine Love' appears in the section of the dialogue that is, in effect, a repetition of the League view of the Order that L'Estoile had reported in his diary. The 'Stranger' asks about the Order's insignia, which portrays a dove nailed to a cross. Reviewing what he sees as the mistaken meanings others have seen in the Order (the same meanings L'Estoile had discussed in his diary entry), the 'Inhabitant' answers, 'But the most perceptive / Critics ... give another meaning entirely to the cross and dove. / They see, beneath it all, / The irregularities that inflame our heroic citizens against Masculine / Love ... / The loves that dominate today, / Concealing their passion, have found a dove of Venus / Behind which ... to play at love.'[61]

In my earlier study, I discussed a variety of Renaissance texts in which 'masculine love' was used in the sense of 'a male homosexual orientation' – for example, in England in the 1610s and 1630s, in Italy in the 1620s – texts that, because of limits on their circulation, could not always have been influences on each other. Another especially revealing work here, which I did not encounter until later and which deserves careful study, is the multivolume encyclopedia-like *Theatrum Humanae Vitae* by the Swiss physician-philosopher Theodor Zwinger (1533–1588), which in its third edition of 1586 (only seven years after this L'Estoile text) contains an extensive entry for 'Libido Mascula' that lists eighty-nine individual or group examples from the Bible and classical and medieval literature and history.[62] But even without this kind of background knowledge, a reader can sense that 'Masculine Love' here refers to a substantial and recognized male homosexual orientation: partly, of course, from the erotic content of the surrounding lines ('sex,' 'passion,' 'the love affairs of the King and his *mignons*,' 'the loves that dominate today'); partly from the degree of outrage it is portrayed as provoking (as I suggested earlier, people are unlikely to become 'inflamed' over what they perceive to be only a passing 'act'); and, perhaps most interestingly, from the fact that the term is capitalized here (and is the only such phrase in the speech of the 'Inhabitant'), as if it were a recognized cultural institution.

The most popular past language for homosexuality in the *Mémoires-Journaux* is 'ganymede' terminology. The word is often used as a label for the *mignons*, signifying what we would call 'a homosexual male' now, the same general sense John Boswell found for the term in medieval writing.[63] In some Renaissance writing about homosexuality, the word 'ganymede' does refer only to the younger (and putatively passive) partner in a male homosexual relationship or act, a more limited meaning that might seem to uphold new-inventionism's view that the age had no conception of a categorical homosexual orientation. Milton uses the term in that way in notes he wrote in the early 1640s for a tragedy to be called 'Cupid's Funeral Pile,' based on the biblical story of Sodom; here he proposes portraying 'every one with mistresse, or Ganymed, gitterning along the streets, or solacing on the banks of Jordan, or down the stream.'[64] But when 'ganymede' is applied to the *mignons* in the *Mémoires-Journaux*, it typically is accompanied by some indication of a persistent, categorical, sexual orientation. For example, the August 1580 Latin poem satirizing the *mignons*' siege of La Fère – the one that ends by declaring that the *mignons* 'couldn't protect their behinds [and] can scarcely protect their fronts' – is entitled 'The Siege of the Ganymedes.'[65] Relatedly, the *mignons* are addressed as 'Shameless Ganymedes' in the bawdy 1577 sonnet that describes them as 'perverted in spirit, fucking each other.'[66] A similar recognition of 'a homosexual' is implied by an arresting construction that appears later in the ironic 1576 'Virtue and Purity of the Mignons' poem – here the *mignons* are called a 'herd / Of ganymede faces.'[67] It is difficult to tell what the author literally means by this expression, or whether he/she means to be taken literally at all – does he/she believe, for example, that there is such a thing as a 'homosexual look' or 'expression'? But for present purposes the more important point is the notion of 'a male homosexual' contained in the phrase – one cannot conceive of 'a ganymede face' without first believing that there is such a thing as 'a ganymede,' that is, a homosexual 'person.'

One of the most telling conventions in the *Mémoires-Journaux* is the use of 'ganymede' terminology to denote not just 'male homosexuals' but 'male homosexuality' as an orientation. Elsewhere in the 1576 'Virtue and Purity of the Mignons' poem, for example, one of the speaker's most forceful condemnations of the *mignons* is: 'They practise among themselves the art / Of lewd Ganymede.'[68] The phrase 'the art of ... Ganymede' seems a clear recognition in figurative terms of a male–male erotic orientation. Its use of the language of 'art' rather than 'act' implicitly portrays this eroticism it as an affective and substantial phenomenon, not a passing kind of 'behaviour.' Relatedly, the fact that the *mignons*, all age peers, 'practise' this 'art' '*among* themselves' means that 'the art of ... Ganymede' must denote a generalized 'homosexuality' rather than just the subordinate role played by the younger partner in a transient homosexual 'act.' The same meaning is conveyed by 'the rites of Ganymede,' a related phrase that appears twice in L'Estoile's Latin scrapbook documents, first in the January 1579 verse dialogue about the Order of the Knights of the Holy Spirit that I discussed above, and then in an April 1583 epigram about the confraternity of penitents. In the 1579 dialogue the Parisian 'Inhabitant' follows his remark about 'Masculine Love' by saying, 'Such sacrifices are due / Quélus and the shades that accompanied him ... / So that the rites of Ganymede will flourish again.'[69] Conversely, the 1583 epigram begins by protesting that 'these penitents have practised the rites of Ganymede for a long time.'[70] In evoking both something established and something religious (in a cogent parallel to the use of the language of 'art' in the earlier example), the phrase 'the rites of Ganymede' figuratively depicts, not a passing, unremarkable, 'act,' but a recognized category of erotic attractedness with all the substantialness and persistence of what we would now call a 'sexual orientation.'

The final earlier evocation of homosexuality that should be noted in the *Mémoires-Journaux* is not technically a 'language' but a historical reference that may reflect a shared contemporary cultural symbolism for the subject. As mentioned, Henri III's final favourite was Jean-Louis de La Valette, whom he made the Duke d'Epernon in November 1581 and whose 'possession' of the king was satirized in several of L'Estoile's scrapbook documents (the 1581 'Courtier's Libel,' the 1585 'On the Duke d'Epernon's Cancer'). Reflecting the same concern, but with greater gravity and intensity as hostility to the king and the *mignons* mounted in the last year of the king's life, in a July 1588 diary entry L'Estoile remarks, 'The League printed and circulated in Paris the *History or Tale of Peirs Gaveston,* drawing a parallel between his life and fate and the Duke d'Epernon ... This braggart Gaveston, beloved and uniquely favoured by king Edward II of England, ... was finally ... exiled from the country ... and ... beheaded. The same tragedy should befall the Duke d'Epernon in France, under King Henry III.'[71] L'Estoile does not include this pamphlet in his scrapbook, but the mere fact of its existence is doubly suggestive. First, the pamphlet seems to presume its audience's knowledge of Henri's homosexuality. Even more significant, its use of a near-topical analogy for the king's sexuality (Edward r. 1307–27) suggests that the Edward II–Gaveston story functioned widely in informed European Renaissance culture as a symbol of male homosexual attraction, indicating in that audience something like a shared body of contemporary cultural symbolism for male homosexuality.[72] The fact that the two best-known English texts about Edward–Gaveston, Marlowe's *Edward II* (first performed 1592) and Drayton's *Peirs Gaveston* (1593), could not have been influences on the League pamphlet seems further evidence of this possibility. The existence of the League's *History or Tale of Peirs Gaveston* compels us to see those English works in a new light as well, as participants in a larger Renaissance sexual tradition rather than as singular undertakings.

L'Estoile's *Mémoires-Journaux*, then, demonstrates its culture's definite awareness of what we would now call 'a homosexual orientation.' Ironically, even those few moments in the work that seem to echo or uphold a new-inventionist position end up, under closer scrutiny, supporting the opposite view. For instance, there is one text, another 1580 scrapbook satire on the *mignons* at the siege of La Fère, called 'The Mignons Depart for the Siege at La Fère,' that uses the language of 'activeness' and 'passiveness' associated with the notion of homosexuality as a kind of fixed-role 'behaviour' rather than as a categorical orientation. But the poem implicitly criticizes the *mignons* for not conforming to that pattern, calling them 'active *and* passive,' not 'active *or* passive.' In an echo of the sexual interchangeability implied in other *Mémoires-Journaux* depictions of the *mignons* such as 'fucking each other' and '[practising] among themselves the art of ... Ganymede,' the incredulous speaker of 'The Mignons Depart for the Siege at La Fère' asks, 'These perfumed poofs, active and passive, / Will they really go into battle?'[73]

There are also two prominent *Mémoires-Journaux* depictions of bisexuality; but, instead of being the mirrors of actuality new-inventionism would take them to be, both seem defences against their texts' profounder recognitions of homosexuality. Unlike homosexuality, bisexuality by definition still encompasses a significant degree of heterosexuality and is thus inherently less threatening to traditional culture – it is still at least partly comprehensible from that culture's heterosexual perspective and is also potentially 'convertible' back to that culture's authorized heterosexual norm (as in its myopia about 'sodomy' that I mentioned above, new-inventionism completely misses this reassuring aspect of bisexuality, implicitly exalting it instead as a more capacious erotic 'fluidity'). Given this comparatively tranquillizing potential of bisexuality, it would not be surprising to find the subject invoked in tandem with emphatic assertions of homosexuality. That is exactly what happens in these texts, which place a bisexual frame around two of the most resounding statements of homo-sexuality in the *Mémoires-Journaux.*

One, a satiric April 1589 sonnet about 'the rare virtues of King Henri the Third!,' technically depicts the king as bisexual, listing among those 'virtues' his 'adorning his body with rouge or powder; ... / Raping nuns [and], the unheard of thing / Making love to men like a sodomite bug-ger.'[74] But the poem's profounder concerns are clearly the king's homo-sexual transgressions. They outnumber his heterosexual ones (assuming we can take the mention of 'rouge and powder' as a coded homosexual reference), and, even more significant, the speaker's greatest consterna-tion seems reserved for the king's final homosexual offence. It is overde-scribed (in contrast to the short 'Raping nuns') and only it is 'unheard of' (an echo of the traditional claim that homosexuality is uniquely 'unspeakable'); the 'raping of nuns' is apparently more bearable to 'hear' about. The other text is the December 1581 'Courtier's Libel,' where the elaborate description of same-sex marriage at court – one of the most glaring representations of homosexuality as an orientation in the entire *Mémoires-Journaux* – is followed, surprisingly, by a bisexual orgy scene. Especially in the case of the 'Courtier's Libel,' where nothing else explains the poem's ultimate incoherence, the final or overall assertion of a bisexuality in these texts seems a mask for the opposite, deeper, and more unsettling perception that actually drives them, the realization that some people have a distinct and abiding 'homosexual orientation.'

Besides indicating a definite Renaissance awareness of a homosexual orientation, L'Estoile's *Mémoires-Journaux* are noteworthy in part for the historical changes they reflect in the public denotation of the subject. Our public vocabulary for same-sex attraction today tends to be narrow and monolithic, dominated by only two terms, 'homosexual' and 'gay'/ 'lesbian.' In contrast, in earlier periods the public denotation of homo-sexuality tended to fall into what I call a 'variegated' pattern, where vari-ous languages for same-sex desire coexisted and were used simul-taneously, but where there typically was no confusion about what those languages meant. The *Mémoires-Journaux* could serve as a paradigm of this earlier pattern of variegation, since, as indicated in my discussion, homosexuality is 'voiced' there through a range of languages – from plain descriptive statements that amount to a *de facto* terminology for the subject ('he really doesn't tend that way,' 'he likes a blond young man better'); to catch-phrases that amount to a shared shorthand ('effeminate men'); to sexual terms that technically had broader meanings but that in practice functioned as synonyms for same-sex desire ('sodomy,' 'buggery'); to categorical terms rooted in the era's practice of labelling reality affectively, in which the emotion involved in a subject was directly stated ('masculine love,' with its evocation of 'males who love other males'); to figurative terms from classical culture that were understood labels for the phenomenon ('the art of Ganymede,' 'the rites of Ganymede'). My title phrase here, the 'masculine love' of the 'princes of Sodom' 'practising the art of Ganymede,' nicely expresses this variegated pattern in microcosm.

This variegated denotation of homosexuality was not a pattern limited to the Renaissance, but continued in broad outline until at least the early twentieth century (though some terms enjoyed more favour than others at certain times and places). For example, Gibbon's influential diatribe against male–male sexuality in volume 4 of the *Decline and Fall* (1788) refers to 'the sin against nature,' 'paederasty,' and 'the lovers of their own sex' all in one page, and even Havelock Ellis and John Addington Symonds's *Sexual Inversion* (1897), often cited by new-inventionists as pivotal in the scientific 'invention' of homosexuality in the late nineteenth century, actually uses a variety of terminology for the subject, from its title phrase to 'homosexuality' to 'sodomy' to 'masculine love' to 'paederasty' to 'sexual attraction between persons of the same sex.'[75] New-inventionists would see this twentieth-century turn from multiplicity to uniformity of language about homosexuality as a shift from a 'confused' or undifferentiated earlier situation to a 'definite' and differentiated modern one.[76] But, as is clear from the *Mémoires-Journaux*, L'Estoile and his anonymous scrapbook authors knew exactly what they were referring to, no matter what particular language for male–male eroticism they were using.

No one has considered this question before, but my speculation now is that our relatively monolithic modern terminology for same-sex attraction is the product of a twentieth-century shift towards uniformity in public language of all kinds, rather than the reflection of any basic change in cultural recognition of the existence of homosexuality (which is not to say, of course, that there have not been other important changes in homosexuality's situation in society between the Renaissance and the present). It could be argued, for example, that we still have a fundamentally 'variegated' language for homosexuality today. For most of us, the first terminology we encountered about the subject was probably not the official scientistic language of 'homosexuality,' but rather the roster of informal, derogatory terms such as 'queer,' 'faggot,' 'sissy,' 'fruit,' 'lezzy,' 'dyke,' and so on. However, because of modern culture's preference for uniform and 'scientific'-sounding language for reality, such terms have now been relegated solely to private speech. Among their many differences from our own time, earlier periods like the Renaissance seem to have allowed several different kinds of vivid language – affective, figurative, and plain *de facto* statements – to coexist in their accepted public vocabulary for a subject, a situation amply illustrated in the denotation of homosexuality in the *Mémoires-Journaux*.

At the same time that they reflect this marked historical change, the *Mémoires-Journaux* also demonstrates a considerable historical continuity. In broad terms, the *Mémoires-Journaux*'s recognition of a distinct 'homosexuality' is in itself continuous with modern understanding. More particularly, it is also notable that, with the exception of their premodern terms that would need to be explicated for general contemporary readers (for example, 'masculine love,' 'ganymedes'), all of the *Mémoires-Journaux*'s *de facto* 'languages' for homosexuality (their plain descriptive phrases, their bawdy depictions) would be as understandable to late-twentieth-century readers as they were assumed to be to late-sixteenth-century ones. This accessible dimension of the *Mémoires-Journaux* poses a considerable challenge to the now-popular 'rupture' school of history, which, under the combined influence of the 'mentalités' movement and postmodernism, typically posits a profound discontinuity between past and present and casts the past as almost an ungraspable 'foreign country' (ungraspable, that is, without the intervention of the powerful critic-interpreter.).

For scholars of homosexual history, the *Mémoires-Journaux* also raises enticing questions beyond the matters of language and awareness I have explored here. Let me end by mentioning two. The first is the question of how the outspoken *Mémoires-Journaux* could have happened at all. Homosexuality had long been considered officially 'unspeakable' (as far as we know now, the first, paradoxical, 'speaking' of this ban in the post-classical West occurred in Peter Cantor's twelfth-century tract, *On Sodomy*, where Cantor denounces 'intercourse of men with men and women with women' as 'ignominious and unspeakable'), and the Renaissance was soon to witness two blatant cultural silencings of homosexual speech,

Michelangelo the Younger's heterosexualizing of Michelangelo's romantic poems to other males when he prepared his grand-uncle's poems for
their first collected edition in 1623, and John Benson's parallel bowdleriz-
ing of Shakespeare's *Sonnets* in his first collected edition of Shakespeare's
poems in 1640.[77] In addition, there are signs in the *Mémoires-Journaux* that
L'Estoile himself recognized the 'unspeakable' nature of his materials; he
sometimes crossed out revealing sexual passages in his diary and scrapbook documents, as if sensing their volatility (fortunately, he often did
not do so vigorously enough to obliterate them, so a great number
remained legible, and the editors of the authoritative *Mémoires-Journaux*
print them fully for the first time.)[78]

How, then, did the *Mémoires-Journaux* happen? (There were at least two
other, somewhat later, French works that either alluded to or directly cas-
tigated Henri III and his *mignons*: the little-known 1605 *Les Hermaphrodites*, whose author is identified by L'Estoile as one Thomas Artus; and
the contentious *Princes*, Book II of the epic poem *Les Tragiques* by the
Protestant polemicist Agrippa D'Aubigné, written sometime in the last
third of the sixteenth century, but not published until 1616.[79] But neither matches the *Mémoires-Journaux* in extent and candour.) At least two
possibilities deserve further study. One is that the era's normally private
or 'secret' speech about homosexuality was catapulted into the open by
France's manifold political, social, and religious crises at the time, which
gave observers licence to 'speak' publicly what they customarily would
have kept 'unspeakable.' This argument would also explain the markedly
different situation that prevailed for the period's best-known other
homosexual monarch, James I of England, where the comparative stability of James's reign and the security of succession after Elizabeth seem to
have kept significant social commentary about his homosexuality in
check and limited homophobic observations to other, 'safer,' public contexts (for example, Bacon's declaration in his *New Atlantis* – written in
1610, published in 1627 – that his utopian land of Bensalem had 'no
touch' of 'masculine love').[80] The other, opposite, possibility is that the
Mémoires-Journaux may not be so singular after all. Since little archival
research has yet been done on premodern documents about homosexuality, perhaps some future scholars may uncover similarly frank personal
and popular writing about the subject from elsewhere in the Renaissance
or earlier.

The other question is the influence the *Mémoires-Journaux*'s subject and
materials may have had on a Renaissance English male homosexual network or subculture. For example, the Bacon brothers, both homosexual,

were both in France during the period of the *Mémoires-Journaux*. Francis was a member of the staff of Sir Amias Paulet, the English ambassador to the French Crown, from September 1576 to February 1579 and thus could have witnessed or heard about several of the most notorious events discussed in the *Mémoires-Journaux* (for example, Quélus's death in spring 1578, the king's solemnization of the Order of the Knights of the Holy Spirit on New Year's Day 1579), as well as actually read some of the broadsides that ended up in L'Estoile's scrapbook. Anthony lived in France for the much longer period of twelve years. He arrived late in the same year his brother left and stayed through 1591. His longest period of residence in one place was from 1585 to 1590 in Montauban, where in 1586 he was arrested and convicted of same-sex sodomy and saved from a death sentence only by the personal intervention of Henri of Navarre, to whose entourage he had become close.[81] Both brothers thus could not possibly have been naïve about their age's awareness, judgment, and language for homosexuality, and it would seem likely that both were conduits for information about the sexuality at Henri's Court once back in England. The more open public discourse about homosexuality during Francis's time in France, even though all of it was hostile, may also have encouraged his relatively daring positive insinuations of homosexuality in his *Essays* (third and final edition 1625), such as his discussion of 'beautiful men' only in 'Of Beauty,' even if he had to paint an officially negative portrait of the subject in his more magisterial, philosophical work, such as *New Atlantis*.

In addition, Marlowe's little-discussed *The Massacre at Paris* (*ca* 1592), which survives only in a fragmentary text, is as much concerned with Henri III's reign as it is with the St Bartholomew's Day massacre of its title (August 1572) and seems based on contemporary reports or sources. The play also clearly implies Marlowe's sense of homosexual affinity with his subject, for example, in his decision to write the piece at all (unique among Marlowe's plays for its topicality), in the passionate addresses he has Henri deliver to the *mignons* ('Our minions, ... / No person, place, or time, or circumstance, / Shall slack my love's affection from his bent'), and in his editing of salient historical facts (he neglects to give Henri a wife in the play).[82] Since so much remains unknown about Marlowe's life, and since we lack a full text of *The Massacre at Paris*, we may never know its exact origins in his experience. The play none the less suggests a knowledge of and strong interest in Henri III and his homosexual milieu among educated, artistic, and political British male homosexuals of the period. For reasons like this, and for the other, major, ones documented here, the previously unexplored materials about the homosexuality of Henri III and his *mignons* in Pierre de L'Estoile's *Mémoires-Journaux* must be a central point of reference in any future discussions of the Renaissance's awareness and language for a homosexual orientation.

NOTES

1 Some L'Estoile materials about Henri III's homosexuality are mentioned, though not examined closely, in David Teasley, 'The Charge of Sodomy as a Political Weapon in Early Modern France: The Case of Henry III in Catholic League Polemic, 1585–1589,' *The Maryland Historian* 18 (Spring/Summer 1987), 17–30.

2 Joseph Cady, '"Masculine Love," Renaissance Writing, and the "New Invention" of Homosexuality,' in *Homosexuality in Renaissance and Enlightenment England: Literary Representations in Historical Context*, ed. Claude J. Summers, 9–40 (New York: Haworth Press/Harrington Park Press 1992; published simultaneously as a special issue of *Journal of Homosexuality* 23 [1992]), and 'Renaissance Awareness and Language for Heterosexuality: "Love" and "Feminine Love,"' in *Renaissance Discourses of Desire*, eds. Claude J. Summers and Ted-Larry Pebworth, 143–58 (Columbia: University of Missouri Press 1993). See 'Masculine Love' for more on the several points below that I can mention only briefly here, such as new-inventionism's outlook and problems, 'masculine love' as a Renaissance language for male homosexuality, the status of 'sodomy' in law, and the Renaissance's characteristically different ways of denoting reality.

3 Nancy Lyman Roelker, ed. and trans., *The Paris of Henry of Navarre as seen by Pierre de L'Estoile: Selections from his Mémoires-Journaux* (Cambridge, MA: Harvard University Press 1958), 21. For more on the content and context of the *Mémoires-Journaux* and for more biographical information about L'Estoile, see Roelker's introduction, which is the most extensive discussion of L'Estoile in English. This one-volume edition is the only English translation of L'Estoile. While concentrating on the reign of Henri IV, it also contains significant materials about Henri III, though very few of the sexual ones I discuss here.

4 *Mémoires-Journaux de Pierre de L'Estoile*, eds. G. Brunet, A. Champollion, E. Halphen, P. Lacroix, C. Read, T. De Larroque, and E. Tricotel, vol. 1 (Paris: Alphonse Lemerre 1888), 1. The complete *Mémoires-Journaux* was published over a twenty-one-year period, with different publishers, and not entirely in the chronological order of the original. All further references to vol. 1 are cited as '1.'

5 'Semé, en ce temps, à Paris, et divulgué partout' (1: 143). I have retained the

original sixteenth-century spelling and usage in quotations. Unless otherwise indicated, all translations are mine. For consultation about the French, I am grateful to Myra Jehlen, Maurice Shroder, and the late Jerome de Romanet. For consultation about the Latin, I am grateful to Jacqueline Murray and Eugene Rice.

6 'Les fous et les meschans,' 'sales et vilains' (1: 246)

7 'Le Roy s'est rendu pénitent / Pource que des enfans il n'a. / Mais, entendez pourquoi cela: / C'est à cause qu'à peine il tend' *Mémoires-Journaux de Pierre de L'Estoile*, eds. G. Brunet, A. Champollion, E. Halphen, P. Lacroix, C. Read, T. De Larroque, and E. Tricotel, vol. 2 (Paris: Librairie de Bibliophiles 1875), 114. All further references to vol. 2 are cited as '2.'

8 'Il a choisi la Bonne Dame / Pour la patrone de ses voeux: / Mais il aime mieux, sur mon ame, / Un jeune fils aux blonds cheveux' (2: 115). 'Aimer mieux' might be translated here as 'prefer,' but the term in English has implications of superficiality and changeability that are not in this text. In addition, some new-inventionists have exploited such implications to promote their view that authentic sexuality – as opposed to the culturally'invented' heterosexuality and homosexuality – is actually in continual, unchartable 'flux,' analogizing, for example, 'sexual preference' and preference in food, and I did not want inadvertently to give any support to that position by using 'prefer.' See, for instance, David M. Halperin, *One Hundred Years of Homosexuality and Other Essays on Greek Love* (New York: Routledge 1990), 26.

9 Boswell, *Christianity, Social Tolerance, and Homosexuality: Gay People in Western Europe from the Beginning of the Christian Era to the Fourteenth Century* (Chicago: University of Chicago Press 1980), 28–30

10 'Par la volonté et exprès commandement du Roy' (1: 233)

11 'Ces belles nopce' ... / De ceste Cour ... / Ma foi, ces nopces [sont] superbes! / ... Mais ce sont mariages tels, / Qu'on n'en vid jamais de pareils: / Un homme à l'autre se marie, / Et la femme à l'autre s'allie. / ... Le Roy aiant repudié / Saint-Luc, son premier marié, / Cherchant une nouvelle queste / S'allie aveques La Valette' (2: 38–9). The title in French is 'Pasquil Courtizan.'

12 'Ils sont accouplés deux à deux / D'Une assez dévote manière / Mais je les trouve vicieux / Quand ils s'enfilent' (2: 114)

13 'Le Roy estoque ses mignons, / Les fait de son lit compagnons' (2: 40)

14 'Alliés / D'un corrumpu esprit, l'un à l'autre enfilés' (1: 335)

15 'Si les fouters, foutus en fesse, / Ne veulent plus être foutus, / Mais très bien fouettés et battus, / Y trouvez-vous quelque finesse?' (2: 116). In the authoritative *Mémoires-Journaux*, the 'foutre' terms here are replaced with ellipses. I have not seen the original manuscript, which is in the Bibliothèque Nation-

ale, so I do not know whether this is censorship by the sixteenth-century writers themselves or by the nineteenth-century editors. The term is bluntly printed as 'foutre' in the one-volume twentieth-century edition of L'Estoile's journal for the reign of Henri III, whose editor had access to the original manuscript, and I adopt that usage here. See *Journal de L'Estoile pour le Règne de Henri III (1574–1589)*, ed. Louis-Raymond Lefèvre (Paris: Gallimard 1943), 346.

16 'Quélus ... / Ne trouve qu'en son cul tout son advancement' (1: 220). In the authoritative *Mémoires-Journaux* the letters of 'cul' are rearranged, and the word is printed as 'luc.' The same situation applies with the 1: 344 'cul' reference I discuss below. Again, I do not know whether this is a slight camouflaging by the sixteenth-century authors or just the product of the nineteenth-century editors' reticence. Here again I follow the usage in the 1943 Lefèvre edition, which prints both as 'cul' (154, 236).

17 'En ... le cul ... marchand' (1: 344)

18 'Mignons, ... / Ne battez le dos seulement, / Mais le Q qui a fait l'offense' (2: 113). The 1943 Lefèvre edition prints 'Q' as 'cul' (328), but the meaning of 'Q' seems clear enough here.

19 'Le derrière, / ... soit la manière, / De nostre Cour' (1: 345)

20 'Samson force aux cheveux avoit, / Et Maugeron l'eust au derrière' (1: 247)

21 'Quélus n'entend pas la manière / De prendre les gens par devant; / S'il eust pris Bussy par derrière, / Il lui eust fourré bien avant' (1: 232)

22 'Sua nam qui terga tueri / Non potuit, vix vix anteriora potest' (1: 368)

23 'La mariée estoit laide ... et contrefaite' (1: 233)

24 'Tu ne peux, ... Saint-Luc, / Recevoir de Brissac aucun fruit ne lignée; / Ta semence se perd en la main pottelée / De ce Grand qui promet te faire nouveau duc' (1: 340)

25 'Grand nombre d'Epitaphes, Tombeaux, Vaudevilles et de ... poésies latines et françoises ... furent semés et divulgués à Paris et à la Cour' (1: 244)

26 'La Mort ... / ... avoir destruit un oeuvre si parfait,' 'On eu mon coeur en sepulture' (1: 293)

27 'Regardez-moi du ciel, voyez vostre Henri, / Triste, pensif, songeant, solitaire et marri, / Qui son ame et sa vie en larmoiant distille' (1: 293)

28 'Que ne puis-je muer ... mon corps ... / Pour m'envoler vers eux ... / ... marchant dans le ciel comme ils font, / Jouir de leur présence et voir tousjours leur face!' (1: 294)

29 'Esprits, en qui je pense et repense à toute heure, / Qu'en songes je contemple et voi toutes les nuits, ... / Que vivre absent de vous je ne veux ni ne puis ... / Mon ame ne fait rien, sinon penser à vous ... / Mon aureille ne peult que vos ... noms entendre' (1: 294–5)

30 'Par son commandement, à ce qu'on disoit' (1: 280); 'En fist cas et le serra lui-mesmes en son cabinet' (1: 295)

31 '[Le] Roy ... l'alloit tous les jours voir, et ne bougeoit du chevet de son lit, et ... avoit promis aux chirurgiens qui le pensoient cent mil francs au cas qu'il revinst en convalescence ... Nonobstant lequelles promesses, il passa de ce monde en l'autre, aiant toujours en la bouche ces mots, ... "Ah! mon Roy, mon Roy!" sans parler autrement de Dieu ne de sa Mère. A la vérité, le Roy portoit à Maugiron et à lui une merveilleuse amitié, car il les baisa tous deux morts, fist tondre leurs testes et emporter et serrer leurs blonds cheveux, osta à Quélus les pendans de ses aureilles, que lui-mesme auparavant lui avoit donnés et attacchés de sa propre main.

'Telles et semblables façons de faire (indignes à la vérité d'un grand Roy et magnanime comme il estoit) causèrent peu à peu le mespris de ce Prince, et le mal qu'on vouloit à ses mignons qui le possédoient' (1: 244)

32 'Regis amorem, / Magnus amor Regis' (1: 251)

33 'Quélus estoit chéri uniquement de vous' (1: 253)

34 'Trop aimé de son Roy' (1: 253)

35 'ses ... enfans' (2: 24)

36 'Le grand Roy des Gaules / A du nom de ses fils ses mignons adopté; / C'est bien raison, puisque ce père ils ont porté / Comme Aenée fit le sien, sur leurs dos et espaules' (2: 115)

37 'Du Cancer Du Duc Despernon' (2: 194)

38 'Un chancreux mal de gorge'; 'Le Roy incontinent le fust voir, et lui-mesme le feit soingner et panser' (2: 194)

39 'Le Lyon, le Belier, la Vierge, les Poissons, / La Chèvre, le Taureau, l'Archer, ni les Bessons, / Ne se ressentent plus de sa chère présence: / Il n'aime, ne chérit qu'un seul Cancer' (2: 195)

40 'Les Vertus et Propriétés des Mignons'; 'ces efféminés, ... ces vilains efféminés' (1: 143, 148–9). 'Gens efféminés' (1: 337)

41 *The Complete Poetry of John Donne*, ed. John T. Shawcross (New York: New York University Press 1968), 165. For more on 'effeminate' in a male heterosexual context in the Renaissance, see my 'Renaissance Awareness and Language for Heterosexuality.'

42 'Le Roy faisoit jouxtes, tournois, ballets et force masquarades, où il se trouvoit ordinairement habillé en femme, ouvroit son pourpoint et descouvroit sa gorge, y portant un collier de perles et trois collets de toile, ... ainsi que lors les portoient les dames de sa Cour' (1: 180)

43 'Du peuple, auquel ils estoient fort odieux, ... pour leurs fards et accoustre-mens efféminés et impudiques'; 'Ces beaux Mignons portoient leurs cheveux longuets, frisés et refrisés par artifices, remontans par dessus leurs petis bonnets de velours, comme font les putains du bordeau' (1: 142–3)

44 'Je n'ause chevaucher une putain publique, / Tant je conçoi d'horreur de ces cons diffamés. / Je ne m'ause attaquer à ces grands cons armés. / ... J'abhorre d'estre bougre ... / Et crains de m'engouffrer dans ces cons affamés. / ... Je veux donc me donner à quelque riche veufve' (1: 337–8). As in the 'cul'/'luc' transposition mentioned earlier, in the authoritative *Mémoires-Journaux*, the letters of 'cons' are rearranged, and the word is printed as 'snoc.' With the same proviso as earlier, I again follow the usage in the 1943 Lefèvre edition, which prints it as 'cons' (234).

45 'Traictant des amours d'une grande dame avec une fille, ... à la Cour ... il estoit commun'; 'Pasquils descrivans une Cour de Sodome, et les affections vilaines et contre nature de nos courtizans et courtizannes, telles que nous les lisons en S. Pol aux Romm., Ier chap' (2: 54)

46 The *Mémoires-Journaux* editors include the information about the appended passage from Romans in a footnote. Though indicating that it appears in French in the manuscript, they render the passage in Latin in the book: 'Feminae eorum immutaverunt naturalem usum in eum usum qui est contra naturam. Similiter autem et masculi, relicto naturali usu feminae, exaserunt in desi-deriis suis in invicem, masculi in masculos turpitudinem operantes ...' (2: 54).

47 'DIEU PARLE'; 'Vous, princes de Sodome, escoutez le Seingneur' (1: 301)

48 See Michel Foucault, *The History of Sexuality*. Volume I: *An Introduction* (New York: Pantheon 1978), 38.

49 Coke, *The Third Part of the Institutes of the Laws of England*, 6th ed. (London: W. Rawlins 1680), 58

50 'J'abhorre d'estre bougre' (1: 337)

51 'Sagonne, est un peu bougre' (1: 220)

52 'Suitte': 'La Valette ... / ... le plus aimé ... / ... est un peu bougre' (2: 48)

53 'N'y avoit-il fils de bonne mère à Paris qui ne vomist injures et brocards contre le Roy, qu'ils apeloient "Henri de Valois, bougre, fils de putain, tiran"': *Mémoires-Journaux de Pierre de L'Estoile*, ed. G. Brunet, A. Champollion, E. Halphen, P. Lacroix, C. Read, T. De Larroque, and E. Tricotel, vol. 3 (Paris: Librairie des Bibliophiles 1876), 242. All further references to vol. 3 are cited as '3.'

54 'Petit bougre'; 'chéri d'un plus grand bougre maistre' (1: 340–1)

55 The contemporary lexicographer Randle Cotgrave glosses 'Bougiron' and 'Bougre' as equivalent to each other ('A Buggerer, a Sodomite') in his 1611 *A Dictionarie of the French and English Tongues* (repr. Columbia: University of South Carolina Press 1950), n.p. Similarly, Wayne R. Dynes calls 'bougeron' a variant of 'bougre' in his entry on 'Buggery' in *Encyclopedia of Homosexuality*, ed. Wayne R. Dynes, 2 vols. (New York: Garland 1990), vol. 1: 173. But the usage in the *Mémoires-Journaux* argues for giving 'bougeron' a qualitatively distinct meaning.

56 'Suitte': 'un bougeron,' 'un peu bougre' (2: 49); 'Veux-tu estre ... / ... des favorits retunu? / Premier te faut estre ... / ... bon bougeron' (2: 50)

57 'Vaudeville sur le Combat des Mignons le 27e Avril 1578': 'Voici là Monsieur Bougeron, / Qui estoit grand ami du Roy' (1: 245)

58 'Ils sont advisés et bien sages / D'ainsi se couvrir les visages; / Car on verroit, entre les bons, / Les bougres et les bougerons' (2: 114)

59 'Suitte': 'Bougres, putains, et bougerons: / Au demeurant' (2: 53); 'Tu ne peux, bougeron, petit bougre Saint-Luc, / Recevoir de Brissac aucun fruit ne lignée' (1: 340)

60 'Les autres, plus malins, calomnians les actions de leur prince, le référoient à la volupté, et disoient que toute ceste cérimonie n'éstoit que le masque des amours du Roy and de ses mignons. Qui éstoit le langage des chefs de la Ligue, lesquels, à desseins, faisoient courrir ce bruit entre le peuple' (1: 298)

61 'Hospes,' 'Incola'; 'Naris at emunctae ... / Censores, aliam multo crucis atque colombae / Adsignant causam et repetunt ab origine prima / Dissidia Heroas quae acuere adversus Amorem / Masculum ... / Hinc memores irae qui nunc dominantur amores, / Invenisse viam obvolucro Cytheraea columbae, / Qua fieret ... lusus amoris' (1: 299)

62 Theodor Zwinger, *Theatrum Humanae Vitae*, 3d. ed. (Basil, 1586), 2301–4.

63 Boswell, *Christianity, Social Tolerance, and Homosexuality*, ch. 9 passim.

64 *Complete Prose Works of John Milton*, ed. Don M. Wolfe, 8 vols. (New Haven and London: Yale University Press 1953–82), vol. 8: 559

65 'In Catamithos Obsides' (1: 367)

66 'Ganimèdes effrontés' (1: 335)

67 'Troupeau / De faces ganimédiennes' (1: 147)

68 'Entre eux ils prattiquent l'art / De l'impudique Ganimède' (1: 146)

69 'Quelusiis tales et concomitantibus umbris / Deberi inferias, ... / ... vigeant ... iterum Ganimedis honores' (1: 299)

70 'Poenitet hos coluisse diu Ganimedis honores' (2: 116)

71 'La Ligue fist courir et imprimer à Paris l'*Histoire ou Fable de Pierre de Gaverston*, de la vie et fortune duquel elle faisoit un parangon avec le duc Desparnon ... Ce gascon, Gaverston, aimé et uniquement favorizé du roy Edouard II d'Angleterre, ... fut finablement ... exilé du pays ... et ... décapité, le duc Desparnon acheveroit ceste même tragoedie en France, sous le Roy Henri III' (3: 174–5)

72 Teasley (23) mentions that, in July 1588, the League preacher Jean Boucher published a *Histoire Tragique et Mémorable de Gaverston* that also compares Henri/d'Epernon with Edward/Gaveston. Teasley does not cite his source, but the National Union Catalogue does list such a work in the collection of the Folger Library (which I was unable to consult). It is not clear if this is the same

as the work mentioned by L'Estoile. L'Estoile mentions no other League work on this subject in his diary for that month, but the title L'Estoile cites is not the same as this one, and L'Estoile does not mention Boucher. If there were indeed two different publications in Paris that month making this comparison, that would only give stronger support to the point that the Edward/ Gaveston relationship was a widely recognized symbol of male homosexuality in the period.

73 'Des Mignons Allans Au Siége De La Fère'; 'Ces fraizés mus[e]quins, agens et patients, / Iront-ils à l'assault?'(1: 363)

74 'Les rares vertus du Roy Henri Troisiesme!'; 'Or' de rouge son corps, or' de blanc, tapisser; ... / Violer les nonnains [et], ô chose inaudite! / En bougre sodomit' les hommes embrasser' (3: 284)

75 Edward Gibbon, *The History of the Decline and Fall of the Roman Empire*, ed. J.B. Bury, vol. 4 (London: Methuen 1909), 536; Ellis and Symonds, *Sexual Inversion* (1897; repr., New York: Arno Press 1985), 1, 4, 6, 8

76 See, for instance, Michel Foucault's contrasting view that 'sodomy' in earlier discourse about sexuality was an 'utterly confused category': *The History of Sexuality*. vol 1: 101.

77 The exact date of 'On Sodomy' is unknown; Cantor died in 1192. 'On Sodomy' is translated and reprinted in full by John Boswell in *Christianity, Social Tolerance, and Homosexuality*, 375–8; the quoted phrases appear on 376 and 377. For the bowdlerizings by Michelangelo the Younger and John Benson, and for more on the entire tradition of homosexuality's 'unspeakableness,' see my 'Censorship,'in *The Gay and Lesbian Literary Heritage*, ed. Claude J. Summers, 151–6 (New York: Henry Holt 1995).

78 The editors place such materials between asterisks in the text, but it does not seem necessary to duplicate that practice here. Introduction, 1: vii.

79 For *Les Hermaphrodites*, see Donald Stone, Jr, 'The Sexual Outlaw in France, 1605,' *Journal of the History of Sexuality* 2 (1992), 597–608. For *Princes*, see Henry A. Sauerwein, Jr, *Agrippa D'Aubigné's LES TRAGIQUES: A Study in Structure and Poetic Method* (Baltimore: Johns Hopkins University Press 1953).

80 For more on Francis Bacon here and below, see my 'Sir Francis Bacon,' in *The Gay and Lesbian Literary Heritage*, 70–1. In my point about James I here, I clearly differ with Robert Shephard's article in this volume, 'Sexual Rumours in English Politics: The Cases of Elizabeth I and James I,' which accepts a new-inventionist understanding of the situation.

81 The chief source for Anthony Bacon's biography from his years in France until his death has been his correspondence, and, since this incident went unmentioned in it, its existence was unknown until Daphne duMaurier discovered it in the Archives Départmentales at Montauban in 1973 during her research for

her biography of the Bacon brothers and their circle. See her *Golden Lads: Sir Francis Bacon, Anthony Bacon and Their Friends* (Garden City, NY: Doubleday 1975), 49–55, 227, 231.

82 *The Massacre at Paris*, III, ii, 16–20. Marlowe, *The Complete Plays*, ed. J.B. Steane (Harmondsworth: Penguin 1969), 561

Masculinities and Homosexualities in French Renaissance Accounts of Travel to the Middle East and North Africa

GUY POIRIER

During the past two decades, many scholarly publications have established that French Renaissance travel accounts are both different from those written by Spaniards and English explorers and embedded in a literary discourse that is linked to what today we call literature, philosophy, geography, and history. Travel accounts were read by a wide range of people, and even the king had his official cosmographers. Unlike their Spanish counterparts, which – in many cases, and in addition, of course, to Las Casas's – witnessed the Conquista from a European point of view, French travel accounts could rely only on ephemeral attempts to establish settlements in Brazil, Florida, and, later, Nova Scotia. As Claude Lévi-Strauss has demonstrated in his *Tristes tropiques*,[1] many of the French explorers who were part of those first enterprises could not have survived without the help of Native people. At the same time, these same travellers had to place into perspective their own European culture, and thus they became reliable sources of modern anthropological data.

As Atkinson already stated at the beginning of the century,[2] the French were looking less towards America than towards the mysterious East: Jerusalem, the Middle East, and the Ottoman Empire – which was, at the beginning of the sixteenth century, at its high point. Unfortunately, the open-mindness that characterizes travel accounts to the Americas cannot always be found in works describing the manners of Middle Eastern Muslim empires, something that may certainly have much to do with geographical proximity and the inevitable struggle for commercial and maritime routes.

In fact, since the Middle Ages, the image of the Muslim had developed in France along different patterns and at different levels. In the twelfth century, two types of discourse were simultaneously produced. One, a public discourse, was composed and used mostly by authors and artists dealing with the *Chansons de geste*. For them, Saracens were not necessarily perverted people, but, rather, enemies. Christian writers were in fact generally ignorant of Eastern manners and religion. A theological and official discourse also developed, which was not necessarily better informed. This second discourse slowly took the place of the first one and was inclined to discuss, in part, Muslim religious beliefs and behaviour.[3] Differences in sexual behaviour between the Christian and the Muslim were emphasized and became one of the main aspects of the split between the Christian identity and that of the Other, the Muslim.

The fall of Constantinople in 1453 and the penetration of Turkish armies into Europe in the following century were determining factors in the construction of the image of the Muslim, not only as the Other, but also as an Other who could one day wipe Christendom from the face of the earth. Like Venice, France did not always consider the Ottomans mortal enemies. When Charles V of Spain became emperor, in 1519, Francis I found in Suleiman the Magnificent a precious ally.[4] Such an unnatural union was continued by subsequent Valois kings, though it did not always serve their reputations well. While Protestants and Ultra-Catholics decided to contest the monarchy, during the Religious Wars, the Turkish file was ready to be used against the king: if an ally could be found in the Turkish leader, did it mean that the kingdom of France looked increasingly like the Ottoman Empire? The pamphlet *La France-Turquie* presents a different hypothesis along those lines. According to the authors of this work, a certain Chevalier Poncet had advised the Queen Mother to run the country as the Ottoman Empire was run: the king should surround himself only with those people whom he had chosen, and who would always agree with him; he should also show intolerance for religions other than his own.[5] A second pamphlet is bound together with the first one and bears the title 'Pour servir de contre-poison à l'Anti-pharmaque, du Chevalier Poncet.' It, of course, defends the king's reputation and point of view. One of the arguments it advances opens a new door to our own comprehension of the vision that the French had of the Ottomans, and suggests how a set of images, not logically linked to one another, could well be associated within a particular social discourse. The extract compares the situation of the Chevalier Poncet, who supposedly had lived for some time in Turkey and then brought Ottoman manners back to France, to the way the sin of *bougrerie* (buggery), which travellers to Rome were often accused of helping to spread, was introduced to the kingdom. If we set aside the political aspects of the pamphlet and the response, we note that the association of ideas and images – from Turkey to Rome, and from political life to buggery – reveals how sixteenth-century pamphleteers could construct stereotypes. Why such links could be drawn is not, however, obvious, but our reading of travel accounts will help to establish a better understanding of their discursive construction.

Other surprising constructions and associations can be identified in philosophical and non-canonical literatures. Frank Lestringant already noted the change in some writers' feelings about the Turks in the middle of the century, probably owing to both a rejection of the antiquity motives and anger directed towards Eastern Orthodox Christians who were too weak to keep the Turks out of Europe.[6] While reading Brantôme, one also discovers how the French borrowed yet another Middle Eastern sin that by Counter-Reformation standards was unacceptable. In the *Dames galantes*, the abbé describes how Sapphism, a fashionable practice of some of the ladies at the court, came from the sexual practices of Turkish women.[7]

The semiotics of the images of the sultan, as well as of North Africans, can be confusing. The study of their origins in accounts written by Renaissance travellers and cosmographers shows how the close-up pictures given by both actual and second-hand witnesses were the keystone to the system we have described, and also carried information that was incorporated into the image of the Muslim as perceived by French Renaissance women and men. At first, the stereotypes linked to the sexual practices of the Muslim all look alike. Clarence Dana Rouillard noted in 1941 how, generally speaking, Muslim people were described: 'All these men live on a false appearance of virtue, are for the most part sodomists, and lead a "vie de bestes brutes."'[8] Similar remarks are made by Guy Turbet-Delof about the way the sexual life of North Africans was described; two words could express it: extreme lubricity.[9] Strangely enough, the various allusions to acts against nature found in accounts of travel to the Muslim countries are not all comparable. If we try to classify them and imagine a typology, we realize that even if, generally speaking, the Muslim Turks or Arabs are accused of being abominable sodomites, some extracts give more information about certain lifestyles. Moreover, even if, for many early sixteenth-century authors and pamphleteers, the difference between Ottomans and Arabs was not always clear,[10] two types of allusions could then be identified; the first one linked to the sultan of the Ottoman Empire, and the other to the Arabic priests and hoteliers of North Africa.

The work of Georgiewitz, many times read, used, and copied by the authors of travel accounts during the sixteenth century, could well be seen as a first level of discourse or a matrix. He was an important witness of the presence of the Turks in Southeastern Europe and obviously influenced Western writers. The abuse of Christian children captured by the Turks is a well-known theme used by many authors, each one adding a few more details to the basic text. Georgiewitz points out that the Turks abuse children – sometimes those six and seven years of age – of both genders, qualifying them as sodomites and describing their desire as 'abominables volontez contre nature.'[11] The same type of description, exhibiting a high level of anxiety, can be found in Henry Pierre's translation of the Münster *Cosmographie universelle*, which presents information primarily about the horrific destiny of the young men captured by the Turks. The most beautiful were castrated – to the peril of their life – and then become interesting for only one reason: they pleased their master and allowed him to exhibit his voluptuous desire.[12]

It seems obvious, at first, that the horror inspired by the travel accounts and, at the same time, probably felt by authors such as Georgiewitz and Münster, served a similar purpose: to convince the European monarchies of the necessity to start a Holy War and to minimize the Turks' power. It is also true that most of the anxiety expressed or embedded in the texts describing such behaviours was more a response to a passive situation imposed on the Christian children than to examples of an act against nature. In a way, the uncontrolled violence of acts against nature seems to be the logical companion of lasciviousness.

Nicolas de Nicolay, a French traveller sent by Francis I to the Empire of Suleiman, provides more details about the different aspects of the Turkish abominations. His description of the sexual behaviour of the Turks reproduces, in part, the usual vocabulary: 'paillardise,' 'sodomie,' 'larrecins,' and so on.[13] But Nicolas de Nicolay not only describes the different cruelties committed by the Turks, but also gives a well-balanced and quite vivid description of an anti-world. The Christian city of Constantinople is undergoing a metamorphosis. The Hagia Sophia Church is transformed into a brothel for both female and male prostitutes.[14] A similar phenomenon takes away the Christian nature of the children captured by the Ottomans or given as an annual tribute to the sultan. These youngsters are not to be devoured by the Minotaur, but rather enter the anti-world of the seraglio. The youngsters then go from the liberty given by nature to a bestial enslavement. Many symbols are turned inside out: baptism becomes circumcision, and love for parents is transformed into a raving madness against their former Christian fellows. Castrated in order to take away all the marks of their manhood, they become, finally, when their beauty vanishes, eunuchs, servants, or cooks.

If we browse various travel accounts, it is more and more obvious that the destiny of young Christians is more complex than first identified. Some travel accounts give a description of the life of young Christians without revealing too many anxious details.[15] According to François de Belleforest, however, the Turks know quite well how effectively to select young Christians who will become close advisers to the sultan: the physiognomy of a young man has no secrets for them and reveals whether a young person will serve the sultan adequately.[16] It seems also that the tragic aspect of those descriptions is maximized when we reach the end of the century. For example, René de Lusinge does not hesitate to write extensively about the fate of Christian slaves captured by Muslim armies and pirates. According to his sources, young children (who have just reached six years of age) are abused as their mothers cry in despair. The anxiety is then shared by new witnesses, and the level of anxiety in the overall situation is raised.[17]

For French travellers, the seraglio was also a constant source of interest and curiosity. Nicolas de Nicolay and Philippe Du Fresne-Canaye are only two of those who tried to give the best and most complete description of these sites. Different attempts to reveal the secrets of the seraglio and of Muslim women – the two seem to go together – were undertaken by Nicolas de Nicolay.[18] Portraits of Turkish women were added to his travel account, and intrusions were made into women's private discussions. Du Fresne-Canaye also tried to penetrate the private world of the sultan, to satisfy a certain voyeurism,[19] but also to minimize the secrecy surrounding the sultan's majestic court. Such an interest also shows that the seraglio was obviously an eroticized site, where the sultan, his concubines, and eunuchs were revolving in a mysterious pattern.

According to Malek Chebel, the eunuch of the seraglio symbolizes for Muslim people an early state in the ageing of the normally constituted man.[20] He is the reflection, in other words, of the pre-nubile sultan who still does not have access to his desire. The image has to be used with caution, but it is quite surprising how abused and sodomized Christian male children first lose their symbol of virility, and then are put at the very centre of the sultan's private, secret, but also prestigious living area. Many reasons could be found in order to explain the interest, as well as the contradictory descriptions of life in the seraglio: one could believe that the imprisonment of the castrated young Christians and the fear that is produced mirror the situation of Christians who fear the power of the Other. From his capture to his life as an eunuch and renegade, the young captive can also be seen as an eschatological symbol. His description, sometimes limited to a few details, will of course have a dramatic effect on the reader. As for travellers such as Nicolay and Cayet, the interest in the seraglio makes it possible to reveal, and at the same time control, a situation.

It seems obvious to we who read travel account after travel account that the simple act of sodomy does not appear in an isolated pattern. Moreover, a complex discourse about manners and desire is intimately linked to it. The impact of the act itself refers not only to God, but especially to a questioning of Christian masculinities and eroticism. Montaigne, in Essay III, 3, is not far from such an affirmation, while he tries to extricate the roots of masculine and feminine beauty: women have their own, but men's is mixed with theirs; and the Great Turk knows about it, since he thanks his young lads at the age of twenty-two.[21]

Another aspect is evident in François de Belleforest and Artus Thomas. The former, in his *Histoire universelle*, violently attacks Greek antiquity. According to him, Athens helped to spread immoral and bestial laws and manners. Greek philosophers such as Aristippe and Epicure are the ones who turned men into beasts without reason.[22] The same kind of accusation is to be found in Belleforest's translation of Münster's *Cosmographiae universalis*. What he called 'detestables amours' is, however, not really clear to us, for it is unusual for Renaissance writers to associate love affairs with homoerotic relationships.[23] We can find a few examples of this in political pamphlets written during the final years of Henri III's reign. It is obvious that people who were part of the intellectual life of the time knew quite well from Plato's *Symposium* or from translations of Anacreon's and Sappho's poetry that love relationships between people of the same sex were part of the private and public life of ancient Greece. At this point, what would be surprising is the association made between 'detestables amours' and the acts against nature committed by the Turks. In fact, another step is needed by Belleforest to establish the link, and he finds it in the difficult political situation and the effeminization of some Greek people – the Cypriots, for example – that slowly prepared the decline of the Greek cities and the invasion of the Balkans by the Turks.[24] The same logical pattern is to be found in Artus Thomas's edition of Chalcondyle's work.[25] Such a filiation between antiquity and the Muslim religion provided a link between the sodomite gods of the ancient Greeks and the beliefs of the Turks. Finally, one could believe that, during the second part of the sixteenth and early part of the seventeeth centuries, Christian writers of travel accounts did not have available to them a wide variety of suitable images and references. Looking towards the Middle East brought only counter-examples that forced them to reaffirm their own identity – the past belonged to the pagan Greeks, their sodomite gods, and their 'detestables amours'; the future, with the perceived Turkish threat, could easily become a reflection of the past. The Christian Eastern Roman Empire, which fell between the pagan past and the Turkish future, could also be placed, according to Frank Lestringant, into this equation. The Orthodox Schism, certainly seen by the French as a prelude to the decline of Christianity in Eastern countries and to the sixteenth-century French Reformation, provided another basis on which to accuse the Greeks of sins similar to those of the Turks.[26]

If we move from the Ottoman Empire to the Arabic countries, the vision of the Other's sexuality changes again. The brutal sodomite reappears between Constantinople and Fez as a stereotype, as a simple characteristic that is automatically associated with Muslim Arabs. Religious men are stigmatized to a greater extent, primarily because they seduce young men during different types of public ceremonies associated with weddings or funerals.[27]

Most of the travel accounts I have examined were written by Christians and Europeans who did not necessarily travel to the countries they described. The work of many cosmographers consisted primarily in translating or copying what an original traveller had written, patching the holes in the narration with extracts sometimes taken from the Ancients.

One travel account, however, is different. It is the *Historiale description de l'Afrique* by Jean Léon L'Africain. Though born in Spain, L'Africain lived part of his life in North Africa. Captured by Christian corsairs, he was offered to Pope Leo X, and eventually converted to Christianity. L'Africain's work is usually seen by scholars as one of the last examples of an act of communication between Western powers and North African Muslim countries. After this date, the European countries would slowly impose their own thoughts and rules on contacts with North Africa.[28] Because of his personal experience, we would expect Léon L'Africain to describe the different aspects of North African sexuality from a more direct and better-informed point of view, but at first glance his descriptions seem more inclined to elicit a strong reaction from his readers. Aware of this, he literally excuses himself for such descriptions, calling on his duty as a historian to write truthfully about what he saw.[29]

What is most surprising in L'Africain's work is the chapter on Fez, a city that is linked to a more complex set of images. Here, L'Africain describes a type of hotel inhabited by transvestite men called 'Elchevas.' It is not easy to imagine what exactly those hostelries were. Obviously, they formed part of a network of institutions where travellers and sick or lonely people could find shelter. The hoteliers, sometimes wearing women's clothes, also imitated women in gesture and voice. L'Africain indicates that they lived with male partners as couples.[30] Moreover, even if the Elchevas were despised by the population of Fez, they had important social duties: they sold wine, and served in the army as cooks. With this description L'Africain reveals the existence of a true homosexual subculture. Unlike the accounts describing the Ottomans' cruelty, and more akin to descriptions of the ancient Greeks, L'Africain's depiction of the Elchevas reveals that they were effeminate men who did not hesitate to behave and dress as women. They do not, however, appear to be similar to the American 'berdache.' L'Africain, who obviously was well acquainted with the sociological organization of Maghrebin culture, insists mostly on the marginalization of the Elchevas.

As we have already seen, the episode of the Fez hostelries was used and rewritten by other cosmographers. Belleforest, in his version of Münster's *Cosmographiae universalis*, introduced an interesting comparison with European brothels. He compared Christian and Muslim legislation and indicated his surprise that the latter was more severe than the former. Obviously, Belleforest was not surprised by the description of such a subculture and could relate to a social pattern almost non-existent at that time in Europe.[31] One could, however, try to imagine how Belleforest would have understood such an extract if the marginalization of brothels had not already started at that time in France. We know, for a fact, that most municipal brothels closed in France during the sixteenth century, probably under pressure from the Reformation and Counter-Reformation, but probably also to reduce the spread of syphilis.

Other cosmographers read the Fez hostelries episode differently and mixed up some aspects of it. For Gabriel Chappuys, for example, many different groups of people seem to live in what he calls 'hospital' and 'hostelry.' From what could be read in his *Estat, description et gouvernement des royaumes et republiques du monde*, both institutions seem to be part of the same complex, where sick but poor nobles and strangers, a few foreign doctors, fools, widows, and Elchevas live, all of whom could today be seen as marginals.[32]

It seems more and more obvious that the structure of the different imageries or stereotypes describing or applied to Muslim unnatural sexualities is more complex than we first imagined. More than just an attribute associated with a group of pagans, the practice of sodomy has more to do, in the case of the Ottoman Empire and the hostelries of Fez, with behaviours repressed by Christianity, theatrical use of Christian fate, and highly symbolic sites. The seraglio, but also the Fez hostelries, and even the Christian cities brutally invaded at night by child rapists, become vivid 'lieux de mémoire,' to which different writers can appeal effectively to produce distress in their readers. Within those sites, no strict rules of description or veracity prevail. The different symbolic extracts wander from text to text, with details that have been moved around and sometimes even mixed up. The important aim of such passages was to remind readers that these 'lieux' existed, that they were linked by little-known lands – whose inhabitants are vaguely described – and that they could swallow Christendom.

The anxiety that originates from this complex of fearful sites has not much to do, surprisingly, with fear of God's punishment. In French political pamphlets written during the Religious Wars, for example, Protestants or immoral princes were cursed and accused of being the cause of both natural disasters and political troubles. In the case of the Ottomans, the logic is different and the apprehension more pervasive. The different acts against nature are described as more intimate phenomena.

It is almost as if Christianity was once again put into a situation similar to that of the Apostles. As the Reformation was trying to return to the faith of the primitive Church, those early fears about the identity of Christians and their reactions to living among pagans were once again appearing. Christian cities occupied by the Muslims and the seraglio, where young castrated Christians were trapped forever in their juvenile bodies, become not only an object of voyeurism, but also a battlefield that had to be thoroughly known so as to allow Christians to face it and prevent it. As scholars and writers in the later Renaissance became more and more sceptical about the moral value of their own ties to antiquity, the Muslim world could well have been seen and imagined as an example of what Christianity could have become without the Reformation. Muslims then became brothers, siblings who shared a common past but who had become dreadful enemies. The Renegade – which will be the last stage of the metamorphosis of the young Christian – becomes the figure in which all fears of the Brother could crystallize.

Should we then be surprised to see how Belleforest used the Fez hostelry episode in order to show the way to legislate against European brothels? Obviously not, especially if we follow our logic. Fez, like ancient Rome or Paris, faced the same moral problems. In North Africa, however, heterosexual prostitution is transformed into same-sex prostitution. Such a parallelism of the two brotherhoods is not necessarily sterile. The French translation of Léon L'Africain's *Historiale description de l'Afrique* and Belleforest's works show that French readers were still curious about *mirabilia*. The Renaissance desire for knowledge, its juvenile curiosity so well defined by Charpentier, Céard, and Mathieu-Castellani,[33] represents perhaps a unique moment during which France had the chance to come to know Muslim countries in a better way. Soon replaced at the beginning of the seventeenth century by the Counter-Reformation need to convert, and by a new exoticism, Renaissance curiosity about the Ottoman Empire and the Maghreb countries could finally be seen as a key to the Muslim world, a key that could well be compared to the ephemeral but so philosophically rich attempts of sixteenth-century France to colonize and write the New World.

NOTES

The research that led to the writing of this article was funded by the Social Science and Humanities Research Council of Canada. The author also wishes to thank Jacqueline Murray and Konrad Eisenbichler for their help editing the English version.

1 Claude Lévi-Strauss, *Tristes tropiques* (Paris: Plon 1955); see the account of the Villegaignon and Léry stay in the Bay of Rio de Janeiro.
2 Geoffrey Atkinson, *Les Nouveaux Horizons de la Renaissance française* (Paris: Droz 1927), 11
3 Cf. Norman Daniel, 'La Persistance des perceptions médiévales du monde arabe,' in *D'un Orient l'autre*, vol. I (Paris: CNRS 1991), 75–84.
4 Cf. Victor Segesvary, *L'Islam et la Réforme* (Geneva: L'Âge d'Homme 1977).
5 *La France-Turquie, c'est à dire Conseils et moyens tenus par les ennemis de la Couronne de France, pour reduire le royaume en tel estat que la Tyrannie Turquesque* (Orléans: Thibaut des Murs 1576), 7–8
6 Cf. Frank Lestringant, 'Altérités critiques: Du bon usage du Turc à la Renaissance,' in *D'un Orient l'autre* (Paris: CNRS 1991), 85–105; and Frank Lestringant, 'La Monarchie française au miroir ottoman: le portrait de Soliman le Magnifique, de Charles IX à Henri III,' in *Soliman le Magnifique et son temps* (Paris: La Documentation française 1992), 51–68.

7 Brantôme, *Recueil des dames* (Paris: Gallimard, [La Pleiade], 1991), 364

8 Clarence Dana Rouillard, *The Turk in French History, Thought and Literature (1520–1660)* (Paris: Boivin et Cie 1941), 216–17

9 'Nous voici par là conduits à nous demander quelles idées se faisaient les Français sur la vie sexuelle des Turcs et des Maures de Barbarie. Elles se résument d'un mot: extrême lubricité': Guy Turbet-Delof, *L'Afrique barbaresque dans la littérature française aux XVIe et XVIIe siècles* (Geneva: Droz 1973), 91.

10 Both were usually considered as Ottomans: cf. Yvelise Bernard, *L'Orient du XVIe siècle, une société musulmane florissante* (Paris: L'Harmattan 1988).

11 'Vous ouïeriez la nuit les plaintes et pleurs de la jeunesse de tout sexe, dont ils abusent: ny voire l'aage de six à sept ans n'empesche que tels miserables Sodomites n'exercent leur vilennie, et ne mettent à execution leurs abominables volontez contre nature': Georgiewitz, *Discours parenetique sur les choses turques* (Chavigny's translation) (Lyons: Pierre Rigaud 1606), 10.

12 'Les autres qui ont plus grande beauté, sont tellement chastrez (chose malheureuse) qu'il n'apparoist en eux rien de viril, ce qui se fait avec grand peril de leur vie. Et s'ilz eschappent, ils ne servent a autre chose que à accomplir leur execrable volupté': Münster, *Cosmographie universelle* (Basel: Henry Pierre 1556), 1209.

13 Nicolas de Nicolay, *Les Navigations peregrinations et voyages faicts en la Turquie* (Anvers 1576), 16–17

14 'Par trois jours que dura ce saccagement, il n'y eut espece de paillardise, Sodomie, sacrilège et cruauté qui ne fust par eux perpetree. Ils despouillerent l'incomparable temple de Sainte Sophie, (jadis avec tant admirable despence edifié par l'empereur Justinian), de tous ses adornements et vaisseaux sacrez, et en firent estable et bordeau à bardaches et putains': ibid., 90–1.

15 'En ce Saray sont noriz environ cinq uns jeunes enfans de laage de huict jusque a vingt ans, lesquelz le dict grant Turc faict instruire et endoctriner tant es letres, que aux armes, sur tout les faict apprendre a lire et escripre, scavoir leur loy, chevaucher, tirer de larc, et autres exercices de la guerre, et de letres, ainsi qui les y trouve enclins et adonnez': F. Antoine Geuffroy, *Briesve description de la court du grant turc* (Paris: Chrestien Wechel 1546), fol. b. III ro.

16 'Ils sont choisis à l'eslite entre sept ou huit cens esclaves fils de Chrestiens, nourris au Serrail, et ne ayants plus haut de 20 à 22 ans, beaux en perfection et esleus selon le jugement de la Phisiognomie, à laquelle les Turcs sont fort adonnez, et se cognoissent presque jusques à en donner certitude': Münster (François de Belleforest), *Cosmographie universelle, beaucoup plus augmentée, ornée et enrichie, par François de Belleforest* (Paris: Michel Sonnius 1575), 627.

17 'Et qui est le pis, et le plus execrable, c'est que la maudite concupiscence et libidineuse volupté de ces barbares passe si avant, et jusques là, qu'ils ne par-

donnent pour exercer cest acte deshonneste, à masle ny femelle, qui n'ont à peine encore atteint l'aage de 6 ans, parmi lesquelles impudicitez s'entendent les voix pitoyables des meres, qui ne peuvent patiemment endurer ny souffrir qu'on extorque de leurs bras leurs propres genitures, ny encores moins leur voir partir telles impuretez et violences abominables, non seulement devant Dieu, mais encore devant les hommes': René de Lusinge, *Histoire de l'origine, progrez, et declin, de l'Empire des Turcs* (Paris: Pierre Chevalier 1614), 343.

18 Cf. Nicolas de Nicolay, *Dans l'Empire de Soliman le Magnifique*, eds. Marie-Christine Gomez-Geraud and Stéphane Yérasimos (Paris: CNRS 1989), 28, 29, 137–40.

19 Cf. Marie-Christine Gomez-Geraud, 'Prise de vues pour un album d'images: l'Orient de Philippe Canaye, Seigneur du Fresne, 1573,' in *D'un Orient l'autre*, vol. I (Paris: CNRS 1991), 329–41.

20 Malek Chebel, *L'Esprit de Sérail, perversions et marginalités sexuelles au Maghreb* (Paris: Lieu Commun 1988), 39

21 'Au demeurant, je faisois grand conte de l'esprit, mais pourveu que le corps n'en fut pas à dire: car, à respondre en conscience, si l'une ou l'autre des deux beautez devoit necessairement y faillir, j'eusse choisi de quitter plutost la spiri-tuelle: elle a son usage en meilleures choses; mais, au subject de l'amour, subject qui principallement se rapporte à la veue et à l'atouchement, on faict quelque chose sans les graces de l'esprit, rien sans les graces corporelles. C'est le vray avantage des dames que la beauté. Elle est si leur que la nostre, quoy qu'elle desire des traicts un peu autres, n'est en son point que confuse avec la leur, puerile et imberbe. On dict que chez le grand Seigneur ceux qui le ser-vent sous titre de beauté, qui sont en nombre infini, ont leur congé, au plus loin, à vingt et deux ans': Michel de Montaigne, *Essais* (Paris: PUF 1978), III,3, 826–7.

22 'Entendez aussi que de celle grande université, et fameuse escole d'Athenes sont sortis les pourceaux Aristippe, et Epicure, lesquelz ont appris la volupté aux hommes, et les ont dressez, et conduitz à une vie plus digne d'une beste, que d'homme ayant quelque usage de raison': François de Belleforest, *Histoire universelle* (Paris: Gervais Mallot 1570), fol. tt.i ro.

23 'Et pour ne nous point arrester aux folles, et detestables amours, qui ont infamé le nom Grec, et desquelles sont pleins les livres de leurs poëtes': Mün-ster (Belleforest), *Cosmographie universelle*, 25.

24 'la vaillance des Rhodiots, l'effemination des Chipriots, et en general la gloire Grecque font cognoistre au Chrestien quel fondement il y a en ce qui est de l'heur mondain, puis que tous ces peuples sont à present les esclaves de la plus vile, et infame nation de l'univers': François de Belleforest, *Histoire universelle*, fol. tt.i ro.

25 'se monstrant mesme plus impie que les Payens qui faisoient leurs Dieux

impudiques, sanguinaires, vindicatifs, incestueux, sodomìtes': Artus Thomas, *L'Histoire de la décadence de l'Empire grec et establissement de celuy des Turcs* (Paris: Veufve l'Angelier 1620), addendum, 11

26 Cf. about anti-Hellenism: Frank Lestringant, 'Le Grec Bâtard,' 282–6, of 'Guillaume Postel et l'obsession turque,' in *Guillaume Postel, 1581-1981*, 265–98 (Paris: Éditions de La Maisnie 1985).

27 We can find descriptions of the Muslim religious men in Léon L'Africain, *Historiale description de l'Afrique* (Lyon: Temporale 1556), 166; Nicolas de Nicolay, *Les Navigations peregrinations et voyages*, 180; and Thomas, *L'Histoire de la decadence de l'Empire grec*, figure 22.

28 For a comprehensive study on Léon L'Africain, cf. Oumelbarine Zhiri, *L'Afrique au miroir de l'Europe* (Geneva: Droz 1991), 27: 'Léon L'Africain est un des derniers maillons avant que s'inverse le chemin des influences. Bientôt l'Europe en plein essor ne cherchera plus de modèles ou des connaissances dans l'Islam, et au contraire celui-ci, à la recherche d'un nouveau souffle, se mettra à l'école de l'Europe.'

29 'que je me fusse voulentiers deporté de m'avancer de tant, avec une grande envie de remettre cecy sous silence, pour ne publier, et découvrir si abhominables vices, qui rendent obscur la gloire de cette cité, ou j'ay prins la plus grande partie de ma nourriture': Léon L'Africain, *Historiale description de l'Afrique*, 136

30 'Ils sont d'une generation appellée Elcheva, et se parent d'habis lubriques, et dissolus, qu'ilz acoutrent à la mode fémine, portans la barbe rase, s'estudians de tout leur esprit à imiter en tout, les gestes, et façons des femmes: voire jusques à la parolle mesmes. Quoy plus? ils se rendent si mols, et delicas, qu'ils n'ont point honte s'abaisser de tant, que de prendre la quenouille, pour filer: et n'y a celuy de ces infames paillars qui ne tienne un concubin, usant avec luy, et se viennent à conjoindre ensemble, ne plus ne moins que fait le mary avec la femme': ibid., 135–6

31 'en quoy il fault loüer plus la modestie de ce peuple vivant soubs la loy du plus lascif legislateur qui fut onc, que des Chrestiens, lesquels souffrent les bordeaux, et maquerelages en leurs villes, et ne se soucient de chastier les insolences des ruffiens, et teneurs de berlans': Münster (Belleforest), *Cosmographie universelle*, 1830–1

32 'Il y a en cest Hospital quelques chambres deputees pour les fols et insensez, à sçavoir ceux qui ruent des pierres, et font autres maulx, où ils sont tenus enfermez et enchainez': Gabriel Chappuys, *L'Estat, description et gouvernement des royaumes et republiques du monde, tant anciennes que modernes* (Paris: Pierre Cavellat 1585), fol. 121 vo.

33 Françoise Charpentier, Jean Céard, and Gisèle Mathieu-Castellani, 'Préliminaires,' in *La Curiosité à la Renaissance*, 7–23 (Paris: SEDES 1986)

Bernardino of Siena versus
the Marriage Debt[1]

DYAN ELLIOTT

The concept of the conjugal debt began with Saint Paul's statement that husband and wife lost proprietary rights over their own bodies, each becoming the property of the other (1 Cor. 7: 4). Over the course of the Middle Ages, clerical authorities elaborated a complex discourse on the marriage debt which was applied as a kind of touchstone for conjugal relations. The apparent thrust of this discourse, one that is warmly embraced by modern scholars, is that the debt would ensure sexual equality in marriage, thus effacing the sexual double standard.

The theory of an equitable debt has been sustained by a dramatic over-investment, and an equally dramatic argumentative oversimplification, on the part of both its promulgators and its subsequent interpreters.[2] This program founders in both medieval commentary and twentieth-century metacommentary, first because an uncritical presumption of equality masks a consistent inequality of application. Moreover, the very terms of the discussion, medieval and modern, presuppose an identicality of interests between husband and wife. This paper discloses some of the more obvious inequalities latent within the tradition, as well as the clerical and historical complicity in their concealment.

The very fervour with which the notion of equality has been sustained raises the further issue of where and how resistance to the presumption of equality might arise and how it might be supported. I address this issue by first focusing on the female mystical tradition as an important site of resistance. Then I turn to Bernardino of Siena's singular, though admittedly late, extenuation of this resistance.

The Debt and Its Actual 'Interest'

Our point of departure is the twelfth century, a time of considerable ferment in the theology and canon law of marriage. Marriage was under attack by dualist detractors.[3] Orthodox defenders responded by making marriage a sacrament, a move which they hoped would secure its dignity. But marriage's sacramental status was achieved by emphasizing the consensual nature of the contract, thereby divorcing it from the sex act.[4] This strategy stimulated a marked reaction that can best be described as over-compensation: twelfth-century canonists and theologians became extremely sensitive, perhaps even oversensitive, to the spousal responsibility of paying the conjugal debt.[5] Gratian, while listing the traditional penitential periods for sexual abstinence, made them contingent on the consent of both spouses in a ground-breaking *dictum*.[6] This sexual relaxation was soon corroborated by Alexander III's statement that abstinence during the penitential periods had the status of a counsel as opposed to a precept.[7] Even the taboos around the woman's biological cycle were frequently waived: according to some pastoral advisers, a wife must pay the conjugal debt during pregnancy, prior to purification, and even during menstruation, if she suspects that her husband may otherwise turn to some extramarital vice.[8] The clerical concern for the ready payment of the debt often took on burlesque urgency: theorists debated, but generally sanctioned, the payment of the debt, not only in holy seasons, but even in holy places.[9]

In our own century, where sexual repression is associated with neurosis, the liberalization of the Church's teaching on married sexuality is typically regarded as a positive trend. Contemporary values may also determine the almost univocal nature of scholarly assessments of the conjugal debt. Most scholars are inclined to take the medieval rhetoric of equality at face value – a stance that not only coincides with the modern endorsement of sexual liberation and parity, but may also reflect a strain in women's studies which frequently attempts to locate reassuring examples or, better still, authoritative endorsements of female agency against an otherwise grim landscape. Elizabeth Makowski, for example, claims a role in this rehabilitative exercise: 'Women, traditional inferiors in both canon and [civil] law, were, surprisingly, at no disadvantage with reference to the conjugal duty.'[10] James Brundage goes considerably further, adducing an impressive set of claims from the allegedly progressive focus of the canonists:

The doctrine of sexual equality in some sense legitimized female sexuality itself, even if only within narrow limits. The canonists' doctrines implicitly conceded not only that it was natural for women to have sexual desires, just as men did, but also that their right to satisfy these desires within marriage was just as important as the satisfaction of men's sexual urges ... Recognition of the sexual equality of spouses was almost certainly connected with the growth of the idea that an emotional bond between partners ought to be an essential constituent of any marriage ... The development among the canonists of notions of sexual equality may have been symptomatic of the beginning of a breakdown of the ambivalence that earlier Christian authorities had shown toward the position of women in society. [11]

As appealing as Brundage's optimism might be, there are important counter-arguments to his claims. With regard to the strengthening of the emotional bond between partners, the canonists' tendency to project husband and wife into the role of creditor and debtor might operate more as a liability than as an asset, considering the widespread disparagement of business relations in this period. Moreover, the less savoury sexual contract between the prostitute and her client cannot help but resonate. Indeed, the action of Chaucer's *Shipman's Tale* depends precisely on the exploitation of such ambiguities in the debt tradition.[12]

But the effort to relate the canonistic focus on the debt to greater sensitivity to women is especially tenuous. The debt cannot be extracted from the entire discourse surrounding the sexual hierarchy by which it was framed. As concern for the debt escalates, so does a concurrent and apparently contradictory insistence on female subordination. All of the authorities are relentless in their reminders that the debt is a singular and privileged zone – the only one in which husband and wife are equal. Gratian, one of the most important ideologues of the debt in the high Middle Ages, also contributed more than any authority since the Church Fathers to the distinction between the order of creation, in which women were uneqivocally subordinated to men, and the order of salvation, in which the souls of men and women were equal.[13] The discrepancy between the equality claims of the marriage debt and the hierarchical matrix from which discussions of the debt are generated casts doubt upon the reliability of these claims. In fact, I would argue that this vigorously defended equality masks an irresponsibility tinged with misogyny: it is grounded on the assumption that the same structure would necessarily benefit both husbands and wives.

The apparently equitable principle of the marriage debt was actually differentially applied in a manner sympathetic to male physiology. No matter how clerical advisers might insist that the husband pay the debt on demand, they frequently deferred to the unreliability of masculine sexual performance. If, for example, a husband's 'permitted' fasting resulted in temporary impotence, pastoral advisers maintained he was guilty of no sin.[14] If the husband is temporarily impotent from having recently paid the debt, 'the wife has no right to ask again, and in doing so she behaves as a harlot rather than a wife.'[15] On the other hand, medieval gender constructions in many ways turned upon the male's physical domination of the female. Thus, the seventh-century Isidore of Seville reasoned: 'The bodies of each [man and woman] are distinguished by strength and weakness. Therefore the greater strength of the man and the lesser strength of the woman is in order that she should submit to the man. Otherwise, with women resisting, libido would force men to seize another thing or to fall upon another sex.'[16] Scholars, such as the thirteenth-century encyclopaedist Vincent of Beauvais, continue to cite without comment Isidore's etymologically inspired reconstruction of gender.[17] Medieval matrimonial law concurred with this vision of the wife's sexual instrumentality in so far as it had evolved no concept of matrimonial rape.[18] The rhetoric of the conjugal debt should be viewed on a continuum with other aspects of this tradition: the insistence on mutual consent for sexual abstinence, but not for sexual activity, covertly sanctioned masculine aggression.[19] Moreover, by the institutional removal of traditional impediments to sex, the wife was rendered infinitely more accessible to the husband.

The wife's sexual subordination was further corroborated by changes in the intellectual world. The scholastic milieu's adaptation of Aristotle had the effect of emphasizing the active/passive dichotomies inherent in the sexual hierarchy. These dichotomies were, in turn, more deeply inscribed in discussions of the debt. Thus, Aquinas, while refuting the contention that an active male and a passive female must necessarily undermine the equality of the debt, argues that (though the active role is nobler) equality resides in the fact that the wife's degree of passivity is proportionate to the husband's activity.[20] Of particular consequence is the eventual domination of the Aristotelian theory of conception, whereby a woman (now believed to provide no 'seed' in conception) was reduced to little more than a passive incubator for the foetus. This view contrasts with the Galenic 'two-seed' theory, whereby conception would be contingent on the woman's sexual arousal, which ensured her emission of seed.[21] Thus, from an Aristotelian perspective, female pleasure was excised as a requirement in a completed sex act, as was female agency in conception. And yet it was the wife who risked all the dangers and discomforts of pregnancy and parturition.

When pastoral counsel is at its most sympathetic to a married sexuality, the emphasis on the debt is still subtly inscribed with presumption of a woman's passive and instrumental sexuality. Certain pastoral counsellors such as Thomas of Chobham curtail a woman's fasting since 'fleshy members befit the office of the flesh.'[22] The Dominicans permit and occasionally encourage a woman to adorn herself so that she will be attractive to her husband.[23] Dominican John Nider seems to push these efforts to accommodate the male furthest:

> Certain great men even say that the wife is bound to deliver herself to her husband for familiar kisses if he requires it and that she does not sin venially by kissing and embracing the husband even if he does not ask, if this is done in a fitting way and with good intention – namely that she divert him from anger or another sin. And Scripture seems to agree with these things in the advice of Solomon, Proverbs 5, which says: Rejoice with the wife of your youth: Let her be thy dearest hind, and most agreeable fawn: let her breasts inebriate you at all times.[24]

Nider also permits a husband to use manual stimulation on himself and his wife so that he can achieve multiple orgasms, provided the correct motives are present.[25] The potential ambivalence created by such counsel is clear when it is contrasted with more mainstream opinion. Thomas of Cantimpré tells a lurid story about a husband who heightened his pleasure by touching his resisting wife's genitalia. In the course of this unwelcome foreplay, the wretched wife appealed to God to vindicate her, and the husband was visited with a horrendous punishment.[26]

The wife's presumed sexual instrumentality finds no echo in a parallel attitude to the husband. The rare efforts to recognize gender differences or disparate sexual biorhythmns for husband and wife all seem to work to the husband's advantage. Thus, Aquinas argues that a female adulterer sins more than a male, owing to the potential harm done to lineage. Likewise, while a menstruating wife is required to render the debt, she is not permitted to seek it.[27] Similarly, Nider, though perceiving pregnancy as increasing a woman's desire for sex, nevertheless considered a pregnant wife more sinful in seeking the debt than would her husband be, owing to the purported danger of abortion and her heightened responsibility for the foetus. While Nider permits a healthy spouse to withold the debt from a leprous one when there is danger of contagion, he is careful to note that doctors claim women are more likely to be infectious than men.[28]

The continued privileging of male sexuality was rather craftily concealed by a stubborn insistence on the female's greater sexual appetite.[29] A potentially sinister twist was added to this perception by the more liberal Dominican theologians. Aquinas, while never challenging women's heightened lasciviousness, nevertheless argued that they felt greater inhibitions over expressing their sexual needs. He thus not only encouraged husbands but presented it as an obligation that they render the debt to their wives when they did not expressly seek it, but presumably indicated their desires in other ways: 'Through the rendering of the debt a medication is furnished for the wife's concupiscence. Now the doctor to whom some sick person is committed is bound to treat the sickness even if the patient does not ask. Therefore the husband is bound to render to his wife when she does not ask.'[30] Many of Aquinas's views on sexuality were rejected by his contemporaries as too daring,[31] but this piece of advice almost instantly became standard fare among a wide assortment of pastoral advisers. The counsel was popular not only with the more sexually permissive Dominican authorities, but among the more conservative Franciscans as well.[32] Some scholars are quick to accept the surface explanation that this advice evinces a new sensitivity to married sexuality generally, but women's sexuality specifically.[33] But it is also arguable that, by making female initiative so subtle, medieval authorities stand in danger of annexing it entirely and transferring it to the husband. Moreover, a sexually insensitive husband was now, potentially, provided with the most altruistic reasons for making unwelcome sexual demands on his wife.

As mentioned earlier, the emphasis on the debt, intertwined with a seemingly benign paternalism, corresponds with canon lawyers' growing precision about the husband's dominance and the dramatic increase in his control over his wife's person – an influence that eddied out into property law.[34] This trend is inseparable from the concomitant emphasis on the wife's submission and unquestioning obedience. Certain authorities, such as the Dominican Raymond of Peñafort, even justified the wife's acquiescence to the husband's quasi-sinful orders, arguing that, in obeying the husband, she was obeying God.[35] Thus, in the high Middle Ages, the wife was remorselessly rendered *sub virga*: a phrase usually translated as 'under the rod of the husband,' signifying his rule, but which can also be translated as 'under the penis.'[36]

The pastoral insistence on the woman's compliance with her husband's sexual demands during biological intervals that were formerly off-limits would inevitably have a tremendous impact on a sensitive psyche. The situation of the menstruous wife is especially indicative. She was, of course, expected to dissuade her husband from so untimely an exaction. Yet a number of pastoral advisers, following Aquinas, assume that, if the wife referred to her condition openly, the husband's revulsion would be so strong that he would turn to sodomy.[37] While the wife's acquiescence was considered sinless by most theorists, her suspect condition automatically cast her into the role of pollutant. She may well have saved her husband from the sin of adultery, or an even more heinous offence, but she nevertheless stained him with a sin ranging in gravity from venial to mortal, depending on the authority consulted.[38] Moreover, the Church's sexual concessions were significantly introduced at the same time that newly translated medical treatises, fresh from the Arab world, added scientific 'certainty' to the traditional correlation between menstruation and the conception of leprous offspring – a period in which leprosy was on the rise, as was the panic which it inspired.[39] An examination of the lurid *exempla* which peppered sermons would suggest that women were subjected to a torturously divided discourse: on the one hand, they were urged to pay the debt; on the other, they were warned against the monstrous offspring that was alleged to result from an unpropitious conception.[40] Couples who trangressed against holy times or places received uncanny punishments: some were depicted as miraculously stuck together during the sex act; others were struck dead.[41]

Mysticism and Resistance

The emphasis on the conjugal debt and the rise of the mystical matron is hardly adventitious.[42] While teachings on marriage and new images of sainthood were sufficiently elastic to accommodate sexual activity, Weinstein and Bell's examination of gender-specific patterns in sanctity suggests that the conscience of the aspirant female saint was less flexible: the saintly matrons of the high and later Middle Ages, like their pious predecessors, were generally possessed of a childhood vocation to chastity and were married against their will.[43] In this new climate of sexual acceptance, moreover, it is unlikely that they would find much clerical support for their efforts to resist marriage or consummation. In fact, in the lives of individuals such as Christine of Markyate, Dauphine of Puimichel, and Paula Gambara Costa, we find priests corroborating parental pressure to marry.[44] The young woman's sorrow over her broken vow determined her virtuosity in a life of penitence. In the cases of Mary of Oignies,

Bridget of Sweden, Dorothea of Montau, Frances of Rome, and many others, marriage inevitably brought on a marked increase in austerities.[45] The conjugal debt itself becomes a new locus for the exemplary female virtue of obedience: discussions of obligatory payment are frequently linked with descriptions of physical revulsion and self-mutilation.[46]

For such women, forced into marriage and denied all pretext for sexual refusal, the newly ascendant realm of intentionality provided a forum in which they could vindicate themselves, in spite of their sexual activity. Both Gratian and Peter Lombard drew attention to the Augustinian distinction between the spouse exacting the debt, whose action ranged from a neutral act to a mortal sin, depending on the circumstances, and the rendering spouse, whose compliance was deemed meritorious.[47] This distinction, reiterated in most lay catechetical works, would encourage spiritually scrupulous spouses to look inward and identify with their sinless intentions. Many pastoral counsellors take this one step further, recommending that such a spouse submit to a sinful exaction with a grieving and sorrowful heart. Some even went so far as to suggest that this level of grieving disinvestment was deserving of merit.[48]

The married woman's propensity to identify with the inner self is of crucial importance to the evolution of a distinctly mystical female spirituality in the later Middle Ages. Scholars such as John Benton and Caroline Bynum have shown that the inner self was identified with God.[49] Thus a woman's enforced and multiply determined passivity and growing reliance on the internal forum might act as a spiritual stimulant; her compensatory act of grieving during sexual intercourse had the potential for fostering a direct communication with the divine.[50] Indeed, the examples of women such as Dorothea of Montau, Frances of Rome, and post-conversion Margery Kempe suggest that the greater the aversion to the conjugal debt, the greater a woman's predisposition for mysticism during the sexually active part of her career.[51] Occasionally we get tantalizing hints of how mystical raptures may have been provoked by the sex act, providing a transcendent escape. Thus, in the life of Dorothea of Montau, 'the Lord wounded her instantly with the arrows of love, and inflaming her with burning love he said: "You are capable of loving me exceedingly well. For frequently I seized you [*rapui te*] from your husband when he still lived and thought he possessed you."'[52] In Dorothea's case, there may in fact have been an inverse relation between the sex act and mystical raptures. But it is not necessary to pinpoint a precise relation between sexual intercourse and mysticism in order to understand how they are functionally linked. The divine assurances that the woman receives in the course of her mystical experiences are essential for rebuilding her vocation by transferring her allegiance from virginity to penitence. Thus, in one of Bridget of Sweden's visions, the virginal Agnes makes the following remarks concerning Bridget:

> You may marvel that a lady coming into favour has been corrupted. I answer you that there are certain women who have continence but do not love ... On that account sometimes pride and presumption arises from their continence ... Yet if someone were of the intention that they would not for the whole world, if it were offered to them, wish to be stained, it would be impossible that such a one would abandon herself to filthy things. But indeed if God were to permit from his hidden justice that such a one should fall, it would be more a crown than a sin for her: as long as it were against her will.[53]

The close relation between the conjugal debt and mysticism is certainly suggestive, but hagiographers would be reluctant to acknowledge such a link out of deference to the quasi-dualist tradition embedded in Christian thought. From the time of the early Church, Paul's remarks about the distractions of marriage, and especially his suggestions that couples separate for prayer, led commentators to maintain a basic contradiction between marriage and the life of the spirit (1 Cor. 7: 5, 32–5). Theologians such as Alexander of Hales and Thomas Aquinas, for example, discuss the ways in which marital relations interfere with mystical rapture and the spirit of prophecy. The late-thirteenth-century *Summa virtutum de remediis anime* is further representative in citing two of the most damning authorities on this score: Origen's declaration that 'in marital intercourse the Holy Spirit is not present' and Augustine's disparaging remark that 'there the soul becomes totally flesh.'[54]

Such implacable prejudices required that the men responsible for processing the lives and visions of holy women, frequently confessors who were attempting to win recognition for their penitents, should make every effort to dissociate the woman's mystical aptitude from marriage altogether or, failing that, from the sexually active part of her marriage. John Mattiotti, confessor and hagiographer to Frances of Rome, is typical in this respect:

> Blessed Frances ... lived with her husband for twenty-eight years and six months: for twelve years she lived with him separated from carnal union by the common consent of the parties: and then marvellously she was changed

... For by such sweetness of the soul and delight of the mind she took part in supernal things, and freed from all earthly things she was united to Christ ... and frequently after such meditations and prayers she was seized in ecstasy.[55]

In fact, Frances experienced visions and ecstasies long before her conversion to chastity. Likewise, Bridget of Sweden's life places her first dramatic encounter with Christ after the death of her husband.[56] But the next rubric in the life reports, rather anti-climactically, 'how even before the death of her husband she saw certain things.'[57]

Bernardino's Revisionary Challenge

The hagiographical tradition may tacitly imply a relation between sexual activity and visions, but one must move outside this tradition to find clearer ratification for this association. John Nider's *Formicarium*, a veritable miscellany of spiritual anecdotage, provides one of the most transparent accounts of the pattern I have been attempting to trace. John describes the life of a certain Margaret, a pious matron in the diocese of Basel, who was the recipient of celestial visions and prophecies in the midst of her conjugal and domestic responsibilities.[58] Though reluctantly rendering the debt: 'She however never reciprocally exacted it, but, lest her chaste mind be occupied by these things, she began to increase her prayers to the blessed virgin (who she loved especially) that by her most pure son, she would give to her husband the gift of greater continence than he had hitherto.' She knew that Mary had heard her request when her husband, knowing nothing of her prayers, confided that he had become frigid.[59]

The fact that John was not Margaret's hagiographer, but simply an acquaintance and admirer, permitted greater latitude in the representation of a possible concurrence in her sexual and spiritual activities. However, while not lobbying for an official recognition of her sanctity, John certainly perceived and presented Margaret as an anomalous exemplar: she is one of only two examples that he provides of the holy life in marriage. In view of her atypicality, there was neither need nor utility in drawing parallels between Margaret's spiritual well-being and her attitudes to sex, at least from John's perspective.

But the pastoral expertise of the Franciscan preacher Bernardino of Siena (d. 1444) seems to support the view that Margaret's experience of the debt was not as anomalous as John Nider's treatment might imply. Bernardino was one of the few men of his day who was prepared to challenge the dominant pastoral discourse on questions as delicate as the nature of female sexuality, the exigencies of the conjugal debt, and the way these two factors interacted with a woman's spirituality.[60] Thus married women in general, but those with a spiritual vocation in particular, eventually found a champion in the early fifteenth century.

Bernardino's originality is first evinced by the fact that he was prepared to broach subjects like the conjugal debt from the pulpit at all, thus uprooting them from their traditional consignment to the confessional. With a Juvenal quotation he quips: '"Indeed a rare bird in this land" is a sermon of this sort, and even more rarely preached.' Quick to acknowledge his departure, he is equally quick to defend it on the grounds that worse scandal would result from silence.[61] But other equally surprising tropes soon follow which tend to muffle the shock of his initial transgression. As a more pastorally oriented, less scholastic member of the clergy, his sermons deny the commonly held view that women were more lustful than men, instead arguing in favour of their greater natural chastity. This premise is advanced at a number of different points throughout the Bernardine corpus. Against potential spurners and detractors of women, whom Bernardino styles as sodomites, for example, he maintains that women are 'cleaner' and 'more precious' in the body.[62] In an exposition of Paul's remonstrance that spouses not defraud one another with regard to the debt (1 Cor. 7: 2), Bernardino is still more direct: 'Behold that the wife comes to the husband's defence in that area, namely in the flesh where man is weaker.'[63] Because this affirmation is intended to gloss the wife's position as helpmate to her husband, it thus runs the risk of positioning the wife's strength in an ancillary, prophylactic relation to the husband's weakness. Had this been the case, Bernardino's praise of women's greater purity would be largely cosmetic: it would accord women greater dignity, but their sexual subservience, though perhaps now understood as more tragic, would nevertheless remain unchallenged.

But unlike most theorists of the debt, Bernardino was not satisfied to let the weaker and more carnal party invariably dominate the stronger and more spiritual.[64] Though quick to affirm that, if the debt is properly exacted in a licit time, denial is a mortal sin,[65] he nevertheless develops a number of strategies for conjugal restraint against less timely exactions. As will become clear, such strategies are directed to the wife.

I mentioned earlier that canonistic treatments of the debt drew largely on what Brundage has described as the 'morally neutral' relationship between the debtor and the creditor.[66] But the equity of this scenario is contingent on the regular alternation of roles between the one who exacts and the one who renders. Thus, Dominicans tended to discourage a one-sided vow in which one party would vow not to exact the debt, though still bound to render, on the assumption that it would be odious for the other (preponderantly male) to be put in the position of always exacting. In fact, Albert the Great protested against the stupidity of such vows, arguing that the foolish vowee should instantly be released from the vow's implications by the bishop.[67] Two comments are in order here. First, that according to a number of authorities, the vow not to exact the debt is the only vow that a woman could make that the husband could not revoke. And second, that in keeping with the prevalent prejudice in favour of the debt, it is suggestive that authorities such as Albert do not show any particular sympathy or concern for the individual (preponderantly female) who is always compelled to render.

Bernardino implicitly challenges the alleged equality of the debt through his core assumption that the husband was the sexual aggressor – a role that presumably accorded with his propensity towards lust: 'Oh in how many unspeakable and incredible ways husbands abuse their wives! Who ever can speak about it honestly? Certainly they do not seem to be conjugal couplings, but piggish abuses that are beyond bestial. And although wives may be unhappy, nevertheless they agree to [sex] in whatever manner.'[68] The same preconception underwrites his mobilization of the familiar 'shy wife' *topos*:

> There is a great difference between the harassments and orders which oblige wives to render the debt and those which oblige husbands, because wives can expect more obvious harassments than husbands. There is a threefold reason for this. First, because women are more modest about seeking than men. Second, because such a petition is viler and more ignominious for a woman than a man. Whence from natural instinct and direction they have rather the condition of suffering and accepting than of exacting and exciting, and the condition of submission than of domination; and on that account the impudence of seeking savours of greater imprudence and is more unseemly in them than in men. The third reason is that women are more under the rule of men than the converse.[69]

Though hardly an image of women that would directly foster progressive change, it has the merit of externalizing some of the factors militating against an equitable sexual rapport. Bernardino's second and third reasons, in particular, indicate an awareness that the wife's position of subjection must necessarily intrude on this one area of theoretical equality.

Bernardino creatively responds to this perceived imbalance by removing the debt from the debt tradition. In other words, he bypasses the usual economically flavoured paradigm of creditor and debtor, instead choosing to recast this obligation in terms of conjugal obedience. These new terms of discussion permit the enlistment of a religious and hierarchical model as a point of comparison: the obedience owed to a superior. Not only is the religious model shorn of all concupiscence, and thus undoubtedly loftier than any secular loyalties, it also has more built-in protections for the individual. Saint Francis's rule of 1221 counselled a brother to disregard the order of a superior if it conflicted with either the rule itself or the subject friar's conscience.[70] (And Bernardino was a Franciscan of the Observance.) Thus, Bernardino challenges the prevailing interpretation of conjugal obedience as both stricter and yet less discriminating. Why is it, he asks, that the level of obedience evinced by the debt so far exceeds that of a religious vow such as a monk would make to his superior?[71]

The religious analogy is especially propitious for its refraction of the sexual hierarchy in marriage which Bernardino believes to be latently in effect with the exercise of the debt. Although Bernardino refrains from explicitly identifying the corrupt superior with the husband, the examples he enlists imply as much. Thus, he argues that even regular obedience has its limits: a monk is not bound to obey his superior if he orders anything sinful. Nor should a wife 'always be bound to spend time in the mud and be shaken in it like a sow.'[72] A husband cannot require his wife to do anything contrary to the good of her body or soul. Bernardino supports this contention with an example which marks the difference between his own and the most 'progressive' pastoral counsel: 'Just as no one of a sane mind would say that a wife ought to obey her husband by having sex on the sacred altar or some holy spot, so neither ought he to say that she should obey by having sex day and night and almost infinite times.'[73] Bernardino clearly believed that even a sorrowful rendering of the debt on a feast day constituted a venial sin; by applying Augustine's comment – that one should not even sin venially on behalf of another – to this delicate subject he upholds the wife's right of refusal, even if the husband is in danger of fornication.[74] On another occasion he dramatically heightens this point, arguing that, even if the wife knew that one of her sins would save all the souls in hell, she would not be justified: her first obligation is charity towards herself.[75]

By equating the wife with an abused religious subordinate, Bernardino suspends the temporal considerations of a domestic and conjugal milieu and places her in a position in which she can benefit more directly from a pristine and supernal set of priorities. Excessive sex causes spiritual dissipation, thus the obligation to render the conjugal debt is reconfigured accordingly: love of God comes first; love of one's self is second; love of one's neighbour, a category in which the husband is included in an undifferentiated way, comes last.[76] The imperative of the debt is subservient to this hierarchy of love. Elsewhere, Bernardino explicitly rejects the prevailing tendency to amalgamate the husband's will with God's will, arguing for the wife's right to resist any ribaldry that is potentially sinful on the grounds that it is more pious to obey God than your husband.[77] In deep agreement with the Augustinian counsel that a wife should resist unnatural sex acts to her utmost, Bernardino is prepared to carry the struggle forward into death. Moreover, in line with his sensitivity to supernal consequences, he assures such heroically resistant women that they will die martyrs and go straight to heaven.[78]

Inseparable from Bernardino's critique of current pastoral teaching on the debt is his ready acknowledgment that women were more inclined to spiritual things than were men,[79] and that a link exists between forced sexual complicity and recourse to visions. This becomes especially apparent in his assessment of the external factors that govern sexual relations when, amidst questions of an individual's constitution and temperament, Bernardino introduces a spiritual dark horse:

> Thirdly, [one must consider] the extent of divine infusions and spiritual visitations; for to certain married individuals, as I have already many times discovered, such a horror of carnal things is sent by God and such an appetite for spiritual devotions and tastes that they cannot render the conjugal debt without great difficulty and the utmost horror; and then surely God, in part, seems in some way to impede the rendering of the debt, through the private law [*per ... privatam legem*] of the Holy Spirit which prejudices the common law.[80]

The 'private law of the Holy Spirit' is especially suggestive. And yet, such spiritual gifts do not necessarily constitute cast-iron rules for sexual refusal. Bernardino acknowledges that from time to time the more spiritual party of the marriage must give in to the will of the other, a situation he compares with voluntarily ascending the gallows.[81] But individual spiritual needs are still an important consideration in the payment of the debt. Thus he portrays a woman inspired by God who derives no pleasure from the marriage act as follows: 'She will have a husband who is but bad flesh and mud. If God's grace loosens her ties and her good sense helps her, in this way she won't cause scandal to her husband, but will render him the debt. But she can't do this every time, as if she were not in that grace, without sin.'[82]

But how is one to know when to render the debt and when to withold it? Bernardino encourages women to embark on an introspective journey – a process which he fondly characterizes as a series of consultations with the three Madonnas: prudence, conscience, and charity.[83] Should such soundings prove inconclusive, however, the wife is then advised to seek the assistance of a spiritual adviser. But this road is less secure than inner ratification, and it is in this context that we are most directly exposed to Bernardino's apprehension of, or even hostility towards, contemporary marital counsel. He warns women against confessors who are inexperienced in spiritual matters. Such men care little for what Bernardino is pleased to call 'the impediment of spiritual graces' and would be inclined to favour payment of the debt, slighting 'the chains of divine love.'[84] At times, Bernardino's performative strategy becomes parodic:

> If you want good advice, don't go to the monks from Grosseto, because they tend to bind women to their homes, women who should not be bound ... One of these big ones will say: be obedient to your husband! You must follow his advice, you cannot do differently. Don't do anything voluntarily. Go, go, you are excused ... Sometimes you'll go to one who is carnal, and not knowledgeable, and he will tell you that it's permissible for you to please your husband by paying attention to and adorning your body. That one's a beast.[85]

The name Grosseto, a town bordering on Siena and politically subject to it, has the advantage of also being a *double entendre* for 'fathead.'[86] It is tempting to interpret these 'big' and worldly advisers as exponents of Dominican Aristotelianism: a font for both sexual liberalism and the revival of 'natural law,' reinforcing the hierarchy of the sexes. In contrast, Bernardino posits that, if a wife has learned through long and bitter experience that frequent and prompt rendering of the debt does not benefit the carnal husband in any auspicious way, especially if the husband purposefully attempts to draw the wife away from the 'thriving charismatic richness of divine things,' this justifies the refusal of the debt. Moreover, Bernardino contends that 'every divinely inspired person awakened to higher gifts' would judge likewise.[87]

Geneviève Hasenohr's analysis of the the pastoralia addressed to married women in the later Middle Ages indicates that the clergy did not even attempt to reconcile women's active and contemplative life, generally focusing on one to the exclusion of the other. She tends to regard Bernardino as a part of this general pattern, owing to the fact that he stresses charitable acts over private devotions.[88] But this generalization seems inappropriate in view of his preaching on the conjugal debt. His efforts to dissociate the debt from the ostensibly equitable and secular debt tradition by placing it in the ostensibly less equitable and more hierarchical, but actually more protected, order of obedience were not simply manoeuvres for evading a discussion of secular life – far from it. The model of religious obedience which he enlists is simply a corridor to the order of salvation, the only context in which men and women were indeed equal.

Historians of women in the Christian tradition would be right to be suspicious of the order of salvation. It was generally used to offset the apparent injustice of the sexual hierarchy in the temporal world by a fictive deferral of equality to the next world. But Bernardino's evocation demonstrates a bold originality in that he brings the order of salvation to bear on the present world. In fact, he creatively superimposes it on the marriage bed – a novel but essential device for his delineation of the 'middle road' between worldly pleasure and contemplation.[89]

The daring of Bernardino's strategies comes into sharper focus when contrasted with the climate of pastoral deference to married sexuality, generally, and the husband's prerogatives in particular, as evidenced by his contemporaries. For example, the Dominican Giovanni Dominici (d. 1419), an influential preacher who was active in many of the same cities as Bernardino, wrote a detailed rule of life for the well-born matron Bartolomea degli Alberti in 1403. Though his alleged fear and shame is used to justify his very cursory treatment of the debt, a number of parallels with Bernardino can still be adduced. For instance, Giovanni also subscribes to the minority position that women are more chaste than men.[90] Moreover, the fact that he interprets Eve's punishment, first and foremost, in terms of her unpropitious role in the marriage act, detailing the various evasions a husband can use not to render the debt, indicates a similar recognition of inequity to that of Bernardino's.[91] But these perceptions do not impel Giovanni to stage any real interference. Though opposed to sex during penitential periods and prepared to give his female penitent advice on how to make herself scarce at bedtime, these remarks are prefaced, and thus undercut, by the reflection that the wife is to some extent excused in God's eyes by her obligation of obedience, while her husband is not.[92] The discussion of sexuality is, moreover, cordoned off from the discussion of the wife's spirituality and penitential practices, while the latter area is made radically contingent on the husband's permission. The wife's infractions in matters such as sumptuous dressing and fast-breaking are routinely excused out of obedience to the husband.[93]

Likewise, Franciscan writers, who worked within a more sexually reticent tradition than the Dominicans, refused Bernardino's lead. For instance, Francis de Plathea of Bologna (d. 1460) wrote a rather singular treatise, in so far as it was exclusively dedicated to the subject of the conjugal debt. Yet the work seems devoid of Bernardino's influence. Francis's list of twelve possible reasons for legitimately witholding the debt are rather conventional, and entirely aloof from spiritual concerns.[94] Even the *Regole della vita matrimoniale*, written by Bernardino's student and confrère Cherubino of Spoleto (d. 1484) and indebted to his master on many points, is disappointing on this score.[95] Writing for a female audience and solicitous for their souls, Cherubino warns wives that they sin in letting their husbands see them naked, and offend God by engaging in dishonest touches and embraces.[96] But the wife's spiritual life *per se* is not at issue, except in the context of explicit sins. The closest Cherubino comes to discussing possible tensions between sexual and spiritual demands is when he argues that excessive sex is harmful to the life of the spirit, citing authorities such as Jerome, Augustine, and Bernard of Clairvaux to demonstrate the resulting fleshly engorgement of the soul. He further adapts biblical instances in support of this position. Sex robbed the prophet of the spirit of prophecy; sex robbed the apocryphal Sara of her seven husbands, who were all suffocated by a demon for their lust in the marital bed.[97] But these examples reinforce the binary of the sexually active person versus the mystic. And no attempt is made to structure evidence of spiritual enervation into a pretext for sexual refusal.

But despite its very localized effect, Bernardino's intervention is still remarkable for its provocative critique of some of the most entrenched and protected aspects of the Christian sexual tradition. He challenges the myth of the conjugal debt's equality by pointing to a husband's and wife's disparate sexual needs. In so doing, he rejects the stereotype of women's greater lasciviousness in favour of his own perceptions of their greater spiritual aptitude. He firmly attests to the fact that mystical raptures are often the domain of sexually obligated women. Moreover, he structures his observations and his apparent sympathy for female spirituality into an important rationale for sexual refusal. But especially significant is that, in pursuit of these ends, Bernardino affirmatively emphasizes the possibility of an inward journey that is more accessible than the mystic's singular quest: the consultation with the three Madonnas. This incitement to self-exploration, while perhaps beginning as a defensive retreat from outward coercion, can then be structured into active resistance. In other words, Bernardino attempts to rescue female agency from the narrow register of masculine sinfulness, thus restoring the wife to a measure of the autonomy that had been so seriously eroded by solicitude for the debt.

NOTES

1 The problem posed in the first part of this paper – namely, the relation between payment of the conjugal debt and women's propensity towards mysticism – is discussed at greater length in chapters 4 and 5 of my book *Spiritual Marriage: Sexual Abstinence in Medieval Wedlock* (Princeton, NJ: Princeton University Press 1993).

2 For a refreshing exception to this general rule see Eleanor McLaughlin, 'Equality of Souls, Inequality of Sexes: Women in Medieval Theology,' in *Religion and Sexism: Images of Woman in the Jewish and Christian Tradition*, ed. Rosemary Ruether (New York: Simon and Schuster 1974), esp. 225–8.

3 See John T. Noonan, *Contraception: A History of Its Treatment by Catholic Theologians and Canonists* (Cambridge, MA: Harvard University Press 1966), 179–93.

4 The definitive theological statement of the consensual vision of marriage is Peter Lombard's *Sententiae* 4.26.6, which essentially follows the lead of Hugh of St Victor's *De sacramentis* 2.11.3–5, *PL* 176, cols. 481–8. Alexander III upheld the consensual view of marriage, and this position was ratified by Innocent III: see Charles Donahue, 'The Policy of Alexander III's Consent Theory of Marriage,' *Proceedings of the 4th International Congress of Canon Law*, ed. Stephan Kuttner, 259–77 (Vatican City: Biblioteca Apostolica Vaticana 1976) and James Brundage, *Law, Sex, and Christian Society in Medieval Europe* (Chicago: University of Chicago Press 1987), 331–41. On the evolution of the sacramental aspect of marriage, see G. Le Bras, 'La Doctrine du mariage chez les théologiens et les canonistes depuis l'an mille,' *Dictionnaire de théologie catholique*, (Paris: Letouzey et Ané 1927), vol. 9, pt. 2, cols. 2196–2216, and Christopher Brooke, *The Medieval Idea of Marriage* (Oxford: Oxford University Press 1989), 273–80.

5 For a discussion of the conjugal debt, see Elizabeth Makowski, 'The Conjugal Debt and Medieval Canon Law,' *Journal of Medieval History* 3 (1977), 99–114.

Also see Pierre J. Payer, *The Bridling of Desire: Views of Sex in the Later Middle Ages* (Toronto: University of Toronto Press 1993), 89–97.

6 'Hec [i.e., periods of sexual abstinence] autem seruanda sunt, si uxor consensum adhibere uoluerit; ceterum sine eius consensu nec causa orationis continentia seruari debet': C. 33 q. 4 d.p.c. 11. See Brundage, *Law, Sex, and Christian Society*, 242.

7 André Vauchez, *La Spiritualité du Moyen Âge* (Paris: Presses Universitaires de France 1975), 128

8 This kind of leniency is especially true of later pastoral manuals, such as that of John of Freiburg (*ca* 1297), which were influenced by Dominican-Aristotelianism. See his *Summa confessorum* 4.2.44–6 (Rome: s.n. 1518), fol. 220v. See Leonard E. Boyle, 'The *Summa Confessorum* of John of Freiburg and the Popularization of the Moral Teaching of St Thomas Aquinas and Some of His Contemporaries,' in *St Thomas Aquinas*, ed. Armand A. Maurer (Toronto: Pontifical Institute of Mediaeval Studies 1974), vol. 2: 245–68; repr. in *Pastoral Care, Clerical Education, and Canon Law* (London: Variorum Reprints 1981). Cf. the contribution of William of Rennes, the glossator of Raymond of Peñafort writing between 1240 and 1245, who lines up various authorities for and against the payment of the debt during menstruation: *Summa de poenitentia et matrimonio Sancti Raymundi de Penafort* 4.2.10 (Rome: Ioannes Tallini 1603), gloss k ad v. *abstinendum*, 516. On Raymond's significance, see Pierre Michaud-Quantin, *Sommes de casuistique et manuels de confession au Moyen Âge*, Analecta Mediaevalia Namurcensia no. 13 (Louvain: Nauwelaerts 1962), 35–42; also see A. Teetaert, 'La Doctrine pénitentielle de saint Raymond de Penyafort, O.P.' *Analecta Sacra Tarraconensia* 5 (1929), 121–82, esp. 121–5.

9 See Thomas of Chobham, *Summa confessorum* 7.2.2.3, ed. F. Broomfield (Louvain and Paris: Nauwelaerts 1968), 336–7. On Thomas, who wrote *ca* 1215, see John W. Baldwin, *Masters, Princes, and Merchants: The Social Views of Peter the Chanter and His Circle* (Princeton, NJ: Princeton University Press 1970), vol. 1: 21–4; also see Pierre Michaud-Quantin, 'A propos des premières *Summae confessorum*,' *Recherches de théologie ancienne et médiévale* 26 (1959), 284–90. Cf. Raymond of Peñafort, *Summa de poenitentia* 4.2.10, 516; John of Freiburg, *Summa confessorum* 4.2.43, fol. 220; Jean Gerson, *Regulae mandatorum* c. 154, in *Oeuvres complètes*, ed. Mgr Glorieux (Paris: Desclée et Cie 1973), vol. 9: 132. Note, however, that Gerson is one of the few who explicitly denies that the spouse is obliged to render the debt if it endangers his or her health: 'Nullus conjugum tenetur reddere debitum in detrimentum notabile et certum sui corporis vel foetus nascituri. Et secundum hoc cognoscitur quando leprosis vel praegnantibus aut menstruatis aut furiosis aut epidimiacis et similibus casibus, reddi vel non reddi debitum oporteat.' Also see Thomas N. Tentler, *Sin and Confession*

on the Eve of the Reformation (Princeton, NJ: Princeton University Press 1977),
171–4, and Dyan Elliott, 'Sex in Holy Places: An Exploration of a Medieval
Anxiety,' *Journal of Women's History* 6 (1994), 6–34.

10 Makowski, 'The Conjugal Debt,' 111; cf. René Metz, 'Le Statut de la femme en
droit canonique médiéval,' *Recueils de société Jean Bodin pour l'histoire comparative
des instititutions* 12 (1962), 88–9

11 Brundage, 'Sexual Equality in Medieval Canon Law,' in *Medieval Women and
the Sources of Medieval History*, ed. Joel T. Rosenthal (Athens: University of
Georgia Press 1990), 70–2

12 The merchant's wife prostitutes herself to a monk, who fraudulently pays her
with money that he borrowed from her husband. When the husband asks his
wife for the money owed, since he is given to understand that the monk payed
the debt to her, she brazenly tells him that she will pay him with the marriage
debt: *The Shipman's Tale*, esp. ll. 373 ff., in *The Riverside Chaucer*, 3d ed., ed.
Larry D. Benson (Boston: Houghton Mifflin, 1987), 207–8.

13 See especially C. 33 q. 5, which addresses both the equality of the debt and
female subordination in the order of nature in such a way that the two issues
are conflated. Peter Lombard derived most of his sources from Gratian (see
Sententiae 4.32.2). Also see Metz, 'Le Statut de la femme en droit canonique,'
81–2.

14 See, for example, John of Freiburg's *Summa confessorum* 4.2.36, fol. 220r.

15 'Mulier non habet jus plus petendi, et in petendo ulterius se magis mere-
tricem quam conjugem exhibet': Thomas Aquinas, *Commentaria in Sententias*
4.32.1.1, in *Opera omnia*, ed. S.E. Fretté (Paris: L. Vivès 1874), vol. 11: 131.

16 'Utrique enim fortitudine et imbecillitate corporum separantur. Sed ideo virtus maxima viri, mulieris minor, ut patiens viro esset, scilicet, ne feminis
repugnantibus, libido cogeret viros aliud appetere, aut in alium sexum pro-
ruere': Isidore of Seville, *Etymologiae* 11.2.19, *PL* 82, col. 417

17 Vincent of Beauvais, *Speculum naturale* 31.114, vol. 1 of *Speculum quadruplex; sive
speculum maius* (Douai: Baltazar Belleri 1624; repr. Graz: Akademischen Druck-
u. Verlagsanstalt 1964–5), col. 2384, cf. the entry in the twelfth-century Latin
bestiary, trans. by T.H. White as *The Book of Beasts* (New York: Putnam's 1954;
Capricorn Edition 1960), 222.

18 See James Brundage, 'Rape and Marriage in the Medieval Canon Law,' *Revue
de droit canonique* 28 (1978), 70–1. Note that even a betrothed girl, violently
abducted and known against her will by her intended, was not considered to
have been raped: see Thomas Aquinas, *Summa theologica* 2 2ae q. 154 art. 7,
resp. to obj. 3, trans. Fathers of the English Dominican Province (London:
Burns, Oates, and Washbourne 1921), vol. 13: 149–50; Alexander of Hales,
Summa theologica 2 2ae inq. 3 tract. 5 sect. 2, q. 1 tit. 5 c. 1, resp. to obj. 3, ed.

Fathers of the College of St Bonaventure (Florence: College of St Bonaventure 1930), vol. 3: 642.

19 For the insistence on mutuality in married vows of chastity, see C. 33 q. 5 c. 1–4.

20 'Ad primum ergo dicendum, quod quamvis agere sit nobilius quam pati; tamen eadem est proportio patientis ad patiendum, et agentis ad agendum; et secundum hoc est ibi aequalitas proportionis': Aquinas, *Commentaria in Sententias* 4.32.1.3, in *Opera*, vol. 11: 134. For a general indication of the degree to which Aquinas leans on the active/passive binary as a marker of gender, see the entry for *femina* in *Index Thomisticus* (Stuttgart-Bad Cannstatt: Fromann-Holzboog 1974), sect. 2, pt. 1, vol. 9, no. 32337.

21 See Danielle Jacquart and Claude Thomasset, *Sexuality and Medicine in the Middle Ages*, trans. Matthew Adamson (Princeton, NJ: Princeton University Press, 1988), 128, 154, and Joan Cadden, *The Meanings of Sex Difference in the Middle Ages: Medicine, Science, and Culture* (Cambridge: Cambridge University Press 1993), 108–9, 117–19.

22 'Immo debet illud nutrire et fovere ut sit idoneum ad usus viriles, quia carnis ad officium carnea membra placent': Thomas of Chobham, *Summa confessorum* 7.2.9.3, 363; cf. 4.2.7.11, 157, and 7.12.3, 560.

23 John of Freiburg follows Aquinas in permitting women to adorn themselves in order to please their husbands. He also cites Albert the Great's advice that, in the event that a husband has difficulty consummating the marriage, the woman should be counselled to dress more provocatively: *Summa confessorum* 3.34.284, fol. 214r; 4.16.23, fol. 236r. Cf. Dyan Elliott, 'Dress as Mediator between Inner and Outer Self: The Pious Matron of the High and Later Middle Ages,' *Mediaeval Studies* 53 (1991), esp. 288–9.

24 'Dicunt etiam quidam magni quod vxor tenetur se exhibere viro suo ad oscula consueta si exigit et quod nec venialiter peccat virum etiam non petentem amplexando et osculando debito modo et bona intentione, vt scilicet eum ab ira vel ab alio peccato reuocet. His videtur textus scripture concordare consilio Salomonis prouer.v. dicentis. Letare cum muliere adolescentie tue. Cerua carissima et gratissimus bimnulus vbera eius inebrient te in omni tempore': John Nider, *De morali lepra* c. 16 (Louvain: Johann von Paderborn *ca* 1481), fol. 82r.

25 Ibid., c. 16, fol. 81r–v. If such acts were motivated by the desire to have children, to avoid fornication, or to render the debt when the husband might otherwise be impotent, they were sinless. However, John also permits illicit rubbings to keep the husband from going outside the marriage bed to satisfy his desires. In such a case, it would be a very grave sin, but still not classified as mortal.

26 'Virum quemdam fuisse percipimus qui tali vitio subiacebat, vt non ei sufficeret delectatio coitus cum vxore; quin etiam eam contrectationibus illicitis molestaret. Ergo, vbi nocte quadam, vxore reclamante, Deique vindictam imprecante, maritus, perpetrato violenter scelere, ad ventris officium surrexit: mox soluto ventre, per secreta naturae in cloacam eius viscera descenderunt': Thomas of Cantimpré, *Miraculorum, et exemplorum memorabilium sui temporis, libri dvo. In quibus praeterea, ex mirifica apum repub. vniuersa vitae bene et christiane instituendae ratio (quo vetus, boni vniversalis, alludit inscriptio) traditur* 2.30.55, ed. George Colvener (Douai: Baltazar Belleri 1597), 292. After voiding his entrails, the husband was carried back to bed screaming to have his hands cut off. He died the third hour of the day.

27 Thomas Aquinas, *Commentaria in Sententias* 4.35.1.4; 4.32.2.2–3, in *Opera*, vol. 11: 176, 131–3

28 John Nider, *De morali lepra* c. 16, fol. 78v; c. 17, fols. 84v–85r. Note that the possible witholding of the debt from the leprous spouse is a softening of the strict letter of canon law (see X.4.8.2).

29 See James Brundage, 'Carnal Delight: Canonistic Theories of Sexuality,' *Proceedings of the 5th International Congress of Medieval Canon Law*, eds. Stephan Kuttner and Kenneth Pennington (Vatican City: Biblioteca Apostolica Vaticana 1980), 374–6; *Law, Sex, and Christian Society*, 350–1, 426–8.

30 'Sed contra per redditionem debiti medicamentum praestatur contra uxoris concupiscentiam. Sed medicus cui est infirmus aliquis commissus, tenetur morbo ejus subvenire, etiam si ipse non petat. Ergo vir uxori non petenti tenetur debitum reddere': Aquinas, *Commentaria in Sententias* 4.32.1.2, in *Opera*, vol. 11: 131; cf. *Summa theologica* Supp. q. 64 art. 2, vol. 11: 314–15. Also see Noonan, *Contraception*, 285. Noonan notes that Thomas's position is in fact a modification of Albert the Great's statement that a spouse, intuiting sinful desires in the other, should render without being explicitly requested to do so. Albert, however, does not identify the respective genders of the actors in this scenario.

31 For example, see Thomas's conclusions that a pious rendering of the conjugal act was deserving of merit and that marriage conferred grace: *Commentaria in Sententias* 4.26.2.1 and 3, vol. 11: 70–1, 73–4. See Fabian Parmisano, 'Love and Marriage in the Middle Ages – II,' *New Blackfriars* 50 (1969), 659–60; Servais Pinckaers, 'Ce que le Moyen Âge pensait du mariage,' *La Vie spirituelle* Supp. 20 (1967), 432–3.

32 See Dominican John of Freiburg, *Summa confessorum*, 4.2.40, fol. 220r; cf. Franciscan Francis de Plathea's treatment: *Tractatus de debito conjugali* q. 11, Bologna, Biblioteca communale dell'Archiginnasio, MS A170, fol. 71r. Note, however, that Francis attaches the important rider that to exact is never a

necessity as this goes beyond apostolic law: a person cannot be compelled to seek his own indebtedness. Franciscan Bernardino of Siena also employs this motif, as will be seen below. Jean Gerson, the chancellor of Paris and a secular master with Franciscan leanings, adopts it (*Regulae mandatorum* c. 149, in *Oeuvres complètes*, vol. 9: 131), as does Denis the Carthusian, who was deeply influenced by Gerson (*De laudabili vita conjugatorum* art. 5, in *Doctoris Ecstatici D. Dionysii Cartusiani Opera omnia*, ed. by the monks of the Carthusian Order, vol. 37; *Opera minora*, vol. 6 [Tournai: Typis Cartusiae S.M. de Pratis 1909], 63). Note that Denis is rather unusual in that he extends a parallel obligation to the wife to render the debt when her husband does not expressly require it, but the circumstances are different. The examples Denis gives are if the husband wants another woman, and his wife is aware of it, or if he made a simple vow of chastity (which generally means that he can render and not exact). John of Freiburg, on the other hand, states explicitly that the bashful-spouse motif applied to the wife alone and that the wife should not render the debt unless the husband is explicitly seeking it.

33 See, for example, Parmisano, 'Love and Marriage in the Middle Ages,' 658.

34 See Susan Mosher Stuard's discussion of how civil lawyers actually looked to Gratian for guidance in solidifying the husband's control: 'From Women to Woman: New Thinking about Gender c. 1140,' *Thought* 64 (1989), esp. 213–15; also 'Burdens of Matrimony: Husbanding and Gender in Medieval Italy,' in *Medieval Masculinities: Regarding Men in the Middle Ages*, ed. Clare A. Lees, 61–71 (Minneapolis: University of Minnesota 1994).

35 The context for this discussion is the issue of whether or not the wife should obey a husband who sinfully recalls a vow to God after he had formally authorized it: Raymond of Peñafort, *Summa de poenitentia* 3.33.4, 383.

36 For the use of this phrase, see Frederick Pollock and Frederic William Maitland, *The History of English Law*, 2d ed. (Cambridge: Cambridge University Press 1952), vol. 2: 407 and n.3. *Virga* was a common word for 'penis' (see J.F. Niermeyer, *Mediae Latinitatis Lexicon Minus* [Leiden: E.J. Brill 1954–6], 1110) and is used as such in a number of pastoral manuals (see Robert of Flamborough, *Liber poenitentialis* 2.2.15, ed. J.J. Francis Firth [Toronto: Pontifical Institute of Mediaeval Studies 1971], 65, and John of Freiburg, *Summa confessorum* 4.16.19, fol. 236r). Robert's manual was written between 1208 and 1213. On his work, see Michaud-Quantin, 'A propos des premières *summae confessorum*,' 276–8, and Baldwin, *Masters, Princes, and Merchants*, vol. 1: 32–3.

37 *Commentaria in Sententias* 4.32.1.2.3, in *Opera*, vol. 11: 133. Bernardino of Siena refers to Aquinas directly: 'Thomas autem addit quod mulierem passionem suam non semper est tutum viro proprio indicare, maxime si sodomitico peccato infectus est, ne exinde ei uxor abominabilis fiat, sicuti talibus facile fieri

solet. Si autem uxori de viri prudentia et bonitate constat, tunc ei honeste revelare potest': Serm. 17, art. 1, c. 1, in *Opera*, ed. Fathers of the College of St Bonaventure (Florence: College of St Bonaventure 1950), vol. 1: 209; also see Serm. 20, ed. Luciano Banchi, *Le prediche volgari di San Bernardino da Siena, dette nella Piazza del Campa l'anno MCCCCXXVII* (Siena: San Bernardino 1884), vol. 2: 141–2; Serm. 24, ed. Ciro Cannarozzi, *Le prediche volgari di San Bernardino da Siena* (Pistoia: Alberto Pacinotti 1934), vol. 1: 387. Cf. Cherubino of Spoleto: 'E se vedesse lo suo marito essere timoroso di Dio e conscienziato, dicagli apertamente la sua passione, acciò ch'egli per non peccare lassi stare. Ma se vede che il marito non ha timore di Dio, e ha mala consciencia, non gli debbe dire niente di questa sua passione, acciocchè non la venga ad abominare': *Regole della vita matrimoniale*, eds. Francesco Zambrini and Carlo Negroni, Scelta di curiosita letterarie inedite o rare dal secolo XIII al XVII, no. 228 (Bologna: Romagnoli-dall'Acqua 1888), 69.

38 John of Freiburg summarizes the debate over rendering and exacting the debt during menstruation in *Summa confessorum* 4.2.46, fol. 220v.

39 See Jacquart and Thomasset, *Sexuality and Medicine*, 72–8, 183–8; and Payer, *The Bridling of Desire*, 106–9. With respect to the possible rise of incidents of leprosy in the high Middle Ages, though more archaeological research is still required, R.I. Moore states: 'It is an acceptable working hypothesis that the explosion of anxiety in the twelfth century had its basis in a real epidemic of lepromatous leprosy, to which the population of north-western Europe was at first highly vulnerable': *The Formation of a Persecuting Society* (Oxford: Basil Blackwell 1987), 78. Pastoral manuals also articulate this concern over leprous and otherwise diseased offspring. See, for example, Thomas of Chobham's *Summa confessorum* 7.2.2.3, 338–9. The same anxieties are reiterated in John of Freiburg's later, and more sexually permissive, collection cited *supra*, note 38.

40 See, for example, Rudolf von Schlettstadt's *Historiae memorabiles*, ed. Erich Kleinschmidt (Cologne and Vienna: Böhlau 1974), no. 35, 96.

41 Robert of Brunne's *Handlyng Synne* gives a lurid discussion of the first penalty (ed. Frederick J. Furnivall, *EETS*, O.S., no. 119, pt. 1 [London: K. Paul, Trench, Trübner 1901], 281–2). For this motif, see Frederic C. Tubach, *Index exemplorum*, Folklore Fellows Communications, no. 204 (Helsinki: Akademia Scientiarum Fennica 1969), no. 1056. For sex on a vigil resulting in death and damnation see J. Th. Welter, *Le Speculum laicorum* (Paris: Auguste Picard 1914), c.35, 'De festis sanctorum colendis,' 58–9. One wonders if the *exemplum* concerning a woman who goes mad at the sight of her husband (and is cured when she confesses, at the suggestion of a Dominican) might not be intended to allude to the ambiguities of the marriage bed: see Tubach, *Index exemplorum*, no. 1164, and J.A. Herbert's description from a collection of *exempla* in

MS Additional 33956, fol. 83, *Catalogue of Romances in the Department of Manuscripts in the British Museum* (London: Trustees of the Museum 1910), vol. 3: 633, no. 85. Cf. Gregory the Great's anecdote regarding a wife who became possessed by a demon when she attended a dedication of a church after having marital intercourse: *Dialogues* 1.10, trans. O.J. Zimmerman, Fathers of the Church, vol. 39 (Washington, DC: Fathers of the Church 1959; repr. 1983), 42–3.

42 On the democratization and feminization of sanctity, see André Vauchez, *La Sainteté en Occident aux dernières siècles du Moyen Âge* (Rome: Ecole Française de Rome 1981), 243–9, 412–13; *Les Laïcs au Moyen Âge* (Paris: Cerf 1987), 79–82, 189–95. On the rise of female saints, also see Donald Weinstein and Rudolph Bell, *Saints and Society: The Two Worlds of Western Christendom, 1000–1700* (Chicago: University of Chicago Press 1982), 220–1; cf. Michael Goodich, 'The Contours of Female Piety in Later Medieval Hagiography,' *Church History* 50 (1981), 20–1. On the number of female mystics who were at one time married and the mothers of families, see Vauchez, *La Sainteté*, 442.

43 *Saints and Society*, 42–4, 234–5; cf. Richard Kieckhefer, *Unquiet Souls: Fourteenth-Century Saints and Their Religious Milieu* (Chicago: University of Chicago Press 1984), 142–3.

44 See *The Life of Christina of Markyate*, ed. and trans. C.H. Talbot (Oxford: Clarendon Press 1959), 59–65; for Dauphine, see *Vies Occitanes de saint Auzias et de sainte Dauphine* 2.3, ed. Jacques Cambell (Rome: Pontificium Athenaeum Antonianum 1963), 144; for Paula Gambara Costa, see *Bibliotheca Sanctorum* (Rome: Città Nuova 1966) vol. 6, cols. 28–9. Also note the efforts of Cunegund of Poland's confessor to make her consummate her marriage: *AA SS*, July, 5: 683.

45 For Mary of Oignies, see *AA SS*, June, 5: 550; for Bridget of Sweden, see the life of the two Peter Olavs which was used for her process of canonization: *Acta et processus canonizacionis Beate Birgitte*, ed. Isak Collijn (Uppsala: Almqvist and Wiksells 1924–31), 78; also see *AA SS*, October, 4: 488. For Dorothea of Montau, see *Die Akten des Kanonisationsprozesses Dorotheas von Montau von 1394 bis 1521*, ed. Richard Stachnik (Cologne and Vienna: Böhlau 1978), 204, and *Vita Dorotheae Montoviensis Magistri Johannis Marienwerder* 2.4–6, ed. Hans Westpfahl (Cologne and Graz: Böhlau 1964), 68–72; for Frances of Rome, see *I Processi inediti per Francesca Bussa dei Ponziani*, ed. P.T. Lugano (Vatican City: Biblioteca Apostolica Vaticana 1945), 240–1.

46 This is especially true for Frances of Rome: see *Processi*, ed. Lugano, 39, 57–8, and the later sixteenth-century life of Frances, in *AA SS*, March, 2: 138, and Dorothea of Montau, *Akten*, ed. Stachnik, 204, 272–3, 306; *Vita Dorotheae* 2.12, ed. Westpfahl, 75–6.

47 C. 33 q. 5 c. 1 and c. 5; Peter Lombard, *Sententiae* 4.32.2

48 With respect to paying the debt in a church, for example, John of Freiburg, following Albert the Great, says that, if no other place can be found, one should submit with sorrow in one's heart: *Summa confessorum* 4.2.43, fol. 220v. For Bernardino of Siena's discussion of a sorrowful rendering of the debt, see note 81, below.

49 Benton, 'Consciousness of Self and Perception of Individuality,' in *Renaissance and Renewal in the Twelfth Century*, eds. Robert L. Benson and Giles Constable (Cambridge, MA: Harvard University Press 1982), 284–5; Bynum, 'Did the Twelfth Century Discover the Individual?' in *Jesus as Mother: Studies in the Spirituality of the High Middle Ages* (Berkeley and Los Angeles: University of California Press 1982), 87

50 Cf. Elliott, 'Dress as Mediator,' 303–5.

51 On Dorothea and Frances, see *supra*, note 45; for Margery, see *The Book of Margery Kempe* 1.3, 1.4, eds. Sanford Brown Meech and Hope Emily Allen, *EETS*, O.S., no. 212 (London: H. Milford, Oxford University Press 1940), 11–12, 14.

52 'Illico eam Dominus spiculis amoris vulneravit, et eam incendens caritate ferventer ardente dicebat: "Tu potes me bene magnifice diligere. Nam frequenter a viro rapui te, quando adhuc vixit et estimavit te possidere"': *Vita Dorotheae* 3.13, ed. Westpfahl, 131.

53 'Quod vero mirabaris de domina que ad indulgentias veniens corrupta est. Repondio [*sic*] tibi. Sunt quedam mulieres qui [*sic*] continentiam habent sed non diligunt ... Et ideo ex continentia aliquando oritur superbia et presumptio ... Si vero aliqua talis esset intentionis: quod nec propter totum mundum si ei preberetur vellet semel maculari: impossibile est talem relinqui ad turpia. Veruntamen si deus permitteret ex occulta iusticia sua talem cadere: plus fieret ei ad coronam quam ad peccatum: dummodo esset contra eius voluntatem': Bridget of Sweden, *Revelationes* 4.20, ed. Florian Waldauf von Waldenstein (Nuremberg: Anton Koberger 1500).

54 Alexander of Hales, *Quaestiones disputatae: 'Antequam esset frater'* q. 68, membrum 7, ed. Fathers of the College of St Bonaventure (Florence: College of St Bonaventure 1960), vol. 3: 1357–8; Thomas Aquinas, *Summa theologica* 2 2ae q. 172 art. 3, vol. 14: 24–5; *Summa virtutum de remediis anime*, ed. Siegfried Wenzel (Athens: University of Georgia Press 1984), 284–5. Although this work was probably intended for the instruction of the clergy, it was nevertheless a major source for Chaucer's *Parson's Tale*.

55 'Vixit ... B. Francisca cum viro suo annis viginti octo, et sex mensibus: duodecim annis habitavit cum eo a carnis copula separata de communi partium voluntate: et tunc mirabiliter commutata est ... Nam tanta animi suavitate, et mentis oblectatione supernis intererat, et a cunctis erat exuta terrenis et

194   Dyan Elliott

Christo unita... et frequenter post tales meditationes et orationes in extasi
rapiebatur': *AA SS*, March, 2: 96.

56 *Vita* in *Acta et processus*, ed. Collijn, 80. This account is taken from *Revelaciones*
5.11, ed. Birger Bergh (Uppsala: Almqvist and Wiksell 1971), 163); also see
Extravagantes 47 (*Den Heliga Birgittas Revelaciones Extravagantes*, ed. Lennart
Hollman [Uppsala: Almqvist and Wiksell 1956]), 162–3.

57 'Quomodo eciam ante obitum viri sui vidit quedam': *vita* in *Acta et processus*,
ed. Collijn, 81

58 'Ceterum (quod dictu vix est credible) occupata in domus distractiuis labori-
bus, vel vexata debilitate in puerperio, aut in necessitatibus proprijs ministrans
proprijs infantulis, mens sanctae feminae inter ista saepius altiorem et deuo-
tiorem de rebus diuinis Christum concernentibus contemplationis gradum
actu habuit, quam me triginta annorum religiosum professione et nomine
vnquam scio habuisse. Inter quas visiones, prout in ea sepe didici, diuino spir-
itu praeuidit, quae humanitus praescire non poterat, de quibus tamen reuela-
tionibus modicam aestimationem faciebat, sed de diligendo Deum, et de
obseruandis Christi praeceptis et consilijs sine peccato maxime curabat':
Nider, *Formicarium* 2.9 (Douai: Baltazar Belleri 1602), 155.

59 'Id tamen reciproce nullatenus ipsa exigebat, sed ne istis casta mens occup-
aretur, preces ad virginem beatissimam (quam dilexit plurimum) coepit mul-
tiplicare, vt a suo filio purissimo, marito donum daretur maioris continentiae,
quam hactenus habuerat in matrimonio ... Quae casta petitio feminae tam
fuit efficax, vt Venus in viro pene eradicata esse videretur. Nam maritus de se
postmodum admirabatur saepius, vunde sibi hoc castimonie munus, quod in
se sentiebat praeter solitum, aduenisset: Sciuit quippe nec abstinentia, nec
precibus, nec ieiunijs id petisse a Deo, quod vxoris merito a Deo dabatur.
Propterea quadam vice satis benigne secreto vxori dixit: Credo, inquit, (ni fallar) me frigidum esse, sed nescio qualiter procurasti': Nider, *Formicarium* 2.9,
154.

60 Bernardino recorded his Latin sermons for his own and for his fellow-Fran-
ciscans' use. His vernacular sermons, however, were recorded by scribes while
he was preaching. Of particular interest from the standpoint of married sexuality are the Latin sermons 17–18, in *Opera*, vol. 1: 204–26; sermons 19–21 from
the Lenten course preached at Siena in 1427, in *Prediche volgari*, ed. Banchi,
vol. 2: 85–172; and sermons 24–5 of his Florentine Lenten sermons for the
year 1424, in *Prediche volgari*, ed. Cannarozzi, vol. 1: 381–423. For an introduction to Bernardino's preaching, see Iris Origo, *The World of San Bernardino*
(New York: Harcourt, Brace and World 1962), esp. ch. 2, 43–76. Also see Cuth-
bert Gumbinger, 'St Bernardine's Unedited *Prediche Volgari*,' *Franciscan Studies*
25 n.s., 4,1 (1944), esp. 14–16, for translated excerpts on women and marriage.

61 '"Rara siquidem avis in terra" (Juvenal, *Satirae*, 6, 165) est huiuscedmodi
   sermo, et rarissime praedicatus': Serm. 18, *Opera*, vol. 1: 217; cf. Serm. 17, 204;
   Serm. 24, ed. Cannarozzi, *Prediche volgari*, vol. 1: 381–2. For the custom of leaving sexually explicit discussions to the confessional, see A. Lecoy de la
   Marche, *La chaire française au Moyen Âge*, 2d ed. (Paris: Renouard, H. Laurens
   1886), 434.

62 'Che alla barba di tutti i sodomiti io voglio tenere colle donne, e dico che la
   donna è più pulita e preziosa nella carne sua, che non è l'uomo': Serm. 19, ed.
   Banchi, *Prediche volgari*, vol. 2: 108. He does, however, ascribe greater reason to
   the male. Women's deficient reason renders her more fragile, which explains
   why Eve was susceptible to temptation: ibid., Serm. 20, 134.

63 'Ecce quod uxor in ea parte, id est in carne, in qua vir infirmior est, in eius
   defensionem venit': Serm. 48, c. 2, *Opera*, vol. 2: 107.

64 This attitude is exemplified in Augustine's letter to Ecdicia, a noble matron
   who took a vow of chastity before she had gained her husband's permission.
   Augustine, recognizing her greater spiritual strength, argues that this imposes
   greater responsibilities on her and denounces her precipitous vow: Ep. 262, c.
   5, *Epistolae*, ed. A Goldbacher, *CSEL*, vol. 57 (Vienna: F. Tempski; Leipzig: G.
   Freytag 1911), 623; cf. 625. This letter and the spirit of the letter were reiterated throughout the Middle Ages. It was especially central to Gratian's vision
   of the conjugal debt.

65 See, for example, Serm. 17, art. 3, c. 1, *Opera*, vol. 1: 215, and Serm. 24, ed.
   Cannarozzi, *Prediche volgari*, vol. 1: 393. Bernardino's position as traditional
   defender and innovative restrainer of the debt is a calculated balancing act
   that is open to misrepresentation. Margaret L. King, for example, stresses the
   former at the expense of the latter in *Women of the Renaissance* (Chicago: University of Chicago Press 1991), 40–1.

66 Brundage, 'Sexual Equality in Medieval Canon Law,' 69

67 See John of Freiburg's discussion of this question and his summary of varying
   views: *Summa confessorum* 1.8.43, fol. 21v.

68 'Oh quot indicibilibus et quot incredibilibus modis viri abutuntur uxoribus
   suis! Quis umquam honeste exprimere posset? Non utique videntur copulae
   coniugales, sed abusiones porcinae et ultra quam bestiales. Et licet quandoque
   uxores sint male contentae, tamen quocumque modo assentiant': Serm. 17,
   art. 1, c. 1, *Opera*, vol. 1: 210. For shock value, Bernardino goes on to argue that
   consent to such acts is worse than the wife having intercourse with her own
   father.

69 'Magna tamen differentia est inter vexationes et praecepta, quae obligant ad
   debitum reddendum uxores, et illa quae obligant viros, quia evidentiores vexationes exspectare possunt coniuges quam mariti. Cuius triplex potest esse

ratio. – Primo, quia mulieres verecundiores sunt ad petendum quam viri. – Secundo, quia talis petitio vilior et ignominiosior est mulieri quam viro. Unde secundum naturalem instinctum et cursum potius habent rationem patientis et suscipientis quam exigentis et stimulantis, et rationem subditi plusquam dominantis; et ideo petitionis improbitas maiorem impudentiam sapit et turpius stat in eis quam in viris. – Tertia ratio est, quia mulieres sunt magis sub regimine viri quam econverso': Serm. 17, art. 3, c. 1, *Opera*, vol. 1: 215. For the shy wife topos, also see Serm. 24, ed. Cannarozzi, *Prediche volgari*, vol. 1: 393.

70 See Lester K. Little, *Religious Poverty and the Profit Economy* (Ithaca, NY: Cornell University Press 1978), 166.

71 Serm. 17, art. 1, c. 2, *Opera*, vol. 1: 210

72 '… semper in luto degere teneatur semperque in illo agitari, ut porca': Serm. 17, art. 1, c. 2, *Opera*, vol. 1: 210. For the comparison of regular versus matrimonial obedience, also see Serm. 20, ed. Banchi, *Prediche volgari*, vol. 2: 142–3; Serm. 24, ed. Cannarozzi, *Prediche volgari*, vol. 1: 389–90.

73 'Unde sicut nemo sanae mentis diceret quod uxor debeat obedire compari suo ad concubendum in sacro altari vel in alio sancto loco, sic nec dicere debet quod ad concubendum die noctuque, et quasi infinities sibi debeat obedire': Serm. 17, art. 1, c. 2, *Opera*, vol. 1: 211; cf. Serm. 18, art. 3, c.2, 223; Serm. 21, ed. Banchi, *Prediche volgari*, vol. 2: 172.

74 Serm. 17, art. 2, c. 1, *Opera*, vol. 1: 213. Bernardino's conviction that rendering on a holy day is still a venial sin can be gleaned from his inflected remark that, if performed 'cum displicentia,' this does not constitute a mortal sin: Serm. 18, art. 2, c. 3, 224.

75 Serm. 20, ed. Banchi, *Prediche volgari*, vol. 2: 150

76 Serm. 21, ed. Banchi, *Prediche volgari*, vol. 2: 164; cf. Serm. 24, ed. Canarrozzi, *Prediche volgari*, vol. 1: 392–3. Also see Serm. 18, art. 2, c. 2, *Opera*, vol. 1: 221. Note, however, that in this last instance the three are not prioritized as they are in the vernacular sermons.

77 'Se la mala ventura nel porta, lascianelo portare, non v'andare tu, non gli ubbidire a niuna ribalderia di peccato. Meglio t'è d'avere pace con Dio che con lui. Piuttosto debbi ubbidre a Dio che a lui': Serm. 24, ed. Cannarozzi, *Prediche volgari*, vol. 1: 394.

78 'E se elli t'uccidesse per quello, sappi e siane certa che l'anima tua andarà subito nella gloria di vita eterna': Serm. 20, ed. Banchi, *Prediche volgari*, vol. 2: 139; cf. Serm. 24, ed. Cannarozzi, *Prediche volgari*, vol. 1: 388–9, and Serm. 17, art. 1, c. 1, *Opera*, vol. 1: 209–10. See Augustine, *De nuptiis et concupiscentia* 1.8.9, eds. C.F. Urba and J. Zycha, *CSEL*, vol. 42 (Prague and Vienna: F. Tempski; and Leipzig: G. Freytag 1902), 220–1, and *De bono coniugali* 11.12, ed. J. Zycha, *CSEL*, vol. 41 (Prague and Vienna: F. Tempski; and Leipzig: G. Freytag 1900),

203–4; cf. Gratian C. 32 q. 7 c. 11. Note, however, that Bernardino's advice about resisting 'unnatural sex' was the rule, not the exception (see notes 92 and 94, below).

79 Women's greater interest in spiritual matters is everywhere assumed. See, for example, his complaint that men are no longer as spiritual as they once were and that this is even true of some women: Serm. 19, ed. Banchi, *Prediche volgari*, vol. 2: 111–12.

80 'Tertio, quoad divinos gratiarum influxus et spirituales visitationes; quibusdam enim coniugum, sicut ego iam pluries reperi, a Deo quandoque immittitur tantus carnalium horror tantusque spiritualium devotionum et gustuum appetitus, quod absque summo horrore et magna difficultate nequeunt debitum reddere coniugale; et tunc certe Deus in parte ad redditionem huiusmodi debiti per Spiritus Sancti privatam legem, quae communi legi praeiudicat, videtur aliqualiter impedire': Serm. 17, art. 1, c. 3, *Opera*, vol. 1: 211; cf. Serm. 20, ed. Banchi, *Prediche volgari*, vol. 2: 147–8; Serm. 24, ed. Cannarozzi, *Prediche volgari*, vol. 1: 392.

81 Serm. 20, ed. Banchi, *Prediche volgari*, vol. 2: 147. Note that is the only instance in which the more spiritual party bears a masculine pronoun. But Bernardino then immediately appeals to women about the ways to assess whether or not one should render the debt ('Credo che ci sieno molte di voi donne, che vorreste sapere queste tre cose ch' io v' ho detto, a ciò che voi vi poteste bene règgiare e non cascare mai in niuno peccato mortale,' 148). Also note that Bernardino has very exacting standards regarding the spirit in which the devout person should render. A wife who desires chastity but, when compelled to render the debt, feels physical pleasure is considered guilty of a venial sin. The preferred scenario is if the pious wife renders the debt, but is tortured in the mind and devoid of all physical pleasure: see Serm. 2, art. 3, c. 3, *Opera*, vol. 6: 241. Significantly, for this example Bernardino draws on the *Trattatti* of Hugh Panziera (d. *ca* 1330) – a treatise on contemplation (eds. Lorenzo de Morgiani and Giovanni da Mugauza [Florence: Antonio di Bartolomeo Miscomini 1492], Tract 8, fol. 52v; on Hugh, see Clément Schmitt's article in *Dictionnaire de spiritualité* [Paris: Beauchesne 1969], vol. 7, pt. 1, cols. 892–3). The context for Hugh's discussion is the ways in which the same action can be interpreted as vicious or virtuous. Note, however, that Hugh invokes the example of a pious man, and that Bernardino changes the gender. For more insight into Bernardino's conception of a pious rendering of the debt, see Serm. 4, art. 1, c. 3, *Opera*, vol. 6: 300, and Serm. 1, art. 3, c. 3, *Opera*, vol. 7: 323–4. Cf. Cherubino of Spoleto, *Regole della vita matrimoniale*, 48.

82 'Arà uno marito che non fia se non carnaccia e broda. Se di tanta grazia di Dio la dislega un poco, e à auto molto senno, in forma non dia iscandolo al mar-

ito, ma rendali el debito suo, non però ogni volta, come se non fusse in quella grazia, sanza peccato': Serm. 24, ed. Cannarozzi, *Prediche volgari*, vol. 1: 392.

83 Serm. 24, ed. Cannarozzi, *Prediche volgari*, vol. 1: 393; cf. Serm. 20, ed. Banchi, *Prediche volgari*, vol. 1: 148; Serm. 17, art. 1, c. 3, *Opera*, vol. 1: 211.

84 'Qui enim talium spiritualium donorum non habent experimentum parvipendunt et negligunt impedimentum spiritualium gratiarum et devotionum in alligatis ad negotia carnis; propterea plus debito stant cum consiliis suis huiusmodi ligamento, et parum pro vinculis divini amoris': Serm. 17, art. 1, c. 3, *Opera*, vol. 1: 212.

85 'Ma se tu vuoi buono consèglio, non andare a frate da Grosseto, chè questi tali sogliono strégnare altrui a casa, che non si díe strégnare ... Che uno che sia di questi grossi, ti dirà – oh, tu se' a ubidienzia del tuo marito! Tu se' tenuta a lui: non puoi fare altro tu. Nol fai volontariamente. Va', va': tu se' scusata ... Che talvolta andrai a uno che sarà carnale, e non dotto, e diratti: – elli t' è lecito per piacere al tuo marito che tu ti lisci, e che tu t'adorni. – Or va', chè elli è una bestia': Serm. 20, ed. Banchi, *Prediche volgari*, vol. 2: 149.

86 Banchi makes this observation: *Prediche volgari*, vol. 2: 149, n.1.

87 'Notabile est quod quando alter coniugum longa experientia didicit quod ex frequenti et prompta redditione debiti suus compar ad meliora nullo modo disponitur, nec a carnali impietate retrahitur, nec in posterum per hoc retrahendus praesumitur, quin potius semper in se perseverat durus, in proximum impius et omnino a Deo separatus et alienus; numquid castae coniugi tantopere est curandum, ut semper ad votum satisfaciat libidini indurati cordis et obstinati, et praecipue ubi divinorum charismatum uberem proventum ex hoc sibi subtrahi apertissime experitur? Puto enim quod omnis divinitus instigatus et accensus ad altiora dona, si in consimili casu talis coniugis poneretur, aliter iudicaret': Serm. 17, art. 2, c. 3, *Opera*, vol. 1: 214.

88 See Hasenohr, 'La Vie quotidienne de la femme vue par l'église: L'enseignement des "Journées chrétiennes" de la fin du Moyen-Âge,' in *Frau und spätmittelalterlicher Alltag*, Internationaler Kongress krems an der Donau 2. bis 5. Oktober 1984, Österreichischen Akademie der Wissenschaften, Philosophisch-Historische Klasse, Sitzungsberichte, 473 (Vienna: Verlag der Österreichischen Akademie der Wissenschaften 1986), 22 ff. With respect to Bernardino, she states: 'On lira dans S. Bernardin un éloge de la femme forte de veine biblique, plus attentif à détailler les effets bénéfiques de son administration avisée et de son dévouement charitable qu'à vanter son esprit de dévotion,' 37–8.

89 'E avete la prima parte principale, e con molta discrezione, la viva dilezione. Non perdere l'uno per l'altro; la via del mezzo!': Serm. 24, ed. Cannarozzi, *Prediche volgari*, vol. 1: 393; cf. Serm. 20, ed. Banchi, *Prediche volgari*, vol. 2: 148.

90 Dominici argues that the husband's greater flexibility in absenting himself from home, hence his greater control over payment of the debt, indirectly shows God's greater trust in female continence: *Regola del governo di cura familiare*, ed. Donato Salvi (Florence: A. Garinei 1860), bk. 2, 88. Later he goes so far as to advance that more women are saved due to their greater chastity (bk. 4, 175–6). For a brief discussion of Dominici and other Italian writers attempting to balance a woman's domestic and spiritual responsibilities in this period, see Silvana Vecchio, 'The Good Wife,' in *Silences of the Middle Ages*, ed. Christiane Klapisch-Zuber, vol. 2 of *A History of Women in the West* (Cambridge, MA: Harvard University Press 1992), 128–33.

91 'Della parte prima rispuoseti Dio glorioso parlando ad Eva, quando disse in pena del peccato: *sub potestate viri eris, et ipse dominabitur tui*. Per la parte prima intendo la signoria nell' atto matrimoniale, del quale scrivo con vergogna e paura, e perciò ne dico poco': Giovanni Dominici, *Regola*, bk. 2, 87.

92 'Di qua arai lo 'ntelletto chiaro, lo sposo è del tempo più signore che non se' tu, e te scusa l' ubedienzia che forse non scuserebbe lui; poi si può per alcuna notte seperare, e non tu. Ma ben debbi essere cauta nelle solennità di non gli dare cagione, e prudentemente occupare il tacito tempo insino il senti adormentato; e così da lungi coricata fa' come se non vi fussi, trovandoti di fuori anzi si desti': Giovanni Dominici, *Regola*, bk. 2, 88. Note, however, that Giovanni, like all authorities, including Bernardino, argues that the wife should resist certain acts (which he specifies as being turned into a beast or a male) until death if necessary (88–9).

93 'La parte seconda di tal penitenzia ditermina la vita della maritata, dicendo: esso signoreggerà te; cioè tu reggerai te, negli ornamenti, cibi, discorsi, guadagni, limosine e orazioni, secondo la sua volontà, e non la tua. Portare oro, ariento, gemme, panni vani, superflui e suntuosi; dipignersi e farsi vana contro la volontà del marito, o per piacere ad altri che a suo marito, è peccato grave. Se veramente esso vuole, o tel comanda, non ornare te, ma le cose sue; e tu se' sua. Fallo per obedienzia, ma non per volontà. E se il puoi pregare di tal voler t' assolva, farai bene ...Volendo tu rompa i digiuni comandati per cenar con esso, fa' quanto puoi di non ubidirlo, ma non tanto ti batta, o se troppo scandalezzi. E arrendendoti a lui, protestali il peccato sarà suo, e mangia per obedienzia, ma non per volontà, temperando sì la gola che Dio t' abbi per iscusata': Giovanni Dominici, *Regola*, bk. 2, 89–90.

94 Francis de Plathea, *Tractatus de debito conjugali* q. 2, fols. 68v–69v. The twelve reasons for refusing the debt, many of which admit to qualification, are: when the exacting spouse's rights are suspended owing to fornication; when one exacts immediately after marriage and the respondent wishes to avail him/herself of the two months of demurral permitted by canon law; when render-

ing is detrimental to health (as with a leprous spouse); when the exacting party is mad; when the husband cannot render without weakening his body; when the foetus would be endangered; during menstruation; in a holy place; in instances of consanguinity; if the husband wishes to know the wife sodomitically or in a 'modo brutali'; if the spouses are spiritual cognates; if the woman is near parturition and believes that rendering would be dangerous to the foetus. On Francis, see Luke Wadding, *Scriptores ordinis minorum* (Rome: Franciscus Albertus Tani 1650), 132, and Jo. Hyacinth Sbaralea, *Supplementum et castigatio ad Scriptores trium ordinum S. Francisci a Waddingo, aliisve descriptos* (Rome: S Michaelis ad Ripam, apud Linum Contedini 1806), 279–80.

95 Cherubino's sermons were considered to be too hyperbolic and secular. These tendencies were reined in after he spent one Lent studying under Bernardino. See Raffaele Piergrossi's discussion of Cherubino in *Dictionnaire de spiritualité*, vol. 2, pt. 1, col. 824. Cherubino often refers to Bernardino in his work. See, for example, *Regole della vita matrimoniale*, 73, 79, 87.

96 Cherubino of Spoleto, *Regole della vita matrimoniale*, 93–8

97 Ibid., 83

Sex, Money, and Prostitution in Medieval English Culture

RUTH MAZO KARRAS

To write the history of prostitution is to impose a modern category on the past. If we look to the past for commercialized sex, we will find it, but that does not mean each society understood or treated these practices in the same way. Conversely, if another culture has labelled women with some word which we habitually translate as 'prostitute,' this does not necessarily mean that those women are what we would think of as prostitutes.[1] More useful than an attempt to locate and describe practices in the past that correspond to a modern understanding of 'prostitution' is an attempt to understand what a particular culture classified that way, and why. England in the later Middle Ages provides a case in point. Although canon law defined prostitution in terms of promiscuity rather than financial exchange, canon lawyers and medieval people generally were certainly aware of the existence of women engaging in commercial sex,[2] and both ecclesiastical and secular courts sought to control these women. A number of scholars have discussed, for other periods in European history, the way in which the legal regulation of prostitution came to be used as a means of controlling all women, and this was certainly the case for medieval England as well.[3] But it was not only legal records that constructed the category of prostitute in such a way as to control all feminine sexuality. The same process can be observed in literary texts, both secular and religious or didactic. The recognition of the existence of commercial prostitutes, whose sin, however, was formally defined as their promiscuity rather than their selling of their bodies, allowed the conflation of all deviant feminine sexuality with venality and the assimilation of all disorderly women with prostitutes.

Detailed depictions of a commercialized subculture of prostitution do not emerge in medieval English literature, although they do appear in the French *fabliaux*, which may also have been known in England. Marie-Thérèse Lorcin argues that in the *fabliaux* the prostitute's greed rather than her sexuality makes her a threat: in seeking to extort more than her legitimate wage from her clients, she becomes the quintessence of feminine sin and threatens to ruin men.[4] Prostitutes are not the only greedy women (or persons) in the *fabliaux*, and the butt of the satire is often not the grasping prostitute but the priest who wants to sleep with her. The woman's greed may be only a backdrop to the lustfulness of the clergy, but those features of the story that are backdrop rather than main focus often indicate clearly the assumptions the society makes, and here the venality of the prostitute is revealed as key.[5]

But the *fabliaux* address the relation between money and sex in other ways than by directly depicting prostitutes. All sexual activity is drawn into the commercial realm. Body parts themselves become commodities: disembodied male and female genitalia are displayed for sale at the market; a wife whose husband's body is 'covered with pricks' describes herself as 'rich.'[6] Greed for sexual organs (which serve as characters in their own right in 13 per cent of the known *fabliaux*) is connected to economic greed.

This connection of sexual desire with covetousness, greed, or avarice appears, not only in the commodification of sexuality in the *fabliaux*, but in similar developments in English literature. Chaucer's Wife of Bath is the most obvious example. For her, sex and money intersect in marriage, not in prostitution, but she still uses a vocabulary of sale and purchase, and connects greed and lust as motives for her marriages. In wedding her five husbands, she 'picked out the best / Both of their lower purse, and of their money-chest.'[7] She despoils her husband's money-box and also drains him sexually.[8] The concept of the 'marriage debt' (that each spouse owed the other sex on demand) was not new, for it was part of Christian doctrine all through the Middle Ages, but the Wife endows it with a more pecuniary connotation through her desire to have her husband 'both my debtor and my thrall'[9] and her description of how she made her husbands work hard and give her land and money. She acknowledges that she exchanged sexual for financial favours: 'For profit I would endure all his pleasure.'[10] Implying that she would be able to get more for sex on the open market than from her husband, she puts the gifts and clothes he bought her on the same level with the profits of prostitution: 'if I would sell my *bele chose*, / I could walk as fresh as is a rose.'[11]

She also uses market metaphors to describe the value of playing hard to get: 'Great demand at market makes dear wares / And too great a bargain is but little prized.'[12] Men and women are adversaries in the market, all trying to fulfil their desire at the least expense.

Chaucer also depicts another case, in the *Shipman's Tale*, of the commodification of feminine sexuality, both through the wife's committing adultery for money and through her repeated use of financial metaphors: 'For I will pay you well and readily / From day to day, and if so be I fail / I am your wife; score it upon my tail'; 'You shall my merry body have as pledge.'[13] The language and ethos of the market pervade the whole tale, in the relations between the two men (husband and adulterous monk) as well as those between the woman and each man.

The Wife of Bath and the merchant's wife in the *Shipman's Tale* are both willing to exchange sexual favours for gifts or cash. Chaucer also presents, in the fragmentary *Cook's Tale*, one woman who is a commercial prostitute. Her husband is connected with a criminal underworld of gambling and riotous living, and she 'held for appearance / a shop, and swived for her sustenance.'[14] The difference between this woman and the two respectable wives who none the less can be bought could be seen in class terms: one sells her body to support herself and her husband, the others for luxuries. Chaucer calls none of them whores, and makes no moral distinction among them. Indeed, Chaucer's Manciple, in his *Tale*, explains that there is no difference in the moral evaluation of the sexual behaviour of women of different classes:

There is no difference, truly,
Between a wife that is of high degree,
If of her body dishonest she be,
And a poor wench, other than this –
If so be they both do amiss –
But that the gentlewoman, in estate above,
She shall be called his lady, as in love;
And because that other is a poor woman,
She shall be called his wench or his leman.
And, God knows, my own dear brother,
Men lay the one as low as lies the other.[15]

Not all women may be commercial prostitutes, but any woman, whether a lady or a wench, who is 'dishonest of her body' is a whore; thus all may be assimilated to the image of the commercial prostitute.

The venality of feminine sexuality appears elsewhere in English secular literature as well. Langland's *Piers Plowman* connects the sin of lust with greed:

> Lechery loves no poor man   for he hath but little silver
> Nor do they dine delicately   or drink wine often.
> A straw for the stews!   they would not stand long
> If they had no other custom   but of poor people![16]

The reference to lechery leads in the next breath to a reference to the stews, the locus of commercial prostitution. Once again, although commercial prostitution was a recognized institution and medieval people would have grasped the distinction between prostitutes and other loose women, in a moral sense the line was very often blurred, and immoral women were conflated with the venal.

This same connection can be found in religious literature, both in its explicit depictions of prostitutes and in its treatment of venality and sexuality more generally. Religious literature is particularly important because it was so pervasive: through preaching, these narratives and modes of classification found their way into the consciousness of the illiterate. People might and did reinterpret what they heard, but preachers provided a great deal of raw material and set some of the basic parameters within which people understood their world.

The image of the prostitute constructed in religious literature grew out of a complex understanding of gender that the Church taught, one aspect of which was the embodiment of lust by women. On the face of it the negative attitude of the Church towards sex generally was not gender-biased, since both man and woman sinned in sexual desire and behaviour. But, given that the majority of writers were heterosexual men, and women the objects of their desire, women came to take the blame for arousing that desire.

The antisexual and misogynistic tradition had flourished mainly within the monastery, but by the later Middle Ages it had emerged. Preachers to the medieval laity were not trying to contest the institution of marriage, but they told the same stories about sinful feminine behaviour as had the monks, and if this did not discourage marriage it certainly must have affected attitudes towards women, both married and unmarried. The emphasis here on the misogynistic aspects of the Church's teaching, because these are relevant to the development of attitudes towards prostitution, should not obscure the existence at the same time of other more positive images of women that may have mitigated it. The positive images, however, tended to focus on individual women (virgin saints and martyrs, nuns, and worthy matrons) and not on women as a group.[17]

Even within the genre of Miracles of the Virgin, the connection of feminine sexuality with prostitution appears. One tale concerns the nun Beatrice, the trusted sacristan of her convent, who has been devoted to the Virgin Mary all her life, yet leaves the convent for a lover (in itself a comment on the vulnerability of women to temptation). Years later she returns as a beggar, only to find that the Virgin has impersonated her the whole time so that no one has noticed her absence. Earlier versions of the story describe her life of sin without reference to commercial sex: of two thirteenth-century Anglo-Norman texts, one says only that she led an evil life of debauchery, the other that she lived with her lover for seven years and bore his children.[18] Fifteenth-century versions of the story describe her as having become a prostitute, and acknowledge a financial motive for this: 'And when he had defiled her, within a few days he left her and went away; and she had nothing to live on and was ashamed to go home again to her cloister, and she became a common woman.'[19]

The legend reveals the slippage between categories of immoral women. There is a clear distinction between the nun who lives in sin with a man, and the prostitute. The deflowered nun was not *ipso facto* a common woman (a term commonly used in the fifteenth century for commercial prostitutes); rather, she became one only after she was abandoned. But it was easy enough for her to become one, both in the realistic sense that such a woman would have nowhere else to turn, and in the literary sense that a woman who in one version is a concubine or mistress, in another becomes a prostitute.

Biographies of prostitute saints were also popular throughout the Middle Ages. Whereas early versions considered the prostitute saint constituted simply by promiscuity, versions from late-medieval England make the links between money and feminine sexuality clear.[20] The most important prostitute saint – indeed, the most important penitent of any sort – was Mary Magdalen. Although the Magdalen became the patron saint of repentant prostitutes, she was rarely depicted as a professional prostitute making her living by sexual intercourse. Some of the French and German dramas about her explicitly state that she refused money when it was offered, or that she offered her body without fee to anyone. The English texts, however, either are ambiguous or explicitly show her accepting money. According to the *Early South English Legendary,* 'many rich men lay with her and gave her great reward.'[21] This does not necessarily mean that she was envisioned as accepting specific payment for specific acts, but it does indicate that venality was part of her sexual activity, a connection apparently made in England but not elsewhere.

The financial connection comes out more clearly in the lives of the other prostitute saints, especially that of Mary of Egypt. In the original Latin translation from the Greek, Mary tells the monk Zosimus that she lived promiscuously in Alexandria for seventeen years, but never accepted money for sex, because she thought she would have more partners if she did not charge. This version of the story found its way into most European vernaculars. Even those versions that tell the story much more briefly, like Adgar's Anglo-Norman collection of Miracles of the Virgin, pick up the detail of her not charging for sex: 'She received everyone, and not for goods / But to fulfil her mad desire.'[22] Another textual tradition emerged, however, beginning in twelfth-century France, in which Mary's life of promiscuity was specifically described as being in a brothel and in which she did take money. William Caxton, who first printed the story in England, adopts this line: in his late-fifteenth-century translation of the *Lives of the Fathers*, he follows his French exemplar in describing her life: 'And during the time of seventeen years and more she had continually made residence at the public brothel of the same town with other common women there being, and with no other thing got her living.'[23] In the earlier Middle Ages, writers who translated or retold the story did not question their sources' statement about Mary's refusal to accept money for sex, but by the fifteenth century the financial motive seems to have claimed priority.

Those versions that follow the original treat Mary's sin as aggravated by her refusal to accept payment. Although canon lawyers did not believe that financial need could ever excuse a woman's becoming a prostitute, as it could a man's becoming a thief, financial need could at least make the sin more understandable.[24] The texts make her accept the blame for those she leads into sin: when she refuses payment for sex, out of fear that a charge would stand in the way of her gratification, she both entices men and makes the sin easier for them. Yet later versions which present money as a motive are not sympathetic – they do not mention the force of financial necessity – but combine the motive of greed with that of lust. Awareness of the importance of commerce did not imply an understanding of how the money economy contributed to sexual exploitation; it merely led to the condemnation of the prostitute's avarice.

In the lives of all the prostitute saints, money plays the greatest role in that of Thaïs. The medieval versions make her a woman of beauty and refinement and keep her price high: the shilling Paphnutius gives her in Caxton's translation of the *Golden Legend* is far more than the typical price of a prostitute in the fifteenth century.[25] The value of the gold and other goods she burns upon repentance comes to thousands of pounds. Yet, despite her riches, she is still described, not as a courtesan, but as a 'common strumpet' or 'common of her body.'[26] The texts make clear that she takes whoever will pay her most, stress the money Paphnutius gives her, and equate renouncing her life of prostitution with burning her gold. The ascetic life Thaïs undertakes after her conversion involves being walled in a cell, in which she has to perform all her bodily functions. The use of excrement as an image in this story is not coincidental: it resulted from the financial aspect of her sin. The excrement image appeared most vividly in the earlier Middle Ages, in the tenth-century dramatic work of Hrotswitha of Gandersheim, but later versions make the role of money much more specific: she despoils men, not of their wealth generally, but of a specific payment for a specific act: 'She was always ready to take / Whoever would the first payment make.'[27]

The legend of Pelagia presents her as an actress, a profession notorious in antiquity and the Middle Ages for loose morals but lacking the explicit financial exchange that accompanies prostitution in the case of the other saints. Once again, although most texts do not mention money, the exception is from England: 'A fair enough woman was she / And she drew many a man to sin / For she made her body common / In pleasure of the flesh, and lechery /... / And she sold her flesh at a good price.'[28] The loose woman has crossed the blurred line into the commercial prostitute.

Prostitution as a business also appears in the life of Saint Nicholas, who performs the miracle of the dowry for the poor girls. The legend shows an awareness of the financial constraints that forced women into prostitution – but the constraints are on the family and not on the woman. It is the father who 'because of great need ... ordered his daughters to be common women and earn both their living and his.'[29] Prostitution is presented as an alternative, not to other sorts of work, but only to marriage; the many women who were neither married nor prostitutes are ignored in this tale. Still, this story and that of Beatrice are practically alone in medieval literature in imagining the forces that might compel women to prostitution.

The lives of the harlot saints in many English versions all place an emphasis on the element of monetary exchange, even where Continental texts do not. Though it was not the monetary element which made them sinful – their sin was lust rather than greed – this type of sinner was expected also to be venal. These legends constituted the teaching about prostitution that most medieval people would have received, and what they taught was that women who enjoyed their sexuality were whores. By making the foremost examples of penitents women who were completely abandoned to their sexuality, medieval culture emphasized the equation of women and lust and made the whore a paradigm of the feminine.

The medieval image of the prostitute was also constructed via other types of texts. Collections of exempla, model sermons, and didactic works intended for lay reading circulated in the fourteenth and fifteenth centuries, and extant manuscripts indicate a great degree of borrowing among them. The result was the development of a common pool of moral teaching. Many of these texts are organized around the Seven Deadly Sins, one of the important subjects on which each parish priest was required to preach four times a year.[30] The treatises on sin divide each sin into branches; the sin of lust (*luxuria*) was generally divided into grades of increasing seriousness. John Bromyard, the Dominican compiler of the mid-fourteenth-century *Summa Praedicantium*, for example, follows one tradition which does not specifically mention prostitution: first comes simple fornication, then *stuprum* (the deflowering of a virgin), adultery, ravishment, sacrilege (sex with a nun), incest, and 'the vice against nature.' Many other texts, including one by John Wycliffe, the founder of Lollardy, follow this schema with minor variations: some omit sacrilege, and some add flirting and impudence as levels below fornication.[31]

Other texts specifically mention prostitution as a category of lust. The *Fasciculus Morum*, a popular fourteenth-century compendium, includes sex with prostitutes as a subdivision of fornication, and therefore less serious than other varieties of lust. It defines fornication as follows: 'Therefore, we must understand that while fornication is any forbidden sexual intercourse, it particularly refers to intercourse with widows, prostitutes [*meretrices*], or concubines. But the term 'prostitute' must be applied only to those women who give themselves to anyone and will refuse none, and that for monetary gain.'[32] The author here assumes that a woman would be a virgin (in which case sex with her was *stuprum* or sacrilege); a wife (in which case it was adultery); or a widow, concubine, or prostitute. There is no category for a single woman who engages in sex other than for money; this suggests that any single woman who was not chaste would risk being cast and treated as a prostitute. Similarly another tract, stressing the mortal sin inherent in fornication, points out that, if a man asks a woman to be his lover, it means he considers her a prostitute (*meretrix*); if he thought she were chaste, he would not ask, and if she is not chaste, she is a prostitute.[33]

While these texts all seem to take prostitution as a subset of fornication, another textual tradition, that of the fourteenth-century *Speculum Vitae*, explicitly considers prostitution as the second branch of lust, falling between simple fornication (between two single people) and sex with a widow:

> The second degree the deed may be
> Between a single man, it seems to me,
> And a common women of the brothel
> That offers her body often to sell.
> This is a sin that is far graver
> And with the Devil more in favour
> For it is held more vile
> And it may more the soul defile,
> Because such women of life unclean
> Perhaps are married, as often is seen,
> Or are women of religion
> Who have forsaken their profession,
>
> ...
>
> And forsake none of a group of kin
> Who have the urge with them to sin
> Father, nor son, nor cousin, nor brother.
> This sin is more grave than any other.[34]

The *Speculum Vitae* also classes prostitution under the sin of avarice, the ninth branch of which consists of sinful trades. Whereas the passage quoted above stresses the indiscriminate nature of sexuality and mentions the selling only in passing, under avarice the text mentions the indiscriminateness only in passing – 'they deny no man' – and stresses the financial gain: 'For their livelihood they do nought else ... By charging they earn their sustenance, they have no other merchandise.'[35] This text and the textual tradition to which it belongs (including the fourteenth-century *Ayenbite of Inwit*, the fifteenth-century allegorical devotional handbook *Jacob's Well*, and a fifteenth-century prose reworking of the *Speculum*), even more than the *Fasciculus Morum*, make the connection between the prostitute's lust and her greed. Although these texts rely heavily on French sources, this connection is more fully developed in the English versions.[36]

Another group of texts, based on the thirteenth-century Anglo-Norman work *Manuel des Pechiez*, had a great deal of popularity in England, probably among both confessors and the laity. This group classifies prostitution as a separate branch of lust. Its early-fourteenth-century Middle English translation, Robert of Brunne's *Handlyng Synne*, gives a list of reasons why this seventh branch is the worst:

> One is, she may take thy brother,
> Father, or kinsman, as well as another.
> Another, for conflict and foul strife,
> You may, through her, lose your life.
> The third is the worst defilement:
> Lepers, people say, use them;
> And, whoever takes them in that heat,
> Purity of body he may soon lose.
> Much woe, then, it is to take such women
> For the sake of these three lacks;
> And much may be that woman's moaning,
> For she shall answer for them, every one,
> That have done any sin with her,
> On Judgment Day, the day of wrath.[37]

Here, once again, along with the warnings against prostitutes on the grounds of incest and disease, is the attribution to them of responsibility for men's souls, although this text does not mention their greed.

John Myrc's fifteenth-century manual of instruction for parish priests gives some indication of the way the clergy were supposed to interrogate their flock in the confessional. Concerning the sin of lust, they were to ask those confessing whether they had had sex, with whom, under what circumstances, and, in the case of a woman, 'whether it were for covetousness / Of gold or silver, or anything of his. / Then the sin would be double / And need penance much more.'[38] Any woman who engages in extramarital sex is suspected of a financial motive.

The connection of female sexuality to money permeated religious as well as secular literature, and the prostitute was a significant point of connection. Fear of woman's venality led to the notion that no woman could be trusted; they were all out to deceive for money. Prostitutes represented something that men distrusted in all women. A prostitute was someone who brought her sexuality out of the private into the public realm, a 'common woman' or a 'fille publique,' to use some of the medieval terms. Even a concubine did not make her sexuality public. A prostitute was someone who did so, by putting it on the market or by being available to the public in general. But any woman who made her sexuality public by making a public scandal of herself could also be considered under the category of 'prostitute,' and was classified with the venal women who sold their bodies.

It was not only the distrust of money (and hence the fear of feminine venality) that made the prostitute such an important figure in medieval culture's control of women. It was also her independence. Any woman who was not under the direct control of a man – any woman who remained single and earned her own living, or indeed any married woman who earned her own living as well – was a threat to masculine control. The figure of the prostitute allowed for the sexualization of this threat. Not all practising prostitutes were in fact independent of men – pimps and husbands were heavily involved in the trade – nor was prostitution the most lucrative career for a woman, and hence the one that led most directly to financial independence. Prostitution became so important symbolically, not because of its practical importance, but because of the medieval connection of the feminine with the sexual.

A woman's sexual behaviour that did not conform to the norms was more important than a man's that did not conform, because a woman was defined much more entirely by her sexuality than was a man. This was why the redeemed prostitute had such power as a symbol of repentance. But, by the same token, scrutiny of women's sexual behaviour was a major means of social control. Labelling some women as prostitutes was a way of deterring others from undesirable behaviour. Taking money for sex did not distinguish one kind of prostitute from another, because the prostitute was simply the extreme case of the overall venality and sinfulness of feminine sexuality.

NOTES

Financial support for this research from the National Endowment for the Humanities (Travel to Collections Grant No. FE-23167-89) and the American Philosophical Society is gratefully acknowledged. I am also grateful to the Department of Western Manuscripts, British Library, and the Rare Book Room, Van Pelt Library, University of Pennsylvania, for access to research materials. A version of this paper was presented at the meeting of the American Historical Association in December 1991, and I thank Judith Bennett for her helpful comments on that occasion, as well as at other times; I also thank Ann Matter and David Boyd for assistance with issues raised in this paper. This material appears in somewhat different form in chapters 5 and 6 of *Common Women: Prostitution and Sexuality in Medieval England* by Ruth Mazo Karras, copyright 1996 by Oxford University Press. Used by permission.

1 In other words, the category 'prostitute' is socially constructed. On the social construction of sexuality, see John Boswell, 'Revolutions, Universals, and Sexual Categories'; David Halperin, 'Sex Before Sexuality: Pederasty, Politics, and Power in Classical Athens'; and Robert Padgug, 'Sexual Matters: Rethinking Sexuality in History,' in *Hidden from History: Reclaiming the Gay and Lesbian Past*, eds. Martin Duberman, Martha Vicinus, and George Chauncey, Jr, 17–64 (New York: Penguin 1990), and the other works cited there.

2 James A. Brundage, *Law, Sex, and Christian Society in Medieval Europe* (Chicago: University of Chicago Press 1987), 248, 390, 464–5

3 See, e.g., Judith Walkowitz, *Prostitution and Victorian Society: Women, Class, and the State* (Cambridge: Cambridge University Press 1980); Lyndal Roper, *The Holy Household: Women and Morals in Reformation Augsburg* (Oxford: Clarendon Press 1989); Ruth Mazo Karras, 'The Regulation of Brothels in Later Medieval England,' *Signs: Journal of Women in Culture and Society* 14 (1989), 399–433.

4 Marie-Thérèse Lorcin, *Façons de sentir et de penser: les fabliaux français* (Paris: H. Champion 1979), 66

5 R. Howard Bloch, *The Scandal of the Fabliaux* (Chicago: University of Chicago Press 1986), 5–6, cautions against the danger of assuming that the literary relations depicted in the *fabliaux* correspond to social reality; however, here they are being used not to discuss sociological detail, but rather the accepted values or ethos of the culture.

6 Sarah Melhado White, 'Sexual Language and Human Conflict in Old French Fabliaux,' *Comparative Studies in Society and History* 24 (1982), 185–210. See also Bloch, *Scandal*, 59–100.

7 'pyked out the beste, / Bothe of here nether purs and of here cheste': *Wife of Bath's Tale*, ll. 441–4b. All quotations from Chaucer are from *The Riverside Chaucer*, 3d ed., ed. Larry D. Benson (Boston: Houghton Mifflin 1987). Modernizations are mine.

8 On the Wife of Bath, see also Carolyn Dinshaw, *Chaucer's Sexual Poetics* (Madison: University of Wisconsin Press 1989), 118; R.A. Shoaf, *Dante, Chaucer and the Currency of the Word: Money, Images and Reference in Late Medieval Poetry* (Norman, OK: Pilgrim Books 1983), 174–7; Sheila Delany, 'Sexual Economics, Chaucer's Wife of Bath, and *The Book of Margery Kempe*,' in *Writing Woman:*

Women Writers and Women in Literature, Medieval to Modern (New York: Schocken 1983), 76–92.

9 'bothe my dettour and my thral': *Wife of Bath's Tale*, l. 155

10 'For wynnyng wolde I al his lust endure': *Wife of Bath's Tale*, l. 416

11 ' ... if I wolde selle my *bele chose*, / I koude walke as fressh as is a rose': *Wife of Bath's Tale*, ll. 447–8

12 'Greet prees at market maketh deere ware, / And to greet cheep is holde at litel prys': *Wife of Bath's Tale*, ll. 522–3

13 'For I wol paye yow wel and redily / Fro day to day, and if so be I faille, / I am youre wyf; score it upon my taille': Shipman's Tale, ll. 414–16; 'Ye shal my joly body have to wedde': Shipman's Tale, l. 423. On the role of money and monetary terminology in this tale, see, e.g., Albert H. Silverman, 'Sex and Money in Chaucer's *Shipman's Tale*,' *Philological Quarterly* 32 (1953), 329–36; V.J. Scattergood, 'The Originality of the *Shipman's Tale*,' *Chaucer Review* 11 (1976–7), 210–31; Mary Flowers Braswell, 'Chaucer's 'Queinte Termes of Lawe': A Legal View of the *Shipman's Tale*,' *Chaucer Review* 22 (1988), 295–304; Paul Strohm, *Social Chaucer* (Cambridge, MA: Harvard University Press 1989), 100; Lee Patterson, *Chaucer and the Subject of History* (Madison: University of Wisconsin Press 1991), 349–59. The concluding pun, 'God us sende / Taillynge ynough unto oure lyves ende' (ll. 433–4), underscores the double entendre of the *taille.*

14 'heeld for contenance / A shoppe, and swyved for hir sustenance': *Cook's Tale*, ll. 4421–2

15 'Ther nys no difference, trewely, / Bitwixe a wyf that is of heigh degree, / If of hir body dishonest she bee, / And a povre wenche, oother than this – / If it so be they werke bothe amys – / But that the gentile, in estaat above, / She shal be cleped his lady, as in love; / And for that oother is a povre womman, / She shal be cleped his wenche or his lemman. / And, God it woot, myn owene deere brother, / Men leyn that oon as lowe as lith that oother': *Manciple's Tale*, ll. 212–22

16 Lecherye loueth none poure for   he hath bote lytel seluer, / Ne doth men dyne dylicatliche   neyther drynk wyne ofte. / A straw for the stywes!   hy stod nat ful longe / And they hadde non other haunt   bote of poure peple!: William Langland, *The Vision of William Concerning Piers the Plowman*, ed. Walter W. Skeat (Oxford: Clarendon Press 1886), C: 17, ll. 91–4, vol. 1: 429

17 R. Howard Bloch, *Medieval Misogyny and the Invention of Western Romantic Love* (Chicago: University of Chicago Press 1991), argues that the simultaneous idealization and condemnation of women were not opposites but both constituted misogyny.

18 Hilding Kjellman, ed., *La deuxième collection anglo-normande des miracles de la sainte vierge* (Paris: Edouard Champion 1922), 70, ll. 102–19; Adgar, *Marienleg-*

enden, ed. Carl Neuhaus (Heilbronn: Gebr. Henninger 1886), Altfranzösische Bibliothek 9, p. 230, ll. 244–7

19 'And when he had defowlid hur, with-in a few dayes he lefte hur & went away; & sho had nothyng at liff on & thoght shame to gang home agayn vnto hur clostre, and sho fell to be a common woman': *An Alphabet of Tales: An English 15th Century translation of the Alphabetum Narrationum,* ed. Mary Macleod Banks (London: Kegan Paul, Trench, Trübner 1904), Early English Text Society, Original Series 126–7, no. 468, 2: 320. See also [Wynkyn de Worde], *The Myracles of Oure Blessyd Lady* [London, 1496], fol. E1v, using the word 'strumpet.' The nun is not named in any of the English versions, although 'Beatrice' is the name she is given elsewhere.

20 The saints discussed here are treated in more detail, along with others, in Ruth Mazo Karras, 'Holy Harlots: Prostitute Saints in Medieval Legend,' *Journal of the History of Sexuality* 1 (1990), 3–32.

21 'Manie riche Men hire leiȝen bi / and ȝeven hire gret mede': *The Early South-English Legendary or Lives of Saints,* ed. Carl Horstmann (London: N. Trübner 1887), E.E.T.S. O.S. 87, p. 463, l. 54

22 'Tuz receut e nient pur aueir / Mais pur emplir sun fol voleir': Adgar, *Marienlegenden,* 194, ll. 9–10

23 'And durynge the tyme of seuentene yeres and more she hadde contynuelly made resydence atte the open bordell of the same towne wyth other comyn wymen there beynge. In Abandonnynge and usynge her propre body to all that came And wyth noo other thynge gate her lyvynge': [William Caxton, trans.], *Vitas Patrum* (London 1495), fol. 68r; his use of sources is discussed in Constance L. Rosenthal, 'The *Vitae Patrum* in Old and Middle English Literature' Ph.D. Diss., University of Pennsylvania, 1936, 134.

24 James A. Brundage, 'Prostitution in the Medieval Canon Law,' *Signs* 1 (1976), 835–6

25 Jacobus de Voragine, *Lives of the Saints as Englished by William Caxton,* ed. F.S. Ellis (London: J.M. Dent 1900; repr. New York 1973), vol. 5: 241

26 *Alphabet of Tales,* ch. 3, p. 3; *Jacob's Well,* ed. Arthur Brandeis (London: Kegan Paul, Trench, Trübner 1900), E.E.T.S. O.S. 115, 22

27 'Scho wes ay redy to take / quha wald þe first payment mak': *Legends of the Saints in Scottish Dialect of the Fourteenth Century,* ed. W.M. Metcalfe (Edinburgh: William Blackwood & Sons 1896), Scottish Text Society vols. 13, 23, 35, 2: 215, ll. 11–12

28 'ffeir wommon heo was I. nouh / And mony a Mon to synne heo drouh: / ffor Comune made heo hire bodi / In fflessches lust and Lecheri / ... / And good chep hire flesch heo sold': Carl Horstmann, ed., 'Die Evangelien-Geschichten der Homiliensammlung des Ms. Vernon,' *Archiv für die Erforschung der neueren Sprachen* 57 (1877), 300, ll. 5–8, 16

29 'for grete neede ... ordeyned his daughtirs to be common wommenne and gett thaire lyuing and his both': British Library, Harleian MS 2371, fol. 54v. See also *Golden Legend*, vol. 2: 110; C. Horstmann, ed., *Altenglische Legenden, neue folge* (Heilbronn: Gebr. Henninger 1881), 12, ll. 111–20. Karl Meisen, *Nikolauskult und Nikolausbrauch im Abendlande. Eine kultgeographisch-volkskundliche Untersuchung* (Düsseldorf: L. Schwann 1931), Forschungen zur Volkskunde 9–12, pp. 232–45, discusses this legend.

30 See Siegfried Wenzel, 'Vices, Virtues and Popular Preaching,' in *Medieval and Renaissance Studies: Proceedings of the Southeastern Institute of Medieval and Renaissance Studies, Summer, 1974*, ed. Dale B.J. Randall, 28–54 (Durham, NC: Duke University Press 1976), on this set of sermon themes.

31 John of Bromyard, *Summa Praedicantium* (Venice: Domenico Nicolino 1586), s.v. luxuria, fol. 1: 457; '*Memoriale Credencium*. A Late Middle English Manual of Theology for Lay People, Edited from Bodley MS Tanner 201,' ed. J.H.L. Kengen, Ph.D. Diss, University of Nijmegen, 1979, 138 ff.; John of Wales, *Monoloquium*, in B.L. MS Harley 632, fols. 312r-312v; Robert Rypon, *Sermones*, in B.L. MS Harley 4894, fol. 16r; John Wyclif, *On the Seven Deadly Sins*, in *Select English Works of John Wyclif*, ed. Thomas Arnold (Oxford: Clarendon Press 1871), vol. 3: 119–67; B.L. MS Add. 11579, fol. 128r

32 Siegfried Wenzel, ed. and trans., *Fasciculus Morum: A Fourteenth-Century Preacher's Handbook* (University Park: Pennsylvania State University Press 1989), 7.7, p. 669

33 British Library, MS Harleian 665, fol. 69r (fifteenth century); MS Add. 11579, fol. 19v (fourteenth century)

34 'þe secund degre may þe dede be / Bytwen a syngle man, thynk me, / And a comon woman of bordelle / þat byddys hir body oft to selle, / þis ys a synne þat ys mare greif / And to þe fend of helle mare leif, / For it ys halden mare wyle / And mare it may þe saule fyle, / For why swylk woman of lyf vnclene / Perchance er wedded, as oft ys sene, / Or er women of religyoun / þat has forseken þair professioun, / ... / And for sakes nan of alle of kyn / þat has wille with þam to syn / Fader, ne sone, ne cosyn, ne brodere, / þis synne ys mare greif þan þe todere': John W. Smeltz, '*Speculum Vitae*: An Edition of British Museum Manuscript Royal 17.C.viii,' Dissertation, Duquesne University, 1977, 441. The reasons given for the harm of prostitution – that it amounts to adultery, sacrilege, or incest – would seem to place it at the most serious end of the scale, yet it ranks only as worse than simple fornication. The author probably got his ranking from elsewhere and embellished the description of the sin without changing its ranking.

35 'For þair lyflede þai do noȝt ellys ... With fyne wynne þai þar sustinance/þai do na other chevysance': ibid., 354–5

36 See Hope Emily Allen, 'The Speculum Vitae: Addendum,' *Publications of the Modern Language Association* 32 (1917), 161–2.

37 'One ys, she may take þy broþer, / Fadyr, or sybkynd, as wel as ouþer. / Anoþer, for contek and foule stryfe, / Þou mayst, þurgh here, lese þy lyfe. / Þe þredde ys þe werstë wem; / Meseles, men seye, vsen hem; / And, who takeþ hem yn þat hete, / Clennesse of body he may sone lete. / Moche wo þan, ys swyche to take, / For þesë þre lakkës sake; / And moche may be þat wommans mone, / For she schal answere for hem echone / Þat haue ydo any synne wyþ hyre, / At domes day, þe day of Ire': *Robert of Brunne's 'Handlyng Synne,'* ed. Frederick J. Furnivall (London: Kegan Paul, Trench, Trübner 1901), E.E.T.S. O.S. 123, ll. 7433–56, pp. 237–8. Judging from the manuscript tradition, the English version was not as widely known as the Anglo-Norman.

38 'wheþer hyt were for couetyse / Of gold or seluer, or oght of hyse, / þenne þe synne dowbul were / And neded penawnce myche more': John Myrc, *Instructions for Parish Priests*, ed. Edward Peacock (London: Kegan Paul, Trench, Trübner 1902), E.E.T.S. O.S. 31, 40

Wives and Mothers: Adultery, Madness, and Marital Misery in Titian's Paduan Frescoes

RONA GOFFEN

Sex is presumed guilty until proven innocent.
                                            – *Gayle Rubin*[1]

The misogyny that characterizes Western societies is two-edged: it encompasses both the unreasoned, often violent, hatred of women and their equally unreasoned exaltation.[2] Completed in 1511, Titian's three frescoes in the Scuola di Sant'Antonio in Padua illustrate both of these misogynies, and, doing so, they reflect much about the actual situation of sixteenth-century women (figs. 1–3).[3] The primary literary source for his three narratives – *Miracle of the Speaking Infant, Miracle of the Jealous Husband,* and *St Anthony Reattaching the Foot of the Irascible Son* – was the Latin *leggenda* by Sicco Polentone, written in Padua *ca* 1435 as Anthony's 'quasi-official'. biography (a copy was chained to a lectern in the sacristy of the Basilica del Santo).[4] Yet Titian's frescoes are not the straightforward visualizations of Saint Anthony's legends which they have always been taken to be; in reality, they depart from the hagiographical source(s) and are more fully understood in relation to the laws regarding adultery, illegitimacy, insanity, and a wife's legal subjugation to her husband. Civil and canon law explain what Titian and his contemporaries read between the lines of the hagiographical script.

The *Miracle of the Speaking Infant* and the *Jealous Husband* reveal the common negative attitude towards wives – a deep misogyny that was losing ground in the sixteenth century but that perservered none the less (figs. 1 and 2). The exalted attitude towards mothers, on the contrary, is

Figure 1. Titian, *Miracle of the Speaking Infant*, fresco, Padua, Scuola di
Sant'Antonio, 1511

Figure 2. Titian, *Miracle of the Jealous Husband*, fresco, Padua, Scuola di Sant'Antonio, 1511

suggested in Titian's third mural for the cycle, in which Saint Anthony reattaches the foot of a youth who, having kicked his mother, then severed his own offending member (fig. 3).

None too bright, the lad had taken literally a preacher's allusion to Christ's metaphoric injunction: 'And if your foot causes you to sin, cut it off; it is better for you to enter life lame than with two feet to be thrown into hell' (Mk. 9: 45).[5] While one woman, perhaps his sister, comforts the hapless hero, his mother implores Saint Anthony to intervene. To be sure, the fundamental purpose of this scene, as of the entire cycle, is to demonstrate Anthony's sanctity and his intervention on behalf of the faithful. The mother's prayers will indeed be answered presently, and her son's wound healed, but the subtext of the story seems to be a warning against emotional extremism – not only of penitence, but of love. Love of a woman, even one's mother, may be dangerous, leading one (admittedly a dim-witted one) to pathological self-destruction. At the same time, reclining on the ground with one arm limp at his side and the other in his lap, with his head supported by his sister, and with blood from his wound spilling around his feet, the youth recalls the Dead Christ in scenes of the Pietà and Lamentation. In short, while one's mother is like the Virgin Mary, one's wife may be Eve. And, in either case, a man's association with a woman is fraught with danger. Inherently bound to the presumptive guilt of sex is the presumed guilt of the female sex object; as Titian shows us in the other two scenes, only the miraculous speech of the newborn who knows his father can vindicate his mother, only heaven-sent reassurance can answer the doubts of the murderous husband who also suspects adultery.

The *Miracle of the Speaking Infant* is a scene of little physical action but considerable psychological tension. The baby's mother, a beautiful Ferrarese noblewoman, had been harshly mistreated and unfairly suspected by her husband, a very distinguished ('primarius') but jealous man ('de uxore suspicio'), as the hagiographer Sicco Polentone described him.[6] In early-modern Europe, an adulteress could be deprived of her dowry (in effect, her means of survival) and would suffer the ignominious disapprobation of the community – hence her means of psychological survival. Under civil law, she could be imprisoned, even executed or murdered – her murder, by the 'offended' male parties, being officially condoned.[7] According to the Venetian law of 11 April 1443, for example, adultery may be punished by jail and a fine, even by death in some cases.[8] Such statutes have origins in Roman law, though in ancient Rome only her father could legally kill an adulterous wife.[9] In medieval and Renaissance

Figure 3. Titian, *St Anthony Reattaching the Foot of the Irascible Son*, fresco, Padua, Scuola di Sant'Antonio, 1511

law, as in ancient times, precisely because adultery was considered a private crime, only those who had an interest in the matter could make an accusation – namely, the woman's husband, father, and/or brothers. A wife's natal kinsmen were thus both her greatest defenders and her greatest danger. They would seek to defend her honour, and hence her dowry, which a wronged husband could confiscate. But, if they were compelled to consider her guilty, her kinsmen were even more likely than her husband to expunge this crime by murdering the offender – their daughter, sister, niece.

The adulterous wife adulterates both herself and – more to the Renaissance heart of the matter – her kinsmen's clan. Hence the law recognized their right to revenge and expiation. This sense of defilement explains, moreover, why a child born of adultery was considered 'more odious than even the bastards born of single, unmarried parents.'[10] For this same reason – because she can contaminate the lineage – the adulterous wife was held to be more guilty under the law than an adulterous husband. Indeed, a wronged wife could not bring a legal accusation of adultery against her unfaithful husband.[11]

In short, the accusations and the consequences of adultery were most severe, and in this case only the intervention of the saint can save the innocent. In the *Miracle of the Speaking Infant*, Anthony calls the one irrefutable witness, the newborn himself, who knows his own father. 'Taking the child in his hands, Saint Anthony ... [said]: "I abjure you ... in everyone's hearing now respond to me and say, who then is your father?" Then the infant, not at all slurring his speech as children are wont, but with clear voice ..., looking his father in the eye, ... [declared]: "Behold, ... this is my father."' Then the saint turning to the father [said]: "Behold, accept your son; and ... as every good man must, love your wife."'[12] The implied message, often repeated by and to early-modern Europeans, is that female sexuality is guilty until proven innocent. In fact, earlier versions of this generic miracle, as ascribed to numerous other saints, and even to the Madonna herself, had involved the vindication of *men* (often priests) wrongly accused of paternity by wicked women.[13] In the most common variant of this first version of the miracle, an illegitimate baby vindicates a falsely accused man. In a second variant, the baby denounces the real adulterer, which likewise achieves the vindication of an innocent man. Only in the later emendation – that ascribed to Saint Anthony and depicted by Titian – does the *legitimate* child exonerate his *mother* by identifying his father as her husband.

Sixteenth-century people viewing Titian's fresco or reading the story in

Polentone's *vita* would surely have known at least some of these other variants on the recurring theme – indeed, the variants were rather more familiar than Anthony's edition of the miracle. Given this hagiographical context, it may be that the fundamental change of the female role from false witness to innocent victim was understood by contemporaries to reflect improving attitudes towards women. Yet, even in sixteenth-century Padua, chastity, the quintessential wifely virtue, was evidently still presumed to be as rare as hen's teeth. No disapprobation of the husband's groundless suspicion is suggested, an indication that his mistrust is understood to be completely plausible, his preoccupation (obsession) natural: he is entitled to supernatural reassurance. Moreover, unlike everyone else in the fresco, the husband and the smiling older man standing next to him are individualized compared with the other, more generalized types. Perhaps these two men are portraits of *scuola* members; confraternity brothers were frequently represented in such paintings, including Titian's *Miracle of the Reattached Foot* and other scenes in this cycle. (This physiognomic specificity and Titian's use of contemporary costumes, here and throughout the cycle, give the scene a sense of actuality.) Even if the two individualized men in the *Miracle of the Speaking Infant* are not portraits, the fact remains that here the husband is effectively rewarded with certainty, not chastised for his false accusations.

The misogynies of the *scuola* miracles are implicit in the literary sources and explicit in the actual situation of Renaissance women. But the Confraternity of Saint Anthony enrolled both women and men: both women and men were the patrons of the *scuola* cycle, therefore, and this may have influenced Titian's conception of his narratives.[14] For whatever reason, however, in conceiving the characters and events he was told to paint, Titian editorialized, interpreting his women in a far more sympathetic light than the stories themselves suggest. In other words, we may see an emotive disjunction between the stories as written and their depiction in the frescoes. Titian contradicted sometimes the spirit and sometimes the letter of his narratives.

Size and colour establish the innocent mother as the heroine of the *Miracle of the Speaking Infant*: broad planes and coinciding contours (for example, snood and gown, sleeve and undergarment) monumentalize the woman, implying her nobility of character. We may recall – as did Titian himself – the grandeur of Giotto's frescoes in the Scrovegni Chapel.[15] But Titian consulted another precedent for the composition, Antonio Lombardo's marble relief completed in 1501 for the Cappella dell'Arca, the saint's funerary chapel in the basilica of the Santo (fig. 4).

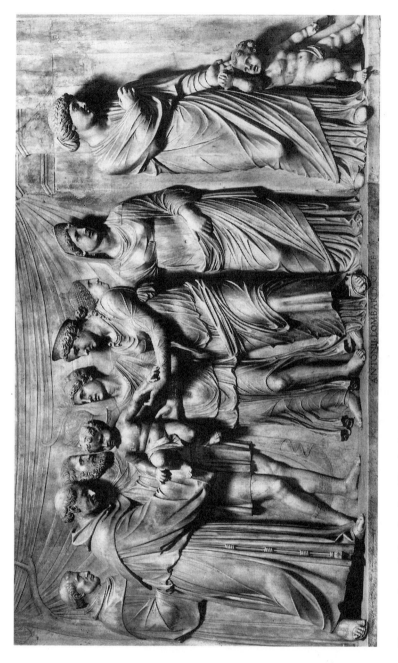

Figure 4. Antonio Lombardo, *Miracle of the Speaking Infant*, marble relief, Padua, Basilica del Santo, Cappella dell'Arca, 1501

The resemblance is general, involving Titian's energetic reshuffling and recasting of Lombardo's figures. Surely the evocation of the sculpture was a purposeful, albeit indirect, reminder of its venerated and miraculous site in the Cappella dell'Arca.[16]

Despite these similarities, the impact of the narratives is very different, most significantly in the presentation of the innocent mother. Even without the painter's dramatic advantage of colour, the sculptor might have distinguished her by adjusting the composition or by redefining her figure – precisely the means later employed by Titian. Lombardo instead chose to minimalize the woman and to glorify Anthony's role, an emphasis to be expected in this relief decorating the saint's chapel. In Titian's version, the saint's importance is more limited – which is certainly unexpected. Not the saint but an anonymous, extraneous confrère holds the loquacious baby, partially concealing Anthony's figure in the process. This friar is unmentioned in Polentone's text: presumably Titian adapted the kneeling figure from Donatello's mob scene representing the same miracle, the bronze relief cast for the high altar of the Santo between 1446 and 1450 (fig. 5).[17] In the relief, however, the primacy of Saint Anthony is maintained despite the crowds. And in the painting, in any case, Anthony cannot compete for attention with Titian's grandiose figure of the mother. Moreover, Titian manipulated the scene to evince the viewer's sympathy with the innocent woman. The room's doorway is perpendicular to this fresco, and one's first view of the miracle is from the right, where the approaching visitor effectively joins the group of women associated with the mother. Lombardo had included two women, one with her child, in a comparable position. Titian added a third woman and eliminated the child, while condensing the group into a solid mass visually buttressing, psychologically endorsing, the female protagonist. Sharing their viewpoint, following their movement, the beholder is invited to adopt their supportive role as well – to stand with the women in this scene where one woman is vindicated.

The setting underscores this sense of movement and psychological identification. Titian has bisected the scene with almost mathematical precision, dividing his fourteen adult figures into two equal groups separated by their different background. Open sky, a grassy hill, and slender trees provide the background for the husband and wife, her companions and his associate, the saint, and the child (the fifteenth figure); the flank of a building is the backdrop for the kneeling friar and six male onlookers. (The elegant youth in the foreground, wearing striped hose and a sweeping white cape, seems to be dressed as a member of a *compagnia delle*

Figure 5. Donatello, *Miracle of the Speaking Infant*, bronze relief, Padua, Basilica del Santo, High Altar, 1446–50

Calze.) The vertical edge of the building leads one's eye directly to Saint Anthony's gesticulating right hand. A large niche enframes almost all of the bystanders at left. Above this, a smaller niche is decorated with a red cross in the semidome, and to the left, a fictive antique classical statue stands in another niche cut into the projecting corner of the structure. This sculpture has long been recognized as Titian's allusion to a figure from a marble relief honouring the Augustan dynasty.[18] Though now identified as Drusus the Elder, the figure was traditionally considered a portrait of Marcus Agrippa, the second (and unwilling) husband of Augustus's daughter Julia, perhaps the most infamous unfaithful wife of ancient Rome. If, then, Titian believed that the sculpted figure represented her cockolded husband, he may have intended an indirect, ironic commentary on Julia's notoriety as an adulteress. In contrast to pagan Julia, Titian seems to say, the Christian wife of the *Miracle* is chaste. Given the uncertainty regarding the identity of the Roman soldier, however, this interpretation must remain uncertain.[19]

Titian's *Miracle of the Speaking Infant* focuses on the moment of the saint's intervention on behalf of the chaste mother. But, in the *Miracle of the Jealous Husband*, no one intervenes to save this 'beautiful and modest' wife from her murderous spouse, a Tuscan knight.[20] The implication of the miracle, recounted for the first time in the legend by Polentone (who specifies that 'the story is not known here,' in Padua), is that violent retribution is warranted, or at least forgivable, when there is suspicion of adulterous fornication. Hence the jealous husband is not punished for the attempted murder of his faithful wife: she *might* have been guilty, and presumably this would have justified her husband's 'biblical' action. Based on the scriptural subjugation of wife to husband, he possesses the *Ius corrigendi*, the legal right to 'correct' her presumed failings, with physical force. Adultery is frequently punished by death in the Bible, for example in Genesis 38, Leviticus 20, Deuteronomy 22, and Daniel 13 – all cited as legal precedents in Renaissance statutes.[21] The contrary example of forgiveness offered to an adulteress by Christ himself was honoured in art but evidently not in the law.[22] A wife, moreover, did not have a corresponding right in regard to her husband, whose faults she might seek to correct only by means of advice, offered sparingly and unassertively. Thus a mid-fifteenth-century marriage manual by the Franciscan Frate Cherubino da Siena, the 'Rules of Matrimonial Life,' advises that, when a husband sins, his wife should exhort him gently to stop: 'my master, my lord, what you are doing is a sin; I pray you, for the love you bear me, do not do that anymore ... ; give this consolation to me ... , who cannot have greater consolation than to see you live without mortal sin.' But the friar also explains that a husband owes his wife instruction and correction, which means that it may be necessary to beat her. If so, he should start with a moderate beating, as with egg white ('come fusse bianco d'uovo'), then intensify his efforts, if need be, for her own good, because it is better to beat the body and save the soul.[23]

To be sure, civil law did not generally intend that the husband's beating be a fatal corrective, though this might be condoned in cases of adultery – as suspected here; but even were this husband brought up on charges for attempted murder, he could plead insanity, because, as Polentone describes him, 'he was quick to anger, and when angered lost all sense of reason.' The determination of insanity was a legal (not medical) matter in medieval and Renaissance Venice; and the fourteenth-century Venetian courts found that 'it is not in the interest of the commune ... to hold [imprison] such an insane person ... instead he may be given over to the custody of his relatives.'[24] There is no hint of trouble with the law in the biography or in the fresco, however; on the contrary, in Titian's emendation of the text, we see a scene of pardon.

Notwithstanding the knight's irrational brutality and the fundamental fact that his wife was innocent, Titian suggests that the husband is forgiven by God through his saint. Thus, Anthony blesses the kneeling husband – but the more remarkable fact that the moribund woman was resuscitated by the saint is omitted from the composition. In point of fact, according to the text, the repentant husband had sought Anthony's intervention, not for himself, but to save his wife. The saint then rushed to her bedside, where, 'making the sign of the Cross continuously, he bent his knee on the ground and prayed to God to restore life to the dying woman.' In the legend, the saint's raising her from her deathbed is the miraculous climax of the narrative, the obvious choice from the traditional hagiographical point of view, and the setting for this story of domestic violence is the household itself, where both the attack and the recovery occur. But in Titian's fresco, the husband's blessing becomes the denouement; the pardon of the criminal, not the salvation of the victim, is commemorated. The crime itself, not the miraculous cure, is depicted front and centre – and it occurs in a landscape far from the trappings of civilization.

On one level, the landscape is a compositional device that Titian exploits to subdivide the two moments of the narrative. But architecture could have done that job just as well, and would have been consistent with the text, which describes the couple's household. Instead, Titian painted pulsating rocks, their contours broken by the sharp diagonals of a few branches – nature that is uncultivated, uninhabited, suggesting that the husband's fury is likewise uncontrolled. Indeed, Titian himself had described the scene as representing 'that man who murdered his wife' ('quello amazò soa mogiera'), even though the text specified that she was not slain but only injured.[25] That Titian intended this as a murderous assault is made clear by the husband's knife and its bloody wound in the wife's breast. And yet neither knife nor wounds – the most horribly conspicuous details of Titian's tragic scene – are in fact mentioned in the literary source.

How are we to explain Titian's misrepresentation, his 'sin of omission' regarding the woman's resuscitation and his 'sins of addition,' the knife and wound? Is it conceivable that he misunderstand the text? To be sure, Polentone's *vita* was written in Latin, and the Italian translation may have become available only after the frescoes were completed – but the Latin is so simple that surely even Titian could have read it, and it was certainly known to some of the *scuola* members who commissioned the cycle. In any case, assumptions regarding Titian's ignorance of Latin are probably exaggerated. Admittedly, he was not well educated; but fluency in Italian combined with frequent exposure to Latin (in church, in civic rituals) certainly gave Titian some knowledge of it, and presumably also the ability to understand simpler texts.[26] It seems unlikely that Titian and/or his patrons confused the Italian and Latin *pugio*, 'dagger,' with the similar word for 'fist,' *pugno* (Italian) or *pugnus* (Latin), because of the context: '... multis pugnis et calcibus percutit ...' ('he beat her with numerous punches [fists] and kicks').[27] For Titian, however, a severe beating had become murder, and it may be that this seemingly wilful mistake reflects his own feelings about the matter. But do these feelings represent sympathy for the victim or misogynistic hostility?

Titian's composition is surely one of the most terrible assaults in art, more violent and more personalized than many saints' martyrdoms, and infinitely more so than the later relief in the Cappella dell'Arca. Giovanni Rubino (called Dentone) and Silvio Cosini began their relief in 1524, thirteen years after Titian's *Jealous Husband* was completed (fig. 6). The two sculptors clearly adapted the husband's pose from the fresco.[28] Like Titian, the sculptors also depicted the attack but not the resuscitation of the wife. There the resemblance ends. In the relief, the victim falls in a graceful swoon – she suggests a classical quotation rather than an anguished death – while two men restrain her husband from striking further blows. The deed is done, calm is being restored. Moreover, the sculp-

Figure 6. Giovanni Rubino (Il Dentone) and Silvio Cosini, *Miracle of the Jealous Husband*, marble relief, Padua, Basilica del Santo, Cappella dell'Arca, begun 1524

tors depicted the wife in profile instead of revealing her anguished face, as Titian had done; and they omitted the deadly knife. Their narrative is thus profoundly different from his bloody drama. Perhaps considering Titian's savage interpretation inappropriate for the saint's tomb, the friars themselves may have required certain changes when they ordered the episode to be represented in the relief. At any rate, Titian's focal point is the attack, and his cast essentially limited to the man and wife. No bystanders intervene, the brutality is undiluted, and the saint's forgiveness, though peripheral in the composition, is none the less clearly represented, another interpolation not mentioned in the text.

Sprawled on the ground and bleeding, the wife struggles to ward off her husband's attack – but his knife is just above her hand, and he pulls her head back by the hair: cruel and conclusive details that anticipate the deadly outcome of the struggle. The knife and wound, as noted, were Titian's additions to the story, but the saint's biographer had in fact specifically mentioned that the husband pulled his wife by the hair, admired as her crowing glory. Perhaps Polentone recalled an earlier legend crediting Saint Anthony with saving a similarly endowed beautiful woman of Limoges whose jealous husband had given her an unwanted haircut: a woman's hair is not only a primary attribute of her loveliness but is invested with specifically sexual significance in Italian culture.[29] Only maidens (including brides), harlots, and hermits such as Mary Magdalen may wear their hair loose; wives, widows, and nuns conceal theirs as a matter of modesty and propriety. And so, when the husband of Limoges crops his wife's coiffure, or when the knight of Tuscany pulls his wife's hair, the sexual nature of the suspected crime is implied, the sexual character of the men's rage specified.

Like the mother of the *Speaking Infant*, the innocent wife is a large woman, her size enhanced by her garments; under normal circumstances she would resemble that beautiful and heroic figure, but her features are distorted by fear and by the skewed viewpoint. (Titian had surely seen the expressive foreshortening of Mantegna's frescoes in the Ovetari Chapel of the Paduan church of the Eremitani.) The methods Titian used to empower the mother now serve to emphasize the wife's pathos and desperation. This inversion or contradiction, the juxtaposition of her natural grandeur and her horrible destruction, conveys the tragedy of her death with far greater concern for the victim than the written narrative suggests. Interpreting her story as a secular martyrdom, Titian compels our sympathy for her and her plight.

Horror is exacerbated by the abstract means of colour and pattern, the husband's oscillating red and white, the wife's hot, intense yellow-orange. Red and white, we recall, are colours traditionally associated with beauty, whereas yellow may signify jealousy: this colouristic 'exchange' suggests a projection of the husband's jealousy onto the wife, of her (distorted) beauty onto her murderer.[30] His garment is perforce repeated in the denouement, showing the saint's forgiveness – though the stripes are calmer now, in response to the husband's kneeling. But no narrative consistency required that Titian also repeat the wife's yellow-orange in the garment worn by one of Saint Anthony's companions. Her colouristic surrogate in the background returns our attention to the suffering woman in the foreground. God and his saint may forgive her murderer, and this forgiveness is all the more wonderful, given the viciousness of the crime. Yet, arousing our pity for the victim, as in the *Miracle of the Speaking Infant*, Titian encourages our empathetic identification with the woman, thereby inverting the misogynistic subtext of the saint's legend. Thus we see the husband's attacking his wife and not her resuscitation – the far more obvious choice from the traditional hagiographical point of view, with numerous comparable precedents in literature and in art, such as Masaccio's and Masolino's *Raising of Drusiana* in the Brancacci Chapel of S. Maria del Carmine in Florence.[31] In the *Miracle of the Speaking Infant*, on the contrary, the choice of moment is almost to be taken for granted; the other possibility, to show Anthony handing the child to his father, would be less revealing and less dramatic.

The actual husbands and fathers who commissioned these murals could see in them situations that were sociologically and psychologically relevant to their own lives. (Their women who were *scuola* members were evidently forbidden to enter this room; presumably they never saw the frescoes.)[32] Indeed, the confrères themselves had effectively related life and art by the fundamental choice of narratives and the sequence of events. If the patrons decided which miracles would be included in the cycle – in keeping with customary practice – it is impossible to say who determined the moment represented.[33] These decisions may have been the result of collaborative consultation, though it is more likely in Titian's case that the master himself made these determinations: the originality of narrative choices in his three murals indicates that this was the case. As saintly *topoi*, however, these three episodes, like all the others in the cycle, confirm expectations, representing miracles (or the kinds of miracles) and accomplishments that Renaissance people required of their saints. Anthony is seen as a healer, a compelling preacher, a miracle worker, and so on. His death is also represented here, as in most such cycles, for an obvious reason: only after a saint's death can he enter the kingdom of heaven.

The program is introduced by the kind of composition that can be seen as a *sine qua non* of *scuola* cycles, the representation of an exemplary action by the guardian of the confraternity, who in this case distributes blessed bread to his confrères. (This fresco, located immediately inside the entrance, is attributed to Titian's brother, Francesco Vecellio, in 1511, and sometimes, fancifully, to Titian himself.) Three of the seventeen narratives of the saint's life depict episodes of particular significance for the confraternity as a Paduan institution – namely, the saint's arrival in the city, his appearance to the Blessed Luca Belludi as a sign of approbation of that friar's preaching the liberation of Padua, and the translation of Saint Anthony's body in 1350 from one funerary chapel to another in the Santo.[34] That the frescoes should reflect local interests in this way is natural, and indeed reminiscent of other such cycles of saints' lives, both in confraternities and in church settings.

In another respect, however, the *scuola* cycle seems to be exceptional, perhaps unique: of the seventeen episodes representing stories of Saint Anthony's life and posthumous miracles, an extraordinary eight deal with family matters. Moreover, seven of the eight 'familial' miracles occur as a mini-cycle within the cycle, including Titian's *Jealous Husband* and the adjacent *Miracle of the Reattached Foot*. The domestic significance of these seven scenes is underscored by the very fact of their proximity. That is to say, the depiction of such domestic events as the saint's saving an infant from drowning is in itself unexceptional; many, if not all, medieval saints performed the same miracle. What makes it remarkable here is the emphatic repetition of these kinds of miracles. Surely this reiteration of domestic subjects reflects the patrons' fundamental concern with family.

The seven-episode familial cycle unfolds to the dexter or gospel side of the altar, decorated with Riccio's sculpture of the Virgin and Child flanked by frescoes of Saints Anthony and Francis. (The placement on the 'superior' side of the altar is significant in itself, and the evocation of Mary's perfect motherhood also germane in this familial context.) The group of seven family miracles is introduced by Corona's depiction of the saint's arrival in Padua, dated 1509 and not coincidentally the first mural commissioned and completed for the cycle: thus civic pride is vaunted, and Anthony's role in the private lives of his followers is literally brought home to the citizens of his adopted city. (This is the implication of the arrangement, even though some of the events that follow, including the *Miracle of the Jealous Husband*, may have taken place elsewhere.) Next to the *Saint's Arrival in Padua* is Titian's *Jealous Husband*, followed by his *Miracle of the Reattached Foot* and the other 'family' miracles: the *Resurrection of a Child Who Had Fallen into Boiling Water* (attributed to Girolamo del Santo, 1524), the *Resurrection of a Man Who Can Attest to the Innocence of Anthony's Father* (an anonymous canvas, not part of the original cycle), *Anthony's Resurrection of a Drowned Girl* (an undated work by Domenico Campagnola), and the *Resurrection of a Drowned Baby* (attributed to Francesco Vecellio, 1511). Within this sequence, the late eighteenth-century composition of the saint's death is both an interruption and a redundancy, because the *Death of the Saint* had already been represented in a fresco by Girolamo del Santo (1513) on the entrance wall.[35] It seems that the eighteenth-century work was painted to replace a damaged fresco, and it is tempting to imagine that this lost composition depicted yet another domestic subject. Be that as it may, the domestic theme is also invoked (or introduced) on the entrance wall by Titian's *Miracle of the Speaking Infant*.

This mural, by virtue of its site the first 'family miracle,' is located just inside the entrance to the chapter room on the wall opposite the altar. Its conspicuous location suggests another means of asserting the primacy of familial concerns in the cycle. The *Speaking Infant* was the first work executed by Titian for the *scuola* and also the earliest of all the family miracles represented there. The very inclusion of this first domestic miracle demonstrates that the confrères were concerned from the start with this kind of subject-matter, though the other episodes on this wall are more exclusively associated with Saint Anthony. These are miracles dealing with the saint as a preacher and teacher who proves the truth of his faith by finding a miser's heart with his money, by inspiring a mule to venerate the consecrated Host, by preventing a glass from shattering, by reproaching the heretic Ezzelino. With the exception of the *Speaking Infant*, however, every episode on the entrance wall is an *unicum*. That is to say, no other saint but Anthony caused a mule to kneel before the Host, and so on. In this context, the inclusion of the *Miracle of the Speaking Infant* – a rather commonplace sort of miracle, as we recall – suggests the confraternity's determination to demonstrate the saint's efficacy as a family counsellor, even at the expense of hagiographic banality.

On the gospel wall, the genus is entirely domestic and the events portrayed are more generic, in this sense also like the *Speaking Infant*. The domestic cycle-within-the-cycle deals with precisely the kinds of mundane problems that concerned the members of the confraternity in their daily lives: threats to the safety of their children (viz., drowning and scalding);

the recalcitrance of liminal youths (the *Miracle of the Reattached Foot*); the violence of unhappy marriages (the *Jealous Husband*) – and the patron saint's effectiveness in helping the faithful to deal with these matters. These narrative choices indicate that the confraternity's overriding interest was more personal than public, intimate rather than civic.

The emphasis on domestic episodes is, then, a departure from the usual criteria of cycles of saints' lives, wherein one or two such miracles were considered to be sufficient to make the point. These narrative idiosyncracies are surely related to the avowed concern of the members of the Scuola di Sant'Antonio as described in their fifteenth-century statutes – namely, to live a Christian life as laymen, and as laywomen. Membership of the confraternity included both men and women. We have seen, however, that only the male confrères generally met in this upstairs *capitolo*, which was also used for boys' catechism classes (to the evident detriment of the frescoes' condition). Women members met instead in the ground-floor rooms that had been part of the original *scuola* building, and likewise girls went there to study their catechism.[36] If indeed women were effectively barred from the upstairs *capitolo*, as the statutes imply, it appears that the audience for these frescoes was exclusively male, while the patronage was both male and female. Perhaps the fresco cycle may be seen as flattering or comforting the women (their innocence will be proved, their children will be saved) while offering redoubled reassurance to the men about a fundamental concern of Renaissance husbands – namely, the chastity and virtue of their wives.

Even within this familial context, however, Titian's two scenes dealing with adultery, like their counterparts in the Santo chapel, seem anomalous. The *Miracle of the Jealous Husband*, we remember, was represented for the first time in his fresco and for the second time in the Santo relief;[37] and the *Miracle of the Speaking Infant* is likewise one of the few monumental depictions of that story. To be sure, versions of the latter miracle were much recounted in other saints' lives, but the corresponding depictions of the story are comparatively few in number and largely limited to manuscript illuminations. In Padua, however, the story was depicted twice on the grand scale, in Titian's fresco and in the funerary chapel of Saint Anthony in the Santo; and twice the Paduans ordered scenes of the obscure *Miracle of the Jealous Husband*.

Titian's two 'adultery' frescoes are also anomalous in presenting events that did not take place in Padua but elsewhere, according to Polentone: the chaste mother is Ferrarese, the murderous husband a Tuscan. Presumably not wishing to impute wrongdoing to Paduan husbands and wives, the biographer, himself a *padovano*, specified the foreign nationalities of these troubled characters. But in the frescoes, such distinctions vanish: Titian clothed his characters as contemporaries of the Veneto, and the actors become everyman and -woman, figures with whom the viewer is invited to identify. The omnipresent fear of adultery is thus brought home – but so, too, the possibility that some wives are chaste, that the lineage is safe, because these wives, at least, have been falsely accused.

To be sure, all Europeans shared the concern with these matters, and everywhere in Europe, wifely chastity was extolled. 'Nothing,' Alberti declared, 'is so important for yourself, so acceptable to God, so pleasing to ... [your husband], and precious in the sight of your children as your chastity.' A woman's virtue is her family's 'jewel,' he explained; it enriches her dowry and is more important by far than her beauty.[38] But in the Venetian Republic, including Padua, visceral jealousy and its theological garb were bound with money and politics: the patrician's exclusive right to rule (and the original citizen's exclusive right to assist the rulers in the chancellery) derived from legitimate descent. Thus, in the Serenissima, female chastity was institutionalized, and exhortations to women more specific than elsewhere. A flurry of legislation enacted during the fifteenth century had specified that a child's social class was determined not only by his father's station but also by his mother's: the child must be the legitimate issue of noble parents in order to inherit their position. Comparable legislation concerning original citizens soon followed.[39] As a concomitant to this legal insistence on a wife's status, and in part deriving from the same vital dependence on her indisputable virtue, Veneto authors and husbands increasingly expressed appreciation of their helpmeets in treatises and in such unpublished familial writings as testaments.[40] The Paduans reflected these mores. It may be that they wished to reiterate their fidelity to Venetian customs and morality in this particular site – the Scuola was one of the most prestigious public buildings in Padua – at this particular time, immediately after their capitulation to Imperial forces in the war of the League of Cambrai and subsequent reconquest by the Republic.

The *scuola* wives are legendary, and their stories, like others in the lives of Saint Anthony (and of all saints), were of course conceived to demonstrate his sanctity in a variety of ways and arenas – in this case, in family court. As in all such sagas, Anthony's biographers are quite explicit about the piety and the worthiness of the beneficiaries: the saint intervenes to help those who are particularly devoted to him, including these two chaste women. It should have gone without saying – but was none the less incessantly repeated in Renaissance marriage treatises – that these same virtues of piety and chastity describe the ideal wife. 'Romantic' love had little if anything to do with this ideal.

To be sure, the fact that families negotiated marriage between individuals certainly did not preclude their loving each other.[41] The authors of treatises regularly urged couples to do so – albeit within the bounds of reason. Unbridled passion, which becomes violent in the *Jealous Husband*, is inappropriate between man and wife. Wisemen, pagan and Christian alike, from Aristotle to Saint Augustine and onward, had explained why this is so: sexual passion robs men of sound judgment. Thus, reiterating the patriarchal commonplace that virginity is superior to marriage, Saint Thomas Aquinas asserted that sex is always sinful, at best a venial sin. To clinch his argument, he quoted Augustine: 'nothing so casts down the manly mind from its height as the fondling of a woman.' Indeed, Aquinas concluded, to love one's wife too ardently is adultery – adultery against God, who must have the greatest love.[42]

Closer in time to Titian, Alessandro Piccolomini asserted bluntly that love and marriage are irreconcilable. Man and wife should share affection and goodwill, but not love: marriage is an obligation, not a free relationship.[43] Unlike the mysogynistic theologians, Piccolomini was unconcerned with the moral issues of sexual love in marriage. Rather, it was simply that he saw no particular association between love and marriage, and no objection to extramarital love, where sexual passion seemed appropriate, and even exalted.[44] In a second version of his treatise, published in Venice some twenty years after the first, in 1542, Piccolimini changed his tune – but a very different ideal was extolled in most contemporary literature, which was probably closer to the mark of patrician reality and psychology. The *scuola*'s two adultery frescoes are in effect illustrations of this mentality, while the *Miracle of the Reattached Foot* represents the other side of the misogynistic coin. And yet Titian, often variously praised and/or blamed by critics for what they commonly perceive to be his mindless or single-minded eroticism, was rather more sympathetic to woman than has been realized.

NOTES

This essay is taken from the first chapter of my forthcoming book, *Titian's Women* (New Haven and London: Yale University Press 1997).

1 Gayle Rubin, 'Thinking Sex: Notes for a Radical theory of the Politics of Sexu-

ality,' in *Pleasure and Danger: Exploring Female Sexuality*, ed. Carole S. Vance (Boston: Routledge and Kegan Paul 1984), 278

2 See R. Howard Bloch, *Medieval Misogyny and the Invention of Western Romantic Love* (Chicago and London: University of Chicago Press 1991), 177 and *passim*, on both aspects of misogyny.

3 Saint Anthony died in 1231 and was canonized the following year. The purpose of his confraternity in Padua was not so much to promote Anthony's cult but to foster Christian morality and religion among the members, as reflected in the statutes of 1439: see Antonio Sartori, *L'Arciconfraternita del Santo* (Padua: Tipografia della Provincia Patavina di S. Antonio dei Frati Minori Conventuali 1955), 38. The project for expanding the *scuola*'s building with the addition of a second storey was approved by the confrères on 8 April 1504 by a vote of 83 to 1: ibid., 52, citing documents in Padua, Biblioteca Civica, B.P. 573, carta 48v. Work on the building was in progress by 19 February 1505: Sartori cites records of that date in Padua, Archivio di Stato, Scuola del Santo, Busta 13, fascicolo 1502, carta 9). First mentioned in the *scuola* register on 1 December 1510, Titian was the third painter to work in the second-storey *capitolo*, or 'chapter room': Sartori (63) transcribes the record of this first payment to Titian in the Archivio di Stato, Scuola del Santo, Registro 124, carta 119. Other accounts record payments to Titian on 23 April, 9 and 21 May, and 19 July 1511. The final payment or *saldo* is dated 2 December, when Titian was already back in Venice: Registro 124, carta 121 verso.

4 For the text, see Vergilio Gamboso, 'La "Sancti Antonii Confessoris de Padua vita" di Sicco Ricci Polentone (c. 1435),' *Il Santo* 11 (1971) (hereinafter cited as Polentone-Gamboso). Polentone's biography was in fact the only source for the *Miracle of the Jealous Husband*.

5 In the Vulgate, Mk. 9: 44; see also Mt. 18: 8. Sartori, *Arciconfraternita*, identifies the second woman as the boy's sister and notes that the fresco was already damaged by 6 June 1518, when Antonio Pignata was paid to repair it: Sartori cites Padua, Archivio di Stato, Scuola del Santo, Registro 124, carta 27. For the episode in the official life of the saint, see Polentone-Gamboso, 51, paragraph 45: 'Ille autem simplex homo et sancti verba rudem ad corticem non ad medullam intelligens, ut rediit domum, quo matrem percusserat pedem gladio mutilavit.' See also Polentone-Gamboso's n. 49 for other textual sources.

6 Polentone-Gamboso, 241–2, paragraph 37: 'Morte istam in Tuscia [referring to the previous miracle in the text, that of the Jealous Husband], sed alteram Ferariae suspicione maxima liberavit. Maritum namque, qui esset vir spectatus atque primarius, reconciliavit uxori; et, quod longe fuit maius ac vere miraculum, quod puer infans, paucos ante dies natus, loqueretur, ac sibi ad quae

sanctus peteret, responderet, effecit. Inerat quidem marito tanta de uxore suspicio, quod natum sibi diebus proximis filium, quasi matre adultera ac semine
alieno conceptum, neque tangere nec videre vellet. Puellum hunc sanctus
Antonius inter manus accipiens: "Adiuro te, inquit ad puerum, per virtutem
Iesu Christi, qui verus est Deus et homo Maria de virgine natus, ut audientibus
cunctis nunc mihi respondeas ac dicas, quisnam est pater tuus."'

7 See Marco Ferro, *Dizionario del diritto comune e veneto* ..., 9 vols. in 5 (Venice: A.
Santini 1778–81), vol. 1: 121–6, with citations of the relevant fifteenth-century
statutes.

8 For the law of 1443, see Lorenzo Priori, *Prattica criminale secondo il ritto delle leggi
della Serenissima Republica di Venetia* (Venice: Pietro Pinelli 1644), 175–9.

9 See Amy Richlin, 'Approaches to the Sources on Adultery at Rome,' *Women's
Studies* 8 (1981), 227–8. Jewish law similarly 'treated the act [rape] primarily as
an offence against the girl's family': see James A. Brundage, 'Rape and Marriage in the Medieval Canon Law,' *Revue de droit canonique* 1 (1978), 63n3 and
62–75, for the evolution of sexual-crime laws from Roman times to the Middle
Ages.

10 Ferro, *Dizionario*, vol. 1: 114, defines the 'adulterino' as the child born of adultery, adding: 'I figliuoli adulterini sono più odiosi, che gl'illegittimi nati da
persone sciolte.' He seems to be paraphrasing the wording of a Venetian stat-
ute or statutes.

11 Ibid., 120. In other matters of law, false accusations might well be penalized
and, in any case, were certainly not answered with approbation for the accuser.
Adultery was a principal exception, largely because marital infidelity was considered a private matter, to be settled by the family: see also ibid., 114. Why,
then, are Titian's 'adultery cases' being resolved in the sacred and public
venue of the *scuola*? An answer to this rhetorical question is offered at the end
of this essay.

12 See *supra*, note 6.

13 For the history of this miracle in various saints' lives, see Paul Canart, 'Le Nou-
veau-né qui dénonce son père. Les avatars d'un conte populaire dans la littérature hagiographique,' *Analecta Bollandiana* 84 (1966), 309–33.

14 On the membership, see Sartori, *Arciconfraternita*, 51; Giuseppina de Sandre
Gasparini, 'La devozione antoniana nella scuola del Santo di Padova nel sec-
olo XV. Da un'indagine su testamenti di soci e simpatizzanti,' *Il Santo* 16/2–3
(May–December 1976), 189–200; and 'Lineamenti e vicende della confrater-
nita di S. Antonio di Padova (secoli XIV e XV),' in *Liturgia, pietà e ministeri al
Santo*, ed. Antonino Poppi (Vicenza: Neri Pozzi 1978), 217–35.

15 On this artistic debt, see Allen Rosenbaum, 'Titian and Giotto in Padua,' *Mars-
yas* 13 (1966–7), 1–7. A black-pencil portrait drawing in Florence, Galleria

degli Uffizi, Gabinetto dei Disegni, Inv. no. 718E, is closely related to this figure (more so, in my opinion, than to the subject of *La Schiavona*). See Harold
E. Wethey, *Titian and His Drawings with Reference to Giorgione and Some Close Contemporaries* (Princeton, NJ: Princeton University Press 1987), 10–11, 147, cat.
23; and M. Agnese Chiari Moretto Wiel, *Titian Drawings* [1989], trans. Jeremy
Scott (New York: Rizzoli 1990), 84, cat. 8. W.R. Rearick also related the drawing and the woman sketched on the verso to the mother and a bystander in
the Santo fresco: see his *Tiziano e il disegno veneziano del suo tempo*, trans. Anna
Maria Petrioli Tofani, Gabinetto Disegni e Stampe degli Uffizi 45 (Florence:
Leo S. Olschki 1976), 37–8, cat. 16.

16 Sarah Blake McHam first recognized the importance of the reliefs of Saint
Anthony's funerary chapel for Titian's compositions: see Blake Wilk
[McHam], 'Titian's Paduan Experience and Its Influence on His Style,' *Art
Bulletin* 65 (1983), 51–60. A conspicuous exception to this rule is Titian's *Mira-
cle of the Reattached Foot.* On the funerary chapel itself, see her *The Chapel of St.
Anthony at the Santo and the Development of Venetian Renaissance Sculpture* (Cam-
bridge, Eng., and New York: Cambridge University Press 1994).

17 See Janson, *Donatello* (Princeton: Princeton University Press 1963), 162–87,
and fig. 84b; and John White, 'Donatello,' in *Le sculture del Santo di Padova*, ed.
Giovanni Lorenzoni (Vicenza: N. Pozza 1984), 51–94.

18 For this relief from a Claudian monument, *ca.* 45–50, in Ravenna, Museo Nazi-
onale, see Diana E.E. Kleiner, *Roman Sculpture* (New Haven and London: Yale
University Press 1992), 146 and fig. 121. Kleiner identifies the figure as Drusus
the Elder, father of Claudius. Titian's allusion to this monument was first recognized by Ludwig Curtius, 'Zum Antikenstudium Tizians,' *Archiv für Kulturge-
schichte* 28 (1938), 233–4, followed by Ruth Wedgwood Kennedy, *Novelty and
Tradition in Titian's Art*, The Katharine Asher Engel Lectures (Northampton,
MA: Smith College 1963), 12. Kennedy repeats the traditional and probably
incorrect identification of the figure as Agrippa. She suggests that Titian
would have known the monument from a cast and comments on his transforming the relief into a statue.

19 Titian's illusionistic statue (and, indeed, his fictive architecture) is perhaps his
first salvo in a lifelong engagement with the *paragone*, his first declaration of his
ambition to redo and outdo the ancients, and his first assertion of painting's
superiority to sculpture – and *this* painter's superiority to any sculptor, living or
dead. For the *paragone*, the modern term now used to describe the Renaissance
debate regarding the comparative virtues of the arts, see Claire J. Farago,
*Leonardo da Vinci's 'Paragone': A Critical Interpretation with a New Edition of the Text
in the 'Codex Urbinas,'* Brill's Studies in Intellectual History 25 (Leiden and New
York: E.S. Brill 1992); and for the *paragone* in Titian's art, my *Titian's Women*.

20 Polentone describes her with these words in Polentone-Gamboso, 241, paragraph 36: 'Fueritne quod miraculum sequitur eisdem loco et tempore nescio, sed fuisse in Tuscia certa res est. Miles erat tuscus, cum nobilitate generis tum opibus strenuus, sed irascebatur facile; atque tanta saepe exardebat ira, quod furentis in modum neque quid diceret, nec quid faceret ulla ratione cognosceret.

'Uxorem hic, feminam nobilem atque pudicam, quod fortasse quicquam minus congrue respondisset, ira subita, ut solebat, accensus, multis pugnis et calcibus percutit, totam per domum trahit, capillos – carissimum mulierum decus – evellit, atque tandem semianimem alto e solario supinam in curiam iacit.

'Ad eam rem domus accurrit tota, et qui aderant omnes moesti famuli et famulae dominam, ut possunt commodius, in lectum ferunt. Ipse vero miles, scelere patrato dolens ac poenitens, santum Antonium ... Quid dixerim? Properat cum milite sanctus et manu iacentis ulcera leniens ac crucis signo continuo signans, genua in terram flectit, Deum ut moribundae restituat vitam et sanitatem orat. Mulier autem, quae membris confractis iaceret ac mortua videretur, sancto exorante sana et libera assurrexit.'

21 Ferro, *Dizionario*, vol. 1: 127. These reprehensible traditions unfortunately continue to our own day; for a recent report on the mild sentences meted out to men who beat or murder their women, see Jan Hoffman, 'Defending Men Who Kill Their Loved Ones,' *New York Times*, 10 July 1994, Section 4, p. 3.

22 N.B. the painting attributed to Titian, *ca.* 1507, in Glasgow, the Glasgow Art Gallery and Museum, traditionally labelled *Christ and the Adulteress* but more recently identified as *Susanna and Daniel*. See Alessandro Ballarin, '*Suzanne et Daniel*,' in *Le Siècle de Titien: L'âge d'or de la peinture à Venise*, exh. cat., eds. Michel Laclotte and Giovanna Nepi Scirè (Paris: Réunion des Musées Nationaux 1993), 327–39, cat. 42a, with previous bibliography.

23 Cherubino da Siena, *Regole della vita matrimoniale* (*ca.* 1450–81), ed. Francesco Zambrini and Carlo Negroni (Bologna: Romagnoli-dall'Acqua 1858), 7, 11–14

24 Guido Ruggiero, 'Excusable Murder: Insanity and Reason in Early Renaissance Venice,' *Journal of Social History* 16 (1982), 111

25 Sartori, *Arciconfraternita*, 63, cites the *scuola* register entry dated 1 December 1510 in which Titian accepted the conditions for painting the three frescoes: 'M[aestr]o Tician depentore die haver depenzando lo primo quadro che xè a man destra intrando de sopra in capitolo ... ducati dodexe doro a tutte soe spexe – L[ire] 74 s[oldi] 8. E de' haver per la depentura de dui quadrj pizoli che sono dalla porta de la canzelaria nostra zoè quel dal pè et quello amazò soa mogiera ducatj disdotto doro val L[ire] 111 s[oldi] 12': Padua, Archivio di Stato, Scuola del Santo, Registro 124, carta 122.

26 Regarding his knowledge of Latin, see F.R. Martin, 'A Patriotic Speech by
    Titian,' *Burlington Magazine* 43 (1923), 304–5, kindly brought to my attention
    by Z.B. Smetana. Martin reproduced the frontispiece of a published Latin ora-
    tion by Titian, delivered 6 January 1572 (just four years before his death). To
    be sure, the oration, honouring the Venetian victory at Lepanto, would have
    been ghost-written for him; but the fact remains that Titian himself, in his
    capacity as ambassador from Cadore to the Serenissima, read the Latin text in
    the presence of Doge Alvise Mocenigo and the Great Council. In it, he speaks
    of 'Italia,' at a time when, as Martin notes, most people spoke only of their
    own region.
27 Polentone-Gamboso, 45
28 See also Blake McHam, 'La decorazione cinquecentesca della Cappella
    dell'Arca di S. Antonio,' in *Sculture del Santo*, 139–41, for a comparison of the
    relief and Titian's fresco. She explains that the sculpture's background scene
    was added over a decade after completion of the relief itself. Executed in
    stucco by an anonymous sculptor, the addition shows Anthony in prayer
    before the Virgin Mary.
29 For this French variant of the story, see the *Liber miraculorum* 11, in *Analecta
    Franciscana* 3 (Quaracchi 1897), 126–7, cited by Gamboso, in Polentone-Gam-
    boso, 45*n*56. For the sexual connotations of a woman's hair, see Daniel Arasse,
    'Il vello di Maddalena,' in *La Maddalena tra sacro e profano, Da Giotto a De Chir-
    ico*, ed. Marilena Mosco, 58 ff. (Milan: A. Mondadori; Florence: Casa Usher
    1986). For another jealous husband who grabs his wife's hair as he beats her,
    see the fifteenth-century mansucript illumination illustrated by Julia
    O'Faolain and Lauro Martines, eds., *Not in God's Image* (London: Temple
    Smith 1973), fig. 7 – a beating that takes place at home (cf. Titian's landscape,
    discussed *supra*, note 25).
30 I thank Professor Bridget Gellert Lyons of Rutgers University for this astute
    suggestion regarding Titian's 'projected' colours.
31 Wendy Stedman Sheard suggests that the 'intrinsic violence' of Titian's subject
    'may have invited an analogous break with visual conventions' and that, by
    foregrounding the husband in the composition, Titian offers him 'as a nega-
    tive example': see Sheard, 'Titian's Paduan Frescoes and the Issue of Deco-
    rum,' in *Decorum in Renaissance Narrative Art*, Papers Delivered at the Annual
    Conference of the Association of Art Historians, London, April 1991, eds.
    Francis Ames-Lewis and Anka Bednarek (London: Department of Art History,
    University of London, 1992), 91.
32 Sartori, *Arciconfraternita*, 38
33 In Venice, for example, the Bellini brothers were given considerable freedom
    in interpreting the narratives for the murals for the Scuola Grande di San

Marco, of which they themselves were confrères; but this freedom was clearly related to their professional status at the time of the commission – and probably also to the fact that their work was donated as a contribution to the *scuola*, which paid only for the materials: see Rona Goffen, *Giovanni Bellini* (New Haven: Yale University Press 1989), 269, 271–3.

34 On the financial benefits of holy relics for their communities, see Patrick Geary, *Furta Sacra: Thefts of Relics in the Central Middle Ages* (Princeton, NJ: Princeton University Press, 1978). On the civic significance of the saint's funerary chapel for Padua, see Blake McHam, *Chapel of Saint Anthony*, 23–8.

35 The death scene by Antonio Buttafuoco, dated 1777, is inserted between the anonymous canvas and Campagnola's fresco, as indicated below. From the right as one enters, the cycle represents: the *Guardian of the Scuola Distributing Blessed Bread to the Confrères*, attributed to Francesco Vecellio (Titian's brother), 1511; *Miracle of the Speaking Infant*, Titian, 1510–11; *Heart of the Avaricious Man*, Francesco Vecellio, 1512; *Miracle of the Mule*, Girolamo del Santo, *ca* 1513; *Apparition of the Saint to B. Luca Belludi Preaching the Liberation of Padua*, Filippo da Verona, 1510; *Death of the Saint*, Girolamo del Santo, 1513; *Cardinal Guido di Monfort Opens the Arca of the Saint in 1350*, Bartolomeo Montagna, 1512; *Miracle of the Glass*, Girolamo del Santo, 1511; *Saint Anthony Reproaches Ezzelino*, Giovanni Antonio Corona, 1510; *Madonna and Child with Saints Anthony and Francis*, polychrome terracotta, altar, Riccio (Andrea Briosco), 1520; *Glory of Angels*, fresco above the altar, Campagnola, 1533; *Saint Anthony's Arrival in Padua*, Corona, 1509; *Miracle of the Jealous Husband*, Titian, 1511; *Miracle of the Reattached Foot*, Titian, 1511; *Saint Anthony Raises the Child Who Had Fallen into Boiling Water*, attributed to Girolamo del Santo, 1524; *Saint Anthony Raises a Dead Man Who Can Attest the Innocence of the Saint's Father*, canvas, anonymous; *Death of the Saint*, Antonio Buttafuoco, 1777; *Saint Anthony Raises a Drowned Girl*, Campagnola, *ca* 1533; the *Saint Riases a Drowned Baby*, attributed to Francesco Vecellio, 1511.

36 Sartori, *Arciconfraternita*, 38

37 There seems to be only one other surviving large-scale depiction of this story, included in the grisaille fresco cycle of Saint Anthony's life by Girolamo da Treviso, *ca* 1526, in the church of San Petronio in Bologna. I owe this information to Professor McHam.

38 Leon Battista Alberti was addressing this exhortation to his own wife. See *Not in God's Image*, eds. O'Faolain and Martines, 189.

39 The culmination was the early-sixteenth-century establishment of the *Libri d'Oro* in which all patrician marriages and births were to be registered. See Stanley Chojnacki, 'Kinship Ties and Young Patricians in Fifteenth-Century Venice,' *Renaissance Quarterly* 38 (1985), 240–70, esp. 246–7 on relevant legisla-

tion; 'Marriage Legislation and Patrician Society in Fifteenth-Century Venice,' in *Law, Custom, and the Social Fabric in Medieval Europe: Essays in Honor of Bryce Lyon*, eds. Bernard S. Bachrach and David Nicholas, Studies in Medieval Culture, XXVIII, 163–84 (Kalamazoo: Medieval Institute Publications 1990); and 'Social Identity in Renaissance Venice: The Second *Serrata*,' *Renaissance Studies* 8 (1994), 341–58; and Goffen, *Giovanni Bellini*, 3–4, 219. Pietro Bembo in *De re uxoria* (among other Venetian authors) provides a quasi-genetic explanation for such laws: the mother's character is most important for that of the child, and noble lineage is the best guarantor of character.

40　For attitudes towards women, see Chojnacki, 'The Power of Love: Wives and Husbands in Late Medieval Venice,' in *Women and Power in the Middle Ages*, eds. Mary Erler and Maryanne Kowalski, 126–48 (Athens, GA, and London: University of Georgia Press 1988), and '"The Most Serious Duty": Motherhood, Gender, and Patrician Culture in Renaissance Venice,' in *Refiguring Woman: Perspectives on Gender and the Italian Renaissance*, eds. Marilyn Migiel and Juliana Schiesari, 133–54 (Ithaca, NY, and London: Cornell University Press 1991). Women had greater liberty in the Veneto (and in Liguria) than elsewhere in Italy. In addition to Chojnacki's publications, see Evelina Rinaldi, 'La donna negli statuti del comune di Forlì, sec. XIV,' *Studi storici* 18 (1909), 185; and Ruggiero, *The Boundaries of Eros: Sex Crime and Sexuality in Renaissance Venice* (New York and Oxford: Oxford University Press, 1985), 63–165. On Venetian feminism in the sixteenth century, see Patricia Labalme, 'Venetian Women on Women: Three Early Modern Feminists,' *Archivio veneto* 152 (1981), 81–109; and Constance Jordan, *Renaissance Feminism: Literary Texts and Political Models* (Ithaca, NY, and London: Cornell University Press 1990), esp. 138–72.

41　For Venetian marriages as family alliances, see Margaret L. King, 'Caldiera and the Barbaros on Marriage and the Family: Humanist Reflections of Venetian Realities,' *Journal of Medieval and Renaissance Studies* 6 (1976), 19–50

42　Quoted in Katharine M. Rogers, *The Troublesome Helpmate: A History of Misogyny in Literature* (Seattle and London: University of Washington Press 1966), 65

43　This was also the view of Andrea Capellano, perhaps the greatest theoretician of courtly love. See Alessandra Del Fante, 'Amore, famiglia e matrimonio nell' 'Institutione' di Alessandro Piccolomini,' *Nuova rivista storica* 68 (1984), 520–1, esp. 511, for Piccolomini's *De la institutione di tutta la vita de l'huomo nato nobile e in città libera* ..., first published in Venice (Hieronumum Scotum) in 1542 and reprinted in 1543. Two years later, in the *Orazione in lode delle donne detta in Siena a gli Intronati* (Venice, Giolito, 1545), however, Piccolomini argued for women's superiority in matters of virtue: discussed by Del Fante, 520.

44　Rogers, *Troublesome Helpmate*, 58

Freedom through Renunciation?
Women's Voices, Women's Bodies,
and the Phallic Order

BARRIE RUTH STRAUS

What do women want? This is a question that puzzled many men, medieval and modern, including Freud[1] and the knight in Chaucer's *Wife of Bath's Tale*, who is given a chance to save his life by being sent on a quest to find the answer. Few have followed the attempt of the knight in the Wife's *Tale* to ask women themselves what they want. And perhaps that is just as well; for recent studies of language, taking Freud's theory of the unconscious into account, make us aware of the extent to which we have no way of knowing what 'woman' might want, since the phallocentric discourse by which our thinking is constituted constructs 'woman' as man's other.[2] In three fourteenth-century English works, however – Chaucer's *Parliament of Fowls*, his *Knight's Tale* from *The Canterbury Tales*, and *The Book of Margery Kempe* – a female character is given a chance to express a desire about men who are sexually interested in her – with results that contrast with the traditional picture, promoted by such Church Fathers as Tertullian and Saint Jerome, of women as bedevilled by an excessive sexuality.[3] In each case the female characters express a desire that does not conform with that of the males. On the brink of marriage, the characters in Chaucer's poems ask to delay or renounce heterosexual activity. After many years of marriage and children, the fictional representation of a real-life Margery Kempe also seeks release from the marriage debt that the Church obligates her to perform. In this paper, I shall suggest that the presence of these voices of renunciation implies a freedom that the context belies. I shall question the possibilities, limits, and ramifications of such attempts at renunciation in order to examine what can be learned from these voices in three works attributed to both men and women[4] in fourteenth-century England, about the relationship between such voices and the larger sociosemiotic system of which they are a part.

Both Chaucer's *Parliament* and the *Knight's Tale* are concerned with the place of sexuality in the world. The voice of a female who – when consulted – chooses *not* to participate in heterosexuality appears in the birds' debate towards the end of Chaucer's *Parliament*. The female object of desire does not completely reject heterosexual activity, but simply requests a delay. The debate is part of a dream vision that is given to an obtuse and frightened narrator who needs to learn more about the experience of love that he knows only from books. It is part of a St Valentine's Day ritual, conducted by the goddess Nature, in which all the birds will choose their sexual partners. Since the goddess Nature is described as vice-regent of God, 'the almyghty Lord' (379),[5] and since the birds choose their mates as Nature 'pricks' or inspires them with desire ('As I prike yow with plesaunce,' 389), the St Valentine's Day ritual presents sexual mating as part of God's 'natural' plan.

Throughout most of the debate, the female eagle serves mainly as the silent witness and object of desire of her suitors' elaborate rhetorical pleas. But the description of the debate repeatedly emphasizes that all the females will ultimately have *some* voice by reiterating the males' need to obtain the females' consent to mate. Before the ritual begins, the narrator reports that *each* of the birds assembled took pains to choose or take his 'formel' or mate *considerately, with her agreement*: 'And ech of hem dide his besy cure / Benygnely to chese or for to take, / *By hire acord,* his formel or his make' (369-71). Indeed, the goddess Nature begins the ritual by reminding the birds that the tradition ('This is oure usage alwey, for yer to yeere,' 411) insists that the *only* condition of each male's choice must be that each female agree to the choice of whomever wants her as a mate: 'But natheles, in this condicioun / Mot be the choys of everich that is heere, / That she agre to his eleccioun, / Whoso he be that shulde be hire feere' (407–10). Nature enforces this condition when she ends the debate by turning the decision over to the female eagle, emphatically reiterating that the choice of whom *she* desires shall be up to the female, *no matter whom it angers or makes happy,* insistently adding, he that *she* chooses shall have her *when* she chooses: 'But fynally, this is my conclusioun, / That she hireself shal han *hir* eleccioun / Of whom hire lest; whoso be wroth or blythe, / Hym that she cheest, he shal hire han as swithe' (620–3).

Before the decision is turned over to the female eagle, however, and before she utters any words, her *body* speaks – as a direct response to her first suitor's plea. The narrator tells us that, immediately after the first suitor finished his plea, the female eagle blushed, which the narrator describes in a strikingly artificial way as arising 'naturally' from the female eagle's sense of 'shame' – shame, modesty, or embarrassment – by comparing the way the colour spread over the female to the way a 'fresh' new rose is reddened anew against the summer sun: 'Ryght as the freshe, rede rose newe / Ayeyn the somer sonne coloured is, / Ryght so for shame al wexen gan the hewe / Of this formel, whan she herde al this' (442–5). Moreover, as he continues, the narrator emphasizes his reading of the formel eagle's bodily sign as based on a modesty and embarrassment that are rooted in fear, a reading that seems shared by the goddess Nature. For the narrator relates that the female eagle was so deeply embarrassed, dismayed, and frightened ('so sore abasht') she was speechless – neither answering well nor saying anything wrong – so that Nature intervened, reassuring her not to be afraid: 'She neyther answerde wel, ne seyde amys, / So sore abasht was she, tyl that Nature / Seyde, 'Doughter, drede yow nought, I yow assure' (446–8).

While the narrator attributes the signs of the female's body – her blush and her silence – to a modesty and embarrassment which the goddess Nature might find appropriate and with which she might agree, her reassurance leaves us wondering what it is that the female eagle might fear. Scrutiny of the first suitor's speech reveals the rhetoric of a conventional plea. Beginning by assuming a humble posture, 'With hed enclyned and with humble cheere' (414), he emphasizes his *choice* of the formel eagle as his superior, rather than simply his equal or mate: '"Unto my soverayn lady, and not my fere, / I *chese*, and *chese* with wil, and herte, and thought"' (416–17) and reiterates his total devotion to her, no matter what she might do: '"Whos I am al, and evere wol hire serve, / Do what hire lest"' (419–20). As he does so, he also calls attention to the part that bodies play in his desire: he refers to the female's body as extremely well made ('so wel iwrought,' 418), attributes to her the choice to let his body live or die ('"Do what hire lest, to do me lyve or sterve,"' 420), and declares that without her mercy and her grace, he will die: '"Besekynge hire of merci and of grace, / As she that is my lady sovereyne; / Or let me deye present in this place. / For certes, longe may I nat lyve in payne"' (421–4). Vowing to serve her no matter what she decides, he asks to be torn to pieces if he is ever found disobedient, wilfully negligent, boastful, or unfaithful: '"I preye to yow this be my jugement: / That with these foules I be al torent, / That ilke day that evere she me fynde / To hir untrewe, or in my gilt unkynde"' (431–4).

Most critics have seen the female eagle as equally conventional.[6] Perhaps this is the case: suffering from virginal modesty, embarrassment, humility, and fitting inability to speak, she might be a timid, fearful, tongue-tied, blushing bride-to-be in need of rescue by the goddess Nature. Perhaps she is overwhelmed by the presumed honour of this public pursuit, by a presumed violation of the courtly code of secrecy in the public declaration, or by being asked to be a paramour rather than a wife. Perhaps the threats to her suitor's body involved in his declaration of his cut, bleeding heart ('for in myn herte is korven every veyne,' 425), and willingness to have his body pulled apart if she ever finds him untrue or cruel, lead her to fear some violence to her own body entailed by the implied sexual act itself. But all these possibilities are left to speculation. We simply do not know. And the female eagle's body remains silent throughout the other suitors' pleas and the birds' debate about their merits.

But when Nature finally turns the decision about the suitors over to the female eagle, the words of her very brief speech (13 out of the poem's 699 lines) create the possibility that the female's initial blushing silence involves something beyond her 'feminine instincts' or concern for the conventions of courtly love.[7] She begins modestly, addressing Nature timidly and deferentially, as she sets up a request. But even as she defers to Nature, phrasing her request as a favour, and acknowledging that she is and always will be subject to Nature's control, she outlines the limits of her freedom:

> 'My rightful lady, goddesse of Nature!
> Soth is that I am evere under youre yerde,
> As is everich other creature,
> And mot be youres whil my lyf may dure;
> And therfore graunteth me my firste bone,
> And myn entente I wol yow sey right sone.' (639–44)

She frames her actual request in the same deferential and measured way; addressing Nature as 'Almyghty queen!,' she asks for a year's *respite* to take counsel with herself ('"Almyghty queen, unto this yer be don, / I axe respit for to avise me,"' 647–8). But the female's speech does not end with this request; as it continues for four more lines, a different tone surfaces. First, the limitations of freedom are foregrounded again, as she asks that, after the year is over, she might have her choice – not just freely, but *completely* freely: 'And after that to have my choys al fre' (649) – as if she fears that the year's delay, rather than giving her freedom, might lead to its loss, voicing the idea that the freedom of the year's delay might be purchased at a cost.[8] Next, she switches from asking favours to asserting her will as she urgently insists – twice – not only that she will say and speak no more: "'This al and som that I wol speke and seye'" (650), but also that no one will get *anything else* from her: "'Ye gete no more'" (651). And she does not stop there, but continues in a way that raises questions about a threat to her body and her life. Matching her suitors' hyperbolic declarations that they would die if she did *not* grant them her favours, she dramatically and emphatically asserts that no one will get speech or *anything else* from her – even if they should try to make her die: "'Ye gete no more, although ye do me deye!'" (651). Finally she ends with an emphatic assertion, in triple negation, of what seems to be *her* desire and her will not to participate in heterosexuality, stating that she *will* not serve Venus or Cupid, truly yet, in *any* sort of way: "'I wol nat serve Venus ne Cupide, / Forsothe as yit, by no manere weye'" (652–3).

The increasing confidence and intensity of what seems to be these final assertions of the female's desire, as opposed to that of her suitors, make it possible, although by no means certain then, that her silence and her colour after the plea of the first suitor came, not from being tongue-tied at or modest about her good fortune in being pursued, but rather from her embarrassment, annoyance, or distress at having a different idea about participating at all.[9] Perhaps she feels annoyance or disdain for having a choice which is less than free and exerted only after the males have chosen first. Perhaps she reads in the suitor's address to her as 'sovereign lady' and 'not my feere' neither the 'degredation' of being addressed as paramour rather than wife, nor the 'compliment' of being elevated above the mere position of wife, but the unasked-for responsibility of having to sustain masculine desire and fantasies of what women want. For, while this moment of the female's refusal to choose – or confirm being chosen as – a mate *at this time* opens up the possibility of woman's desire to delay or not participate in heterosexuality at all, the text reveals how even the female's decision to delay neither subverts nor jams the semiotic system in which women's bodies are inscribed as objects of exchange. Nature exhibits neither surprise nor displeasure at the female's request for a delay, but grants that request. Moreover, as she does so, she not only stresses the limitation of the female's 'freedom' *to* only one year, but also shows how that lack of freedom is inscribed both in courtly love and in marriage. Far from admonishing the female eagle for her 'indifference,' she uses that indifference to encourage the male eagles to fuel and sustain their ardour:

> 'To yow speke I, ye tercelets,' quod Nature,
> 'Beth of good herte, and serveth alle thre.
> A yer is nat so longe to endure,
> And ech of yow peyne him in his degre
> For to do wel, for, God wot, quyt is she
> Fro yow this yer; what after so befalle,
> This entremes is dressed for yow alle.' (659–65)

For, in urging the suitors to persevere in serving the female despite the indifference she has just displayed, Nature shows how the female's indifference is in fact the basis of the systems of both courtly love and marriage in which women's bodies are exchanged among men – regardless of 'what women want' – to serve masculine desire for masculine status and self-esteem.

What is merely suggested about a gender difference in desire in the *Parliament* is made much more explicit in the *Knight's Tale*, a romance told by a nostalgic and patriarchal old knight.[10] The knight's description of Emily associates her with a sexuality that is both natural and innocent;[11] he calls her fairer than a lily and compares her colour to that of a rose: 'That Emelye, that fairer was to sene / Than is the lylie upon his stalke grene, / And fressher than the May with floures newe – / For with the rose colour stroof hire hewe' (1035–8).[12] He also attributes her early rising to being 'priked' or inspired (like the birds in the *Parliament*) to perform the rites of May:

> Er it were day, as was hir wone to do,
> She was arisen and al redy dight,
> For May wole have no slogardie anyght.
> The sesoun priketh every gentil herte,
> And maketh it out of his slep to sterte,
> And seith, 'Arys, and do thyn observaunce.' (1040–5)[13]

Just as this sexuality is seen as naturally disruptive of Emily's (and every other noble person's) sleep, the mere sight of Emily walking in a garden beneath the tower where two knights are imprisoned becomes emblematic of the disruptive force of sexuality on the male bonding that holds the world of the *Knight's Tale* in place. For, as soon as Palamon and Arcite, who are both kinsmen and brothers in arms, simply *view* Emily from their tower, all their oaths are dissolved into rivalry over her. As Theseus, ruler of Athens, points out, at a later stage, when he comes across the two men (each having escaped from prison in different ways) fighting over Emily, ankle-deep in blood, the joke is that this rivalry is conducted despite the fact that Emily neither knows about it, nor (perhaps like the female eagle in the *Parliament*) cares:

> But this is yet the beste game of alle,
> That she for whom they han this jolitee
> Kan hem therfore as muche thank as me.
> She woot namoore of al this hoote fare,
> By God, than woot a cokkow or an hare! (1806–10)

And Theseus, after sparing the lives of these rivals in response to the entreaties of women, in effect attempts to channel the young men's passion and aggression into a more useful social (and political) cause by turning their private quarrel into a public tournament to take place in the same spot a year later. Emily – unconsulted (Theseus states 'I speke as for my suster Emelye,' 1833) – will become the prize conquered through war, as her sister, Hippolyta, was when Theseus conquered and married that Amazon queen.

Emily, like the female eagle, speaks only once – uttering thirty-one lines in a poem famous for its length. While Palamon and Arcite pray to their respective gods, Mars and Venus, for victory and possession of Emily (which ultimately amount to the same thing: control of and through her body), she prays to the goddess Diana for freedom. And where the eagle only gave us hints about what her reluctance involved, Emily's speech is specific. She begins her prayer by emphasizing Diana as the goddess of chastity, whose devotee she has been, and as a woman who knows what young maidens desire: '"O chaste goddesse of the wodes grene, / ... / Goddesse of maydens, that myn herte hast knowe / Ful many a yeer, and woost what I desire"' (2297–2301). Unlike the female eagle who asks only for a year's delay, Emily asserts that the desire Diana knows is Emily's desire to remain a virgin *all her life*, which – as her use of a triple negation underscores – involves the desire *never* to be a lover or a wife: '"Chaste goddesse, wel wostow that I / Desire to ben a mayden al my lyf, / Ne nevere wol I be no love ne wyf"' (2304–6). As she reiterates this desire, Emily relates virginity to a desire to continue the freedom she enjoys: '"I am, thow woost, yet of thy compaignye, / A mayde, and love huntynge and venerye, / And for to walken in the wodes wilde"' (2307–9).[14] She not

only emphatically rejects any interest in becoming a wife or being pregnant, but also explicitly states that she does not want to know the company of men: '"And noght to ben a wyf and be with childe. / Noght wol I
knowe compaignye of man"' (2310–11).[15] Emily's assertion of a desire *not*
to be a wife and *not* to be pregnant appeals to the triple aspect of her goddess Diana – as protectress of virginity; as Luna or Lucina, presider over
childbirth; and as Proserpina, the maid who becomes a wife through
abduction and rape. Her articulation of this desire points to what the
female eagle of the *Parliament* did not state: while marriage is socially
desirable for women's status and prestige in Western culture, especially in
a Catholic culture that prohibits birth control, marriage can take place
only at the expense of at least two kinds of violence to women's bodies,
not comparably experienced by men: penetration of the hymen and
pregnancy. In this way, Emily's rejection of heterosexuality not only
points to the restrictions of freedom involved in women's loss of chastity
and the roles of wife and mother the knights' desires would ask Emily to
undertake. It also relates that rejection to the physical effects of heterosexuality that are only restricted to and restrictive of women's bodies.

As Emily continues, asking that Diana replace the love Palamon and
Arcite have for her with love and peace between them instead –

> Now help me, lady, sith ye may and kan,
> For tho thre formes that thou hast in thee.
> And Palamon, that hath swich love to me,
> And eek Arcite, that loveth me so soore,
> This grace I preye thee withoute moore,
> As sende love and pees bitwixe hem two,
> And fro me turne awey hir hertes so (2312–18), –

she makes clear that she neither shares nor enjoys the two knights'
desires, and requests that those desires be directed elsewhere, if they cannot be extinguished. Moreover, her description of the knights' desires as
their hot love, *their* desire, and all *their* busy torment and *their* fire (emphasis mine) – 'That al hire hoote love and hir desir, / And al hir bisy torment, and hir fir / Be queynt, or turned in another place' (2319–21) –
does not *simply* convey her own distance, distaste, and disparagement of
these two knight's desires, but also reasserts the lack of desire for physical
sexuality – at least with men – she had previously expressed.[16]

Emily's fear that the world in which she lives will not allow *her* desires to
be granted is expressed in her brief request – that if she *must* have one of

the two men, she might get the one that desires *her* most – through her use of double hypotheticals (two ifs) and passive constructions that emphasize her lack of control: 'And *if* so be *thou* wolt nat do me grace, / Or *if* my destynee *be* shapen so / That I *shal nedes have oon* of hem two, / As *sende* me hym that moost desireth me' (2322–5). Nevertheless, she ends her prayer strongly by emphatically reasserting – now with 'bitter tears'- her desire to have her maidenhood kept intact:

> Bihoold, goddesse of clene chastitee, .
> The bittre teeris that on my chekes falle.
> Syn thou art mayde and kepere of us alle,
> My maydenhede thou kepe and wel conserve,
> And whil I lyve, a mayde I wol thee serve.' (2326–30)

Interestingly, the Knight's description of Emily's preparation for and response to the omens that appear after her prayer frame that prayer with a sense of violation of Emily's body similar to that depicted in her prayer, underscoring what it is that Emily might well fear. In contrast to his descriptions of the preparations of Palamon and Arcite, the Knight's description of Emily's preparations dwell on her body in what is best described as a leering way.[17] Not content to stop at telling us that Emily 'Hir body wessh with water of a welle' (2284), the Knight goes on to titil-late his audience: 'But hou she dide hir ryte I dar nat tell, / But it be any thing in general' (2284–5), and tease: 'And yet it were a game to heeren al. / To hym that meneth wel it were no charge; / But it is good a man been at his large' (2286–8).

Ultimately, as he suggests that voyeurism is most safely experienced through books, the Knight connects his voyeuristic invasion of Emily's sexual secrets with our own acts of reading: 'Two fyres on the auter gan she beete, / And dide hir thynges, as men may biholde / In Stace of Thebes and thise bookes olde' (2292–4). Reading, voyeurism, and vio-lence against Emily's body are connected in the Knight's description of Emily's response to the omens that appear after her prayer as well. It is hard to ignore the suppressed sexuality in general in the Knight's descrip-tion of fires that are quenched or die and come to life again, and are compared to burning pieces of wood that squeak when wet and drip with moisture that looks like drops of blood. Moreover, the fact that the Knight uses the word 'queynt' four times within six lines in his descrip-tion makes it impossible to deny that, while the word means 'strange' or 'curious' and 'quenched,' it also means 'women's private parts,' or more accurately 'cunt.' The resultant pun creates a sense of the Knight's inappropriate obsession with Emily's body and sexuality. And this sense is reinforced by the way the Knight relates Emily's response to the 'queynt' sight of the fires. Right after he describes the burning logs as looking as if they are dripping with drops of blood, he tells us rather ambiguously that, *for this reason* (presumably because she saw the phallic logs dripping with blood), Emily was so terrified that she was nearly out of her mind and began to cry: 'For which so soore agast was Emelye / That she was wel ny mad and gan to crye' (2341–2). As he does so, the Knight replaces the idea that Emily might lack heterosexual desire for the two young knights, with its threat to phallocentric ideas of masculinity, with the more flattering notion to a patriarchal mentality (a mentality clearly conveyed by January in Chaucer's *Merchant's Tale*), that she feared their very male strength, prowess, and perhaps even the violation implicit in the dripping blood. At the same time, however, the description of that fear seems to diminish Emily by depicting her as so frightened she is practically out of her mind, as does the Knight's next attribution that Emily is crying because she didn't know how to read the signs. Whatever the cause(s), however, when the Knight continues to relate that Emily was crying 'oonly for the "feere,"' combining fire, fear, and passion, we know that at some level Emily does understand what Diana immediately confirms: the gods have decreed that Emily will have to marry one of the two men who suffered so much over her: 'Among the goddes hye it is affermed, / And by eterne word writen and confermed, / Thou shalt ben wedded unto oon of tho / That han for thee so muchel care and wo' (2349–52). The men's desires and suffering take precedence over Emily's. Her function as the sacrificial weaver of peace on which the patriarchal social order depends is underscored by her fate in the rest of the poem.[18] We do not hear of *her* desires again. She remains silent as she is passed from one rival to the next. We hear of Arcite's desire, as he obtains his wish and wins victory over her in battle first, but, then on the verge of death, before being able to marry her, passes her on to Palamon. Arcite's gesture is often attributed to his magnanimity, but as a gesture of reconciliation with the blood brother from whom Arcite has been estranged, the gesture points out the way Emily functions as booty and as a medium of exchange.[19] Moreover, since Palamon had promised to wage eternal war on chastity if he were granted his desire to possess Emily, the exchange points out the sacrifice of Emily's desire on which it is based. Emily's sacrifice is ratified by Theseus and his parliament to cement peace between Thebes and Athens. But far from being acknowledged or credited by any of the men, her silent acquiescence to her role would undoubtedly be subsumed by the Knight as woman's fickle following of Fortune: '(For wommen, as to speken in comune, / Thei folwen alle the favour of Fortune)' (2681–2).

The voices of females in the *Parliament of Fowls* and the *Knight's Tale* speak on the brink of a marriage which they ultimately cannot avoid. The female eagle's attempt at least to delay heterosexuality depicts a female who is not immediately interested in it. Emily's attempt to reject this mode of sexuality describes a desire for women that is ultimately not allowed. In *The Book of Margery Kempe*, the voice of the female who attempts to renounce heterosexuality seems at first glance to have more in common with Chaucer's married, middle-class, middle-aged (or old, in medieval terms) Wife of Bath[20] than the youthful, aristocratic, about to be married-off female eagle and Emily. While Margery shares the Wife's class, ambition, and focus on (if not obsession with) heterosexual relations, she differs from the Wife in having sustained a lengthy marriage to the same man, and produced fourteen children. Like the Wife, Margery is far from being sexually inexperienced. The Wife reports lack of sexual enjoyment with her three old husbands, flirtations with other men, but sexual pleasure only with her younger husband, Jankyn, who verbally and physically abused her. By contrast, Margery reports an enjoyment of carnal relations with her non-abusive husband that was mutual, and describes being greatly tempted by the sexual advances of another man.

For Margery, however, knowledge of the pleasure she and her husband had felt during married sexual relations is a source of pain. The Wife is content to remind the pilgrims that, according to the Church, it is better to wed than to burn (in the fires of passion and fornication). However, Margery, after a lengthy marriage and children, and several failed business ventures, aspires to the Church's highest goal of chastity. While the female eagle and Emily seem to operate in a world more secular than religious, and the Wife of Bath struggled to define herself *against* Church proscriptions about sexuality, Margery ultimately seeks to find an outlet for her energies under the Church-sanctioned rubric of the religious mystic. Telling her husband, John, that she well knew that they often 'had displeased God by their inordinate love, and the great delectation they each had in using the other,' Margery suggests that they cease that behaviour and begin 'to punish and chastise themselves wilfully by abstaining from the lust of their bodies' (6).[21]

Although Margery's circumstances differ from the fictive voices of Chaucer, her desire for freedom through chastity at a later stage of married life emphasizes further problematics of heterosexuality, similar to those Chaucer's Wife reveals, that might well shed light on the hesitation of the younger and more inexperienced female voices. The narrative of Margery's desire for freedom through chastity points to women's bodies as the site of a power struggle between women and such agencies of the sociosemiotic order as husbands and the Church. In so doing, it also relates the way sexuality in marriage involves a commercial exchange where both women and money are objects of a masculine desire for power and status.

The struggle for control of women's bodies through the regulation of female sexuality is illuminated in a scene near the beginning of *The Book of Margery Kempe* that articulates what delays or renunciations of heterosexuality attempt to escape. This vignette depicts a physical and spiritual crisis that occurs when Margery was in her twenties, newly married and quickly pregnant, initially described as a form of perinatal or post-partum depression: 'and after she had conceived, she was belaboured with great accesses till the child was born and then, what with the labour she had in childing, and the sickness going before, she despaired of her life, weening she might not live' (1). Thinking herself on the verge of death, Margery sends for a priest in order to confess some 'thing' she had on her conscience that she had never revealed before. This 'thing' is never spelled out in the account of her life, but all indications point to some aspect of Margery's sexuality for which she feels Church-induced guilt.

The narrator's description of the priest's interaction with Margery in this delicate situation underscores how, far from relieving her conscience, that priest's unempathic and judgmental injunctions exacerbated Margery's crisis. We are informed that, just as Margery was about to reveal what 'she had so long concealed,' her confessor 'began sharply to reprove her,' so that 'she would no more say for aught he might do.' The narrator then explicitly attributes Margery's resultant breakdown *both* to her guilt *and* to the priest's harsh condemnation, relating that, because of her fear of damnation 'on the one side, and his sharp reproving of her on the other side, this creature went out of her mind and was wondrously vexed and laboured with spirits for half a year, eight weeks and odd days' (1). After a period of 'madness,' Margery experiences a vision of Christ, in the likeness of a man, and becoming 'calmed in her wits and reason, as well as ever she was before,' asks her husband for 'the keys of the buttery to take her meat and drink as she had done before' (2). Interestingly, 'her maidens and keepers,' mirroring the priest's harsh attitude, advise her husband against this. But 'her husband ever having tenderness and compassion for her, commanded that they should deliver to her the keys; and she took her meat and drink as her bodily strength would serve her' (3), restoring her to health.

This early scene depicting a struggle between a priest and a woman whose mind and body are ravaged through Church-sanctioned heterosexuality and childbirth seems symptomatic of the struggle for control of women's bodies and their sexuality by the Church. The fact that Margery's 'secret sin' is never revealed seems to imply the inarticulate nature of women's desire in phallocentric discourse. The suspicion that her guilt might be about masturbation, which the Church of course condemns, would also make the scene emblematic of the heterosexual imperative of Catholicism and Western society. The divergences in the way the priest and Margery's husband express concern over Margery's body reflect an important difference in attitude, but nevertheless point to the way both men are in control of her spiritual and physical health.

In the opening vignette, John supports his wife in her struggle for control over her body and her life. However, although as the daughter of the mayor of Lynn, Margery has greater social status and wealth than her husband, crucial scenes throughout the narrative reiterate Margery's struggle with her husband, as agent of Church and societal authority, for control of her body and her life. In Margery's attempt to gain freedom through chastity, her struggles with external as well as internalized Church authority, and with the authority of her husband, poignantly articulate the limitations of freedom for women in phallocentric discourse. The marital relationship as a struggle for control, and sexuality in marriage as a commercial exchange, are revealed in the narrator's description of the inspiration for Margery's desire to give up sexuality for chastity. We are told that one night, when she lay in bed with her husband, she heard such sweet and delightful melodies that she thought she had been in Paradise, 'and therewith she started out of her bed and said: – "Alas, that ever I did sin! It is full merry in Heaven"' (5). After this vision, the narrator continues, 'she had never desired to commune fleshly with her husband, for the debt of matrimony was so abominable to her that she would rather, she thought, have eaten or drunk the ooze and the muck in the gutter than consent to any fleshly communing, save only for obedience' (6). When her husband insists on having his will, she obeys weeping and sorrowing, and counsels chastity, a practice he agrees would be good, but states he is not yet ready for.

Margery's lack of control over her body and her sexuality is further made clear in the narrator's contrasting descriptions of Margery's and her husband's behaviour during their several years' disagreement about chastity. When her husband refuses to 'spare her,' and continues to 'use' her 'as he had done before'(6), Margery admits that she cannot deny him her body, but proclaims that she will withdraw her love and affections from all earthly creatures and direct them towards God instead. That Margery's lack of control over her body is not limited to carnal relations *within* marriage is emphasized by the insertion of the narration of her temptation to adultery during the course of the above vignette. The narrator relates that during this period Margery leads such a strict life of such bodily penance as fasts, vigils, and wearing hair-shirts secretly by day – in addition to multiple daily confession, especially of 'that sin she so long had (hid), concealed and covered' (6) – that she is slandered and reproved. She continues to have 'no lust to commune with her husband,' but, praying to God to be able to live chastely, lays with her husband every night in his bed, and bears him children, despite finding carnal relations with him both 'very painful and horrible' (8). Not surprisingly to a modern reader aware of the theory of repression, after a year of strength, while continuing to feel repulsed by her husband's advances, Margery falls prey to the desire to commit adultery with a man whose proposition sounds suspiciously like a threat of rape: a man she likes tells her that 'he would lie by her and have his lust of his body, and she should not withstand him, for if he did not have his will that time, he said he would anyhow have it another time; she should not choose' (8). The narrator's explanation that Margery took too seriously what the man intended as a test makes clear the struggle for power inherent in the sexual temptation, and the way what might be considered Margery's desire is raised only to be denied. Reminding us again that Margery is repulsed by carnal relations with her husband, even though they were 'lawful' and 'in lawful time' (9), the narrator presents Margery as so obsessed with the man's words that she seeks him out two times. The first time, the man made 'such simulation' (8) she was unable to detect what he meant, but the second time, the man's brutal and violent rejection again reveals sexuality as a power struggle, and connects heterosexuality with violence and money: 'At last, through the importunity of temptation, and lack of discretion, she was overcome and consented in her mind, and went to the man to know if he would then consent to her, and he said he never would, for all the gold in this world; he would rather be hewn as small as flesh for the pot' (9).

Sexuality and money are related in the Church discourse of married sexuality as well.[22] The commercialism implicit in the Church description of married intercourse as obligatory payment of the 'marriage debt' is made explicit in the description of the way, several years later, Margery persuades her husband to grant her desire that they live chastely. Margery's desire to live chastely with her husband is described as effected through the immediate intercession of Christ. We are told that Margery's prayer to Christ to grant this desire is answered by Christ's promise to her in a vision to 'suddenly slay (the fleshly lust)' of her husband in exchange for her fasting. The following Easter, when her husband tries to resume carnal relations, she calls on Jesus's help, with the result that her husband 'had no power to touch her at that time in that way, nor ever after with any fleshly knowledge' (14). Margery's lack of control over her body and the explicit commercialism of married sexuality are made clear in the subsequent vignette, when the narrator describes both Margery's need to obtain her husband's permission to go on a pilgrimage, and the bargain by which she finally obtains his agreement to live in chastity.

After eight weeks of chastity, Margery's husband, both poignantly and accusingly, asks her whether, if a man came with a sword and threatened to cut off her husband's head unless her husband could 'commune naturally' with her as before, she would permit his decapitation or permit him to 'meddle with' her again as before (16). When Margery reluctantly and sorrowfully replies that she would '"rather see [him] being slain, than ... turn again to our uncleanness"' (16), John responds that she is not a good wife. A short while later, John proposes the following bargain to his wife: if she grants his desire, he will grant hers. His first desire is to resume intercourse; his next, that she pay his debts before going on her pilgrimage; his third, that she stop fasting on Fridays and eat and drink with him. In response to her prayer for the right answer, we are told that 'Our Lord Jesus Christ' tells her to grant her husband what he desires and she will get what she desires, and releases her from the need to fast. As a result, Margery strikes the bargain with her husband, that if he will not come into bed with her any more, she will pay his debts, and eat and drink with him on Fridays. When John agrees, Margery seems to have purchased her freedom. But Margery's inability to escape heterosexuality is clear in the way her inscription within heterosexuality reappears in Margery's erotic relationship with Christ as her lover, father, and lord in her visions.

In all these ways, then, the voices of the female eagle in Chaucer's *Parliament of Fowls*, of Emily in his *Knight's Tale*, and of Margery in *The Book of Margery Kempe* each assert a desire for freedom that is not fulfilled: whereas the presence of each voice itself advances the claim that such freedom is possible within heterosexuality, the very assertion of the claim shows the way the inscription of womens' bodies restricts women's freedom in phallocentric culture. Men may ask what women want, but as Luce Irigaray and others have demonstrated, phallocentric discourse is constituted so that we not only do not, but more often cannot, know – for our answers disclose the restriction of women's bodies as they are phallocentrically inscribed, and as they are constrained by the economics of masculine desire.

NOTES

1 See Ernst Jones, *The Life and Work of Sigmund Freud*, vol.2 (New York: Basic Books 1955), 421.
2 For the limitations of phallocentric discourse, see especially Luce Irigaray, *Speculum of the Other Woman*, trans. Gillian C. Gill (Ithaca, NY: Cornell University Press 1985), and *This Sex Which Is Not One*, trans. Catherine Porter (Ithaca, NY: Cornell University Press 1985). I explore the limitations of the knight's quest in relation to phallocentric discourse in 'The Subversive Discourse of the Wife of Bath: Phallocentric Discourse and the Imprisonment of Criticism,' *ELH* 55 (Fall 1988), 527–54.
3 See for example Tertullian's statement to women to remember that as descendants of Eve, they are the 'devil's gateway' to sin: *On the Apparel of Women*, Book 1, in *The Ante Nicene Fathers*, vol. 4, ed. and trans. Alexander Roberts and James Donaldson, American ed. A. Cleveland Coxe (repr.: Grand Rapids: W.B. Eerdmann's 1961); Saint John Chrysostom, *Address on Vainglory and the Right Way for Parents to Bring Up their Children*, in M. Laistner, *Christianity and Pagan Culture* (Ithaca, NY: Cornell University Press 1951), 109–10; and An Exhortation to Theodore after His Fall, in *Nicene and Post Nicene Fathers*, vol. 9, ed. Philip Schaff and Henry Wace, ser. 2 (New York: Scribner's Sons 1893), 346; and Saint Jerome's *Adversus Jovinianum*, in *Patrologiae cursus completus ... series Latina*, vol. 23, ed. J.P. Migne (Paris: Garnier 1844–64).
4 Although *The Book of Margery Kempe* is often promoted as the first autobiography of an Englishwoman, the textual description of the transmission of Margery's story through two male scribes, one a priest, problematizes any simple attribution of the book's voices to one gender. See *The Book of Margery Kempe*, vol. I, The Early English Text Society, eds. Sanford Brown Meech and Hope Emily Allen (New York: Oxford University Press 1940; repr. 1961), 1–5. For useful discussions of this and other issues in this text appearing after this paper was delivered see Karma Lochrie, *Margery Kempe and the Translations of the Flesh* (Philadelphia: University of Pennsylvania Press 1991); Sarah Beckwith, 'Prob-

lems of Authority in Late Medieval English Mysticism: Language, Agency, and Authority in *The Book of Margery Kempe*,' *Exemplaria* 4/1 (Spring 1992), 171–200; and Lynn Staley, *Margery Kempe's Dissenting Fictions* (University Park: Pennsylvania State University Press 1994).

5 All references to Chaucer's *Parliament of Fowls* are to line numbers in *The Riverside Chaucer*, 3d ed., ed. Larry D. Benson (Boston: Houghton Mifflin 1987). Translations and emphases are mine.

6 For example, J.A.W. Bennett refers to the formel's 'instinctive femininity': *The Parlement of Foules: An Interpretation* (Oxford: Oxford University Press 1957), 177; D.S, Brewer states that 'we need not concern ourselves with the formel's feelings and motives. The lady's attitude toward the lover was conventionally and properly remote': *The Parlement of Foulys* (New York: Thomas Nelson and Sons 1972), 24. Charles O. McDonald attributes the formel's blush to her embarrassment at the public declaration as a violation of the courtly code of secrecy: 'An Interpretation of Chaucer's *Parlement of Foules*,' *Chaucer Criticism*, vol. 2, eds, Richard J. Schoeck and Jerome Taylor (Notre Dame: University of Notre Dame Press 1961), 285; D.W. Robertson, Jr, attributes the formel's embarrassment to the result of being addressed as a paramour rather than a mate: *A Preface to Chaucer* (Princeton: Princeton University Press 1962), 377. Stephen Knight also refers to the formel as 'like any much loved courtly lady': *Geoffrey Chaucer* (Oxford: Oxford University Press 1986), 30.

7 Henry M. Leicester, Jr, suggests that, far from being conventional, the formel's request marks her stepping 'out of the role of courtly *domina* ascribed to her by the tercels, and assert[ing] her independence even of the role of mate tacitly assigned to her by everyone else': 'The Harmony of Chaucer's *Parlement*: A Dissonant Voice,' *Chaucer Review* 9 (1974), 28.

8 Interestingly, while A.C. Spearing emphasizes the formel's freedom, his description of that freedom also points to its further limitation through ultimate domination: 'freedom of speech and choice includes a freedom not to choose, or at least to defer choosing ... Human love involves ... the possibility of resisting Nature, or at least of gaining a margin of freedom within which to choose the time and manner of one's submission': *Medieval Dream-Poetry* (Cambridge: Cambridge University Press 1976), 100.

9 For a similar emphasis on the idea that the formel 'simply refuses to make a choice' for 'inscrutable' reasons, see James Dean's 'Artistic Conclusiveness in Chaucer's *Parliament of Fowls*,' *Chaucer Review* 21 (1986), 22. Also, see Jack B. Oruch, who states that 'exactly why the formel postpones her decision is difficult to determine from the text, and no doubt a deliberate ambiguity on Chaucer's part,' in 'Nature's Limitations and the *Demande D'Amour* of Chaucer's *Parlement*,' *Chaucer Review* 19 (1983), 27. For an argument closer to my

own, seen after this paper was presented in 1991 see Elaine Tuttle Hansen's *Chaucer and the Fictions of Gender* (Berkeley: University of California Press 1992), 108–20. Hansen and I agree that the formel's refusal to decide is far from inconsequential, and is related to the absence of female desire in the text. While she argues that the formel's request for a delay is neither ambiguous nor indeterminable, pointing to the way in which female desire is precluded by 'the competing matrimonial models' that are 'feudal and courtly,' I would say that the construction of such matrimonial models by a discourse that is ineluctably phallocentric results in an inability to know or articulate female desire. Thus, whereas Hansen suggests that the formel's request for a delay is neither ambiguous nor indeterminable, I propose that its ambiguity and indeterminacy are constituted by the unknowability of desire, which I see as related to the indeterminacy of the search of the narrator of the poem.

10 For differing accounts of the Knight's relationship to chivalry and his tale, see, for example, R. Neuse, 'The Knight: The First Mover in Chaucer's Human Comedy,' *University of Toronto Quarterly* 31 (1962), 299–315; Donald H. Howard, *The Idea of the Canterbury Tales* (Berkeley: University of California Press 1976), esp. 228–9; Terry Jones, *Chaucer's Knight: The Portrait of a Medieval Mercenary* (New York: Methuen 1980); John H. Pratt, 'Was Chaucer's Knight Really a Mercenary?,' *Chaucer Review* 22 (1987), 8–27; H. Marshall Leicester, Jr, *The Disenchanted Self* (Berkeley: University of California Press 1990), 221–382; Lee Patterson, *Chaucer and the Subject of History* (Madison: University of Wisconsin Press 1992), 164–230.

11 My emphasis on Emily's sexuality as both natural and innocent in this description agrees with that of such critics as E. Talbot Donaldson, *Speaking of Chaucer* (New York: W.W. Norton 1970), 49, and Patterson, *Chaucer and the Subject of History*, 208, on the way the repetition of details in this description constructs Emily *as* 'nature,' May, spring. For an interpretation of Emily and nature that sees her asking for a 'sterile freedom,' see William F. Woods, '"My Sweete Foe": Emelye's Role in *The Knight's Tale*,' *Studies in Philology* 88 (1991), 302.

12 All references to *The Knight's Tale* are to line numbers in *The Riverside Chaucer*, 3d ed., ed. Larry D. Benson (Boston: Houghton Mifflin 1987). Translations and emphases are mine.

13 In contrast to Leicester, *Disenchanted Self*, 233, I would attribute any heterosexual eroticism in the description of Emily here to the Knight, rather than to Emily.

14 V.A. Kolve's statement in *Chaucer and the Imagery of Narrative* (Stanford: Stanford University Press 1984), 222, that 'Emily worships Diana not as a dedicated virgin or a nun bound to chastity but as a young girl not yet awakened to love,

who will consent to marry in the fullness of time,' overlooks the intensity of Emily's expressed request to remaine chaste, free and 'not know the company of man' here. It is true that Emily speaks here as a young woman whose desire to remain free and chaste *could* represent what is only allowed as a *stage* in patriarchal culture; the fact that she has no choice but to limit this desire to a stage of heterosexual development, however, should not nullify the quality of her devotion to her preference to remain chaste. W.F. Bolton's statement that Emily's desire for chastity is undercut by her love of 'venerye' displays a similar heterosexual, and perhaps homophobic, bias in its failure to consider the possiblity of a 'venerye' not directed towards men: 'The Topic of the Knight's Tale,' *Chaucer Review* 22 (1987), 223–4. See also Thomas A. Ross, *Chaucer's Bawdy* (New York: E.P. Dutton 1972), 230. In my reading, the emphasis in this passage is on the way, at this stage, Emily's phallic identity is directed, not at men, but at herself. For useful discussions of homosexuality, lesbianism, and medieval literature and culture that appeared after this paper was delivered in 1991 see Carolyn Dinshaw, 'The Heterosexual Subject of Chaucerian Narrative,' *Medieval Feminist Newsletter* 13 (Spring 1992), 8–10; Susan Schibanoff, 'Chaucer's Lesbians: Drawing Blanks,' *Medieval Feminist Newsletter* 13 (Spring 1992), 11–14; David Lorenzo Boyd, 'On Lesbian and Gay/Queer Medieval Studies,' *Medieval Feminist Newsletter* 15 (Spring 1993), 12–15; and Glenn Burger, 'Queer Chaucer,' *English Studies in Canada* 20 (June 1994), 153–70.

15 Emily's initial rejection of heterosexuality curiously echoes one of the few poems composed by one or more female troubadours in the twelfth century that also emphasizes chastity as a means of freedom, and especially as a means of avoiding the distasteful bodily effects of childbirth: 'Lady Carenza, I'd like to have a husband, / but making babies I think is a huge penitence: / your breasts hang way down / and it's too anguishing to be a wife / ... I therefore advise you, if you want to plant good seed / to take as a husband Coronat de Scienza, / from whom you shall bear as fruit glorious sons: / saved is the chastity of her who marries him': trans. by Meg Bogin, in *The Woman Troubadours*, ed. Meg Bogin (New York: W.W. Norton 1980), 145.

16 Again, W.F. Bolton's disparagement of Emily's plea – 'The final fall is in the coquettish conclusion, but already the wordplay (on "venerye" and "queynt") has undercut the plea,' 224 – seems misdirected. In my reading of this plea, the puns, rather than expressing coyness, reveal Emily's unconscious fear that Diana cannot grant her desire to remain free, as does the unconscious slip in the pun on 'queynt.' The inappropriateness of the level of diction of 'queynt' for Emily, as opposed to the Miller (or the Wife of Bath), in my view, points to the way; rather than expressing an unconscious desire to *be* violated, Emily's anxious statement of her wish that Palamon and Arcite's desire be extin-

guished, or 'queynt,' also reveals the very part of her anatomy she wants to keep concealed and intact, a desire the slip reveals will not be allowed. The pun on 'queynt' as 'cunt' here anticipates the emphasis on that term in subsequent lines by the patriarchal Knight, who is telling us the tale. The coyness that Bolton attributes to Emily seems more properly attributable to a patriarchal construct shared by Bolton and the Knight that must deny a female character's desire to remain free. Moreover, the use of 'queynt' as a description of heterosexual relationships, at this point in the tale, emphasizes the way patriarchal marriage will reduce the subjectivity glimpsed in Emily's plea to be a free and independent woman who scorns the company of men, to a denigrated and objectified body part.

17 For a different view of the Knight's narration that credits the Knight with an attractive self-consciousness, awareness, and growth, and finds the Knight's narration only a little voyeuristic here see Leicester, *Disenchanted Self.* Seeing an amusing ambivalence in the Knight's attitude towards Emily, Leicester feels that, in this passage, 'we see the Knight working through and mastering his own attraction to a point of view he ultimately finds inappropriate and misleading' (309–10).

18 For the notion of 'woman' as the sacrifice on which the social order is grounded in phallocentric culture, see Julia Kristeva, 'Woman's Time,' *Signs* (1981), 13–35.

19 See for example David Aers, *Chaucer, Langland and the Creative Imagination* (London: Routledge & Kegan Paul 1980), 185.

20 For an excellent discussion of the relationship between Chaucer's Wife of Bath and *The Book of Margery Kempe*, see Sheila Delany, 'Sexual Economics, Chaucer's Wife of Bath, and *The Book of Margery Kempe*,' in her *Writing Women* (New York: Schocken Books 1983), 76–92.

21 All textual page references to *The Book of Margery Kempe* are to the modernization by W. Butler-Bowden (New York: Devin-Adair Company 1944).

22 For associations of power, sexuality, money, and marriage in Chaucer's *Wife of Bath's Prologue and Tale* see my article, 'The Subversive Discourse of the Wife of Bath: Phallocentric Discourse and the Imprisonment of Criticism,' *ELH* 55 (Fall 1988), 527–54.

Learning to Write with Venus's Pen: Sexual Regulation in Matthew of Vendôme's *Ars versificatoria*

GARRETT P.J. EPP

Matthew of Vendôme's *Ars versificatoria* (*ca* 1175) was the earliest in a series of poetic manuals produced in the twelfth and thirteenth centuries, and second only to Geoffrey of Vinsauf's *Poetria nova* in its influence upon later writers. While recognizing its historical importance, modern scholars have generally dismissed or disparaged Matthew's work.[1] In particular, critics have attacked the frequent sexual references in the treatise as being inappropriate to its pedagogical purpose. No one seems to have considered that the sexual references might themselves have any pedagogical purpose, other than a dubious respite from tedium.

The contrasting attitudes expressed by two recent translators of the *Ars versificatoria* together typify critical response towards the work. Roger Parr devotes more of his Introduction to the work and reputation of Arnulf of Orléans, Matthew's colleague and rival, than to Matthew or his treatise, which he deems 'considerably dull and repetitious, with its only relief being the scathing attacks on his enemy, Arnulf, referred to as Rufus.'[2] Aubrey Galyon defends dull repetition as pedagogically sound, but finds the work scurrilous and obscene. He briefly summarizes the negative critical reaction that has been generated by Matthew's inclusion of sexually explicit *exempla*, noting that 'Matthew's use of obscenity is not restricted to his attacks on Rufus. There often seems to be no reason for his coarse sexual references except his own whims.'[3] Nor does Galyon offer any potential reason. Citing Curtius on the relative lack of prudishness in the Middle Ages,[4] Galyon quickly passes on to discuss the evidence that Matthew had read widely. However, neither Matthew's reading of some of the more sexually explicit classical authors (he quotes Ovid even more often than he does Virgil, and is fond of Juvenal), nor any lack of prudishness in the period, adequately accounts for the inclusion of a line (apparently of Matthew's own invention) such as 'Syncopat in coitu mentula crebra sonos' (*Ars* II.37.10: 'a thick penis cuts off the sounds of intercourse') as an example of how first-conjugation verbs can best be used. After all, this particular work was explicitly written for the instruction of young school-boys (*Ars* II.12: 'ad informationem puerilis disciplinae'; cf. IV.51.29),[5] and not for the entertainment of lascivious adults.

Yet it is hardly just Matthew's own whim that posits an intimate connection between sex and language. As the very word 'conjugation' should demonstrate, the terminology of grammar is to a large extent the terminology of sex, and one should expect this commonality to be exploited, particularly in an age dominated by etymological explanations in all things. Danielle Jacquart and Claude Thomasset have clearly demonstrated how etymology informed (and obscured) medieval medical knowledge of sexuality; while John A. Alford and Jan Ziolkowsky, among others, have explored the widespread use of grammatical metaphor in medieval writing on sexual matters.[6] The ubiquity of such metaphor should indicate that the connection between sex and language is more than purely philological. In her examination of Renaissance English materials, Patricia Parker has perceived 'an intimate and ideologically motivated link between the need to control the movement of tropes and contemporary exigencies of social control ...'[7] The same link extends back into classical material, as Parker indicates, and is evident in Matthew's *Ars versificatoria*, informing both his choice of poetic examples from others, and the construction of his own. Both sexual activity and writing are to be carefully regulated, as they pose parallel dangers to the emerging masculinity of Matthew's young charges.

In her book on *Meanings of Sexual Difference in the Middle Ages,* Joan Cadden prefaces a discussion of Alan of Lille's *De planctu Naturae* with a warning: 'Our modern cultural assumptions would lead us to believe that when sex and grammar are being compared, sex is the real issue. This is not necessarily the case in the twelfth century, when the seven liberal arts in general and grammar in particular were the foundation not only of a new curriculum and a new approach to learning but also of a new way of reading nature and Scripture.'[8] In Matthew's treatise – unlike Alan's allegory – grammar does indeed take precedence over sex, but that does not mean that sex is not a real issue. Cadden's argument is not that Alan has no real interest in sex, nor that critics should have less interest – sex, after all, is the topic of her book. Rather, her point is that the cultural importance of grammar adds moral weight to Alan's comparisons. That similar comparisons are made in Matthew's treatise may indicate that moral weight shifts both ways. Alan was Matthew's contemporary, and possibly his student; the *Ars versificatoria* and the better known *De planctu Naturae* are clearly interdependent works,[9] highly similar in their use of metaphor and language in general, if different in focus. Whereas Alan uses complex rhetorical and grammatical metaphors explicitly to condemn sexual transgression, Matthew is writing about writing, carefully laying out the basics of what Alan takes for granted. His own commentary on sexuality is therefore mostly implicit and oblique, if not always subtle – and it can be argued that subtlety is itself not appropriate in the instruction of young students, if they are to grasp the issues.

Both works presume that the rules governing sexual activity and language usage are similarly absolute. The *De planctu* opens with a lament regarding rampant homosexual behaviour, metaphorically expressed – here as throughout the work – as an error of writing, a failed trope:

Non tamen ista tropus poterit translatio dici.
In uicium melius ista figura cadit. (*De planctu* m.1.23–4)

This transposition [or metaphor], however, cannot be called a trope. The figure here more correctly falls into the category of defects. (trans. Sheridan)

This error is also represented by a tear, or *diuorcia* (pr.4.162–3),in Nature's embroidered tunic, which, we are told, should ideally resemble the 'texture matrimonio' (pr.4.161–2: 'the interweave of a marriage'; trans. Sheridan). Marriage, personified in the work by Hymenaeus (pr.8), is also Alan's metaphor for the bond between body and soul (pr.3.30 ff.) – a metaphor likewise found in Matthew (*Ars* I.50.43–4) – and for earthly harmony in general. Marriage is a major theme in two of Matthew's other surviving works, the poems *Milo* and *Tobias*,[10] and the *Ars versificatoria* certainly presumes its importance. Matthew opens and closes his treatise with references to good writing as 'venusto verborum matrimonio' (*Ars* I.1: 'the lovely marriage of words;' see IV.26, 45); in between, he uses both quoted and invented examples to inveigh against its violators who, as in Alan, are metaphorically connected with those who violate grammar and rhetoric – those who dare 'dictiones ... conjugare, quae propter mutuam significationum repugnantiam ad discidium quasi anhelantes nullo patiuntur copulari matrimonio' (*Ars* II.42: 'to join words which, due to a mutual repugnance of meaning, gasp out for separation rather than suffer being coupled in marriage').[11]

Matthew's invective, like Alan's, begins very early in the work. Already in the Prologue, having humbly asserted that his treatise is the product of reason and careful deliberation, Matthew introduces his rival, Rufus, and states:

> ex conflatu invidiae meae paginae sine discretione rationis impetuosum praetendat vituperium, sed suo alludens concubinario Thaida rufam complectatur ...
>
>   Si me sustinuit, quamvis mercede, scolarem,
>   Sustineat Rufum rufa capella marem. (*Ars* Prol.2, 3)

> do not let him, puffed up with envy, offer impetuous insult to my writing without reason's discernment, but let him embrace red-haired Thais, playing in her bedroom.
>
>   If he has held me back, a scholar, at some price,
>   Let the red she-goat hold up Rufus, the red male.[12]

That is, unreasoned judgment is a prostitution of scholarly talent and material; conversely, unbridled and unsanctioned sexual behaviour is like careless literary criticism. Neither is beautiful, and beauty matters.

In discussing the art of description, which he deems central to poetic writing, Matthew states that, as a rule, an approving physical description is appropriate only to a female subject. However, he allows that the beauty of a young boy may be described for specific reasons, such as to arouse sympathy. Citing a chaste elegiac example from Statius (notably not from Virgil's popular but more suspect Eclogues), Matthew comments: 'Est autem forma elegans et idonea membrorum coaptatio cum suavitate coloris' (*Ars* I.68: 'Beauty, however, is an elegant and suitable arrangement of members, with pleasing colour'). Later in the work (III.50) he will draw a direct parallel between the 'corporeae venustatem materiae' ('lovely corporeal matter') of a human being and 'superficialis verborum ornatus' ('the external ornament of words'); here, in the earlier example, *membra* could mean either the limbs of the beautiful human subject, or the clauses of a beautiful sentence, and *color* a human complexion, or the use of the colours of rhetoric.[13] He then moves directly to the topic of women, and sex:

> Item matronae debet attribui rigor severitatis, remotio petulantiae, fuga

incontinentiae sive libidinis. Est autem libido res vilis et turpis ex vili et turpi membrorum agitatione proveniens ... (*Ars* I.69)

Likewise, one ought to attribute to a wife strict austerity, lack of impudence, and the avoidance of incontinence and lust. For lust is a vile and repulsive thing produced by the agitation of vile and disgusting members ...

Here the *membra* in question are clearly genital, and just as clearly contrasted with those previously mentioned; these are not properly arranged, or controlled.

In his extended description of an ideal wife (I.55), Matthew attributes these same austere virtues to the fictitious Marcia, and avoids virtually all physical description; in stark contrast to the subsequent portraits of the beautiful Helen and the ugly Beroe, there are no human *membra* here, of any description. Marcia 'femineum sexum festivat' (I.55.33: 'makes the feminine sex delightful'), through her lack of anything that Matthew considers feminine, such as weakness, lust, and deceit. In a later example of personal attributes based on sex, Matthew quotes Juvenal in regard to a woman's prodigal wastefulness, and terms this an argument *a natura* (I.82). His portrait of the ideal wife similarly presumes that woman is vicious by nature, and defines her 'matronale decus' (55.3: 'matronly virtue' or 'ornament') as masculinity:

Mollitiem sexus solidat, fraudesque relegans
    Femineas redolet mente fideque virum.[14]
Visitat infirmam naturam gratia morum;
    Innatum mulier exuit ausa malum.
Est mulier non re, sed nomine; mens epithetum
    Naturae refugit evacuatque dolum.

...

Marcia mente potens vitium captivat et aegrum
    In melius sexum degenerare facit. (55.9–14, 23–4)

She makes the soft sex firm and, banishing feminine frauds, savours of masculine judgment and faithfulness. She visits grace of character upon infirm nature; the bold woman divests herself of innate evil. She is a woman in name only; she flees Nature's epithet and empties it of guile ... By the strength of her judgment Marcia makes vice captive, and makes the feeble sex decline into the better.

The portrait is also rhetorically masculine, overly repetitive (as Matthew tends to be), but otherwise exemplary of a relatively plain or virile style.

As defined by Quintilian, such a style does not lack ornament – for which he claims orators have a justifiable weakness.[15]

Sed hic ornatus ... virilis et fortis et sanctus sit nec effeminatam levitatem et fuco ementitum colorem amet, sanguine et viribius niteat. (*Institutio oratoria* VIII.3, 6)

But such ornament must ... be bold, manly, chaste, free from all effeminate smoothness and the false hues derived from artificial dyes, and must glow with health and vigour. (Trans. Butler)

The writer's *materia* or subject material, like the Latin noun itself, is traditionally characterized as feminine; the ideal rhetorical style is masculine. Matthew's *materia*, here literally female, is brought under masculine order and control, and is refigured as male.

Controlled and therefore acceptable ornament – elegance informed by reason – also figures in Matthew's portrait of Ulysses as (feminine) utterance impregnated by (masculine) thought, in yet another marriage metaphor:

Ne sit lingua potens sensu viduata, maritat
    Se linguae sensus interioris honor.
Foederat ingenium studio, fructusque maritus
    Seminis in messem fructifare studet. (I.52.9–12)

Lest his potent utterance be widowed of judgment, the honour of his inner judgment weds itself to utterance. Genius is coupled with study, and the husband labours that fruit may be borne for the harvest.

Yet the overall passage is remarkably ornate, and thus feminine in style. Matthew betrays here his own fascination with rhetorical ornament, as he does again – on both literal and metaphorical levels – in his two highly physical portraits of the beautiful Helen. Most telling is the second, included specifically as a less ornate example, in which he states:

Haec facit ad Venerem, mihi tales eligo, tales
    Describit quales Windocinensis amat. (I.57.19–20)

He composes these things for Venus, I choose such things myself, the one from Vendôme describes what he loves.

The qualities he chooses to describe are purely physical. The line regarding her 'cella pudoris' (57.5: 'sanctuary of modesty') refers to virtue only very indirectly, and she is not seen to inspire such, either. Rather, according to the poem's last line, she can turn chastity itself into lust: 'Illic Ypolitum pone, Priapus erit' (57.24: 'Put Hippolytus with her, and he will become Priapus').

Of course, Helen was infamously undomesticated, uncontrolled by a husband. The chief difference between her and the prostitutes that Matthew condemns in other examples would seem to be that her charms are real, and theirs false. The latter fall metaphorically into Quintilian's category of vicious and decadent rhetoricians –'qui vitiis utuntur, virtutem tamen iis nomen imponant' (*Inst. Orat.* VIII.3, 7: 'those who employ a vicious style of embellishment disguise their vices with the name of virtue'). Hypocrisy is linked to both physical and verbal ornamentation in the section of the *Ars versificatoria* dealing with the decorous use of verbs. For instance, Matthew juxtaposes maxims of rhetorical practice, such as 'Versificatoris scema *venustat* opus' (II.38.28: 'The poet's figures beautify his work'), with references to apparently less successful attempts at physical ornamentation:

Arte placet species ornata: placere laborans
    Crines *intricat* crinibus aeger amans. (II.38.17–18)

An ornate appearance pleases by its art: trying to please, the agitated lover *entangles* hair with hair.[16]

Matthew further states: 'Hypocritae *phalerant* sub pietate malum' (II.38.7: 'Hypocrites *decorate* evil with piety'), and then adds an explanatory quotation with a distinctly sexual import from Juvenal's second Satire: 'et de virtute locuti, / Clunem agitant' ('and while speaking about virtue they wiggle their buttocks'). Indeed, the verb 'wiggle' does not quite capture the meaning here – J.N. Adams has noted that this phrase refers to the movements of the pathic male in intercourse.[17] These particular lines follow immediately upon a full set of sexual examples. The first two of these are fairly explicit: one indicates the negative effect on a lover of being caught in the act of copulation by his rival, and the other describes Rufus as being irresistibly drawn to prostitutes.[18] The third is more abstract:

Dum dominatur amor, virtus *exorbitat*, aegra
   Mendicat ratio, lex sine lege jacet. (II.38.5–6)

When love prevails, virtue strays; sick reason begs, law is unlawfully neglected.

As with Helen, virtue strays under love's influence, and masculine reason and control are lost.

Yet the implicit proscription here is more specific than that. While the first part of this double example can be read as a general maxim on the power of lust, the reference to *aegra ratio* ('sick reason') in the second part clarifies the nature of the law here neglected as the heterosexual law of Nature, as laid down in *De planctu*. Alan regularly connects sodomy with reason in precisely the same way that Matthew connects *aegra ratio* with law: where sodomy is practised, reason is foolish (*De planctu* m.5.15: 'insipiens ratio') or irrational (pr.5.54–5: 'irrationabilis rationis'); where in Matthew 'lex sine lege jacet' ('law is unlawfully rejected'), in Alan 'ratio rationis egere [est]' (m.5.61: 'reason is to lack reason'). Matthew's use of *jacere* further suggests that where reason is sick, or is not itself, law passively 'lies down' without its legitimate partner, and turns sodomite.[19]

This same illegitimacy may stand behind Matthew's proscription of what he terms 'impropriae verborum positiones,' citing a phrase from Virgil's homoerotic second Eclogue: 'Ardebat Alexim' (*Ars* IV.8: 'He burned for Alexis'). Galyon translates the first phrase as 'improper word usage' and comments: 'Matthew is objecting to *Ardebat, ardeo* (burn or glow) is not a transitive verb.'[20] However, *positio* normally relates to placement or arrangement than to usage in this sense, and *Alexim* is arguably a perfectly acceptable example of the accusative of respect – Virgil's Corydon burns for or in regard to Alexis. It is more likely the relative position of Corydon and Alexis, of grammatical subject and predicate, that worries Matthew. This is precisely the worry, and the metaphor, that Alan repeatedly takes up in *De planctu*, lamenting over those who allow 'subiectionis predicationisque legem relatione mutua' (pr.4.88: 'a law of interchangeability of subject and predicate'; trans. Sheridan).[21] Moreover, Virgil has not even taken the care to disguise this relationship, as Matthew recommends only a short time later: 'Fit iterum peryfrasis, quando foeditas circuitu evitatur' (IV.21: 'Again, periphrasis is made when what is foul is avoided through circumlocution'). Matthew then cites another passage from Virgil along with one of his own making – both describing heterosexual intercourse in 'verbis decentibus' ('decent terms').

Both periphrasis and metaphor embellish Matthew's most infamous reference to sexual activity. The longest of the examples of description in the first section of the work is given over to Davus, a figure closely related to Alan's hedonistic worshipper of Bacchus (*De planctu* pr.6). Matthew's portrait consists mostly of a catalogue of vices, effusive but elegantly stated, and a description of Davus at a feast which culminates in the following passage:

> Vergit ad incestum, Venus excitat aegra bilibres
> Fratres, membra tepent cetera, cauda riget.
> Metri dactilici prior intrat syllaba crebro
> Impulsu quatiunt moenia foeda breves.
> Nequitia rabiem servilem praedicat, actu
> Enucleat servae conditionis onus.
> Urget blanda, furit in libera terga, rebellis
> Naturae vetito limite carpit iter.
> Imbuit innocuos vitiis, exuberat aegri
> Pectoris in multos particulata lues. (*Ars* I.53.77–86)

He turns to unchastity; a sick Venus arouses the two-pound brothers; the other members are warm; the tail stiffens. The first syllable of the dactylic metre enters with repeated thrust, and the short ones batter down the vile defensive walls. In his wickedness he predicates a servile madness, and by his action makes plain the burden of a slavish condition. He presses upon charming backsides, goes mad over naked backsides; rebellious, he takes the path beyond the forbidden bounds of nature. He stains the innocent with vices; this particular infection flows from his sick breast into many.

The passage is perhaps less decorous than it is obscure. The difficulty of translation here might best be illustrated by quoting Galyon's very different version of the first four of these lines:

> He turns to lewdness as a foul passion suffuses his genitals,
> Causing love's orbs to bulge and Venus's lance to stiffen.
> Yet before the lengthy member of this dactyl can pierce home,
> The short syllables shake and destroy the enterprise.[22]

Galyon is obviously not attempting a literal, word-for-word translation, but a free exchange of euphemisms: the *bilibres fratres* ('two-pound brothers') – a phrase adapted from Juvenal[23] – here become 'love's orbs,' and the *cauda* ('tail') becomes 'Venus's lance.'

But more is lost in this exchange than Matthew's own periphrasis. Galyon has transformed what seems to be successful sodomy into an example of apparently heterosexual impotence. The *Venus aegra* ('sick Venus'), like the *aegra ratio* ('sick reason') dealt with earlier, and like Alan's 'solecistic Venus' (*De planctu* pr.4.20), is homosexual desire. This identification is strengthened here by the line 'furit in libera terga,' which Galyon translates: 'He is enflamed at the sight of a naked body.' Parr, on the other hand, translates this as Davus raging 'against the free-born's backs,'[24] apparently remembering that Matthew has earlier quoted a passage from Claudian where this is indeed the meaning of the same phrase: 'servi rabies in libera terga furentis' (*Ars* I.29: 'the passion of a slave raging against the backs of freemen'). But *liber* can mean 'naked' as well as 'free' or 'freeman,' and *tergum* not only 'back' but 'backside' – or, even more specifically, the anus.[25] The rebellion of Davus is not against a human hierarchy, but against Nature. Like Alan in his portrait of the lover of Bacchus, Matthew 'emphasizes the connection between gluttony and lust'[26] – and that lust is of the same variety that Alan most condemns.

I have already cited another of the more explicit sexual examples in the *Ars versificatoria* – namely, 'Syncopat in coitu mentula crebra sonos' (*Ars* II.37.10: 'a thick penis cuts off the sounds of intercourse'). It too has been the victim of mistranslation: again the penis remains, but its activity changes. Galyon translates the line as: 'A thick penis *sounds* sweetly in intercourse,' and Parr as: 'The erect organ *weakens* with sounds of copulation.' *Syncope* is a grammatical term that denotes the omission of a letter or syllable within a word; what is omitted is clearly not the strength of the erection but the sound that its activity creates.[27] Much as Matthew advises the writer to render copulation decorous through periphrasis (IV.21), effecting proper control over his subject-matter, this penis silences all direct and unseemly evidence of copulation, but does not end its appropriate conjugal activity.

Mistranslation here, as in the Davus passage, renders impotent Matthew's implicit advice to his young students and misconstrues his conception of the writer's task, even as it alters the attitudes towards sexual activity that he expresses. Critics have recently commented on the similar impropriety of editorial allegorization and gender-switching in the homo-erotic work of poets such as Michelangelo;[28] ironically, the same impropriety was occasionally used as a rhetorical device by medieval poets, ostensibly to render their own homoerotic verse more decorous, more socially acceptable.[29] However, Matthew wants his young students to know clearly the vices they are to avoid, and not mistake them for elegant expression. Thus, like Alan's Nature, he feels he must occasionally leave the heights of elegant obscurity to produce 'paululum ad pueriles ... infantie fescinnas' (*De planctu* pr.5.18–19: 'the trivial, crude pieces suited to ... undeveloped literary ability'; trans. Sheridan). Mistranslation defeats their purpose.

Just as Matthew does not deem all sexual activity appropriate, regardless of precedent or desire, so too he does not deem the use of all words or figures appropriate for the writer, including some figures accepted by ancient poets; as Matthew states, quoting Juvenal, 'Non enim veritas ... ab his expresse exigenda est, quibus erat "pro ratione voluntas"' (IV.6: 'For clearly truth cannot be expected from these, for whom "desire is taken for reason"').[30] Moreover, not all errors can simply be corrected by a teacher, as Matthew emphasizes (IV.35). In order to avoid error, rhetorical expression is to be subjected to masculine control and authority, like the wife and servants of a household:

> Unde ad hujusmodi offendiculi remedium in venusto dictionum matrimonio usum praecipue debemus aemulari,
>   Quem penes arbitrium est et jus et norma loquendi.
> Usus enim dictiones sunt quasi pedissecae et tributariae, et ei tanquam patrifamilias obsequuntur. (IV.26)

> Thus to remedy offences of this sort, in a lovely marriage of words we ought to emulate usage, 'In whose possession there is judgement, and authority, and the standards of speech' [Horace, *Ars poetica* 72]. For words are the handmaidens and tributaries of usage, and obey it as the father of the household.

However, the possibility of stylistic faults does not render the writer or his pen incapable, any more than sexual vice causes impotence. Alan's 'solecistic Venus' has real power in the sexual world; Davus is successful in his sexual (and gastronomic) endeavours, as is Rufus with his whores. If vice had no potency, one would not need to warn of its dangers. The point is to direct and contain that same potency. As Matthew states in another of his examples, 'Ad *conjunctivas* spirat amica vices' (II.24.14: 'The mistress hopes for *conjugal* duties'). The duty of the writer is to provide these, subjecting his metaphorical mistress in a proper and responsible manner –

imposing order and masculine virtue upon his feminine *materiae*, much as Matthew does in the portrait of the wife Marcia. In the rhetorical tradition that Matthew occupies, good writing is good husbandry; he is merely more explicit than some in his metaphorical description of the husband's role, and his proscription of conjugal vices.

One of Alan's chief metaphors in *De planctu Naturae* is the *calamus* or reed-pen that Nature gives to her ultimately incompetent deputy, Venus; it is made *prepotens* (extra-powerful) 'ne a proprie descriptionis semita in falsigraphie deuia eumdem deuagari minime sustineret' (*De planctu* pr.5.33–4: 'so that she might not suffer the same pen to wander in the smallest degree from the path of proper delineation into the paths of pseudography'; trans. Sheridan). In the words of R. Howard Bloch, 'Nature has endowed her handmaiden with two instruments of rectitude – *ortho*graphy, or straight writing, and *ortho*dox coition, or straight sexuality ...'[31] However, all the power of her pen is insufficient to prevent Venus from slipping into the solecism of sodomy. Likewise, for all his warning of the dangers of excessive rhetorical ornament in the *Ars versificatoria*, Matthew himself occasionally betrays a weakness for its feminine and feminizing charm. His young male students can hardly be expected to do better than either of these, but at least they have been warned. They are expected to learn masculine control over their material, avoiding the parallel feminizations of rhetorical and moral vice, learning the proper use of their pens.

NOTES

1 For an overview of the early reception and reputation of Matthew's *Ars versificatoria*, and of later critical attitudes towards it, see the introduction to Aubrey E. Galyon's translation: *The Art of Versification* (Ames: Iowa State University Press 1980), 19–21. The treatise has also been translated by Roger P. Parr, *Ars Versificatoria (The Art of the Versemaker)* (Milwaukee, WI: Marquette University Press 1981). The Latin text is in Edmond Faral's *Les Arts poétiques du XIIe et du XIIIe siècle* (Paris: Champion 1962), 106–193, henceforth cited as *Ars*. Except where noted, translations included here are my own.

2 Parr, *Art of the Versemaker*, xii

3 Galyon, *Art of Versification*, 16

4 Ibid., 17, citing Ernst R. Curtius, *European Literature and the Latin Middle Ages*, trans. Willard R. Trask, Bollingen Series 36 (New York: Princeton University Press 1953), 50

5 *Puer* generally refers to a boy between the ages of seven (when one commonly began formal schooling) and fourteen; while this usage is by no means absolute or universal, it seems likely that this *Ars* was written for a prepubescent audience – an audience that, according to Philippe Ariès, 'was believed to be unaware of or indifferent to sex': *Centuries of Childhood: A Social History of Family Life*, trans. Robert Baldick (New York: Knopf 1962), 106. On the other hand, Ariès seems to consider joking reference to genitalia commonplace around very young children, if not around school-aged boys (pp. 100–2).

6 Danielle Jacquart and Claude Thomasset, *Sexuality and Medicine in the Middle Ages*, trans. Matthew Adamson (Princeton, NJ: Princeton University Press 1988); see especially ch. 1, 'Anatomy, or the Quest for Words,' 7–47. On grammatical metaphors of sex, see John A. Alford, 'The Grammatical Metaphor: A Survey of Its Use in the Middle Ages,' *Speculum* 57 (1982), 728–60 (esp. 731–3, 745–6); and Jan Ziolkowsky, *Alan of Lille's Grammar of Sex: The Meaning of Grammar to a Twelfth-Century Intellectual* (Cambridge, MA: Medieval Academy of America 1985).

7 Patricia Parker, *Literary Fat Ladies: Rhetoric, Gender, Property* (London & New York: Methuen 1987), 98

8 Joan Cadden, *Meanings of Sex Difference in the Middle Ages: Medicine, Science, and Culture* (Cambridge: Cambridge University Press 1993), 222

9 Unfortunately, neither can be securely dated; see Ziolkowsky, *Alan of Lille's Grammar of Sex*, 60–1, for a brief discussion of the main connections between these works. *De planctu Naturae* has been edited by N.M. Häring, in *Studi Medievali* ser. 3, 19.2 (1978), 797–879, and translated by James J. Sheridan, *Alan of Lille: The Plaint of Nature* (Toronto: Pontifical Institute of Mediaeval Studies 1980).

10 See Bruce Harbert, 'Matthew of Vendôme,' *Medium Ævum* 44 (1975), 229–30.

11 The phrase 'patiuntur copulari' could also be translated as 'being fucked,' given that *patior* is the technical Latin verb for passive sexual activity.

12 The same image is repeated at the end of the work, in IV.48, again in reference to Rufus and Thais.

13 Parr's translation of this line almost obliterates any sense that it might refer to physical beauty, seeming only to refer back to the form of the line quoted, and not the boy referred to therein: 'Here is a form that is elegant with a suitable joining of members and a pleasing complexion.' It is worth noting that Matthew does not actually quote any physical description of the boy. Elsewhere in the poem, Matthew uses *membra* to refer to the three qualities of poetry (defined in II.1 as 'verba polita, decendique color, interiorque favus'), noting that the beauty of poetry depends on the conjuction of all three, citing as example yet another line from Statius (III.49–50).

14 I have here incorporated a possible correction noted in Faral's edition, but not followed in either of the published translations. The uncorrected line ends 'fideque nitet.'

15 See Book VIII.3,1 of *The Institutio Oratoria of Quintilian*, vol.3, ed. and trans. H.E. Butler, Loeb Classics (London: Heinemann 1932). On the question of gender and rhetorical style here and as taken up in the Renaissance, see Parker, *Literary Fat Ladies*.

16 Galyon translates these lines as 'Artful makeup enhances beauty, but the poor coquette, / Striving to be pleasing becomes entangled in a mass of hair.' The 'aeger amans' might well be coquettish, but would seem to be masculine.

17 J.N. Adams, *The Latin Sexual Vocabulary* (Baltimore, MD: Johns Hopkins University Press 1982), 136–7, 194. As an interesting side note one might add that Matthew of Vendôme is one of only a very few medieval authors cited by Adams, who is concerned primarily with classical Latin; citation of Matthew's work, including the *Ars versificatoria* and *Milo*, is second in frequency only to that of the scurrilous play *Babio* (see pp. 24, 37, 39, 71, 84, 155, 152).

18 *Ars* II.38.1–4: 'Pro rivale timens rivalis *apocopat* ictus / Et merita fodiens mentula messe caret' ('Fearing his rival he cuts short his thrust and his delving penis loses its merited harvest') and 'Rufinam coitus meretricis *inebriat*, immo/ Lumina lippa lupae turpis *inescat* amor' ('Intercourse with a prostitute intoxicates Rufinus, while love indeed lures the bleary eyes of a repulsive whoring bitch'). The verb exemplified in the first passage offers a grammatical metaphor for sex, being derived from *apocope*, which can denote both the dropping of a letter or syllable, and castration (see Ziolkowsky, *Alan of Lille's Grammar of Sex*, 55); in *De planctu* Alan uses *apocope* as a metaphor for death (m.8.40) and for a short haircut (pr.8.141).

19 It is worth noting that the verb *iacere* (used with *cum*) is a ubiquitous euphemism for copulation.

20 Galyon, *Art of Versification*, 122 n.54

21 Sheridan, *Alan of Lille*, explains both here (p. 137 n.26) and in regard to the similar lines at the opening of the work (p. 68 n.5) that for Alan the subject represents man and the predicate woman, whereas the opposite is true – only woman is expected to subject herself, and only to man. The same confusion affects Sheridan's explanation of Alan's phrase 'suppositiones appositionesque' in pr.5 (59 ff.), although Alan specifically links woman with the subject, or *supposito* (literally 'that which is put below'), in the same sentence.

22 Galyon, *Art of Versification*, 41.

23 See Juvenal, Satire 6.372; the correspondence has been pointed out by Adams, *Latin Sexual Vocabulary*, 71.

24 Parr, *Art of the Versemaker*, 35

25 See Adams, *Latin Sexual Vocabulary*, 115. Matthew's punning recontextualiza-tion of Claudian's phrase might well have been suggested by the figure of the slave itself, *servio* being a frequent metaphor in classical Latin for (mostly pathic) homosexual activity. The name *Davus* is of course strongly associated with slaves through Latin comedy; see *Ars* I.42 (and Parr's n. 41 p. 27). Mat-thew uses *libera* in another ambiguously sexual example at II.38.16: '*Illaqueat victrix libera colla Venus*' ('May Venus the conqueror ensnare free necks' or 'unfettered [or naked] vaginas') – on *collum*, see Adams, 108 (and n.3).

26 Sheridan, *Alan of Lille*, 170 n.1. Although this portion of Alan's poem is not specifically concerned with homosexuality, there are sodomitical overtones to his metaphorical description: Alan's idolatrous glutton pursues Bacchus, bound to him by *dilectionis*; eventually he captures his god in 'dolio sui ventris' (literally 'the wide-mouthed jar of his belly'). See *De planctu* pr.6.20–9.

27 The word *sonos* is in the accusative case, and acts as direct object of *syncopat*, not – as Parr's translation implies – as cause or agent.

28 See, for instance, James Saslow, *Ganymede in the Renaissance: Homosexuality in Art and Society* (New Haven and London: Yale University Press 1986), 14–15.

29 For one example, see *Medieval Latin Poems of Male Love and Friendship*, ed. and trans. Thomas Stehling (New York and London: Garland 1984), no. 115. Ste-hling comments briefly on this device, termed 'aleotheta,' on p. xxxi.

30 See Galyon, *Art of Versification*, 101. In its original context, the phrase from Juvenal describes the reasoning of an overly headstrong wife (Satire 6.223).

31 R. Howard Bloch, *Etymologies and Genealogies: A Literary Anthropology of the French Middle Ages* (Chicago and London: University of Chicago Press 1983), 133

Reading the Dirty Bits

ANDREW TAYLOR

The presence of unobservable areas of sex activity presents certain barriers to research which are difficult to overcome.

– Margaret Mead

My topic is the distinctly sexual pleasure of fantasizing on a text, whether in compulsive, solitary rereading of certain passages as a sexual substitute or when two people read together as a form of flirtation or seduction, as in Paolo and Francesca's notorious reading of the story of Lancelot.[1] This sexual pleasure has been a recurring attraction of literature, perhaps for as long as there has been literature. No history of sexuality or of reading can afford to ignore the conjuncture of the two. However, the topic presents extreme methodological difficulties.

Let me begin with the response of one of the great modern teachers of vernacular love poetry, E. Talbot Donaldson, to one of Chaucer's female characters, the young woman May in the *Merchant's Tale*. As her husband-to-be, January, lets his mind play on her image, May is presented according to a standard catalogue of beauties:

He purtreyed in his herte and in his thoght
Hir fresshe beautee and hir age tendre,
Hir myddel smal, hire armes longe and sklendre,
Hir wise governaunce, hir gentillesse,
Hir wommanly berynge, and hire sadnesse.[2]　　　　　　(seriousness)

May is no different from hundreds of others. That does not mean, however, that she is a lifeless piece of bad writing that can elicit no response today. Donaldson readily concedes that May is a generalized beauty, but argues that it is for precisely this reason that she so warms the heart: 'She becomes not only the embodiment of all pretty young girls in the Spring, but a proof that the Spring of pretty young girls is a permanent thing, and that May in their persons will always warm the masculine heart as May warms their hearts and sends them out among the flowers.'[3]

Many will find this seductive writing, the vigorous, concrete prose of a manly man whose intellectual sophistication has not chilled his heart nor destroyed his relish for such simple manly pleasures as girl-watching. But Donaldson's reading cannot be expected to appeal to everyone. Its allure lies in a triple homology that links good old Geoffrey, that wise and tolerant man who wore his own education so lightly; Donaldson himself, with his democratic echoes of Maurice Chevalier; and an intended reader, obviously male, whom I envisage (and I imagine Donaldson envisaged) as a promising young undergraduate, a good college man. For the young college man to share Donaldson's and Chaucer's pleasure in May is to become, like them, a connoisseur of both good writing and pretty girls, a master of ironic detachment and well-modulated heterosexual desire, and thus potentially a writer of the masterful and detached prose of the ruling class of heterosexual men; it is to prove himself in all ways 'a manly man, to been an abbot able.'[4]

Today, this is no longer an innocent pleasure. Shifts in the politics of gender allow us to see Donaldson's reading of Criseyde as a form of iconolagnia, a sexual penetration of the kind our culture alternately glamorizes and condemns. The girl-watching Donaldson is reading like a man, as 'a spectator in direct scopophilic contact with the female form displayed for his enjoyment.'[5] It would be naïve, however, to suppose that our sexual liberation and theoretical sophistication have brought us into a world where we see clearly for the first time and may condescend to the naïvety and sexism of our elders. Even as we luxuriate in this volume in our mutual defiance of traditional academic taboos, we must recognize that this defiance and the endless discourse it engenders are no less governed by repression. As Michel Foucault implies when he ponders the condition of a society that on the subject of sex 'speaks verbosely of its own silence,' we, the 'other Victorians,' may be endlessly loquacious about sex and sexual repression, but our curiosity is not innocent and our verbosity is not frank.[6] This is particularly true, I would suggest, about dirty reading.

A stubborn disingenuity haunts the discussion of textual/sexual plea-sure. Medieval literary theory, to begin with, is powerfully evasive. Con-fronting the dual embarrassment of Ovid and Virgil's latinity, which many clerics adored and sought to emulate, and the presence of the Song of Songs among the books regarded as Holy Writ, one of the primary tasks for medieval hermeneutics was to develop a means of purifying sec-ular love stories and erotica.[7] Medieval commentators did so, and did so with an ingenuity and loquaciousness that rivals our own – the Song of Songs is one of the most discussed of all the books of the Bible.[8] But when Peter Abelard tells us that the wood of Lebanon of Solomon's chariot sig-nifies the cross and should remind us of the crucifixion, his personal his-tory makes his exegesis suspect.[9] One may well feel that the medieval pleasures of the text are expressed more truly by the recurring meta-phors of the blank page as the female body, subject to the markings of the pen, or of the written page as the female body, subject to manipulation and penetration as a reader strips aside the veil of rhetorical ornament to penetrate to a deeper meaning.[10]

Our own century is no closer to being frank. Traditional humanism has allowed the aura of high culture to legitimate what might otherwise be considered salacious, developing a critical idiom that consistently implies that the pleasures of reading *Playboy* are simple and utterly different from the complex pleasures of reading the *Merchant's Tale* or *Troilus and Cri-seyde*. Recent attempts to achieve more politically palatable modes of reading vernacular poetry, on the other hand, still tend to elide certain crucial questions. It is easy to object to Donaldson's enjoyment of Cri-seyde as an epitome of male reading from which the woman reader is excluded, for example, and indeed several critics have done so.[11] But this avoids the more difficult question of whether the female reader should in some way be included or whether the pleasure itself is not inherently morally dubious.[12] Whether radical, traditional, or medieval, literary criti-cism has a strong vested interest in denying the question of iconolagnia.

It may seem that I have dwelt at rather excessive length on one sen-tence by one twentieth-century critic rather than getting to the Middle Ages. In a sense, however, I am already there. Donaldson's is ultimately a historicist reading, offering access to the pleasures of the past by appeal-ing to a carnal continuity. The hermeneutic triangle he establishes (Geof-frey Chaucer, Donaldson, and the good college man) invokes a fusion of the horizons of male desire across the ages. For the spring of pretty young girls is a *permanent* thing, and May in their persons will *always* warm the masculine heart. This is a historical claim. It is, in other words, by recognizing the warmth in our own bodies that we have access to the inner world of the past. This raises the methodological paradox that we can know the repressed desire of the past only through the desire we have repressed in ourselves. There is no straight empirical road to follow. As Pierre Payer observes: 'I know of no body of data that could be used to substantiate empirical claims about the actual incidence of particular forms of sexual behaviour, their distribution among particular classes, or their frequency among the population in the early Middle Ages.'[13]

Must male readers then begin by analysing the shape of our particular pleasures if scholars in general are to understand the history of male reading? Ruby Ritch, in discussing modern pornography, makes that very suggestion: 'Here's a proper subject for the legion of feminist men: let them undertake the analysis that can tell us why men like porn (not, piously, why this or that exceptional man does *not*).'[14] Her injunction is in keeping with certain directions in contemporary anthropology and some feminist historiography and literary criticism to deal explicitly with the subjectivity of the commentator.[15] But do we relish the prospect of hearing more about why men like porn? That is, do we wish to invite individual men, to reflect on and then confess the nature of their particular reading pleasures? And, even if they were take the challenge, would they be able to tell us? The sources of our pleasure are often hidden from us, as Saint Augustine found when trying to elucidate his response to one particular image in the Song of Songs:

> Does one learn anything else besides that which he learns when he hears the same thought expressed in plain words without this similitude? Nevertheless, in a strange way, I contemplate the saints more pleasantly when I envisage them as the teeth of the Church cutting off men from their errors and transferring them to her body after their hardness has been softened as if by being bitten and chewed ... But why it seems sweeter to me than if no such similitude were offered in the divine books, since the thing perceived is the same, is difficult to say and is a problem for another discussion.[16]

If even our licit pleasures remain a mystery, it is not surprising that so few men have stepped forward to answer Ruby Ritch's challenge. Since in our culture the only thing more shameful than sexual experience is sexual ignorance, the simple question 'Do *you* like porn?' brings us immediately into a field in which any declaration is perilous. Like its surrogate, masturbation, dirty reading hovers on the edge of what can be socially acknowledged. And since, like masturbation, it usually takes place in the privacy of the chamber and, within that, like lecherous dreams, in the inner privacy of the chamber of the mind, it is normally accessible only as public confession.[17]

If we cannot hope for many readers to confess, we must hope for readers who will somehow give themselves away. We seek material traces – dirty bits – soiled pages that would testify to repeated reading, stains of spittle or semen, physical traces of physiological facts, the erections and ejaculations of the past. Occasionally we find them.

Gower's *Confessio Amantis*, for example, consists in large measure of stories of seduction, sexual conquest by trickery, and rape. Gower's avowed purpose is to lead the reader to a recognition of the evils of worldly love, and thus to a higher love – these are negative *exempla*. As the Confessor says to the Lover at the end of the story of Neptune's attempted rape of Venus, 'Mi Sone, be thou war therfore, / That thou no maidenhode stele.'[18] The need to warn oneself against wickedness has, of course, always been a convenient justification for dubious reading material; it is one of the reasons Pierre Col offers for reading *Le Roman de la rose* in 1402, and two and half centuries later it is the reason Samuel Pepys offers for reading *L'Escholle des filles*, 'a mighty lewd book, but not yet amiss for a sober man *once* to read over to inform himself in the villainy of the world.'[19] So much depends on the word 'once.' You may not believe these men, but unless you can catch them returning to the passage you cannot prove that they lie.

At least one early reader has been caught. In the Osborn *Confessio Amantis*, a handsome folio of *ca* 1400 now in the Beinecke Library at Yale, a reader, presumably an owner, has pencilled in a small hand to direct him back to the passage where Neptune grabs Cornix between the thighs in an attempt to rape her.[20] Similarly, on folio 137v (Book 6, line 1977), someone, possibly the same person, has written 'here is the tale' to direct himself back to the passage where the necromancer Nectanabus sleeps with Queen Olimpias (thus begetting Alexander). It seems fairly clear that such readers do not mark these passages to remind themselves to eschew earthly love, sorcery, and the raping of maidens, but rather to facilitate finding the passages again so that they may do so vicariously.

Here at last are the dirty bits, physical markings testifying to a material practice. In contrast to the narrative reader, who follows the tapeworm of plot avidly to the end, the imitative or fantasizing reader returns compulsively to certain passages – 'the dirty bits' in erotic literature, central confrontations in the literature of violence. This appears to be what the Osborn reader has done. This phenomenon is widely recognized

(although in a age of rapidly scanned paperbacks, no one need do anything as incriminating as marking the passages in order to find them). It
is a habit sufficiently common to have passed into vernacular English
idiom and I can assume that the phrase 'dirty bits' will be generally
understood. But few are prepared to admit that they read this way – to do
so would be to confess to too obvious an extraliterary pleasure. Modern
studies such as Janice Radway's *Reading the Romance* and Victor Nell's *Lost
in a Book*, although they offer much to elucidate the psychology of casual
reading, are surprisingly coy; one searches in vain through their pages for
any direct reference to sexual arousal or the repeated reading of erotic
passages.[21] Even Pepys was only prepared to note the physiological effect
of his reading of *L'Escholle des filles* in his secret shorthand: 'It did hazer
my prick para stand all the while, and una vez to decharger.'[22]

It is no accident that Pepys's copy of *L'Escholle des filles* does not survive.
Pepys ordered the book in a plain binding because he was resolved from
the start to burn it 'that it might not be among my books to my shame' –
a convenient illustration of the extreme fragility of the material evidence.
Some four hundred year earlier, the scribes who produced British Library
MS Harley 978 may have had similar motives in their ordering of the
material, which includes Goliardic poetry; medical texts; an Anglo-Norman treatise on hawking; the *lais* and fables of Marie de France; and a
variety of music, mostly religious, including the famous round 'Sumer Is
Icumen In.' The collection was assembled in the mid-thirteenth century
and soon came into the hands of a monk of Reading Abbey, whose dissolute life makes him all too appropriate an owner.[23] It seems more than a
coincidence that the *lais* of Marie de France, poems in no sense condu-
cive to monastic morality, are placed towards the end of the book, while
the music and medical texts are placed at the front. If other monks of
Reading enjoyed Marie's *lais* or similar material on a regular basis, they
were certainly discreet about it. We have the rare good fortune to possess
an early cartulary from Reading, which contains a list of the contents of
library.[24] The list predates Harley 978 by some fifty years, and even the
later additions to the list would seem to be somewhat earlier, but it does
give a sense of the books the monks were supposed to be reading.[25] The
contents of the library are uniformly moral; there is virtually no mention
of any secular material, and none whatsoever of secular love poetry. Con-
fronted with the more worldly pleasures of Harley 978, one is left with a
suspicion that the library list is misleading. As Proust once remarked, the
discretion of our elders prevents us from forming an accurate picture of
the past.

If dirty reading were merely a nasty adolescent habit, it would matter less that its history is so difficult to track, but considerably more is at stake. Enjoying the dirty bits requires an ability to extrapolate images from a text and place them in a sustained fantasy, and this ability marks a significant extension of the use of the technology of the book. It is of considerable interest then, especially in the context of current debates on the origins of modernity, to determine how and when such reading practices developed. The work of Paul Saenger on the use of private books of hours by the laity suggests that there was a significant correlation among the habit of silent reading, with its stress on the pleasures of the eye, the elaborate visualization encouraged in late-medieval devotion, and the growth of book ownership among the laity.[26] Owning a book one could read silently tended to promote an interior life which could be radically at odds with the reader's public personna; the practice fostered religious individualism as well as erotic pleasure, and the two easily overlapped. As Saenger notes: 'artists took advantage of the privacy afforded by each person's own book of hours to portray erotic scenes unimaginable in public art or publically displayed liturgical texts.'[27] Dirty reading is thus a telling aspect of the growing bookishness of the late-medieval laity and the development of the late-medieval subject.[28]

At the time, however, these new erotic pleasures attracted surprisingly little direct comment. The possibility that the pictures of the naked Susanna or Bathsheba that became so common in late-medieval Books of Hours might encourage lechery,[29] or that reading of earthly love affairs might encourage young people to pursue them, found relatively little expression, or at least little expression outside self-reflexive *integumenta* in the love literature itself.[30]

Dirty reading did not go entirely unnoticed; criticism of clerics for being seduced by the blandishments of rhetoric or marginal illuminations is well known, and we find criticism of lay reading from the fourteenth century on.[31] Guillaume de Deguilleville has his character Oiseuse (Idleness) boast: 'I wishe after festes and sonedays for to rede vanitees to gadere lesinges to gideres and make hem seeme soothe and for to telle trifles and fables and rede romaunces of lesinges.'[32] Christine de Pisan insists that a lady ban immoral books from her home: 'The lady willingly will read books inculcating good habits, as well as studying on occasion devotional books. She will disdain volumes describing dishonest habits or vice. Never allowing them in her household, she will not permit them in the presence of any daughter, relative, or lady-in-waiting.'[33] Jean Gerson, chancellor of the University of Paris, warns against the dangers of books that stir people to lechery, such as works by Ovid or Matheolus or the *Romance of the Rose*, or rondels and ballads, or songs that are too dissolute.[34] For the most part, however, dirty reading is one of the few forms of sexual misbehaviour that is overlooked in late-medieval *pastoralia* and moral commentary. It was not that medieval sexual theory was limited to sexual acts. Drawing on Mathew 5 (omnis qui viderit mulierem ad concupiscendum eam ...), late-medieval sexual theory clearly recognized the existence of unfulfilled lust, lust as a purely mental state, what the *Glossa ordinaria* calls 'internal concupiscence.'[35] For all that, the majority of writers had little to say about a vice they could not observe.

There are a number of possible reasons for this silence. For one thing, dirty reading was severely socially limited. It was only the more luxurious Books of Hours and Psalters whose technical artistry might depict Bathsheba's or Diana's nakedness vividly enough for erotic effect. Modern written pornography, in contrast, developed in close dependence on printing; it is often defined in terms of its mass production, and its widespread availability has given it surprising political ramifications and made it a more obvious social threat.[36] No less important was the force of convention. There was already a fully developed theory of discourse based on the opposition between immoral or excessive speech, *turpiloquium*, and the moral authority of the *logos* and the written page. Reading was thus deeply coded as a clerical activity, a form of the *opus dei*, and a guard against a loose tongue, the snares of the hall and tavern, and the blandishments of women.

For the late Middle Ages, the common perceived threat was not pornographic books but ribaldry, the scurrilous public singing and tale-telling that was said to accompany feasting and lead to fornication.[37] John Lacy, for example, an early fifteenth-century Dominican anchorite, in a treatise on the ten commandments, describes Lechery as a story-teller: 'Then cometh in Lechere, and he lokuth al abowthe the hows, and then he settith him downe on the benche; and then beginneth he to speke and bringe in oolde storius of wemen and of lustus and ribaldry, and faste he rusith himself of olde synnes, and alle lau3en and been glad to here his prechinge.'[38] An anonymous sermon from roughly the same period tells us that, while others are at church, gluttons go to taverns, where they sit 'faste in the devil's seruyce, with many rybald wordes and songes of lecherie, blasfemynge God with many grett othes, backebytynge, slaundur, and envie.'[39] These are the sins of the hall and the tavern, not the chamber; of public, not private, spaces, just as they are the sins of the throat and mouth, or of the ear, not of the eye.

Certainly the eye is the pre-eminent organ of sensual temptation; on this matter medieval commentators as diverse as Bede, Nicholas of Lyre, and Bromyard agree with the conventions of *fin'amour*.[40] But what the eye looks upon is a real flesh-and-blood man or woman, however decorated by artificial trappings. For Robert Mannyng of Brunne, even when sin is both internal and mental ('privity' and 'thilth of thought'), it still has its origin in the sight of an actual human being. His warning against the dangers of erotic dreaming in bed, particularly when it becomes a custom, culminates in the specific admonition not to behold women; 'Behold nat wymmen ouer mykyl: / Here syghte makþ mennes þoghtes fykyl.'[41] Perhaps the clearest example is the preaching image of the devil's five fingers, the five fingers of lechery, widely known through Chaucer's *Parson's Tale*. The devil has five fingers to ensnare a man and a woman into lechery: the first is their foolish looking; the second, their villainous touching; the third, their foolish words; the fourth, their kissing; and the fifth is the stinking deed of lechery itself.[42] The flesh you can see is ultimately the flesh you will touch. The gaze has not yet been transformed into a mode of reception for images that are human products.

Today it has. Let me offer a representative moment. A few years ago I sat at a table in a bar on the edge of a Midwestern campus, jotting down notes for what would become this paper. In one corner of the room was a huge television screen. On the screen a young woman in lingerie was engaging in phone sex. Reclining on a couch, with phone in hand, she writhed in simulated orgasm, whispering words I could not hear. None of the men or women in the room was paying much attention. They seemed genuinely, not studiously, indifferent. The experience, after all, was not unusual; had I not been thinking about sexual representation, I would probably not even remember it. This is our mediatized world, where pornography, while it is enjoyed privately only as a guilty secret, is seen publicly by everyone.

Increasingly, it is the shape of pornography as an electronic commodity that determines our understanding of the moral issues it raises. The staggering capacity of our society to reshape the body and render the fetishized, sexually coded simulacra ubiquitous ensure that, for us, pornography is not just pre-eminently visual but pre-eminently a camera's image. Porno that is merely graphics, merely letters but not pictures, no longer much concerns us.[43] It is its extreme commercial publicity that makes pornography threatening, with its consequent capacity to miseducate, and in particular to promote violence against women. For us it is the body electric, not the living flesh, that is the source of source of temptation, the object of the lascivious gaze.

Pornography thus becomes not just a moral threat magnified electron-ically, but the very measure of our implication in the world of electronic commodification and virtual realities. As Fredric Jameson argues, porno-graphic films are 'only the potentiation of films in general, which ask us to stare at the world as though it were a naked body,' and if we recognize this more clearly today, it is because of our material conditions, because 'our society has begun to offer us the world – now mostly a collection of products of our own making – as just such a body, that you can possess visually, and collect the images of.'[44] It is in this world that is possible to conclude, as Jameson does, that 'the visual is essentially pornographic.'[45] Gerson would easily concur with this position but would understand in a radically different way, and we need to discover what constitutes this dif-ference. If we are to 'think the visual' by grasping 'its historical coming into being' – the defiant possibility that Jameson holds out – then we must disentangle the contemporary understanding of the phallocentric gaze from the older ethics of visual concupiscence upon which it has been grafted and pursue the traces of the illicit visual pleasures of the past, whatever the difficulties in doing so, to see whether they did indeed resemble our own. We need a better sense of the difference between our exposure to videos and earlier exposures to books printed in their thou-sands, and still earlier exposures to handwritten books of strictly limited circulation. Perhaps in understanding what was at stake in the privacy of the medieval chamber and its pleasures, we can better understand what is at stake in our return to the public display of the hall.

NOTES

I would like to thank the Social Sciences and Humanities Research Coun-cil of Canada for supporting this work in its initial stages.

1 *Inferno* V, 118 ff. For commentary on this passage see Susan Noakes, *Timely Reading: Between Exegesis and Interpretation* (Ithaca and London: Cornell Univer-sity Press 1988), 38–48, and 'The Double Reading of Paolo and Francesca,' *Philological Quarterly* 62 (1983), 221–39.

2 *The Riverside Chaucer*, 3d ed., ed. Larry D. Benson (Boston: Houghton Mifflin 1987), IV (E), 1600–4

3 E. Talbot Donaldson, *Speaking of Chaucer* (London: Athlone Press 1970), 49

4 Benson, ed., *Riverside Chaucer, Canterbury Tales*, I (A), 167

5 Laura Mulvey, 'Visual Pleasure and Narrative Cinema,' *Screen* 16 / 3 (Autumn 1975), 13. This classic study has generated extensive debate. See, for example,

Regina Schwartz, 'Rethinking Voyeurism and Patriarchy: The Case of *Paradise Lost*,' *Representations* 34 (1991), 85–103.

6 Michel Foucault, *The History of Sexuality*, Volume I: An Introduction, trans. Robert Hurley (New York: Random House 1980), 86

7 On the purification of Virgil by allegorical interpretation, see Henri de Lubac, *Exégèse médiévale: Les Quatres sens de l'écriture*, Part II, 2 vols. (Paris: Aubier 1961–4), vol. 1: 233–62.

8 That the Song of Songs offered dangerous pleasures was a recurring theme in the commentary, beginning with Origen. See Ann W. Astell, *The Song of Songs in the Middle Ages* (Ithaca and London: Cornell University Press 1990), 1–40; E. Ann Mater, *The Voice of My Beloved: The Song of Songs in Western Medieval Christianity* (Philadelphia: University of Pennsylvania Press 1990), 20–31; and Lee Patterson, 'No Man His Reson Herde,' in *Literary Practice and Social Change in Britain, 1380–1530*, ed. Lee Patterson (Berkeley: University of California Press 1990), 133, n. 48.

9 Abelard, *Sermones et Opuscula Ascetica, Sermones ad Virgines Paraclitenses in Oratorio Ejus Constitutas, Sermo IX*, PL 178, cols. 444–5

10 As their metaphors show, medieval grammarians concur with contemporary critical theory in depicting reading as a sexual or sexually coded pleasure. See further Toril Moi, 'Desire in Language: Andreas Capellanus and the Controversy of Courtly Love,' in *Medieval Literature: Criticism, Ideology and History*, ed. David Aers, 11–33 (New York: St Martin's Press 1986); Alexandre Leupin, *Barbarolexis: Medieval Writing and Sexuality*, trans. Kate M. Cooper (Cambridge: MA,: Harvard University Press 1989), 59–78; and Carolyn Dinshaw, *Chaucer's Sexual Poetics* (Madison: University of Wisconsin Press 1989), esp. 14–25.

11 See, for example, Dinshaw, *Chaucer's Sexual Poetics*, 30–9.

12 Susanne Kappeler, *The Pornography of Representation* (Minneapolis: University of Minnesota Press 1986), pushes the recognition of the phonographic nature of representation itself to its logical conclusion, noting not only that 'equal opportunities are out when what they are equal to is undesirable' (220) but that 'Art will have to go' (221). Elaine Tuttle Hansen believes that the traditional text can still be salvaged for the feminist medievalist: 'Her desire can still be to encounter the masterwork, but from what can be thought of as a partial perspective, in various senses of the word partial'; *Chaucer and the Fictions of Gender* (Berkeley: University of California Press 1992), 290. Similarly, Leslie W. Rabine, when reading classics of Western romanticism, finds herself 'seduced by their beauties and repelled by their active complicity in forming a cultural value system which has systematically excluded women from humanity'; *Reading the Romantic Heroine: Text, History Ideology* (Ann Arbor: University

of Michigan Press 1985), 19.

13 Pierre J. Payer, *Sex and the Penitentials: The Development of a Sexual Code, 550–1150* (Toronto: University of Toronto Press 1984), 120

14 B. Ruby Rich, 'Anti-Porn: Soft Issue, Hard World,' *Feminist Review* 13 (1983), 66

15 See, for example, the statement by Sandra M. Gilbert and Susan Gubar: 'Reading metaphors in this experiential way, we have inevitably ended up reading our own lives as well as the texts we study': *The Madwoman in the Attic: The Woman Writer and the Nineteenth-Century Literary Imagination* (New Haven: Yale University Press 1979), xiii. For examples in anthropology, see Paul Rabinow, *Reflections on Fieldwork in Morocco* (Berkeley: University of California Press 1977), and Gilbert Herdt and Robert J. Stoller, *Intimate Communications: Erotics and the Study of Culture* (New York: Columbia University Press 1990).

16 *On Christian Doctrine*, II, vii, 7–8, trans. D.W. Robertson (Indianapolis: Liberal Arts Press 1958), 37–8. 'Num aliud homo discit, quam cum planissimis uerbis sine similitudinis huius adminiculo audiret? Et tamen nescio quomodo suauius intueor sanctos, cum eos quasi dentes ecclesiae uideo praecidere ab erroribus homines atque in eius corpus emollita duritia quasi demorsos mansosque transferre ... Sed quare suauius uideam, quam si nullam de diuinis libris talis similitudo promeretur, cum res eadam sit eademque cognitio, difficile est dicere et alia quaestio est': *Sancti Aurelii Augustini: De Doctrina Christiana, Corpus Christianorum, Series Latina* 32 (Turnholt: Brepols 1962), 35–6.

17 I deal with this issue more extensively in 'Into His Secret Chamber: Reading and Privacy in Late Medieval England,' in *The Practice and Representation of Reading in Britain*, eds. James Raven, Helen Small, and Naomi Tadmor, 41–61 (Cambridge: Cambridge University Press 1996).

18 G.C. Macaulay, ed. *The English Works of John Gower*, vol. 2 *Confessio Amantis*, EETS ES 82 (London: K. Paul, Trench, Trübner 1901), Book 5, ll. 6218–19

19 *The Diary of Samuel Pepys*, eds. Robert Latham and William Matthews, vol. 9 (1668–9) (Berkeley: University of California Press 1976), 58 (my italics). See Maxwell Luria, *A Reader's Guide to the* Roman de la rose (Hamden, CT: Archon Books 1982), 190, for a translation of Pierre Col's letter of mid-1402 to Christine de Pisan, and Roger Chartier, 'The Practical Impact of Writing,' in *A History of Private Life, III: Passions of the Renaissance*, ed. Roger Chartrier; trans. Arthur Goldhammer (Cambridge, MA: Harvard University Press 1989), 143, for the story of Pepys.

20 New Haven, Yale University, Beinecke Library, MS Osborn fa 1, fols. 114v (Book 5, l. 6177). Similar small hands have also been drawn on fol. 155r (Book 7, l. 2339) and twice on fol. 191r (Book 8, ll. 2403 and 2431). These glosses were first mentioned by Derek Pearsall in a lecture at the Beinecke Library. I

would like to thank Robert Babcock, curator at the Beinecke, for bringing them to my attention.

21 Janice Radway, *Reading the Romance: Women, Patriarchy, and Popular Literature* (Chapel Hill and London: University of North Carolina Press 1984), and Victor Nell, *Lost in a Book: The Psychology of Reading for Pleasure* (New Haven: Yale University Press 1988)

22 Pepys, *Diary*, 59

23 The fullest description of the manuscript to date is that of Christopher Hohler, 'Reflections on Some Manuscripts Containing 13th-Century Polyphony,' *Journal of the Plainsong and Mediaeval Music Society* 1 (1978), 2–38, which supplements C.L. Kingsford, ed., *The Song of Lewes* (Oxford 1890), vii–xviii. Hohler also provides much information about the owner, William of Winchester, a brother of Reading and sometime subprior of Leominster.

24 S. Barfield, 'Lord Fingall's Cartulary of Reading Abbey,' *English Historical Review* 3 (1888), 113–25

25 Barfield misleadingly dates the list to the fifteenth century. B.R. Kempe attributes the list to the original hand which compiled the manuscript in the 1190s and dates the additions to the early thirteenth-century: *Reading Abbey Cartularies: British Library Manuscripts Egerton 3031, Harley 1708, and Cotton Vespasian E XXV*, Camden Society, 4th Series 31, 3 vols. (London: Royal Historical Society 1986), vol. 1: 1–3, 186.

26 Paul Saenger, 'Silent Reading: Its Impact on Late Medieval Script and Society,' *Viator* 13 (1982), 367–414, and 'Books of Hours and the Reading Habits of the Later Middle Ages,' *Scrittura e Civiltà* 9 (1985), 239–69

27 Saenger, 'Books of Hours,' 268

28 Major contributions to our understanding of these interconnected developments include James H. Marrow, *Passion Iconography in Northern European Art of the Late Middle Ages and Early Renaissance* (Kortrijk, Belgium: Van Ghemmert 1979); Caroline Walker Bynum, *Fragmentation and Redemption: Essays on Gender and the Human Body in Medieval Religion* (New York: Zone Books 1992); and Georges Duby, ed., *A History of Private Life, II: Revelations of the Medieval World*, trans. Arthur Goldhammer (Cambridge, MA: Harvard University Press 1988). On the question of periodization, see the spirited critique of David Aers, 'A Whisper in the Ear of Early Modernists; or, Reflections on Literary Critics Writing the "History of the Subject,"' in his *Culture and History, 1350–1600: Essays on English Communities, Identities and Writing*, 177–202 (Detroit: Wayne State University Press 1992).

29 As Michael Camille has noted: 'Often artists explicitly presented the worldly object of the patriarchal voyeur's gaze in a way that suggests that the medieval reader, too, could delight in the curvacious supine forms of the white demure

flesh of Bathsheba': *The Gothic Idol: Ideology and Image-Making in Medieval Art*
(Cambridge: Cambridge University Press 1989), 303, offering Paris, Bibliothèque Nationale MS Lat. 10525, fol. 85v as an example. Cf. Baltimore, Walters
Art Gallery MS W. 297, a Psalter by the Coëtivity Master of *ca* 1460; New York
Public Library MS 150, a Book of Hours of *ca* 1475 by the Master of Morgan
366; and New York, Pierpont Morgan MS 85, a Book of Hours of *ca* 1510–1520,
all showing David watching Bathsheba, plates 49, 60, 118 in John Plummer, *The
Last Flowering: French Painting in Manuscripts, 1420–1530, from American Collections* (Oxford: Oxford University Press 1982). Other moments include Act-
aeon surprising Diana bathing: Paris, Bibliothèque Nationale Fr. 606, fol. 32;
and Saint Catherine stripped to the waist and bound to a column and flogged:
New York, The Cloisters Belles Heures, fols 17 and 17v, plates 102, 438, and
439, in Millard Meiss, *French Painting in the Time of Jean de Berry: The Limbourgs
and Their Contemporaries* (New York: George Braziller 1974).

30 Within poetry there is a rich tradition of self-reference or self-inculpation,
although with varying degrees of indirection. An excellent recent study of the
phenomenon is A.C. Spearing, *The Medieval Poet as Voyeur: Looking and Listen-
ing in Medieval Love-Narratives* (Cambridge: Cambridge University Press 1993).

31 See John Bromyard: 'Just as those who in physical books only have regard
for thick letters and capitals for Play and Curiosity will never be good clerics, so those who only acquire knowledge in the book of God for the sake
of pleasure and curiosity and only have regard for that which is beautiful
and delectable to the eyes, nor use these things for the love and knowledge
of God, will never be led through them to the perfect vision of God':
'Secundo, quia sicut in libro materiali, qui solum respiciunt literas crassas,
& capitales ad ludum, & curiositatem, nunquam erunt boni clerici, nec sic
Dei, uel sui cognitionem acquirent, ita qui creaturis utuntur ad uoluptate*m*,
& curiositatem potius, quam ad utilitate*m*, q*ui* solu*m* respiciunt illud, q*uod*
pulchru*m* & delictabile est oculis, nec eas ordinant, uel eis utuntur ad Dei
cognitionem & amorem, nunquam per eas ad Dei perfectam ducentur
uisionem': *Summa praedicantium* (Venice 1586), vol. 1, s.v. 'Liber,' cap. iv,
fols. 444v–445.

32 Aldis Wright, ed., *The Pilgrimage of the Lyf of the Manhode from the French of Guillaume de Deguilleville* (London: Roxburghe Club 1869), 103

33 Christine de Pizan, *A Medieval Woman's Mirror of Honor, The Treasury of the City
of Ladies* [*Livre des Trois Vertus*], trans. Charity Cannon Willard; ed. Madeleine
Pelner Cosman (New York and Tenafly, NY: Bard Hall Press and Persea Books
1989), 93, cf. 104

34 Jean Gerson, *Oeuvres Complètes*, ed. P. Glorieux, 10 vols. (Paris: Desclée 1960–
73), vol. 7: 829

35 'Quia videre absolute non est malum, sed inquantum ex eo sequitur concupis-centia interior. Et ista concupiscentia sic procedit: quia primo ex aspectu muli-eris causatur concupiscentia in appetitu sensitiuo quod dicitur sensualitas ...' (That looking is not a sin in itself, but inasmuch as internal concupiscence fol-lows from it is. And this concupiscence proceeds in this manner: first, from the appearance of the woman, there arises a desire in the sensual appetite, which is called sensuality ...): Nicholas Lyre, *Bibliorum sacrorum cum glossa ordi-naria* (Lyon 1545), vol. 5: 21. Cf. Bromyard, *Summa praedicantium*, vol. 1, s.v. 'Luxuria,' cap. vii, fol. 457: 'Luxuria est omnis immundicia, pertinens ad libidinosam, & illicitam delectationem, quecunque modo fiat, siue cordis cogi-tationi, siue oculorum defectione, siue oris locutione, sicut in turpiloquio, et huiusmodi siue in quibuscunque, alijs motibus, sicut in osculis tactibus, & amplexibus' (Lechery is any kind of uncleanness pertaining to libidinous desire and illicit pleasure, of whatever sort, whether in the inner thought, or in foul speech and things of this kind, or in anything else, or any motions, such as kisses, touchings, and embraces).

36 See *The Invention of Pornography: Obscenity and the Origins of Modernity, 1500–1800*, ed. Lynn Hunt (New York: Zone Books 1993), 109–23, and Robert Darn-ton, *Édition et sédition: L'Univers de la littérature clandestine au XVIIIe siècle* (Paris: Gallimard 1991). Hunt notes that early-modern pornography 'was linked to free-thinking and heresy, to science and natural philosophy, and to attacks on absolutist political authority' (p. 11).

37 For examples of the *topos* 'earthly minstrelsy as distraction' see *Richard Rolle: Prose and Verse*, ed. S.J. Ogilivie-Thomson, E.E.T.S. 293 (Oxford: Oxford Uni-versity Press 1988), 17, and *Robert Mannyng of Brunne: Handlyng Synne*, ed. Idelle Sullens (Binghamton, NY: Medieval and Renaissance Texts and Studies 1983), 118–20.

38 G.R. Owst, *Literature and Pulpit in Medieval England*, 2d ed. (Oxford: Blackwell 1966), 441

39 Sermon 17, dated *ca* 1380 to *ca* 1415, in Woodburn O. Ross, ed., *Middle English Sermons Edited from British Museum Royal 18 B. xxiii*, E.E.T.S. O.S. 209 (Oxford: Oxford University Press 1940), 101

40 See Lyre, *Glossa Ordinaria*; Bromyard, *Summa Praedicantium* cites Bede in his discussion of 'luxuria.' See *supra*, note 35. Capellanus defines love as 'a certain inborn suffering derived from the sight of and excessive meditation upon the beauty of the opposite sex': *The Art of Courtly Love*, trans. John Jay Parry (New York: Frederick Ungar 1941), 28.

41 Robert Mannyng of Brunne, *Handlyng Synne*, 204

42 Benson, ed., *Riverside Chaucer, Canterbury Tales*, X, ll. 851–61

43 The change is comparatively recent. Andrea Dworkin's *Pornography: Men Pos-*

sessing Women (New York: Perigee Books 1979) is worth noting as an example of a critique that still deals primarily with books.

44 Fredric Jameson, *Signatures of the Visible* (New York: Routledge 1990), 1

45 Ibid.

Did Mystics Have Sex?

NANCY F. PARTNER

Of all the conventionally created objects of historical interest, the *thing* called the 'Middle Ages' is by far the most peculiar, counter-intuitive, and deadening to the imagination. In saying this I don't mean that I think the domestic, social, or political arrangements prevailing during the 'medieval' centuries were notably strange; they are, in fact, easily recognizable to us. Nor do I find the medieval pursuits of agriculture, industry, or commerce foreign to my understanding, or anyone else's. And even the most distinctive (in the sense of distant and exotic) features of medieval culture – a theocentric universe revealed through sacred writings and doctrinal tradition; an international religious institution claiming exclusive privilege to teach and guide humanity to salvation; special forms of art and literature which reflect and comment on a world understood as divinely created and intelligible to the mind in elaborated anagogical tropes – even these most distinctively 'medieval' constructs are readily available to our basic comprehension, and, indeed, sympathy, with only a moderate exertion of the imagination fortified by some acquired knowledge.

And yet our approach to the lives and suffering of men and women who lived, say, seven hundred years ago is rigidly contained and channelled in intellectual structures whose purpose almost perversely works to dehumanize and etiolate this human past. The period of time this chronological 'middle' conventionally covers (from the sixth to, or through, the fifteenth century) is unintelligibly protracted. This amoebic construct is justified by nothing firmer than the uneven thinning out and eventual demise of Roman provincial government in Western Europe for a beginning, and, at the other end, the self-congratulating pronouncements of a few Italian intellectuals that they definitely wrote a better Latin than anyone who had lived since Cicero (or perhaps Saint Augustine).[1] To assist us in handling this thousand-year object, we have the intellectual precision instruments of internal divisions: the Middle is articulated (in what might almost be a deliberate parody of Aristotelian unity) into the early-middle, the 'high' or middle-middle, and the late-middle. (Compare this morphological vacuum with the comparatively sensible and evocative divisions of Graeco-Roman antiquity: Classical, Hellenistic, Republican Rome, and so on.) And we might consider that the imposition of form on the ineluctable seriatim of time is the mental act which announces and accomplishes the primal human demand for *meaning*, for *meaningfulness* as a condition and quality of human life over the generations. Chronology is the first fiction.[2] And we medievalists are stuck with a chronology of 'middleness' which announces as its contribution to the meaningfulness of history that something interesting happened long ago, in some 'beginning' before the great Middle, and interesting things resumed happening much later on, after the protracted vacancy of Middleness had finally concluded. This is almost the chronology of a clinical depression on a hideously enlarged scale.

Medievalists complain about this with ritual regularity; it's one of the things we *do*, a part of the professional obligation. And it should not matter as much as it quietly does. No one cares any longer about the artificial Ciceronian Latinity of Italian humanists. Few people even care about the Renaissance any longer in the old way; *that* Renaissance is rapidly losing its metaphorical romantic substance and is being engulfed in the rapacious maw of the Early Modern academic machine. (One increasingly hears of Early Modern Florence and Rome now.)

But let us pause a moment to contemplate (with shameless, unconcealed envy) the miracles of generation that have come from that twice-happy name, The Early Modern Period. This designation now covers some five hundred years of European history, and it is hardly necessary to describe its magnetic attraction, at least at graduate-study and scholarly levels. All the exciting topics seem to cluster and multiply there. The Early Modern is variously credited with the invention of homosexuality, heterosexuality, neurosis, perversion, tension, subversion, the white-hot fuel core of the modern psyche. But what has been involved in infusing such energy and fascination in what was never so compelling when it was called only The Age of Absolutism, or The Northern Renaissance, or The Reformation or The Ancien Regime (names that cling to life with the pallid inertia of textbook chapters)? The open secret is, of course, attaching the idea of modernity to 'something' at the invisible heart of political, social, economic, and domestic arrangements which, on the face of them, have nothing familiarly or recognizably 'modern' about them.

The baffling and boringly opaque manifest levels of past societies we cannot imagine living in, and historical persons whose ambitions and tastes are lost on us, are made crystalline translucent once we recognize their incipient modernity, and the latent meaning turns out to be excitingly inelligible, recognizable, almost familiar, almost ... ourselves! This triumph of and by the professoriat – for, make no mistake, it *is* a triumph – makes me wish that medievalists would sweep the Middle Ages into the recycle bin along with the Ages of Absolutism, Wars of Religion, and all that; take command of our semiotic destiny; and rename our entire field 'The Really Early Modern Period.'

This may sound like a joke, but if it is, it's a serious joke, or one that ought to get serious when we consider what calling five hundred years of distant history The Almost Modern Period has done for the field that depends on the medieval for its point of departure and first condition. For surely some wonderful hermeneutic sleight of hand has been pulled when so many overeducated people agree to grant historical 'earliness' to the seventeenth century.

I know that the hermeneutically sophisticated must agree that the entire historical Past is equally, ontologically Not-There, *unrepresentable* in any rigorous sense, and thus medieval historians have nothing more to lament than anyone else in a similar line of work. But it is also true that the blight of *absence* afflicts our sense of medieval life more acutely than any other period. In a much-noticed article in a special issue of *Speculum*, Lee Patterson sharply criticized the uncritical and unselfcritical tendency of historians now to accept the 'master narrative' of Western cultural history which assigns, as a novel historical development, 'the emergence of the idea of the individual' to the Renaissance.[3] And not merely the *idea of* the individual as social unit or citizen, but the very human experience of individuated subjectivity, of interior being, of complex and autonomous consciousness, of *mind*, is made contingent on historical developments in the fifteenth, or sixteenth, or seventeenth century, depending on which old or new historicist you are reading.[4] For the enthusiastic quarrels of revisionist scholarship have surprisingly left untouched this one idea: that, in the Middle Ages, people were profoundly different from us. It helps to return to the *locus classicus*, Burckhardt's famous passage from *The Renaissance in Italy*:

In the Middle Ages both sides of human consciousness – that which was turned within as that which was turned without – lay dreaming or half awake beneath a common veil. The veil was woven of faith, illusion, and childish prepossession ... Man was was conscious of himself only as member of a race, people, party, family, or corporation – only through some general category ...[5]

Burckhardt's medieval psyche (the Self under a perpetual self-denying ordinance) exists only rhetorically, a grey, dull ground of barely individuated human matter against which 'the psychological fact' (his term) of the free play of personality, subjectivity, individuality can emerge like fireworks in the Renaissance state.

This view is curiously close to that of Foucault and the Foucaudian New Historicists, who assert, virtually as a premise, that the individuated *subject* is the social-cum-epistemological precondition for the nation-state, for political rights, authorship, private property, sexual identity (that is, modernity); and this same individuated subject is constituted or created *by* the pressures brought to bear by the processes and discourses associated with the historically 'modern.' The cause/effect aspects of this theory are disconcertingly interchangeable: 'the modern' constructs persons who think (falsely) that they are autonomous subjects; and persons who think (falsely) that they are autonomous individuals accept and reinforce the modernness of society. Whether scholars concentrate on the social discourses of power or the social construction of sexuality, Burckhardt's 'psychological fact' of the absence of the medieval individual – which he used only as a rhetorical fact – is the premise. Among a generation of poststructuralists who refuse binary opposites as a description of reality, the Modern exists over against the (suppressed) Medieval, rather as the masculine takes form against the feminine in another discourse of power.

The assertive, conflicted, tensely erotic Modern rests against a Medieval of collective identity, undeveloped subjectivity, and no sexuality at all, under Burckhardt's undifferentiated 'common veil.' The interiorized self (presumably unneeded by medieval social, cultural, economic, and political conditions) was waiting in some platonic sphere to be summoned to its historical debut to preside over pre-capitalist formation and the birth of the bourgeoisie. The Early Modern narrative actually, and quite naïvely, accepts as a premise that the standardized prescriptive doctrines of official religious culture in the Middle Ages (the routine condemnations of pride and self-assertion, of sex, money, and pleasure, issued by the celibate class of professional ecclesiastics) as a literal and sufficient description of medieval human reality, against which everything modern (and interesting) can begin. The infusion of modernity in the Early Modern Period is precisely the interiorized conflicted self, the subject whose death is so often announced now in some quarters, and that is what is absent from everyone's concept of the 'medieval.' I say 'everyone's' because it is one thing to dismiss Burckhardt's romantic metaphors or deconstruct the discourse of Early Modernity, and quite another to offer anything else in their place, anything else as powerful. I am conflating here and being a little unfair, but the overwhelming impression given by medieval studies, by medievalist scholars, is of a world of past persons we really cannot recognize: we can describe their institutions and learn their semantic codes, but they are not human to us. We medievalists are not entirely the victims of the narrative aggressions of scholars in trendier fields. We collaborate even in our best efforts at empathetic understanding, in our reluctance to offend the dead, in our genteelness disguised as scholarship, and especially in our reluctance to explore the full range of meanings of religious experience. Thus, the question in the title of my essay about mystics having sex is so basically foreign to the medievalist enterprise that it strikes even me as simply crude.

My question is addressed to that most distantly religious and 'medieval' form of experience: *mysticism* – direct encounters between humans and God. This is surely a topic which evokes a distinctively medieval culture: intense religiosity, an otherworldly world-view, disdain of secular life, bodily austerities. Mystical experience, in its medieval (and later) Christian forms, was culturally sanctioned, and thus culturally constrained and culturally defined. It had a secular literary tradition reaching at least as far back as the sixth book of Virgil's *Aeneid*; a special poetic vocabulary from the Old Testament Song of Songs, a crucial New Testament anchor in Paul's cryptic utterance in 2 Corinthians (12:2) about the man who was raised up to the third heaven; the institutional approval of Gregory the Great; theological orthodoxy and an elaborated religious psychology from the pseudo-Dionysius, Richard of St Victor, and others, and I have only sketched in the foreground of a densely occupied cultural landscape.[6]

Thus, all specific, recorded instances of mystical experience approach us deeply wrapped and packaged in layers of what we call 'Cultural Context.' The task of historical understanding is usually conceived as one of unpacking the layers of context: biblical, literary, theological, philological, text-exegetical, devotional, social, and so on; arranging and describing them in a paraphrase of contemporary concepts; and then demonstrating how the specific mystical event under investigation makes a coherent, self-explanatory, 'fit' with its contextual packaging.

This is the approach taken by current scholarship to the famous and famously conflicted life of Margery Kempe, mayor's daughter and burgess's wife of King's Lynn in the early fifteenth century. Margery, as most medievalists know, was the courageous and feckless woman who, one night, jumped out of her marriage bed proclaiming that it is far happier in heaven, felt a sudden and complete revulsion from intercourse with her husband (she would sooner 'have eaten and drunk the ooze and muck from the gutter than consent to intercourse' – but with her husband only, this revulsion did not encompass other men, as she candidly admits), and embarked on the career of a visionary witness of God's grace, extended even to sexually initiated women.[7] 'I love wives also,' Jesus assured her once they were on intimate terms and she lamented the loss of her virginity, which left her undeserving of his attentions.[8] Margery's visitations from Jesus were explicitly sexual from the first time he 'ravished her spirit' and commanded her to call him 'Jesus, your love, for I am your love' until, years later, when he insisted that he 'must be intimate with you, and lie in your bed with you,' where she was to love him as a wife does her husband and kiss his mouth, his head, and his feet.[9]

The case of Margery Kempe as a mystic, once an embarrassment to secular and religious scholarship, now rehabilitated along feminist lines, is more interesting for what it reveals about the state of medieval scholarship than for its relation to the medieval mystical tradition, which is really quite straightforward.[10] All the numerous studies of Margery Kempe's life which I have read proceed from the same premise: that Margery experienced a special kind of experience called 'mystical' which can be understood only in the terms the mystical tradition offers us for understanding it. My sentence is circular because the reasoning of this approach is circular. Mystical tradition offers us a coded language: the core or controlling concept is that of an event in which the Soul (gendered female always) 'knows' God in a direct access of 'Knowledge,' more complete and satisfying than any humanly received knowledge, but which is wholly incommunicable, or 'ineffable' in the classic term. Once the 'ineffableness' of the event is established as the premise, the event may be lingeringly and minutely described in metaphor: the Soul languishes with desire, sick with longing; she sighs, weeps, lies awake at night; she is naked and surrenders to the advent of her lover; then union, ecstasy, ravishing, the kiss, eating and tasting; and the prolonged delights, the 'familiarities' of feeling, touching, smelling, and hearing the beloved; finally rest, sleep, death – and rebirth.[11]

This language is regarded as a metaphorical code for the supernatural by doctrinal fiat: a scheme of linked metaphor whose ultimate referent is outside the range of human perception and understanding, and thus can be approached only through figuration, paraphrase, comparison, and displacement. Catholic tradition assures us this is so, and modern scholars comply, whatever they really think about the possibilities of God entering into such direct relations with individuals. Willingness to divulge opinions on this subject seems to violate some deep academic, if not religious, decorum. I frankly admit that I am unable to conceive of a God, under any serious monotheistic conception, who favours individuals in this way, with flattery and gratifications, or even special knowledge unavailable to anyone else. Other medieval scholars who share religious beliefs with the subjects of their studies may well regard my unbelief as a limitation, but this is a case in which I think that authors should come forward and say where they stand, and they rarely do.

Even the anxious candour of Margery Kempe, who wanted to tell us about irrepressible sexual desire, frustration, and pleasure, is primly reconfigured into a known matrix of orthodox, pious meaning. And the primness and piety are not essentially changed when the religious orthodoxy of the fifteenth century is reformulated into the feminist orthodoxy of the twentieth. It is true that current scholarship emphasizes Margery's protofeminism: her brave and stubborn insistence on living the life of her own choice; her perseverence in the face of ridicule and threat; her defiance and self-defence against male authorities; and especially her ingenuity in producing her book. Still, the expressive centre and locus of her life, the sexual encounters with Jesus, are treated only in gingerly paraphrase and left wholly uninterrogated as something 'mystic.' In every essay I have read, the blunt word 'sex' is absent, replaced by the politely distant 'erotic'; the act of intercourse is euphemized as 'marriage,' or disembodied as 'union,' and there are no orgasms at all. The case of Margery Kempe is unusual only in the social and domestic circumstances of the mystic herself; her language and expressive emotions are only a shade less sublimated and disguised than those of more 'respectable' mystics, including her contemporary Dame Julian of Norwich.

The issue of mystical experience is not of major importance in medieval life, but it does offer an interesting test case for a culture in which so very much experience was filtered through the concepts, language, images, and expectations of a specific and institutional religion. Talking about mysticism makes us, or *ought* to make us, come directly to terms with what it is we think we are approaching in the recorded experiences of medieval Christians. Once in a while – not too often, of course, but once in a while – it is not a bad idea to pause in our erudite parsing of the pseudo-Diony-sius, or Bernard's meditations on the Song of Songs, or the Victorine con-cept of negating the soul, or even Foucauldian discourse analysis, and ask rather crudely just what in the world we think we are talking about?

Placing mystical experience in its self-designated and self-defining cul-tural context, as we are all taught to do, arrives at a *paraphrase*, not an interpretation. Since the paraphrase-language is derived from the sanc-tioned, orthodox realms of medieval literature and religious usage, this paraphrase activity of unpacking the 'cultural context' can not only open the way to understanding the specific religious self-interpretation of mys-ticism, but open *out* to the *social functions* of mystic experience in medi-eval society: the personal authority a mystic could attain; the solace and excitement such an authority could offer the laity outside the normal channels of Christian institutions. All successful mystics understood this, and Dame Julian tried to explain some of it to Margery Kempe, who never managed to turn her fraught, intense 'visions' into social capital.[12]

The anthropologist I.M. Lewis, whose erudite and sympathetic book, *Ecstatic Religion*, makes an excellent starting-place for scholars interested in cross-cultural studies of mystical states, is explicit and enlightening on religious ecstasy as a 'social fact.'[13] The 'social fact,' distinctly observable and endlessly recorded, is a pattern (repeated across centuries and cul-tures) in which a certain kind of mental affliction is 'valiantly endured and, in the end, transformed into spiritual grace,' *and* – a special vocation as priest, prophet, shaman, saint.[14] Thus, for our purposes, the line leads directly from Paul on the road to Damascus to Julian of Norwich lying in bed with her body dead below the waist but her thoughts on God.[15] The social transformation achieved by the infliction of spiritual ecstasy on the receptive Soul: from outsider to insider, margin to centre, obscurity to fame, and passivity to authority was a career path notably open to women and to subordinated or marginalized (i.e., 'feminized') men. And among the marginalized, we must include all monastic men, no matter how respected, not forgetting that medieval society never quite overcame a deep ambivalence to the celibate, constrained, demasculinized male.

But social function, a useful concept borrowed from anthropology, is not yet *meaning*, which is a hermeneutic activity and requires a different translation language to approach the mind. Anthropology offers an inter-pretation language which moves *outward* from the conflicted private emotional *event* to recognize the opportunities different societies open to mystics once the secret crisis is reconfigured into a publicly available language. But this ignores the question of meaning with respect to the mind that created and endured its ordeal of pleasure.

In *Ecstatic Religion*, Lewis does consider, cursorily but with more sympathy than most anthropologists would give in the 1960s or 1970s, the psychological possibilities of interpretation.[16] Many more anthropologists today are ready to listen to their own colleague Georges Devereux, pioneer of psychoanalytic anthropology from the 1940s until his fairly recent death, in his basic premise that

> ... in the study of Man ... it is not only possible but mandatory to explain a behavior, already explained in one way, also in another way, – i.e. within another frame of reference ... The simple fact is that a human phenomenon which is explained in one way only is, so to speak, not explained at all ... and this even – and, in fact, chiefly – if this phenomenon's first explanation has made it perfectly comprehensible, controllable and foreseeable in terms of its own specific frame of reference.[17]

Devereux, both a psychoanalyst and a field-work anthropologist, dismissed with contempt the conceptually mushy 'additive, fusioning, synthetic, or parallel' attempts at 'hyphenated' interdisciplinary approaches to human behaviour, and insisted on a rigorous 'double discourse' which would construct two complementary explanations, each complete and valid within its own frame of reference.[18] (To strengthen the epistemological argument, I would refer readers to Louis Mink's discussion of multiple modes of comprehension.)[19]

Thus, when Julian of Norwich tells us of her three petitions to God – to 'know more of the physical suffering of our Saviour'; to suffer a physical illness to the point of dying, suffer bodily and mentally, but not die; and to receive three 'wounds' of a mataphorical nature – we do not have to conform immediately to her frame of reference and her own allegory of her desires.[20] Nothing is being dismissed, permanently ignored, reduced, explained away, or insulted when we note, to begin an *interpretation*, the allegory of sexual fears and frightening desires spoken through Julian's strong images of Christ's body punctured, torn, gouged, multiply penetrated in her explicit visions, and the repeated concentration on blood, fresh, copious, flowing, draining from face and body. The Culture authorizes and offers its own code for Julian's 'passional devotion,' but we know that *meaning*, in any strong hermeneutic sense, is never what announces itself. The frame of reference and symbolic code offered to us at the manifest level of human self-explanation are significant in cultural and social ways, but are not the meaning of the mind's silent and hidden life.

Julian's longing for pain, her equation of suffering with love (interestingly similar to the erotic doctrine of Andre Cappellanus's *Art of Love*, in which love is a sickness contracted by looking too much at beauty), issued in an illness involving anesthesia and paralysis of the lower body, a sinking towards coma so apparently irreversible that her family sent for the parish priest, difficult breathing, encroaching blindness, and then the sudden reversal and end of all symptoms with no after-effects, except for the memory of the visions she had been granted. Excluding the visions, this pattern, notably including the affliction of the limbs, is familiar from the silent mimetic choreography of the classic case histories of hysteria.[21]

This is not a pattern reserved only for women. Two centuries earlier, in 1194, a young monk in the monastery of Eynsham, near Oxford, became ill, finally lapsed into a coma for nearly two days, and when he awoke, invigorated and mysteriously restored to health, he intimated that his soul had visited places not of this world, and his revelations became the substance of a book written by his brother, Adam, known as *The Vision of the Monk of Eynsham*.[22] The visionary, named Edmund, had suffered from anorexia, acute revulsion from food, and a painful ulceration on his leg that would not heal, until he awoke when it healed spontaneously. The period just preceding his ecstatic trance state was reported by him to have included midnight sessions of corporal discipline from older monks, which filled him with such pleasure, such 'unbearably sweet sorrow' with each stroke, that he wanted many more, and when he next discovered a bleeding crucifix in the church, he acted on another overwhelming desire and ate the blood. The older monks steadily denied all of these events. Edmund's visions of the Other World are notable for the number of homosexuals he discovered there, the severity of their fate after death, and his exclamatory discovery that women too are involved in this sin, numberless multitudes of them condemned to obscene tortures for eternity. In spite of the efforts of Edmund's brother, Adam, a talented writer (author of the *Life of St Hugh of Lincoln*) who championed his brother's cause, the mystic's ambition of fame and authority eluded Edmund. The monks of his own house distrusted him, and he is not generally included in the honour roll with Walter Hilton, Richard Rolle, and Julian. Like Margery Kempe, Edmund of Eynsham was too undisguised, insufficiently sublimated.

Observers may not have had our same psychological vocabulary, but they knew; the uneasiness and diffuse suspicion that surrounded Margery and Edmund plainly tell that these aspirant mystics carried an aura of sexual anxiety. It was also only too obvious that Edmund, like Margery, *wanted* the social profits of his private ecstasy. (The social history of mysticism tells us that undisguised desire for respect and social position are fatal to the ambition.)

But anyone who wishes to examine the detail of the visions will see that the revered Dame Julian and the too easy-to-dismiss monk Edmund are psychic twins, however different in their social achievements and command of theologized poetics. The pressures of the unconscious mind, however thoroughly repressed, cannot be erased, and *will*, under certain conditions, demand some form of expression. And although that expression will run through culturally characteristic channels, and use the vocabulary and social forms available to the personality living in its historically local moment, it will still speak of the psychic unity of our kind.

Some of George Devereux's three decades of work in 'enthnopsychiatry' – cross-cultural studies grounded in both cultural anthropology and psychoanalytic theory – should at least be considered before Freud's concept of the mind, of the unconscious and conscious mind in its dynamic process of struggle, is dismissed as a bourgeois patriarchal deception. Similarly, the work of Gilbert Herdt, another psychoanalytically informed anthropologist, on male initiation rites in New Guinea supports the idea that cross-cultural psychiatry has a clear analogue in transhistorical studies.[23] When people who never encountered a European in their isolated mountain villages until the 1950s are discovered to have a social/sexual culture based on a founding myth about the first Man and Wife, and their lustful Son who wished to have sex with his mother, causing the anger of the father ... one has to consider the idea that Oedipal conflict may not be merely an aberration of nineteenth-century Vienna.[24]

Mysticism has always wanted to tell us what it is about psychically without acknowledging it. In the manner of Edgar Allan Poe's 'The Purloined Letter,' this cultural expression of the unconscious has paraded itself in an explicitly sexual language whose actual meaning is blandly denied by recoding it as Metaphor for the Ineffable. But, as Georges Devereux insists, the psychic unity of mankind is both assumed and proven by the congruence of cross-cultural studies and psychoanalytic depth studies; Edmund's embarrassingly explicit unbearable pleasures, the 'unspeakable sweetness' of his hallucinatory episode of being whipped by men, were inadequately coded but the psychic equivalent of whatever rarified sensations inform *The Cloud of Unknowing.*

The psychoanalytic language which allows the passions of the mind to speak openly is not an instrument of modern twice-fallen decadence inflicted on the past. It is, from a medievalist's point of view, the language of love which Augustine used in the *Doctrina Christiana* to explain the dynamic structure of the universe – from the microcosm of the soul tempted to love what it should only use, to the self-contemplating divine love. It is a language analogous with the syntax of desire with which Dante's pilgrim came to understand himself in the divine economy. Freud renewed these languages for the Western tradition, for the explication of modern hearts, so that the invisible things once more can be understood through the opaque film of reality.

The religious culture which offered medieval people a language with which to express their longings found its culminating expression in Dante's poem, which describes a world moved by love at every level, from the incoherent and undisciplined desires of each heart to the harmonious movements of the heavens. This was a world in which human desire, rightly directed to the sole object deserving to be loved for its own sake, found its meaning in the objective correlative, of the universe created by God. This is a world which no longer exists in unselfconscious serenity. The fully articulated medieval universe has shrunk to an artefact, a reconstructed 'context,' made of overlapping texts, posited of and by literature. This God-driven universe of desire is now a 'thing' *in* our universe. It no longer contains us. The literal signs of an invisible reality point inward now, but still to a shared and intelligible world of desire and its objects, negotiated anew by each soul. The unresolved drama fixed timelessly in the unconscious centre of each life in time finds its dignity in the universal drama of human life – moved by desire, thwarted by reality.

Mystical experience is always about desire, about the indefatigable search of the mind for the satisfaction of wishes that are emphatically *not* to be fulfilled, that must at once be denied and yet diverted and expressed, often in allegorized and mimetic forms. Extreme states tell us as nothing else can about the deep and characteristic patterns of mental life in a specific society, but only if we are willing to move beyond paraphrase as our critical activity. Medieval mysticism wants to tell us about the heavy weight of sexual restriction, sexual guilt, and conformity to difficult rules of self-constraint carried by monks and nuns, and by all women, but especially those whose religious conpunctions were sensitive and genuine. The mystic crisis wants to tell us about the fault lines in the medieval construction of ideal mental life. Frankly using a psychoanalytic language of libidinal drives, sublimations, and displacements, acknowledging in medieval people the full mental structure of the unconscious as well as conscious personality, will restore to the life stories we write of and for them the depth, complexity, and fellowship with ourselves they deserve.

NOTES

1 For a philological inquiry into the origins of the 'middle' nomenclature, see George Gordon, 'Medium Aevum and The Middle Age,' *Society for Pure English* Tract No. XIX (Oxford 1925), 3–28.

2 Hayden White's amusing and deliberately provocative suggestion that we regard the medieval annal form as an authentic and unmanipulated expression of reality works nicely as focal centre for his discussion of the constructedness of narrative form: 'The Value of Narrativity in the Representation of Reality,' in *The Content of the Form* (Baltimore and London: Johns Hopkins University Press 1987), 1–25.

3 Lee Patterson, 'On the Margin: Postmodernism, Ironic History, and Medieval Studies,' *Speculum* 65 (1990), 92

4 See Patterson's scathing comments on the predominantly Marxist analysis which has created the absurd idea of a human society without individuated citizens: 'Margins,' 93–7.

5 Jacob Burckhardt. *The Civilization of the Renaissance in Italy*, vol. 1 (New York: Harper & Row 1958), 143. Burckhardt appropriates Dante for the Italian renaissance of individuality: 'Dante's great poem would have been impossible in any other country of Europe, if only for the reason that they all still lay under the spell of race.'

6 Scholarship in this field is comprehensive and erudite; readily available and interesting are Paul E. Szarmach, ed., *An Introduction to the Medieval Mystics of Europe: Fourteen Original Essays* (Albany: State University of New York Press, 1984); Valerie Marie Lagorio, *The Fourteenth-Century English Mystics: A Comprehensive Bibliography* (New York: Garland 1981).

7 *The Book of Margery Kempe*, trans. B.A. Windeatt (Harmondsworth: Penguin 1985), 46. It should be noted that, by the time she composed her book, Margery was quite conscious of her vulnerability to accusations of doctrinal disobedience, and even heresy, and so she made it clear that she never positively *refused* her husband's demands, however distasteful they were to her: 'And so she said to her husband, "I may not deny you my body, but all the love and affection of my heart is withdrawn from all earthly creatures and set on God alone"': *Book*, 46. The Middle English original is currently available only in the

Early English Text Society edition: *The Book of Margery Kempe*, eds. Sanford Brown Meech and Hope Emily Allen, E.E.T.S. 212 (London: Oxford University Press 1940); a new edition is being prepared by Lynn Staley Johnson. I have worked out a reading of Margery's book which combines narrative analysis and psychoanalytic interpretation against a background of medieval culture: 'Reading *The Book of Margery Kempe*,' *Exemplaria* 3 (1991), 29–66.

8 *Book*, 84–5

9 Ibid., 51, 126–7, for the long and explicit passage which makes clear the nature of Margery's experiences: 'For [Jesus tells her] it is appropriate for the wife to be on homely terms with her husband. Be he ever so great a lord and she ever so poor a woman when he weds her, yet they must lie together and rest together in joy and peace. Just so must it be between you and me ... Therefore I must be intimate with you, and lie in your bed with you ... when you are in bed, take me to you as your wedded husband, as your dear darling, and as your sweet son ...'

10 I refer to a number of the many (and constantly increasing) essays on Margery Kempe in my article 'Reading *The Book* ...'; a comprehensive monograph on the subject is that of Clarissa Atkinson, *Mystic and Pilgrim: The Book and the World of Margery Kempe* (Ithaca, NY: Cornell University Press 1983), a very good 'contextual' treatment which wholly sidesteps the sexual issues. A useful anthology with bibliography is *Medieval Women's Visionary Literature*, ed. Elizabeth Alvida Petroff (London: Oxford University Press 1986). Margery becomes more feminist with each successive stage of scholarship: Karma Lochrie's *Margery Kempe and Translations of the Flesh* (Philadelphia: University of Pennsylvania Press 1991) is a fascinating and idiocyncratic excursus into many disembodied directions, leaving the human and ordinary Margery Kempe far behind; Lynn Staley Johnson's *Margery Kempe's Dissenting Fictions* (University Park: Pennsylvania State University Press 1994) also ignores the embarrassments of human sexuality and endows Margery with almost preternatural cunning in manipulating her patriarchal society; selections of characteristic current work are published in Sandra J. McEntire, ed., *Margery Kempe: A Book of Essays* (New York: Garland 1992), and Linda Lomperis and Sarah Stanbury, eds., *Feminist Approaches to the Body in Medieval Literature* (Philadelphia: University of Pennsylvania Press 1993).

11 See Wolfgang Riehle, *The Middle English Mystics*, trans. Bernard Strandring (London: Routledge & Kegan Paul 1981), for the sexual language of mystical experience.

12 *The Book of Margery Kempe*, 77–8. Margery's version of her conversation with Dame Julian seems blurred and self-serving, but also preserves what might be the core of Julian's counsel: 'The anchoress ... advising this creature to be obe-

dient to the will of our Lord and fulfil with all her might whatever he put into her soul, *if it were not against the worship of God and the profit of her fellow Christians* [my emphasis].' There is a gentle advice here to conform better to outward decorum and not shock people.

13 I.M. Lewis, *Ecstatic Religion: An Anthropological Study of Spirit Possession and Shamanism* (Harmonsworth: Penguin 1971), 21. There is, of course, a vast anthropological literature on shamanism of interest to medievalists, but Lewis's knowledge of history and religion, and the nuance and clarity of his writing, make him exceptionally interesting to historians.

14 Ibid., 67, and ch. 3: 'Affliction and Its Apotheosis'

15 Julian of Norwich, *Revelations of Divine Love*, trans. Clifton Wolters (Harmondsworth: Penguin 1966), 65. For a recent study along traditional lines, see Grace Jantzen, *Julian of Norwich: Mystic And Theologian* (London: SPCK 1987).

16 Lewis's ch. 7 'Possession and Psychiatry,' *Ecstatic*, 178–205) is both sympathetic to psychoanalytic concepts (many of which are quietly incorporated into his own interpretations; see p.71, 'what begins as an illness ... ends in ecstasy ...') and quarrels with it on various fronts.

17 George Devereux, *Ethnopsychoanalysis: Psychoanalysis and Anthropology as Complementary Frames of Reference* (Berkeley and Los Angeles: University of California Press 1978), 1, and he continues: 'Moreover, it is precisely the possibility of a human phenomenon being explained 'completely' in *at least* [my emphasis] two (complementary) ways which proves, on the one hand, that the phenomenon in question is both real and explainable and, on the other hand, that *each* of these two explanations is 'complete' (and therefore valid) within its own frame of reference.' Another readily available collection of essays by this extraordinarily interesting scholar is *Basic Problems of Ethnopsychiatry*, trans. Basia Miller Gulati and George Devereux (Chicago: University of Chicago Press 1980).

18 Devereux, *Ethnopsychoanalysis*, 2

19 Louis Mink, *Historical Understanding*, eds. Brian Fay, Eugene O. Golob, and Richard Vann (Ithaca, NY, and London: Cornell University Press 1987), 35–41

20 Julian of Norwich, *Revelations*, 63

21 Readers genuinely interested in the origins of psychoanalysis and the diagnosis of hysteria should begin with the classic text on the subject rather than modern, and often very polemical, reinterpretations: Joseph Breuer and Sigmund Freud, *Studies on Hysteria*, trans. James Strachey (New York: Basic Books, n.d.), which is a reprint of vol. 2 of the *Standard Edition*; the first edition was published 1895.

22 This interesting vision is printed in vol. 2 of *Eynsham Cartulary*, ed. H.E. Salter (Oxford: Clarendon Press 1907), 255–371, with introduction and notes. It

offers a detailed and full instance of a case of male hysteria in very recognizable form; the material concerning the monk's illness, his behaviour just before and after the vision/coma, and his assertions about activities with senior monks at night are found in the introductory and epilogue chapters to the *Vision*, chs. 1–13, and 57–8; homosexuality is encountered in chs. 25 and 26.

23 Gilbert Herdt, *The Sambia: Ritual and Gender in New Guinea* (Chicago: Holt, Rinehart and Winston 1987); this fascinating and well-presented record of field-work and interpretation among an isolated tribal people by a psychoanalytically informed anthropologist deserves to be read and seriously considered by historians of distant times and cultures. If a psychoanalytic paradigm works with flexibility and subtle results for cultural anthropology, there is a distinct argument there for historical studies.

24 Herdt, *Sambia*, 167–8, for the foundation myth of the Sambia and its obvious Oedipal form

Notes on Contributors

James A. Brundage, Ahmanson-Murphy Distinguished Professor of History and Courtesy Professor of Law at the University of Kansas, is the author of nine books, including *Law, Sex, and Christian Society in Medieval Europe* (1987); *Medieval Canon Law* (1995); and, with Vern Bullough, *Handbook of Medieval Sexuality* (1996).

Vern L. Bullough is Distinguished Professor Emeritus, State University of New York at Buffalo, and Visiting Professor at the University of Southern California. He specializes in the history and sociology of human sexuality and has authored or edited some fifty books and two hundred articles on related topics, including *Sex Variance in Society and History* (1976); *Cross-Dressing, Sex and Gender* (1993); and, most recently, with James Brundage, *Handbook of Medieval Sexuality* (1996).

Joseph Cady teaches in the Division of Medical Humanities at the University of Rochester Medical School. His most recent publications are seven essays in *The Gay and Lesbian Literary Heritage*, ed. Claude J. Summers (1995).

Konrad Eisenbichler is Associate Professor of Renaissance Studies/Italian and Director of the Centre for Reformation and Renaissance Studies (Toronto). He has published widely on Italian Renaissance theatre, Michelangelo, and Lorenzo de' Medici, and has recently completed a monograph study of the youth confraternity of the Archangel Raphael (Florence).

Ivana Elbl received her doctorate from the University of Toronto. She is an associate professor at Trent University, where she teaches late medieval and early modern history. Her research deals with the Portuguese overseas expansion in the fifteenth and sixteenth centuries. She is currently finishing a two-volume study of Henry the Navigator.

Dyan Elliott is Associate Professor of History at Indiana University and the author of *Spiritual Marriage: Sexual Abstinence in Medieval Wedlock* (1993). She is currently working on a book analysing the instability of the boundaries between female sanctity and heresy in the later Middle Ages.

Garrett P.J. Epp is Associate Professor in the Department of English, University of Alberta, Edmonton. His current research centres on masculinity, effeminacy, sodomy, and early English drama, and he occasionally directs productions of medieval plays.

Rona Goffen is past chair of the Department of Art History at Rutgers University and was editor of *Renaissance Quarterly* (1988–94). Her most recent book is *Titian's Women* (1997). She is also the author of *Giovanni Bellini* (1989).

Roberto J. González-Casanovas, PhD Harvard, Associate Professor of Spanish at the University of Kentucky, has published many articles on medieval Iberia. His books deal with Llull's utopian *Blanquerna* (1995), Llull's exemplary discourse (1996), and Muntaner and Martorell's crusading propaganda (1997). His research involves cultural rhetoric in Iberian chronicles and travels about the Mediterranean.

Ruth Mazo Karras, Professor of History at Temple University, is the author of *Common Women: Prostitution and Sexuality in Medieval England* (1995) and *Slavery and Society in Medieval Scandinavia* (1988), as well as numerous articles in the area of gender and sexuality.

Carol Kazmierczak Manzione received her PhD in 1989 from the State University of New York at Buffalo, where she also did her undergraduate work. She is currently teaching in the Department of International Studies at the University of Maine at Presque Isle. Her book on Christ's Hospital, *Christ's Hospital of London, 1552–1598: 'a passing deed of pity,'* was published in 1995.

Jacqueline Murray is Associate Professor of History and Director of the Humanities Research Group at the University of Windsor. She has published widely on issues of marriage and family, on gender, and on both female and male sexuality in medieval Europe. She is currently working on a study of the relationship between embodiment and male sexuality in medieval thought.

Nancy F. Partner is Associate Professor of History at McGill University. Her publications on related subjects include 'Reading *The Book of Margery Kempe*,' *Exemplaria* (1991); 'No Sex, No Gender,' *Speculum* (1993); and 'The Family Romance of Guibert of Nogent,' in *Medieval Mothering*, ed. B. Wheeler and J. Parsons (1996). She is currently writing a book on psychoanalytic theory and medieval studies.

Guy Poirier, Assistant Professor in the Department of French at Simon Fraser University, teaches French Renaissance and early-seventeenth-century literature, and contemporary French-Canadian literature. His book *L'Homoséxualité dans l'imaginaire de la Renaissance* is currently in press.

Robert Shephard is Associate Professor of History at Elmira College. He received his PhD from Claremont Graduate School. Currently he is working on a study of the place of royal favourites in the political culture of late Tudor and early Stuart England.

Barrie Ruth Straus, Associate Professor of English at the University of Windsor, specializes in medieval and modern narrative, contemporary theory, women's studies, and cultural studies. The author of *A History of the Catholic Church* (1987), she also edited *Skirting the Texts*, a special issue of *Exemplaria* (1991) on feminisms and medieval and Renaissance texts.

Andrew Taylor is an assistant professor at Northern Kentucky University. His work on medieval reading has appeared in *The Practice and Representation of Reading in England*, eds. James Raven, Helen Small, and Naomi Tadmor (1986), and *Bakhtin and Medieval Voices*, ed. Thomas J. Farrell (1996).